SOUTHERN ELECTRIC

David Brown

Capital Transport

ACKNOWLEDGEMENTS

A large number of fellow enthusiasts, photographers and former railway staff have helped in the production of this book, and the author is most grateful to all for their assistance. Particular thanks are due to Laurie Mack, who freely provided an enormous quantity of material from his extensive records and researches into the subject covering the past fifty years, and who undertook the final editing task. Another deserving of particular mention is the late Richard Riley who, as well as lending his entire collection of Southern Electric photographs, also generously entrusted me with the late G.T. Moody's original notebooks. Others who have kindly allowed me to use photographs from their collections include James H. Aston, Michael H.C. Baker, John H. Bird, Colin Boocock, Dick Coombes, the late Denis Cullum, Alex Dasi-Sutton, Fred Ivey, the late Alan A. Jackson, the late David Jenkinson, Colin Marsden, John H. Meredith, Bryan Rayner, John Scrace, the late John L. Smith (Lens of Sutton), Brian Stephenson and Chris Wilson. I am indebted to the Carriage and Wagon Department of the Bluebell Railway for allowing me to photograph the moquette patterns on their considerable collection of old SR carriage seat cushions. My grateful thanks also go to Alan A. Jackson and to Lawrie Bowles for agreeing to read through parts of the manuscript and for making a number of valuable comments and suggestions, and to Tony Dyer who provided photocopies of many pre-war articles and magazines, notes on braking systems and (not least) encouragement at times when the project was in serious danger of grinding to a halt. Finally I should like to thank my wife Alison and children Jennifer and Iain, who have put up with me disappearing into the 'office' for hours on end when, no doubt, there were more important things I should have been doing.

Title page 4 SUB unit 4302, which started life as three-car unit 1287 in the 1925 Guildford–Dorking batch and was augmented in November 1945, is seen here calling at Ashtead on 17th July 1959 with an evening Waterloo–Effingham Junction service. Fresh from the paint shop a few weeks before, it was withdrawn in November 1960, but the motor brakes then survived for more than a year as match wagons in the removal of the 1945/46 trailers to storage. *Chris Heaps*

CONTENTS

INTRODUCTION

Southern Electric: A New History 1909-83 sets out to give detailed coverage of the electrification schemes carried out by the Southern Railway Company (SR) and its predecessors during the first half of the twentieth century, and to describe fully the rolling stock provided for these schemes. The story is continued, in less detail, through the British Railways Southern Region period until the latter half of 1983, by which time the author would argue that Southern Railway influence had sharply waned with the withdrawal of the last 4 SUB suburban unit from passenger service that September.

Although considered by many railway observers and photographers, and certainly by the general public, as being mundane and without interest, the Southern Electric system is nevertheless fascinating, largely because it possesses a unique combination of characteristics shared by no other comparable railway network. These characteristics are the result of a number of interrelated geographical, historical and technical factors.

Firstly, a significant proportion of the system inherited by the SR in 1923 from its pre-Grouping constituents comprised a dense network of local routes around London (easily the most extensive of any of the four new main line companies), mainly radiating from the City and west end termini into the suburbs of Kent, Surrey and southern Middlesex. The rising costs of steam operation on these lines, together with demographic trends resulting in substantial traffic increases in the period immediately following World War One, made completion or extension of electrification schemes started by its constituents before 1923 a priority for the newly-formed company. Following completion of the first SR schemes by 1926, it was decided for future electrification to standardise on the relatively simple, cheap and robust low-voltage dc system with unprotected third rail, originally chosen in 1912 by the London and South Western Railway for its inner suburban lines. This decision, and a commitment by its Board and management to see virtually the entire suburban system converted, meant that by 1930 the Southern had the largest network using this power supply arrangement in the world. Had the much more complicated and costly high-voltage single-phase ac overhead system chosen by the London, Brighton and South Coast Railway (and finally abandoned in 1929) been adopted instead, the final extent of the SR's electrification would undoubtedly have been smaller. Some minor additions in the suburban area were made over the next ten years, including two entirely new lines. Traffic continued to increase through the following decade, largely as a result of uncontrolled house-building in the areas served, until by 1939 saturation point was being reached on several lines.

Secondly, the SR inherited a number of relatively short main lines which extended from the suburban area through Kent, Sussex and Hampshire to the south coast, little more than fifty miles from London. Following virtual completion of its suburban area the SR commenced electrifying these lines on the same low-voltage dc system, starting with the Brighton main line in 1932-33. Between 1935 and 1939 a rolling programme of electrification saw Hastings via Lewes and two routes to Portsmouth added to the network, together with middle-distance routes to Reading in the west and Maidstone/Gillingham in the east. Quite apart from technical developments which reduced conversion costs and the availability of low-interest Government finance for most of the schemes, this policy owed much to the shortness of the routes concerned and the consequent potential to operate a suburban-type regular-interval timetable, catering for both day-trippers and the ever increasing number of daily commuters (a convenient word, although not actually in use at the time) whom the company was keen to encourage. Further expansion of the electrified network had to be postponed in the run-up to World War Two and post-war conditions made immediate resumption impossible, even though ambitious plans were optimistically announced by the SR Board in 1946.

From 1st January 1948 the Southern Railway became the Southern Region of the nationalised British Railways (BR), and the Kent Coast and Bournemouth main lines were eventually added to the region's third rail system as part of the Modernisation Plan in the 1959-67 period. Before this, however, BR had adopted an industrial-frequency ac system using overhead wire current collection as a standard for electrification schemes elsewhere in Britain. Hence the Southern Electric was now considered non-standard and (arguably) obsolete, and this led directly to a third factor, namely the longevity of much of the SRs electric rolling stock. In particular, the main-line electric multiple units built for the coastal and other longer distance schemes between 1931 and 1939 were based on contemporary steam-hauled stock built over the same period. However, whereas the steam stock of comparable vintage was virtually all withdrawn between 1959 and 1963 concurrent with dieselisation or electrification of the lines over which it ran and the availability of more modern vehicles, much electric stock of similar age lasted a further ten years. Thus in 1971 it was still possible to travel in 1932-vintage Maunsell corridor coaches (in 4 COR units 3159-3168, formed with former Brighton line 6 PUL trailers) complete with wood-framed droplights and not a square inch of plastic laminate internal panelling in sight.

Lastly, the dyed-in-the-wool conservatism of the SR

engineering establishment through the first 25 years of nationalisation ensured that new suburban and main line stock built for the electrified network closely followed the layout and concept of trains the Southern Railway had designed before the war, albeit with updated electrical equipment and braking systems. Hence suburban coaches with closed compartments were still being turned out from Eastleigh Works in 1963, the 1956 Kent Coast main line units were remarkably similar in accommodation and layout to their pre-war equivalents, and the BR-design units which replaced the 1932-39 stock on the main lines between 1964 and 1972 (of which general withdrawal was not completed until 2005) showed little or no improvement from the passengers' point of view over the trains they superseded, other than in ride quality.

It has already been mentioned that the Southern's electric trains encouraged little enthusiasm amongst railway observers and photographers, particularly before 1939, and derogatory descriptions such as 'trams' and 'electric worms' were in widespread use amongst those who preferred their trains with a steam engine in front. One noted railway photographer of the period even moved from suburban Kent to Berkhamstead, ostensibly to get away from them! For present-day authors, an unfortunate result of this attitude is a dearth of good quality photographs of SR electric trains and infrastructure (other than official views) taken during this period. What interest there was in the Southern Electric was undoubtedly kindled during World War Two with the 1943 publication of Ian Allan's *ABC* spotter's guide on the subject. It continued through the 1950s as the SR's extensive fleet of antiquated suburban electric units, mostly with wooden bodywork converted from Victorian and Edwardian-era steam stock, was gradually withdrawn, most to be rebuilt with new steel bodies to become second-generation SUBs and EPBs.

Enthusiast interest undoubtedly waned through the 1960s as the decline of steam and line closures under the Beeching regime drew their attention elsewhere, and the withdrawal of most of the original Brighton and Eastbourne express stock in the 1964-66 period went largely unnoticed until it was too late. Minds were concentrated once more by the end of the decade with the demise of the last of the Brighton line 4 LAVs, and as it became clear that the remainder of the pre-war stock was also shortly destined for the breakers yards. With the primary aim of preserving one of the remaining 2 BIL units, a number of like-minded enthusiasts formed the Southern Electric Group (SEG) in 1970. In the event, a unit of this class was chosen for the National Collection, but the SEG was able to purchase Portsmouth line 4 COR unit No.3142 instead, and this unit has been undergoing restoration.

A surprising number of Southern Electric vehicles from the 1925-52 era survived into preservation and are extant today, although their states of repair vary widely from virtual dereliction to pristine running order. Apart from 2 BIL 2090 and 4 COR 3142, these include (in rough order of age) a 1925 Western section suburban motor coach, two other COR motor coaches, two 4 DD double-decker motor coaches, and complete 4 SUB 4732. Pride of place must however go to the restored 1932 Brighton line Pullmans, of which kitchen parlour firsts *Audrey*, *Vera* and *Gwen* continued to see service as part of the splendid *Venice Simplon Orient Express*, and kitchen composite *Bertha* is now on the Swanage Railway after operating for several years on the Bluebell Railway. A significant number of vehicles from this period were also retained by the railway for departmental use, although all have since been withdrawn.

The author's own interest in the Southern Electric started during pre-school years in the early 1960s, at which time my family lived within sight and sound of the level crossing at Ashtead station, on the former LBSCR/LSWR joint line between Epsom and Leatherhead. Originally electrified in 1925 as part of the Western section Guildford and Dorking scheme, since 1929 this line had enjoyed electrified services serving three London termini (Waterloo, Victoria and London Bridge). In 1960 the frequent suburban trains calling at Ashtead were virtually all formed of 4 SUB units, although in amongst the flat fronted all-steel ones a sprinkling of domed cab roofs was noticed. These would have mainly been the Bulleid '4101' series of 1941-45 vintage, although the odd augmented 1925 '4300' or '4326'-class unit could still turn up at this time. Additionally, two expresses would roar through each hour on their way from London to the coast or back, formed of corridor 4 COR and 4 BUF stock with their end gangway connections swinging alarmingly. In those days, SR electric stock had its own distinctive and well-remembered smell, which seems to have been compounded of green paint, seat upholstery, wood varnish and ozone! Also recalled from the occasional shopping trip to Epsom or Leatherhead were the seats, particularly those covered in the boomerang-patterned moquette in shades of maroon, pink, light blue and black, which developed a shiny tinge when worn.

By 1970 and with the aid of an Ian Allan *Combined Volume* the different types of 4 SUB and other units were being noted more carefully, as the trip to secondary school in Leatherhead was by train (from choice – the 418 bus or even walking were equally convenient). Although the SUBs, by now virtually all blue, remained ubiquitous on suburban services, the expresses were now formed of more modern, and definitely less interesting, CEP and BEP stock. In amongst the SUBs was the occasional 4 EPB – particularly on a peculiar Waterloo – Guildford working which called at Ashtead at 07.55, and a pair of 4 CORs which tore through without stopping at about 09.30 en route from Horsham to London Bridge. There was the odd visit further afield. At Guildford an elderly 2 BIL or (more often) 2 HAL still trundled in from the Aldershot direction every thirty minutes, sometimes even a green one with small yellow warning panels, although by May these had been replaced by CORs. 2 BILs very occasionally turned up at Leatherhead on Horsham – Victoria services, substituting for a SUB – the four minutes in a c.1938 first class compartment on the way home from school was something to be savoured. The author has pleasant memories of two railtours using pre-war SR electric stock in 1971, the first being the

2 BIL farewell trip that January and the second an excursion involving a pair of Portsmouth 4 GRI units – two fully-staffed catering cars ensured that a good time was had by all.

I lost interest in railways generally at about the time the 4 CORs were being withdrawn *en masse* in 1972, and therefore also missed the withdrawal of the compartment SUBs and the introduction of the experimental sliding-door PEP stock which worked on the South Western division (although not through Ashtead) for a few years. Enthusiasm was rekindled in about 1977 whilst at university, and, armed at last with decent photographic equipment, I was able to record on film the last few years of the second-generation 4 SUBs until their demise in 1983. For me, these units had always been the archetypal 'suburban train' and with their withdrawal the atmosphere of the Southern Electric definitely changed for the worse. At the same time, many distinctive features of the 1932-33 Brighton line electrification scheme were being swept away after fifty years with resignalling, junction remodelling in the Selhurst area and replacement of the power supply system.

Although a number of general surveys and photographic albums on SR electric trains have been produced since, no seriously detailed account of the system has been available since the fifth edition of the late G.T. Moody's classic *Southern Electric* was published by Ian Allan in 1979. It is clear that Moody based his text for the original 1957 and subsequent editions of this book on detailed personal observations gathered together since the 1920s, backed up with information provided by official SR press releases and periodicals such as *The Railway Gazette*. Since that time a considerable amount of additional material has been unearthed and published, mainly in the specialist enthusiast journals published by the Electric Railway Society and the Southern Electric Group. In particular, it has been possible in recent years to study Southern Railway archives now held at the National Archives at Kew, and elsewhere. The minutes of the Rolling Stock Committees have proved particularly fruitful, providing background information and reasons for many of the events and decisions previously written about without question.

Inspired by the detailed articles published in the SEG journal *Live Rail* and elsewhere, and by the success of *The 4 Sub Story* which I co-authored in 1984, I assumed when this project was started in earnest in 1992 that most of the necessary information could be gathered together relatively quickly. However, as more and more new material came to light, it was soon obvious that I had opened the proverbial 'can of worms', and it became abundantly clear why no-one else since G.T. Moody had yet achieved anything similar. A reasonably detailed account of the pre-war suburban stock, in particular, has proved extremely complicated to organise. While descriptive details of the origins of all vehicles with bodies converted from steam stock have been included, space limitations have made it impossible to provide complete details of every one of the numerous unit reformations which took place in the 1940-62 period. On the other hand, some detail has been possible with the main-line express and semi-fast stock fleets which were of more manageable size. Intentional omissions include the Waterloo and City Railway, which now has its own detailed history, and the diesel-electric units of the BR era, except where they became involved with the electric stock story. Conversely, a brief history of the BRCW type 3 Bo-Bo diesel-electric locomotives (later class 33) has been included in *Volume 2*, as they formed an important element of the 1967 Bournemouth line electrification.

Southern Electric: A New History 1909-83 is in two parts. *Volume 1* describes the suburban electrification schemes carried out by the Southern Railway and its pre-grouping predecessors and the suburban rolling stock placed in service up to 1951. Appendices list carriage stock numbers and initial unit allocations, and the distinctive letter and numerical headcodes the SR used on its electrified services. *Volume 2* deals with main line electrifications from 1932 onwards and the electric rolling stock provided for those schemes, and covers the Second World War period, the last years of the Southern Railway, and the British Railways era until 1983.

Third class was renamed second class from 3rd June 1956, as part of a change agreed by the railways of Western Europe. Descriptions of vehicles prior to this date refer to third class and with the word 'brake' at the end, reflecting Southern Railway usage; eg motor third brake (MThB). References from this date describe appropriate vehicles as second class, and with the word 'brake' before the class, as in BR usage; eg motor brake second, (MBS). This change in terminology had no effect whatsoever on the standard of accommodation provided.

The 24-hour clock was adopted by British Railways from 14th June 1965. Times quoted prior to that date are in the twelve-hour format suffixed am/pm as appropriate (9.15am, 11.04pm etc), while times quoted after that date are in the 24-hour format (eg 09.15, 23.04).

Sums of money quoted in the text relate to values at the date given. The value of money has declined over the years. An approximation of 'what it would cost now' can be taken by using a retail price index factor. This indicates that prices have more than doubled since 1985, risen 10-fold since 1970, 15-fold since 1960, 23-fold since 1950, about 45-fold since 1935, and 40-fold since 1925 (there was deflation in 1930-35).

In a book of this size some errors and inconsistencies are inevitable, however carefully the completed manuscripts are checked, and for these the author accepts full responsibility. Any reader who feels moved to comment on any aspect of the book is invited to contact the author via the publisher.

Overleaf A Southern Railway suburban area map dating from 1929, showing the extent of the electrified network in that year. The Dartford – Gravesend, Wimbledon – West Croydon and Windsor lines are marked as 'New Electrification in progress'. Other interesting details include the new Wimbledon – Sutton line opened as far as South Merton, and the route of the projected (but never built) 'Southern heights Light Railway' between Orpington and Sanderstead.

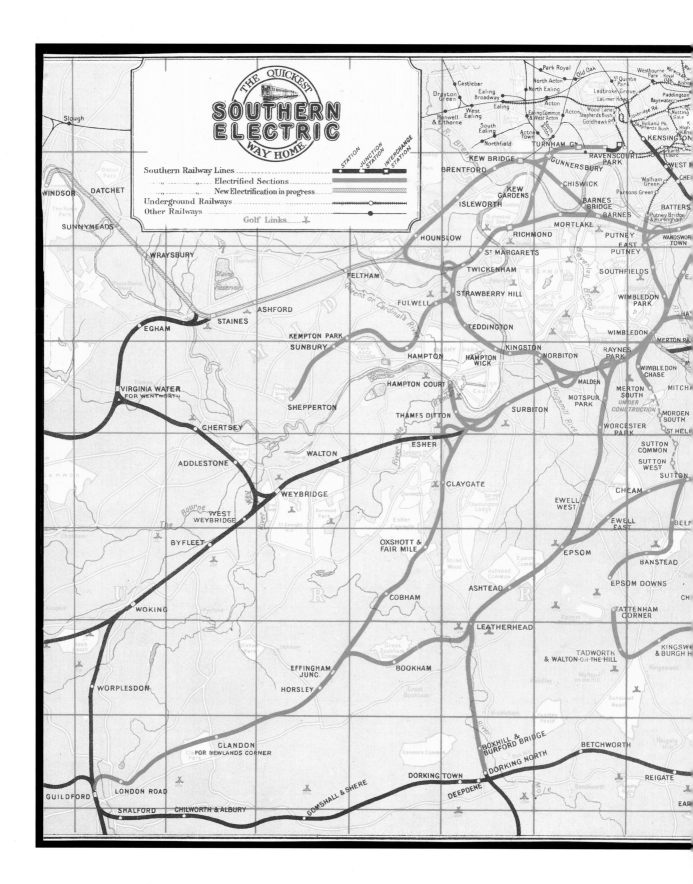

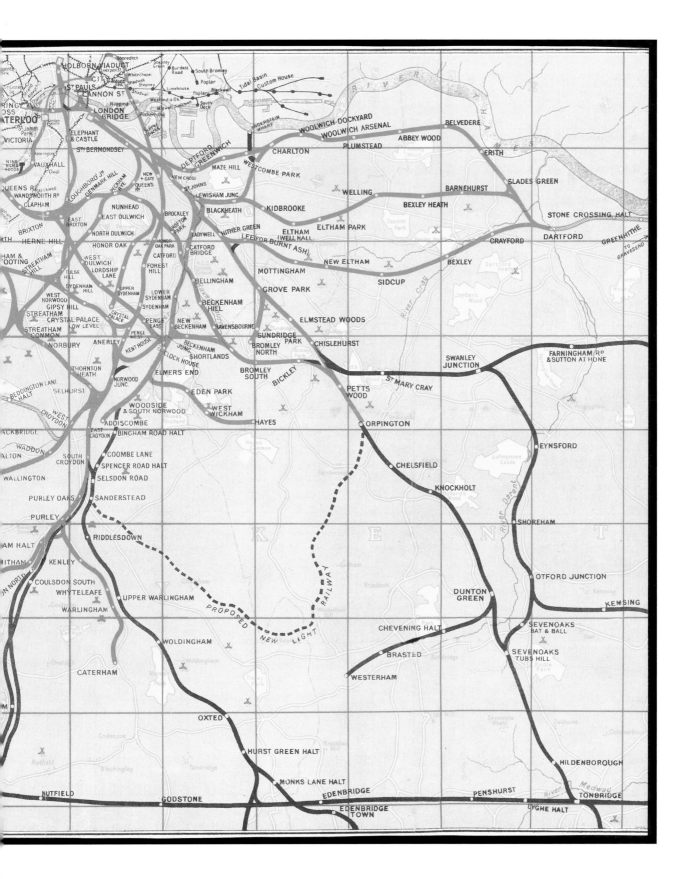

1: PRE-GROUPING ELECTRIFICATION

Although the first practical demonstration of electric traction on railways took place as early as 1879 when Werner von Siemens showed his pioneer electrically-powered train at the Berlin Trades Exhibition, for the following twenty years the main line railway companies in Britain were uninterested in experimenting with this novel and cleaner form of propulsion. The prodigious inventor Magnus Volk began running his diminutive electric tramcars along the seafront at Brighton in August 1883, while on a slightly larger scale the deep level City and South London tube railway was electrically worked from its opening in 1890, as was the Liverpool Overhead Railway which commenced operation in 1893.

It was on urban railway networks that the advantages of electric traction were most obvious, and from around the turn of the century it slowly became more widely used on such lines, the UK lagging behind the United States and some other countries in this respect. For example, electrification of the Metropolitan and District Railways in London was completed in the inner area by 1905, and other early applications were on the Mersey Railway (1903) and the North Eastern Railway's North Tyneside network (1904). All the lines so far mentioned used direct current (dc) of relatively low voltage (c.600V) picked up from a conductor rail situated either inside or outside the running rails, an arrangement also common in North America. Such a system was adopted by the London and South Western Railway in 1912, and later by the Southern Railway following the 1923 Grouping. In the years before and just after World War One, it became standard practice for British railway companies considering electrification to send an engineer to study and report back on installations in the USA.

Elsewhere in Europe, particularly in Switzerland and Italy, experiments had taken place with alternating current (ac), either single or three-phase and at a much higher voltage than comparable dc installations, with the trains picking up current from overhead wires, an arrangement considered more suitable for longer distance main line electrification. In Britain, only the Midland and the London, Brighton and South Coast Railways adopted this system. The Midland Railway electrified its line from Lancaster to Morecambe and Heysham, totalling nine and a half route miles, in 1908, using a 6,700V 25 Hertz (cycles per second) single-phase installation which lasted until 1951. The LBSCR adopted a similar system, with its first route being electrified in 1909, and thus was the first of the constituents of the Southern Railway to operate electric trains over a main line surface route.

THE LBSCR AC *ELEVATED ELECTRIC*

The London Brighton and South Coast Railway had its origins in the London and Brighton Railway, opened southwards as far as Haywards Heath in July 1841 and throughout two months later. The route north of Norwood was owned by the London and Croydon Railway, with whom the LBR amalgamated in 1846 to form the LBSCR. The Act of Parliament authorising construction of the Brighton line ceded ownership of the Coulsdon – Redhill section to the South Eastern Railway (whose own main line headed due east from Redhill to Dover), an arrangement which quickly proved unsatisfactory for both it and the LBSCR. Important milestones in succeeding years were the opening of the cut-off line between East Croydon and the west end terminus at Victoria in 1862, and the construction of what became known as the Quarry Line between Coulsdon and Earlswood, by-passing the congested SER junction at Redhill, in 1899. These works, together with quadrupling as far south as Balcombe Tunnel Junction and at Haywards Heath, resulted in the final form of the Brighton main line by 1910. In addition to a number of secondary main lines and branches, the company had also developed a relatively dense and complicated network of suburban and local lines to the south of London during the same period, many of which formed loops radiating out from the termini at London Bridge and Victoria, giving a considerable number of route permutations. Important centres served by these lines included the Crystal Palace (in which the LBSCR had a financial interest), Croydon, Sutton and Epsom.

With a virtual monopoly of transport between London and Brighton, the LBSCR was regularly accused of abusing its position and providing a poor service, largely the result of an often-precarious financial position. It was unsurprising, therefore, that a number of schemes for rival lines between London and the south coast were promoted from 1863 onwards, some serious and some merely designed to spur the Brighton company to improve its own services, but none reached the statute book. All were proposed as conventional steam-worked lines and most were backed, generally not openly, by either the SER or the London, Chatham and Dover Railway.

Of greater relevance to the present story were a number of rival schemes for electrically-powered lines at the turn of the century, although again none failed to get much beyond the stage of a promoters' pamphlet. The radical idea of an independent railway worked by electricity between London and Brighton was first mooted in 1899, and two years later a 'London and Brighton Electric Railway Company' proposed an almost straight 47 mile route from a metropolitan terminus in Lupus Street, Pimlico. With F.H. Cheesewright as Chief Engineer, the suggested route would have had more than nineteen miles in tunnel and gradients designed to '...allow highest speeds...at the minimum cost of energy' – in other words it was intended to use regeneration. Further unconventional features of this initial scheme included use of the Behr monorail system and a complete lack of intermediate stations, major towns en route such as Croydon and Redhill being served instead by short branches trailing in to the main route and served by separate trains. It was planned that the electric trains would complete their journey in 32-35 minutes, and the first class single fare would be just five shillings. These rather fanciful ideas gradually metamorphosed into a more conventional line, described in a pamphlet dated 1902, now with standard intermediate stations at Beddington, Redhill and Haywards Heath, the twenty-minute interval service calling alternately at each. By this time the planned journey time had risen to forty minutes, and the estimated cost from £6 million to £9 million. A parliamentary bill was submitted for the 1902 session, but was unsurprisingly thrown out that March as it failed to comply with standing orders in several respects. A further monorail scheme dating from 1901, backed by a London syndicate, also sank without trace as did another, more conventional, proposal the following year.

While these schemes aroused considerable interest, they did not greatly concern the LBSCR Board and management of the time. Nevertheless, the General Manager, Sir William Forbes, was quoted as saying that as soon as an electric traction system had been developed capable of running a train at high speed for fifty miles and still produce a return on the capital invested, the company would adopt it, whatever its origin. Anyway, the Brighton line was still being improved (quadrupling as far south as Balcombe Tunnel Junction being finally completed in May 1910) and, in order to show what could be achieved with steam traction, the LBSCR put on a return demonstration run between Victoria and Brighton on 26th July 1903. Billinton B4 class 4-4-0 No. 70 *Holyrood*, hauling three Pullman cars and a van, managed the outward journey in a creditable 48 minutes and 41 seconds at an average speed of 63.4mph, with a maximum of 90mph through Horley. Although the run achieved its purpose in showing that, with a light load, steam was capable of almost matching the performance of the proposed electric trains, such speeds were not feasible on a day-to-day basis due to the complexity of the junctions and the density of the traffic.

As we shall see in a moment, the LBSCR Board was far more concerned about its suburban traffic where, in the period from about 1903 onwards, at a time when road competition was all still horse-drawn, a combination of falling receipts and increased expenses, particularly in the inner area, was causing worry. In this case, electric traction was considered as a means of economising in operating costs, rather than necessarily encouraging traffic. In 1901 the Company's Chief Engineer, Charles E. Morgan, visited Italy to study the relative merits of the low-voltage dc system in use between Milan and Varese and the high voltage three-phase ac system installed on the Sondrio – Lecco line. Morgan reported to the Directors in January 1902, but his report was mainly concerned with listing shortcomings for LBSCR purposes of the dc system as used in Italy. Major Philip Cardew, one of the Directors, continued strongly to extol the advantages of electrification, and as a result the London, Brighton and South Coast Railway obtained powers to electrify all its lines as part of the LBSC Railway Act of 21st July 1903. While the company now had statutory consent to electrify its main line to counter rivals if need be, it could also press ahead with suburban electrification. As a first stage, Philip Dawson was appointed Consulting Engineer to report on practicability and the most suitable method of electrification, looking firstly at the South London line (the innermost loop between Victoria and London Bridge, via East Brixton and Peckham Rye), but with conversion of the Brighton main line firmly in mind.

It has been stated in virtually every previous work covering the LBSCR overhead electrification that the South London line was electrified due to a loss of traffic caused by competition from newly-electrified tramways in the area, and that electrification arrested this decline. This argument seems to have been put about by the LBSCR management, particularly Philip Dawson, and possibly first appeared in print for general consumption in an article on the company entitled 'The Evolution of a Popular Railway', published in *The Railway and Travel Monthly* dated September 1911, in other words some time after the event. In it the author, G.A. Sekon, states '... to meet the competition of the electric tram cars, the Directors ... decided to electrify the South London line ...' (Sekon was the pen-name of G.A. Nokes, who had previously edited *The Railway Magazine* from 1897 until 1910.) Similar statements appeared in the company reports in the same period. It seems that the LBSCR management simply wanted a plausible excuse for the changes to feed to the shareholders, and that it was easy to cast the municipally-run (and therefore 'unfairly' subsidised) trams as villains of the piece against the private enterprise Railway Company.

However, when looked at more closely, it can be seen that statements regarding tramway competition do not ring true. The LBSCR obtained powers for electrification in 1903, but declining suburban receipts had not shown up in the company's books by this time. Direct competition for passengers in the catchment area of the South London line from electric trams was not fully in place until 1906, after it had been decided to convert this route and after the loss of traffic had occurred. The falls in passenger numbers were really due to demographic and economic factors, little understood at the time, and the subsequent rise in traffic following electrification was due to opposing trends of the same type. The losses in the early Edwardian period were the result of a trade recession and also due to a series of wet summers depressing leisure travel, while the later increases were caused by an upturn in trade and also an increase in the travel habit, particularly for local journeys. To illustrate this, passenger bookings at Peckham Rye (about mid-way along the line)

Above Portrait of (Sir) Philip Dawson.

Opposite above Complex catenary arrangements on the approaches to London Bridge, showing a variety of supports. Note that the spool-type insulators, from which the twin catenary wires are suspended, are unusually underneath the lattice girder directly ahead of the signals, presumably for clearance reasons.

Opposite below LBSCR South London line three-coach set, new outside the carriage builder's workshops, late in 1908. Coach 3201, which eventually became the motor third brake of dc unit 1801, is leading.

Below A South London line set on test running under a variety of catenary supports. That nearest the camera is a lattice supported by A frames, while the next two are cantilevers. The catenary wire appears to be set straight, which led to uneven wear in the bow collectors on the motor coaches.

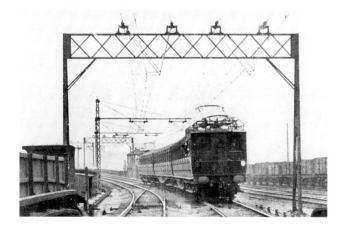

were 1.2 million in 1902, down to only 0.5 million in 1906, and back up to one million in 1910. These factors affected all forms of public transport at the time, not just the railways. Certainly, by 1912 the LBSCR had all the suburban traffic it could handle.

The actual reason why the South London line was chosen as the first electrified route was that it presented most physical features of a local railway over a relatively short distance, including numerous closely-spaced stations, abrupt gradient changes and sharp curves, and was therefore particularly suitable for trial purposes. From its junction off the local lines out of Victoria, just north of Battersea Park station, it curved on a brick-arched viaduct to Wandsworth Road, after which it ran parallel with the Chatham main line in shallow cutting or at ground level through Clapham. It then ascended to cross the LCDR station at Brixton on an iron lattice bridge before descending through East Brixton station to run parallel with the LCDR's Nunhead and Crystal Palace line, still on a viaduct. The route then passed into deep cutting and two tunnels, between which was situated Denmark Hill station, before returning to brick viaduct through Peckham Rye (where it parted company with the LCDR), Queens Road Peckham, Old Kent Road and South Bermondsey, where a junction was made with other LBSCR lines into London Bridge. Although most of the route was double-tracked, between Peckham Rye and South Bermondsey there was a third road. This variety of terrain allowed a selection of catenary mounting arrangements to be tried in most possible railway situations, and enabled engineers to test the system to its likely limits. A further advantage was that the major part of the route was isolated from other traffic flows.

In line with Morgan's earlier study, Dawson's Report to the Directors of June 1904 recommended the use of a high-voltage ac system, using current collection from overhead wires, as being more suited for main-line operation than a dc third-rail arrangement with conductor rails. Power distribution arrangements were also simpler, and the permanent way would be kept clear of live rails. Unlike the Italian model, however, it was decided to use a single-phase system of German origin having only one contact wire, rather than three-phase which had two. Even though the primitive single-phase ac traction motors then available were heavier and less efficient than dc motors and installation of the 'overhead' was expected to be more expensive than an equivalent third-rail dc system, it was envisaged that there would be savings over the whole life of the project. The cost of the electrification was to be met entirely from the Revenue Account. The LBSCR Board generally concurred with Dawson's recommendations, and on this basis minimum specifications were decided upon and tenders invited.

British electrical companies having had virtually no relevant experience, early in 1906 contracts were let to the German company Allgemeine Elektricitäts Gesellschaft (AEG) of Berlin, who sub-contracted with Messrs. R.W. Blackwell and Co. Ltd of Westminster for the supply and erection of the overhead catenary and associated structures. This firm in turn subcontracted with the British Thomson-

LONDON BRIDGE YARD; LOOKING TOWARDS STATION

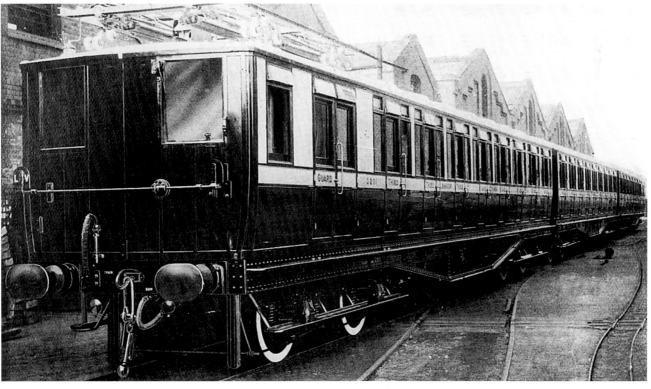

Houston Company (BTH) for switchgear and with Johnson & Phillips and Siemens for cabling. The initial intention was to convert the Battersea Park – Peckham Rye section only, and contracts were let on this basis. Very soon afterwards, following discussions with the SECR who shared facilities at the two termini, it was decided to electrify the line throughout, so a further contract was let to AEG at the end of March 1906 to cover the sections between Victoria and Battersea Park and between Peckham Rye and London Bridge. Tenders for the rolling stock were invited in March 1907, the order being secured by the Metropolitan Amalgamated Carriage and Wagon Company of Birmingham. Electrification work commenced early in 1906 but proceeded slowly as it was mostly done at night or between trains on Sundays, in order to minimise track possessions on this busy route. Thus it was not possible to commence trial running until January 1909.

Unlike the Metropolitan and District Railways, which built their own power stations, the LBSCR had no ambitions in this direction and did not wish to spend unnecessarily on what was initially an experimental installation. It therefore contracted with the London Electric Supply Corporation, already involved in the supply of power for the burgeoning electric tramway network in south London, to provide the electricity to power its trains. Single-phase alternating current at a nominal 6,700V 25Hz was fed from the Deptford Power House of that company to a main switch cabin at Queens Road, Peckham. The simple single-phase traction motors then available would only work satisfactorily at low frequencies, and 25Hz was chosen as it was conveniently already being supplied from Deptford to power the rotary converters of the tramway systems. From Queens Road, the current was then distributed through lineside cables laid in earthenware ducts or wooden casing to further switch cabins located at each station for supply to the overhead wires.

The conductor wires were of round-section copper, suspended every ten feet by droppers from double catenary wires in a vee arrangement, the droppers being attached to the contact wire with phosphor-bronze clips. The catenary wires were of twelve-strand non-continuous steel cable, galvanised and tarred to limit corrosion. These were carried above the tracks on corrugated spool type insulators (the preferred type after tests) mounted horizontally, generally above the catenary supports, on two short bars. The contact wire itself passed below the supports, and there were additional outriggers connecting it to the insulators. This design ensured that the weight of the catenary wires placed only compression loads on the insulators. The double catenary arrangement was chosen both for its stiffness, important as there was no tensioning system, and also to avoid as far as possible the blast from steam locomotive chimneys. Unsurprisingly, however, it was soon found that contact wire deterioration was much faster on those tracks shared with steam trains. Photographic evidence suggests that the contact wire was originally set straight in at least some locations, but this wore grooves in the pick-up bow collectors on the trains. By the time passenger services commenced it seems that the contact wire along the entire route had been aligned to weave

nine inches (six inches had earlier been tried) either side of the track centre-line to avoid this problem. This change may have compounded the delays to the start of services referred to below.

The conductor wires were normally positioned 16ft above rail-level, but this was increased to 19ft 6in at both London Bridge and Victoria to give adequate safe headroom for staff attending to oil-lamps on the roofs of steam-hauled coaches. The minimum clearance between a live conductor and earth stipulated by the Board of Trade for 6,700V was 13ft 11in, five inches above the normal LBSCR loading gauge height. For this reason it was necessary to make certain sections 'dead' (ie not energised) where the wires passed under the limited clearances of Elizabeth, Eccleston and Ebury bridges which spanned Victoria station and its throat. The resulting sudden loss of power did nothing to assist electric trains accelerating out of the terminus ready for the ascent over Grosvenor Bridge. The catenary supports themselves, which typically were situated 150ft apart, were sturdy structures generally consisting of A-frame or lattice girder uprights either side of the track, fixed into the ground with concrete, supporting a horizontal lattice girder span laced to them with wire. There were numerous modifications to this basic design to suit local conditions at various locations, including some centre-pole brackets over Grosvenor Bridge and a number of cantilevers west of Denmark Hill and elsewhere. These latter comprised a lattice girder upright and horizontal steel girder catenary support pulled up by two steel cables, making it necessary to mount the insulators underneath the support. Oddly, little attention seems to have been paid to the siting of signals when the overhead catenary was installed, and many became difficult to observe in the tangle of support poles, girders and wires.

At stations, precautions to enable stray current from a broken conductor wire to be handled safely included facing the platform canopies with sheet zinc and earthing them. Coasting marks, consisting of a small blue plate bearing a white cross, were fixed to overhead support uprights in appropriate locations to indicate to a driver where to shut off current before arriving at the next station. Likewise, plates bearing the numbers 2, 3 or 6, attached to a convenient lamp post or canopy support, showed where to draw-up trains of varying length at each station. Surprisingly, no attempt was made to modernise lighting arrangements on stations served by electric trains, gas lamps continuing in use. These general arrangements continued for the Crystal Palace lines, converted in 1911-12, and the Coulsdon and Sutton routes completed by the Southern Railway in 1925.

Apart from the double track forming the South London line proper, the tracks equipped included the local lines from Victoria to Battersea Park Junction (there being no access from the through lines) and the two outer roads of the three between London Bridge and Peckham Rye. Seven platform lines serving five platforms (the present 9-13) were electrically-equipped at Victoria, and four at London Bridge (19-22 of the old terminus before the 1974 reconstruction).

A feature of the South London line was that there were

Denmark Hill station, looking towards Victoria, about 1923. The South London line is on the left, with the ac catenary and switch cabin prominent.

three tracks from London Bridge as far out as the Victoria end of Peckham Rye station, the centre road designated Up Main and used by some trains running into London Bridge. Although in most places the catenary supports stretched over it, as mentioned above, this centre road was not initially wired up. However as part of the electrification works it was made reversible between London Bridge and South Bermondsey Junction, the signalling being interlocked so it could only be used in one direction at a time. Two new signal-boxes were provided as part of these alterations, which came into effect from 19th October 1909.

The rolling stock originally comprised eight three-coach sets, numbered after delivery 1E-8E, each formed of two third class motor coaches and a first class trailer. All four axles of each motor coach were powered, and current was collected from bow collectors which trailed the direction of travel. Unusual features of these vehicles included a side gangway between compartments to aid passenger flow in crowded conditions, greater-than-standard width and height, an unusually high level of luxury (particularly for suburban stock) and a lack of second class for the first time on LBSCR coaches. A four-road carriage shed for the new stock, each track holding only one three-coach set, was constructed on a restricted site at Peckham Rye, in place of earlier carriage sidings in the vee between the Tulse Hill and South London lines. Adjacent to this, on the south side of the line towards Denmark Hill, was a separate three-bay repair shop incorporating inspection pits and an overhead gantry crane, fully-equipped to enable all electrical repairs and overhauls to be undertaken. There was an additional external pit-equipped loop and several other berthing sidings in the vicinity. Both sheds were of similar appearance with white-painted walls, extensive glazing and twin arc-shaped roofs. A small petrol-powered vehicle was provided in 1908 for over-head repair and maintenance; as it was self-propelled, it could operate when the current was switched-off. Three other similar vehicles (two converted from cars previously in passenger service) were later acquired as the electrified network spread.

Following steam-haulage of the first set over the line to test clearances on 5th January 1909 and the first electrically-powered trial run between Battersea Park and East Brixton later the same month (probably 17th January, but sources vary as to the exact date), extensive testing took place through the year. On one occasion a set ran non-stop between the two termini in just fourteen minutes and eight seconds. Various problems conspired to put back the commencement of passenger services, and as a result it was necessary to arrange storage of most of the new rolling stock at the manufacturers for a time as it was completed. Technically, there were problems with the electrical equipment on the motor coaches to be overcome, and it is also likely that realignment of catenary wires was necessary in certain locations as mentioned above.

It had been hoped to inaugurate the electric service in June but it was then necessary to make adjustments to the power supply arrangements in response to a legal writ served by the Postmaster General, who was concerned over possible interference to his telegraph cables. It was then anticipated that services would start on 1st October following a Board of Trade inspection on 1st August, but the inspecting officer required signalling alterations at London Bridge to be made before approval to commence passenger operation could be given. Eventually, public services started on 1st December.

The LBSCR used electrification as a means to reduce staffing costs on the South London line by putting the drivers of the new electric trains, henceforth known as motormen, on a lower rate of pay than equivalent steam drivers, the sums involved being 25s and 39s per week respectively. For this reason, although steam drivers were given the option of becoming motormen, few took up the offer but moved to other duties. Instead, most motormen were retrained firemen or guards who were already on a comparable rate of pay.

On weekdays and Saturdays the new electric trains ran at roughly fifteen-minute intervals from 7.30am to midnight, although the headways were irregular when compared to the South Western electric services introduced a few years later. On Sundays there was a regular-interval service every half-hour from 7.15am until 11.15pm, except for a two-hour 'church interval' then usual in mid-morning. With nine intermediate stops, the journey time by electric train for the eight miles 51 chains between London Bridge and Victoria was only 24 minutes, enabling each train to do a round trip, plus layovers, in an hour. This compared with a 36 minute journey time for the superseded steam services. Originally, steam trains conveying all three classes ran on weekdays from 4.30 to 7.30am (the current at that time being switched off, probably to enable some works to be completed), but from 1st June 1912 the service was entirely electrically worked. Rush-hour services were initially worked by two of the three-coach sets coupled together, one being used at other times.

The newly electrified services were marketed as *The South London Elevated Electric*, frequently shortened to just *Elevated Electric*, referring both to the means of current collection and the nature of the line, which was mostly on viaduct or embankment. Large green and white enamelled metal signs advertising the new service were erected at

Victoria and London Bridge, and smaller versions appeared at the intermediate stations. To further promote the improved service, a pocket folder was issued to the public giving details of train times and fares. Although normal fares were not much altered, season ticket rates were reduced, an annual ticket between London Bridge and Victoria costing only £7 5s first class or £5 10s third. Another popular innovation was the issue of weekly packets of six third class return tickets at a discount price, for example London Bridge to Victoria for 2s, giving a saving of 6d, the normal third class return between these stations costing 5d.

From the start, the new services proved highly successful, surprisingly so to LBSCR management it would appear. According to Sir William Forbes, a return of 10% on capital had been earned in the first year, passenger numbers rising from four million in 1909 to seven and a half million in 1910. As this large increase was almost entirely in third class, it soon became clear that the balance of accommodation in the electric trains was wrong, a result of incorrect traffic predic-

The maintenance and overhaul shop at Peckham Rye depot, built for the South London line electrification. Dick Kerr petrol railcar No.1, purchased by the LBSCR in 1908 specifically for overhead inspection and repair, stands outside. Three-coach unit 6E is parked in the pit-equipped siding alongside, while sister unit 3E can just be glimpsed inside. The condition of the rolling stock clearly dates this picture to the 1909-10 period.

Overhead wiring and supports at the southern end of Crystal Palace tunnel, the supports generally being a little less substantial than those used on the South London line. The train of CP stock is running into the Down Norwood Junction platform with (according to the headcode) a terminating service from Victoria via Streatham Hill. Part of the Crystal Palace itself can be seen projecting above the wall behind the signal box.

tions. Most of the first class City workers who had moved into the area in the first wave of South London housing development in the 1850-80 period were now retiring. Their place was largely taken by people making more local third class journeys to work in shops, light industry and even crewing the new trams, whose routes did not generally parallel the railway. To counteract this imbalance, and possibly for other technical reasons mentioned later, between 1910 and 1912 the motor coaches were paired with driving trailer composites converted from steam stock, giving a much lower proportion of first class seating, while the original trailer firsts were eventually adapted for steam haulage and transferred to the main line. Following these reformations, off-peak services comprised a single two-coach set and peak hour trains two or three sets coupled together.

With the success of the South London line electrification, further extensions to the electric network were put in hand almost immediately. Plans to extend the Wimbledon branch of the District Railway to the LBSCR stronghold of Sutton, a scheme supported by residents of that town, resulted in a South London line set being steam-hauled there from London Bridge in January 1910. Ostensibly to test clearances, this exercise was really to make the political point that the LBSCR was quite ready to electrify to Sutton if competition made such action necessary. However, the Wimbledon and Sutton scheme made no progress at this time (it was eventually brought to fruition by the Southern Railway in 1929-30, as recounted in Chapter 2) and so early in 1910 it was decided to put conversion of the Crystal Palace lines in hand.

The initial LBSCR route to Crystal Palace to be electrified was that from Battersea Park via Clapham Junction and Streatham Hill, the old West End of London and Crystal Palace line. While planning for this was going ahead, it was decided also to include the section from Peckham Rye to Tulse Hill, whence there were spurs to West Norwood Junction (for the Crystal Palace direction) and Leigham Junction (for Streatham Hill). Past the junction between Crystal Palace tunnel and the platforms, the lines through both sections of Crystal Palace station itself were wired up. Beyond the direct London Bridge platforms, the catenary extended a short distance towards Sydenham, to allow electric stock access to the berthing sidings and pits between them, which were also wired up accordingly. Past the Croydon/Beckenham platforms, the overhead extended to Norwood Junction and on through the platforms at Selhurst, to enable stock to reach the new shed complex and sidings erected in that area. Between Battersea Park Junction and south of the platforms at Clapham Junction only the local lines were electrified, but beyond to Balham all four tracks were wired to enable electric trains to overtake each other. Other short sections converted included the third (reversible) road between London Bridge and South Bermondsey Junction and its continuation as a second Up line to Peckham Rye, and the Down relief in addition to the Up and Down local lines at Norwood Junction. At Clapham Junction, one of the Pig Hill sidings north of the station was wired up, with connections to the Up and Down local lines, to enable electric trains to

reverse there if necessary, while at Streatham Hill the London-facing Up-side bay was converted for the same purpose. At Crystal Palace all three of the Croydon bays, as well as a berthing siding to the south, were electrified, as were two additional platforms at London Bridge.

The Crystal Palace extensions were carried out under similar financial arrangements and by the same contractors as for the South London line and work proceeded very rapidly. The electrification fixed equipment was largely the same as for the previous scheme, but the switch cabins were more widely spaced and there were further large distribution cabins at Peckham Rye and Tulse Hill, fed from the original plant at Queens Road. Experience showed the standard catenary supports could be of lighter section and, as before, a variety of other designs was used where local conditions demanded. The most striking examples were erected between Pouparts Junction and Clapham Junction where, due to the close proximity of parallel LSWR lines, it was necessary to use cantilever supports. These had their uprights adjacent to the Down local line on the edge of the embankment, and reached over all four LBSCR roads to cover possible future requirements, although only the local lines were actually wired. Owing to the length of these cantilevers, it was necessary to have two pairs of upright supports spaced widely apart, and provision was made to run a fifth line between them if this should ever prove necessary. Their distinctive design led to them being dubbed 'guns' during World War One. There were lengthy tunnels at Leigham Court (directly south of the Streatham Hill platforms), Knights Hill (north of Tulse Hill) and Crystal Palace, and in these the overhead catenary was supported on steel beams carried on brackets let into the tunnel lining, the insulators being mounted above the beams in the standard arrangement. Between Bromley Junction and Norwood Junction and around the Norwood Fork spur considerable lengths of single track were to be electrified, and on these sections single wooden poles and lightweight steel arms were used. Finally, where the line ran in deep brick-lined cutting on the approaches to Clapham Junction and elsewhere, the horizontal supports were affixed to concrete blocks let directly into the tops of the retaining walls.

Above right The Sydenham and direct London Bridge side of Crystal Palace (LBSCR), showing the long lattice overhead supports spanning the platforms. The centre tracks were used for berthing and light maintenance outside the peaks. A six-coach train of CP stock departs (as shown by the angle of the bow collector), bound for West Norwood and London.

Right The impressive cantilever overhead supports between Clapham Junction and Pouparts Junction. Erected with future expansion in mind, they spanned all four LBSCR lines at this point and allowed space for an additional track between the uprights on the left. A train of CP stock, in its original formation with motor coach leading, approaches with a Crystal Palace – Victoria working.

Selhurst was the second choice of site for the new electric stock depot, there being insufficient land at the originally preferred location at Streatham Hill. The site chosen, on the west side of the line between Norwood Junction and Selhurst stations, was mostly purchased from Crystal Palace Football Club, who relocated northwards to Selhurst Park, but some farmland was also utilised. Construction commenced in 1910 and was completed by the middle of 1911. It was necessary to lay the access tracks from south of the local platforms at Selhurst due to site considerations, and the lines through these platforms (and slightly beyond, towards Thornton Heath) were therefore wired to enable electric stock to reverse and shunt into the depot, even though no scheduled electric services were due to call there. The depot consisted of ten electrified sidings, four of which ran into an inspection and repair shop constructed of corrugated iron cladding on a steel framework. Electric stock could also be inspected at existing facilities at Peckham Rye, and in the pit-equipped centre roads at Crystal Palace.

Wide-bodied rolling stock of the type used on the South London line was unsuitable for the Crystal Palace routes due to restricted clearances (particularly in the tunnels), and conventional 8ft wide compartment coaches without side gangways were therefore supplied. MACW supplied 34 motor coaches and 34 driving trailer composites, while a further 34 trailers were built at the LBSCR carriage works at Lancing. These vehicles were made up into loose coupled three-coach sets comprising one motor coach and two trailers, but six (two sets) or even eight-coach trains were worked in the rush hours.

Electrification from Battersea Park to Crystal Palace was completed in time for an intensive passenger service to run to and from Victoria on 12th May 1911, the date of the opening of the Festival of Empire at the Crystal Palace by King George V to celebrate his coronation. The extension through to Norwood Junction and Selhurst was also used to cope with the heavy traffic on this occasion. Following this, it appears that some electric services ran to steam timings until 1st June, when the full electric timetable commenced between Victoria and Crystal Palace. In the Down direction on weekdays there were three trains per hour from 7am to 8am, followed by a roughly quarter-hourly interval until 4pm. Five per hour ran until 6pm, following which the service was cut back to a fifteen-minute interval until 9pm and then three per hour until close of service at midnight. Similar services worked in the Up direction, except that the five per hour frequency operated in the morning peak instead. As on the South London line, intervals between trains in a particular hour were not generally even.

Work on the lines from London Bridge via Tulse Hill was also finished in 1911, but in this case electric services could not commence immediately due to the necessary power not being available from the suppliers, who were in the process of extending Deptford Power Station. A strike by coal miners between 1st March and 9th April 1912 did not assist matters either, but a limited service was started on 3rd March as a means of economising on locomotive coal, electric trains

running from London Bridge via Tulse Hill to Crystal Palace, Norwood Junction and Selhurst. The full electric timetable eventually commenced on 3rd June, and from this date trains ran between London Bridge and Crystal Palace with a four per hour frequency from 9am until 11am, and then three per hour until the last train just before midnight. There was also a circular service running between Victoria and London Bridge via Streatham Hill, Leigham Junction and Tulse Hill; this ran approximately every twenty minutes in the morning and evening peaks and hourly at other times. During the middle of the day (11.25am until 2.35pm) these services ran between London Bridge and Streatham Hill only, while a number of others terminated at Clapham Junction, making use of the Pig Hill reversing siding referred to previously. Trains on both these routes from London Bridge ran non-stop as far as Queens Road Peckham, while some peak-hour services missed out East Dulwich and/or North Dulwich. Where particular trains entered or came out of service at Crystal Palace, they normally picked up or set down passengers at Norwood Junction on the journey from/to Selhurst depot, but otherwise there were no electric services normally timetabled between these three points at this time. Other than wartime changes mentioned below, service patterns and frequencies on the South London and Crystal Palace lines remained roughly constant until the ac overhead system was abandoned in 1928/29.

A new feature introduced on the Crystal Palace lines with electrification was the use of numerical headcodes to denote to passengers and staff the destination and route of a particular train. These headcodes consisted of black enamel plates with white numbers, clipped between the cab windows at the front of the train and illuminated from above. The original headcode numbers and the routes to which they refer are listed below:

1 Victoria – Streatham Hill – Crystal Palace
2 Victoria – Streatham Hill
3 Victoria – Streatham Hill – Crystal Palace – Norwood Junction
4 London Bridge – Tulse Hill – Crystal Palace
5 London Bridge – Tulse Hill – Streatham Hill/Clapham Junction/Victoria
6 London Bridge – Tulse Hill – Crystal Palace – Norwood Junction

The Crystal Palace lines proved financially as successful as the South London line had been following electrification, with passenger numbers increasing by 70% in the first year, and also reduced operating costs. As part of their half-yearly report to the shareholders covering the period ending 31st December 1912, the LBSCR Directors therefore announced their decision to electrify the remainder of the suburban network, with the exception of one or two minor lines, as far out as Cheam on the Epsom line and Coulsdon and Smitham Downs on the main line. It was expected that the necessary work as a whole would take four years to complete, but would be carried out in sections with each being brought into service as it became ready. With the detailed planning already done, contracts were quickly let, AEG once more being chosen as main supplier for the electrical installation.

Cheam station, looking towards Ewell East, following the installation of passing loops by the LBSCR in 1911 and third-rail dc electrification between Sutton and Epsom by the Southern Railway in 1929. Through electrification rendered LSBCR plans to interchange terminating ac services here with outer-suburban and coastal trains superfluous, and hence the intended central island platform was never built. *Stations UK*

The routes to be dealt with were as follows:

a) London Bridge – Norwood Junction – Windmill Bridge Junction – East Croydon – Coulsdon and Smitham Downs

b) Sydenham – Crystal Palace

c) Norwood Fork – West Croydon – Sutton – Cheam

d) Tulse Hill – Streatham – Mitcham Junction – Sutton

e) Balham – Windmill Bridge Junction and West Croydon line

f) Streatham – Streatham Common

g) Streatham Junction North – Streatham Junction South.

h) Purley – Tadworth/Tattenham Corner and Caterham*

  *SECR-owned lines. See later in this chapter for explanation.

Additionally, it was intended to extend Streatham Hill sidings to provide further maintenance and berthing accommodation for the extra trains required.

Regarding rolling stock for the projected extensions, it was intended at this time to use two-coach sets formed of a driving motor third brake and a driving trailer composite, similar to the revised South London line stock but with a normal 8ft width Crystal Palace-type motor coach. A contract for 200 motor coaches was placed with MACW on 18th July 1913, the £1 million cost being underwritten by the manufacturers, and shortly afterwards Lancing Works was instructed to commence building trailers. At this time AEG were to supply motors and other electrical equipment, as before. Construction of trailers commenced in 1914.

The line from Norwood Fork through West Croydon, Wallington and Sutton to Cheam was considered first priority, enabling Crystal Palace line services from Victoria to be extended through to these stations. The populations of Croydon and Sutton were rising rapidly in the first years of the century (in the case of Croydon, from 134,000 to 170,000 between 1901 and 1911) and good traffic receipts were expected from these towns. Although considered by the LBSCR to be the edge of its suburban area, the main purpose of extending through to Cheam, the first station out from Sutton towards Epsom, was to provide room for terminating electric services away from the congested junction station at Sutton. Conveniently, loops had been laid in between the south end of the Epsom line platforms there and Cheam in 1911, mainly in order to allow Mid-Sussex expresses to over-take stopping services. As part of this widening the station at Cheam was entirely reconstructed with new side platforms (connected by subway) on the loops, which were designated slow lines. Space was also left between the existing centre fast lines for an island platform which was not built at the time, but featured in plans for extending *Elevated Electric* services. Terminating electric trains would use the Down slow platform, and berth in reversing sidings to be laid on the Down side at the country end before shunting to the Up loop platform to start the return journey to London. Between these manoeuvres, outer-suburban or coastal trains would call at the centre island to connect. It was also expected that traffic at Wallington would be heavy, and it was therefore intended to turn back some electric services there, utilising a new reversing siding. Situated between the running lines at the country end of the station, it was to be provided by laying a new Down line and using the existing Down alignment as the siding.

Work on parts of the Sutton extension pressed ahead with some speed, and in April 1914 the LBSCR published a statement in which it was hoped that electric services from Victoria to West Croydon and Wallington (via Crystal Palace) would commence '...about the summer of next year (1915)'. However, that August World War One broke out and, as it became impossible to obtain materials from the German contractors, installation ceased some time in 1915 as supplies ran out. For the same reason the rolling stock contract was renegotiated in 1915, with MACW now agreeing to provide fully-equipped motor coaches, but it is unclear who would have supplied the electrical equipment. Twelve driving trailers had been completed in 1914 and fifteen more the following year before work at Lancing ceased. Two of the finished vehicles entered service on the Crystal Palace lines but the rest, together with a number of underframes, were immediately placed into store.

The following description of works completed by the summer of 1915 was mainly compiled by the late J. Howard Turner[1] from eyewitness accounts; it is thought that no documentary evidence still exists. Concrete anchorages for the catenary supports had been installed all the way from Norwood Fork to Sutton Home signals (before the junction with the line from Mitcham Junction), while the overhead supports and catenary wire were complete southwards from West Croydon, again as far as Sutton Home signals. Work on the reversing siding at Wallington was half-completed, but nothing had been done at Cheam. A possible reason why the Norwood Fork – West Croydon section had not been wired up is that non-standard catenary was required in the Gloucester Road Junction area, whereas the remainder of the route involved only routine work installing standard structures. Nothing had been done in the Sutton station area because it was intended to remodel the junctions to provide direct connections from the West Croydon line into the Epsom Downs platforms clear of those on the Mitcham Junction – Epsom line. Elsewhere, it seems that overhead catenary had been erected from Tulse Hill through Streatham to a point just beyond Streatham Junction South on the Mitcham Junction line by the end of 1914, as part of the general scheme ((d) and (g) above), and possibly also on the Streatham Junction North – Streatham Junction South spurs. Other work included substantial concrete walls and abutments for electrified berthing sidings, never completed, on the Down side between Balham and Streatham Hill.

In August 1914 the entire British railway network, as a strategic resource, was placed under Government control under the direction of a Railway Executive Committee. Although disruption to the Capital's railway services during World War One was as nothing compared to 1939-45, the *Elevated Electric* network was affected by restrictions imposed. The SECR Metropolitan Extension services between Victoria and Moorgate Street, which closely paralleled the South London line for much of their route, were withdrawn on 3rd April 1916, leaving LBSCR electric trains to cope with all the heavy traffic from stations between Victoria and East Brixton. Later, to release men for the Army, a number of inner-area stations were closed; on the electrified network these included South Bermondsey and Old Kent Road and Hatcham, both on the South London line, from the beginning of 1917. At the same time a number of services and station opening times were curtailed, with Sunday closure of East Brixton and North Dulwich and withdrawal of Sunday trains between London Bridge and Crystal Palace/Streatham Hill. After the War ended a number of these changes were reversed, although some not until after the 1923 Grouping. South Bermondsey was reopened on 1st May 1919, but Old Kent Road remained closed and was eventually demolished by the Southern Railway in 1925, shortly after an edict that it was to reopen. An hourly London Bridge – Crystal Palace Sunday service was reinstated by the SR in July 1923, and East Brixton (but not North Dulwich) reopened on Sundays from 12th July 1925.

After the War it seemed that amalgamation of the existing railway companies, if not outright nationalisation, was inevitable, and it was therefore very difficult for them to make concrete plans for the future. This was not helped by continuing Government controls and the unstable state of the railway manufacturing industry at the time. In the event it proved possible only to continue with schemes started before the war, this meaning electrification in the case of the LBSCR. However AEG could obviously no longer be used as main contractor, and the General Electric Company (GEC) therefore stepped in to supply the remaining electrical equipment, with Blackwell's providing the overhead catenary structures as before. The supports and catenary for the Norwood Fork – West Croydon section were eventually installed in about 1920.

A more serious problem was that the finance authorised in 1913 was not now sufficient to complete the scheme, a result of wartime inflation, and the LBSCR had in the meantime to confine itself to more modest electrification proposals. In view of this, the company asked in May 1921 to be released from the 1915 rolling stock contract with the renamed Metropolitan Carriage, Wagon and Finance Co., who agreed provided that twelve motor coaches were purchased. These, together with the trailers already completed at Lancing, would presumably have provided enough trains to cover the almost-complete West Croydon extension. As before, no work was done immediately by MCWF, but Lancing Works had recommenced construction of trailers late in 1919, a further fifteen being outshopped.

---

1 Howard Turner J.T.: *The London Brighton and South Coast Railway Volume 3 – Completion and Maturity*, ISBN 0 7134 1389 1, 1979, pp197-198

Notwithstanding the financial climate and other uncertainties Philip Dawson, no doubt wishing to justify his consultant's fee, had submitted a comprehensive 201 route mile scheme for further electrification in 1919. His report recommended conversion of not only the remainder of the LBSCR suburban lines as planned before the War, but also the main line to Brighton and its associated branches to West Worthing, Eastbourne and Seaford – it will be recalled that the high-tension ac system was originally chosen with the Brighton main line in mind. Not only this, but the SECR-owned lines to Redhill, Oxted and Dorking Town were also included by agreement with the South Eastern and Chatham Managing Committee. As will be seen later, the SECR was actively itself actively considering electrification, but on an entirely different 3,000V dc system, and this arrangement was designed to avoid duplicate installations on the London – Purley route and beyond. The LBSCR's plans were submitted to the newly formed Ministry of Transport for approval late in 1920.

In January 1921 Dawson submitted a further report, this time covering rolling stock requirements. Three-coach sets formed of two driving motor coaches and a centre trailer were suggested for the remainder of the suburban and outer suburban routes, while locomotives hauling existing stock would have worked main line passenger services, including through trains from outside the electrified area, as well as freight. The LBSCR rejected Dawson's proposals in this field, deciding instead on the use of more flexible 'motor coaches' (basically short motor luggage vans) hauling or propelling driving trailers and non-driving trailers, and it was in this form that the Coulsdon and Sutton electric stock was eventually provided. In December 1921 an electrical specification for this stock was drawn up by Dawson and the equipment contract was won by GEC against the rival bid from the Metropolitan-Vickers Electrical Company Ltd.

With Grouping pending, the LBSCR clearly thought it desirable to obtain a second opinion regarding future main line and suburban electrification, and on 2nd November 1921 the company engaged another consultant, the Swiss engineer Dr D. Heinemann. After reporting on problems with rolling stock electrical equipment, in January 1922 he presented a reduced 109-mile plan covering only the remaining suburban routes and the main line to Brighton. In the same month, however, the Board decided not to go ahead with main line extensions and the parliamentary bill covering Dawson's scheme was withdrawn, consigning both his and Heinemann's plans to history. This was despite Ministry of Transport pressure to proceed, their Advisory Committee on electrification chaired by Sir Alexander Kennedy having come down in favour of the ac system in 1920.

Notwithstanding the foregoing, LBSCR officers remained convinced that wholesale electrification, at least of their suburban lines, was necessary to handle existing traffic, let alone any increases occurring for whatever reason. Following the lifting of Government controls from midnight on 15th August 1921, and in spite of approaching amalgamation with neighbouring railways (LSWR and SECR) unsympathetic to the idea of high-voltage ac electrification, the company then announced in 1922 that it was to continue with the scheme drawn up in 1913 and convert the Balham–Windmill Bridge Junction–East Croydon–Coulsdon and Smitham Downs route, as well as bringing the Sutton line into operation at least as far as Wallington. With the grudging agreement of its neighbours, finance for this was raised by issuing previously authorised debenture stock worth about £300,000. In January 1922 Dawson's consultancy contract was renewed by the LBSCR 'for two years or to see the work through', giving the Board of the Southern Railway little choice but to renew it again in December 1923. The 21 motor luggage vans and six of the trailers were ordered from MCWF, in fulfilment of the 1921 agreement, the remainder of the trailers not already extant coming from railway workshops.

LBSCR track maintenance staff in the suburban area were instructed to '...carry out whatever work remained to complete the equipment of the railway between Balham Junction and West Croydon forthwith' – in effect to put up catenary supports and overhead wires whenever they had time to spare between their regular work. Installation again proceeded rapidly and by the end of the company's separate existence on the last day of 1922 it appears that overhead catenary supports had been erected from Balham as far as Gloucester Road Junction, just before East Croydon. Overhead wiring reached Coulsdon North a year later. The Coulsdon and Sutton ac electrification was eventually brought into service by the Southern Railway in 1925.

Heinemann was still not finished and presented yet another, cheaper, proposal on 22nd November 1922, just weeks before Grouping. The number of suburban lines to be converted was slightly reduced to cover (in addition to those already authorised) just Tulse Hill–Mitcham Junction–Sutton and South Bermondsey–New Cross–Norwood Junction. Main line electrification was to be confined to the Brighton main line plus Preston Park to Dyke Junction (West of Hove). The most interesting parts of this final proposal were an increase in line-voltage south of Coulsdon to 11,000, as also recommended by the Gibbs report (see later) and for which the existing system was already suitable, and three-phase supply to the substations. The suburban routes would have been worked by the same stock as provided for the Coulsdon and Wallington scheme, while main line services from outside the electrified area would have been hauled to London from suitable changeover points by motor luggage vans working singly or in pairs. Only London–Brighton services would have used larger electric locomotives of 2-4-4-2 or 4-4-4-4 wheel arrangements and, as Heinemann was Swiss, he quite possibly envisaged 'Crocodile' types. The *Southern Belle* Pullmans speeding out of Quarry tunnel at Merstham behind one of these would have been a sight to behold!

The final years of the *Elevated Electric* network, under Southern Railway ownership, are dealt with in the next chapter.

THE SOUTH WESTERN ELECTRICS

By the start of the twentieth century, the London and South Western Railway (LSWR) had also developed a comprehensive network of inner and outer-suburban routes, radiating south-westwards from its then sprawling and untidy London terminus at Waterloo. Its lines ran into the prosperous Thames valley, west Surrey and surrounding areas, districts served including the well-heeled outer suburbs of Wimbledon, Richmond, Epsom and Surbiton as well as the more central (but by 1900 rather less desirable) Clapham and Battersea. The steam trains working these routes were often infrequent, slow and relatively uncomfortable, although the LSWR had better quality rolling stock than many of its contemporaries. While the railway was the only means of long distance mobility for the majority, the fare-paying public at large had little choice but to put up with its shortcomings. From 1900 the company began to introduce new bogie carriages for use on its suburban lines, hauled by more powerful locomotives, but there remained major shortcomings to the service frequency and comfort offered.

At this time, demographic trends resulted in a movement of population away from the inner suburbs and, as mentioned earlier, a series of wet summers coupled with a trade recession also conspired to reduce traffic in the years up to 1908. As on the neighbouring LBSCR, the net result of these factors was a steady and worrying drop in passenger loadings and receipts. During the same period, several new and more attractive forms of urban transport were beginning to abstract even more traffic away from the railway. The most important of these were the newly-electrified tramways operated by the London County Council (LCC) in the inner area and London United Tramways (LUT) further out. They had the combined advantages of cheap fares, a frequent and regular interval service, and convenient stopping places. These same advantages were also offered from about 1908 by the developing road motor-bus services, which were not at this time subject to stringent Government controls. The new tube railways, especially the Central London to Shepherds Bush (1900) and the Great Northern, Piccadilly and Brompton line to Hammersmith (1906), also played their part in tempting users away from the LSWR's trains, particularly those on the circuitous route from Clapham Junction to Richmond via Shepherds Bush. Both tube lines gave good connections with tram, and later bus, services which operated into the heart of South Western suburban territory.

Another major new threat to LSWR services at this time was the Metropolitan District Railway (MDR) electric trains operating into the South Western strongholds of Hounslow, Richmond and Wimbledon from 1905. Ironically, District trains running to these destinations did so over metals owned by the main line company, and they were therefore the first electric trains to use LSWR tracks (apart from the Waterloo and City tube, which was a special case). This came about because the MDR had running powers over two short sections of line, from Studland Road Junction (Hammersmith) to Turnham Green and Richmond, and between Putney Bridge and Wimbledon.

An agreement was signed between the companies concerned on 4th December 1903, whereby the LSWR undertook to carry out conversion of both sections of line to electric traction, with the MDR paying interest on the capital. The work, done under the supervision of the District's Chief Electrical Engineer, included the laying of positive and negative conductor rails, energised with a potential between them of 600V dc (300V above ground potential in the outer rail, and 300V below in the inner rail). This electrification system was used by all railways owned by the Underground Company (the District and three tube lines) and was the natural choice of their American promoters under Charles Tyson Yerkes. Power for these systems was provided from the Underground's generating station at Lots Road, Chelsea. The Hammersmith–Turnham Green section was used by scheduled electric services from 1st July 1905, followed closely by the Turnham Green–Richmond and Putney Bridge–Wimbledon lines from 1st and 27th August respectively. The new District electric trains followed North American practice and consisted of saloon-bodied bogie cars with sliding doors opening into wide vestibules (B stock in the MDR's rolling stock classification). Running at frequent intervals, these new trains quickly attracted the public of Wimbledon, Richmond and surrounding areas away from the LSWR's own suburban services. In particular, passenger loadings on Hounslow loop trains, whose route was closely paralleled for almost its entire length by an MDR line electrified in June 1905, fell substantially.

Although the South Western's management could see what was going on around it and was aware of the loss of passengers and revenue on its suburban lines, the rather complacent attitude prevailing at the time meant that little was done to attempt to curb the decline or, more particularly, to encourage traffic. The Chairman of the LSWR Board, Sir Charles Scotter, and its General Manager, Sir Charles Owens, seemed more concerned with developing long-distance traffic to the west country than with the problems of suburban development. However, all was about to change. The elderly Chairman died in December 1910 at the age of 75, and was succeeded by Sir Hugh Drummond. Sir Charles Owens retired at the end of the same year, and the new Chairman went head-hunting for a successor. At the suggestion of the company solicitor, Will Bishop, he chose Herbert Ashcombe Walker, who was appointed to the post of LSWR General Manager as from 1st January 1912. At the age of 43, Walker already had a distinguished record in railway management, latterly in the senior position of Outdoor Goods Manager on the London and North Western Railway. At the LSWR, and later the Southern Railway, he was to become the outstanding railway manager of the first half of the twentieth century. (Unconnected with the development of the Southern Electric for which he was largely responsible, it is convenient to mention here that he was knighted in the New Year Honours list in 1915 and advanced to KCB in 1917, in both cases for his service to the Government in wartime.)

Walker was a man of action and, following his appointment, saw revival of traffic and receipts in the suburban area as a priority. He quickly chose electrification as the best and

Portrait of (Sir) Herbert Walker.

Wimbledon Power station (as originally built) with Durnsford Road electric train shed adjacent.

most cost-effective method of achieving this goal. As well as the more attractive service possible due to the superior acceleration of electric trains, such a conversion also promised operating and maintenance economies. In order to move forward with the planning of a suitable suburban electrification scheme he promoted Herbert Jones to the post of Electrical Engineer. Jones had just about as much experience in railway electric traction as was then possible, having been involved with the pioneer electric tube line, the City and South London Railway. In 1898 he moved to the new Waterloo and City Railway, the second of London's deep level electric tube railways and from its inception a puppet of the LSWR, where he became engineer-in-charge from 1900. Following his promotion, Jones was sent on a fact-finding trip to the United States later in 1912, to look particularly at direct current third-rail installations in use on urban railroads there. He returned to England impressed with what he saw, particularly with regard to the economy of installation and reliability in use of such systems. This resulted in the third-rail dc system being chosen as most suitable for the task by both Jones and Walker, a view reinforced by Mr (later Sir) Alexander Kennedy from the firm Kennedy and Donkin, who was engaged as an additional consulting engineer on electrical matters. A suitable scheme was drawn up very quickly, and was presented to the LSWR Board in December 1912.

Walker and Jones were certainly not interested in the LBSCR's high-tension overhead scheme, parts of which had been in operation for three years when LSWR suburban electrification was first mooted. The company was not at that time concerned about main line electrification as such, the equipment was seen as expensive to install and maintain, and a foreign company was involved. As will be seen later, this lack of a uniform electrification system was to lead to much friction between officials of the two companies before and just after the 1923 Grouping.

In charge of rolling stock for the electrification was Surrey Warner, LSWR Carriage and Wagon Superintendent. Warner had come from the GWR at Swindon in 1905 to replace William Panter in charge of the South Western's carriage works at Eastleigh. Although the original intention had been to provide new stock for the electric services, to save costs it was decided at an early stage to adapt some of the most recent steam-hauled suburban stock, designed by Panter and built between 1902 and 1912, which would otherwise have been made redundant by electrification. Quite apart from the estimated £56,000 cost saving, a further advantage of this course of action was that compartment stock would provide more seats than equivalent new saloon vehicles of the type used on other lines.

The proposals of Walker and Jones to electrify the principal suburban lines of the LSWR were adopted by the Board and announced to shareholders early in 1913. The proposed scheme was to be divided into two stages. Routes to be converted in stage one were Waterloo to Waterloo via both the Kingston and Hounslow loops, the main line out as far as Hampton Court Junction and thence onwards to both Hampton Court and Claygate (a short distance down the Guildford New line), the Shepperton branch, and Wimbledon to East Putney and Point Pleasant Junction. This part of the scheme covered fifty route miles and about 150 track miles, and it was expected that the work involved would take two years to complete, at an estimated cost of £1,159,284. The rest of the scheme, or stage two, was to include all three routes to Guildford, via Epsom, Cobham and Woking, and (possibly) Twickenham/Hounslow to Windsor. Incidental works were to include the construction of flyovers at Hampton Court Junction and Woking, and of electric stock maintenance depots on land already owned at Wimbledon and Strawberry Hill. A power station to provide electricity for the new trains was to be erected, also at Wimbledon.

The London and South Western Railway never obtained Parliamentary powers for electrification, in contrast to the LBSCR and SECR, as it considered that propulsion by electricity was not ruled out under the terms of the original London and Southampton Railway Act of 1838. Certain organisations showed concern at the LSWR plans while their 1913 Bill was being discussed in Parliament however, including the National Physical Laboratory located at Bushy Park, near Teddington, who were worried that stray return currents could affect readings on their delicate magnetic instruments. In spite of initial efforts to prevent this by providing additional insulation to the running rail return, it was proved that stray currents were indeed escaping and further expensive work had therefore to be carried out. Another organisation to complain was the Post Office, concerned about possible effects on the electric telegraph; again additional works had to be undertaken, slowing the introduction of electric services on the Kingston loop.

Unlike the neighbouring Brighton company, which obtained the necessary power for its electric trains from outside sources, the LSWR built its own generating station. This was situated at Durnsford Road, Wimbledon, on the Up side of the line north of Wimbledon station and next to the River Wandle. A large red-brick edifice, its twin chimneys soon became a well-known landmark in the area. The boiler house contained sixteen Babcock and Wilcox boilers with chain-grate stokers, fed with coal from a 1,400 ton capacity bunker. This in turn was supplied from a coal storage area, served by wagons on a 550ft overhead siding. This siding was electrified, and shunting was carried out by a small BoBo steeple-cab electric locomotive which had originally been acquired from Dick, Kerr as early as 1899 for the Waterloo and City Railway. In the turbine room, five 5,000 kilowatt turbo-alternators generated three-phase alternating current at 11,000V, 25Hz. Cooling towers, utilising water from the adjacent River Wandle, were situated at the north end of the power station.

The high-tension current was distributed from Durnsford Road by means of lineside cabling to the substations, of which there were nine in the initial stage of the scheme. Three-core, paper-insulated, lead-sheathed armoured cable was used, mounted on short posts beside the running lines, and the cable arrangements provided duplicate feeds to each substation. The substations were located at Waterloo, Clapham Junction, Raynes Park, Kingston, Twickenham, Barnes, Isleworth, Sunbury and Hampton Court Junction and, with the exception of Clapham Junction (located inside an arch at the country end of what was then Platform 5, now 9-10), were all housed in tall brick buildings of distinctive appearance. Substation electrical equipment was supplied by British Thomson-Houston and consisted of transformers to step-down 11,000V to the nominal line voltage of 600, rotary converters to rectify the current from alternating to direct, and associated switchgear. These converters had to be manned continuously while trains were working, and were therefore expensive to run; unmanned remotely-controlled substations were some years into the future.

From the substations, the electricity was fed to the conductor rails, of 100lb/yard flat-bottomed 'Vignoles' section produced from special high-conductivity steel. They were mounted outside the running rails on porcelain insulators, generally attached to every third sleeper. The surface of the conductor rails was located 3in above the running rails and their centre line was 1ft 4in outside the track gauge. As far as was practicable, they were situated between the running lines; this was especially necessary at stations, where safety considerations made it desirable to keep the conductor rail as far from the platform edge as possible. Negative return to earth was through the running rails, the joints of which were bonded with copper cables. Insulated joints for track-circuiting purposes were fitted with impedance bonds, and it was necessary to convert track-circuits from dc to ac.

Sections of the South Western already electrified for use by District electric trains had insulated return to earth through a fourth rail, and the Wimbledon – East Putney line had to be modified in order that LSWR electric trains could run over it. This involved changing the voltages of the third and fourth rails so the outer rail was at +600V and the centre rail at ground potential. (It was also necessary to alter the control gear on the District electric stock, and a switch was fitted in each cab to change between the two configurations, activated by motormen at Putney Bridge.)

Major civil engineering works carried out for stage one of the electrification scheme included the widening to eight running lines of the route between Vauxhall and Loco. Junction (Nine Elms), the provision of a flyover at Hampton Court Junction, and a new station at Barnes Bridge. The flyover was constructed to carry the Down Hampton Court branch track over the main lines to avoid conflicting movements, necessary if an intensive electric service was to be operated. Consisting of lengthy brick viaducts leading to a 160ft long skew lattice girder span, it was ready for use on 4th July 1915. The station at Barnes Bridge was rather more central to the village than Barnes station itself, situated at the Putney end of Barnes Common. Consisting of two 400ft wooden side platforms, connected by a tiled subway to a modest street level frontage, the new station opened its doors on 12th March 1916, concurrent with the start of electric working on the Hounslow loop.

Apart from these major works, many other changes of a more minor nature were needed before the lines concerned were ready to receive a frequent service of electric trains. Stations were generally tidied up, given new nameboards composed of white lettering on a blue background, and had their gas or oil lighting replaced by a low-voltage electrical installation supplied via lineside cabling from an auxiliary generator at Durnsford Road. Stopping plates, bearing the numbers 3 or 6 in white on a blue enamel square, were affixed to lamp-posts or canopy supports at convenient locations along the platforms. Coasting marks consisting of white diamonds mounted on a short upright (more often than not a length of old rail), told the motorman where to cut off current in order to coast to the next station; their positions were carefully worked out in order to achieve the maximum economy.

Left LSWR three-coach electric unit in service near Hounslow c1920.

Below 74S, One of the two small electric locos built for the Waterloo and City line in 1899, was transferred to Durnsford Road to shunt wagons on the power station coal incline. It survived until the 1950s change of frequency scheme and the closure of the power station; here it is seen in front of the incline, after the rebuilding of part of the power station following war damage, on 9 February 1957, shabby but still functioning. *R.C. Riley*

The rolling stock provided comprised 84 three-coach electric multiple units, numbered E1-E84. Converted from existing compartment steam-hauled stock as mentioned above, each unit comprised two motor coaches and an intermediate trailer, with driving cab and guard's accommodation at the outer end of each motor coach. In order to make best use of the vehicles utilised for conversion there were three varieties of unit, each differing slightly in internal layout and seating capacity, but all had about 180 seats of which just over one third were first class. Almost all seating was in enclosed compartments, but 21 of the units had a small first class saloon in the trailer. As on the neighbouring LBSCR, the electric stock lacked second class seating, some time before this was abolished on other lines.

Maintenance facilities for the new electric units were provided at Wimbledon, adjacent to the generating station, on the site of the former LSWR gasworks; the six-road repair shop and nine-road inspection shed were constructed of corrugated asbestos cladding on a steel frame. In 1915 it was decided to extend these facilities by electrifying some of the adjacent Wimbledon Park sidings and erecting a carriage cleaning shed, which came into use in March 1917. Further berthing sidings were provided at Waterloo, Hounslow, Shepperton and Hampton Court, together with a larger stabling facility at Strawberry Hill.

From the public's point of view, the most important feature of the electrification was the entirely new timetable, offering frequent services with regular headways which were easily memorised. The service interval varied according to the route, with Hounslow loop and Shepperton services every thirty minutes but quarter-hourly trains on the Kingston 'roundabout', for example. At first, there were no extra electric services during the peaks, the trains merely being lengthened from three coaches to six. Trains departed from a particular station at the same minutes past each hour, and prospective passengers therefore no longer had to consult a timetable before travelling. This was a great selling point, placing the railway in effective competition with the frequent trams and underground services. The regular interval timetable was largely Walker's idea, being compiled in his office. He was once quoted as saying 'People don't like timetables, make it easy for them'.

The outbreak of World War One caused unforeseen difficulties and delays with supplies and manpower, but in spite of this the first section was ready by the latter half of 1915. This was the line from Waterloo to Wimbledon via East Putney. After commissioning of electrical equipment and the first of the new trains had taken place the new, more frequent, electric service commenced on 25th October, utilising three units. Power was supplied initially from the Underground Group's Lots Road generating station as Durnsford Road was not quite complete, and much of the route was in any case traversed by District Railway electric trains. Electric services on the rest of the routes involved in the scheme commenced on various dates in 1916 as conversion work was completed and rolling stock became available. The Kingston 'roundabout' and Shepperton branch services began on 30th January, followed by the Hounslow loop on 12th March and the Hampton Court branch on 18th June. Finally, on 20th November, the short section from Hampton Court Junction to Claygate was converted. Off-peak, alternate electric trains from Waterloo connected at Claygate with steam push-and-pull services to Guildford via Cobham, but during rush-hours through Waterloo–Cobham–Guildford steam trains continued to operate. The main reason for electrifying to Claygate seems to have been to provide an alternative terminating point, apart from Hampton Court, for electric services running down the South Western main line and serving the busy but congested Surbiton station. Additionally, by this time some minor suburban housing development at Claygate was already taking place.

Unlike the LBSCR, the motormen to drive the new electric trains were mostly recruited from the ranks of steam drivers, and were on the same rates of pay. The large scale of the conversion and wartime shortages of manpower probably left the LSWR with little choice.

By the time public services commenced, a system of headcodes had been devised to indicate the route and destination of a particular electric train. Although apparently not part of the original plans and designed largely for the benefit of signalmen, they were also useful for passengers and came to feature prominently in LSWR publicity material. They consisted of a metal stencil between the leading cab windows of the train, lit from behind at night. An additional narrow plate displaying a horizontal bar could be slipped in above the main stencil if required, effectively doubling the number of codes available. The initial list of LSWR headcodes is shown below; unless otherwise noted, the same headcode applied in both directions on a given route.

Headcode	Route
P	Waterloo – East Putney – Wimbledon
P (with bar)	Waterloo – East Putney – Wimbledon Park
V	Waterloo – New Malden – Teddington (Kingston 'roundabout')*
V (with bar)	Waterloo – Richmond – Teddington (Kingston 'roundabout')*
S	Waterloo – Wimbledon – Shepperton
S (with bar)	Waterloo – Richmond – Shepperton (peaks only)
O	Waterloo – Barnes Bridge – Hounslow (Hounslow loop)*
O (with bar)	Waterloo – Richmond – Hounslow (Hounslow loop)*
H	Waterloo – Surbiton – Hampton Court
I	Waterloo – Surbiton – Claygate

* On Kingston 'roundabout' services, the headcode was changed over at Teddington.

On Hounslow loop services, the headcode was changed over at Hounslow. The SR changed the practice; Down O and V trains via Richmond carried a bar, but Up O and V were carried unmodified.

Stage one of the LSWR's suburban electrification scheme had been largely completed by the end of 1916, although the last of the 84 three-coach electric units was not delivered from Eastleigh until August 1917. A few steam services which had remained on the electrified lines were turned over to electric traction in April 1917. Conversely, the service to Claygate reverted to steam from July 1919, the reason being a vast and not entirely foreseen increase in traffic on the other electrified sections, stimulated largely by electrification and the new improved timetables, although other sociological factors also played a part, including an influx into the south western suburbs of frightened inner-Londoners following the first German air raids on the capital. The rolling stock thus saved was redeployed on other parts of the electrified network to reduce overcrowding, and further stock became available when the Waterloo – East Putney – Wimbledon service became peak-hour only and limited-stop (East Putney and Clapham Junction) at the same time. It was soon found that the three-coach units had power to spare, and Jones decided to make further seats available in the peaks by lengthening some trains to eight coaches, by inserting a two-coach trailer set between two motor units. Converted in 1919-22 from more of the same vehicle types as had been used for the original units, these trailer sets had no driving cabs and so were an operating nuisance, especially at the beginning and end of each peak when they had to be shunted. They did however prove an effective and cheap solution to overcrowding, and the same arrangement was to be perpetuated by the Southern Railway on almost all the electrified suburban lines.

Work on stage two of the electrification was left to await the end of the War, following which detailed planning commenced. In 1920 South Western management looked seriously at electrifying to Guildford via Epsom and via Cobham, but found that contractors were unable to submit reliable tenders at reasonable prices, so further work was postponed. The planned flyover at Woking Junction was never constructed, and the electrification work was left to the Southern Railway who inherited the lines concerned at Grouping in 1923. As recounted in Chapter 2, the routes to Guildford via Epsom and via Cobham were eventually electrified in 1925, but residents of Windsor and Woking had to wait until 1930 and 1937 respectively for electric trains to serve their towns.

Although not directly concerned with the electrification, a significant event took place on 21st March 1922 when the rebuilt Waterloo station was officially opened by Queen Mary, the King being too ill to attend. The LSWR's London terminus had been in the throes of reconstruction since the turn of the century, but Walker's arrival in 1912 gave the project a new impetus. Although certain alterations to the original plans were made for economic reasons, the new station was a fitting London terminus for the new electric trains. A large concourse, equally suitable for dealing with throngs of home-going workers and with holiday crowds, led onto 21 platforms, covered by a train shed measuring 550ft by 740ft. These statistics made Waterloo now the largest station in Britain.

By the start of 1923, it could confidently be said that the London and South Western Railway under Sir Herbert Walker had achieved its aims in electrifying its inner-suburban network. Operating economies had been attained and the cleaner, more frequent trains in their smart new green livery attracted the public in ever-increasing numbers, leading to a pleasing increase in the railway's, and consequently shareholders', profits. In particular, the excellent train service was to become a factor in encouraging London's white-collar workforce to move out into the suburbs, travelling into London to work each weekday. When the Southern Railway took over the LSWR suburban network at the start of 1923, it inherited a system which would form the nucleus of the largest electrified suburban railway in the world.

THE SOUTH EASTERN AND CHATHAM PLANS

The two railways working outwards from London to the south eastern suburbs and Kent – the South Eastern Railway (SER) and the London Chatham and Dover Railway (LCDR) – had come under single management control only in 1899 through the formation of the South Eastern and Chatham Railways Managing Committee (SECR). Prior to that date the two companies had been in more or less direct competition for business in a common operating area. Inevitably this rivalry, known during its most acrimonious period as 'the feud' and fuelled by the mutual animosity of their respective Chairmen, had left both companies financially weaker than the LSWR or even the LBSCR, itself no great generator of dividends at this time. On the suburban side, the legacy of former competition was the inheritance by the SECR of two complex and virtually unconnected suburban networks and two fleets of outdated rolling stock with incompatible braking systems.

Although poor economic health meant that neither company could contemplate the investment required, the SECR Managing Committee did not let this difficulty prevent it from investigating electrification of its suburban lines and on 11th August 1903 obtained parliamentary powers to electrify its entire system, probably as a publicity gesture. An important clause in the 1903 Act, insisted on by the Admiralty, required the railway to protect the instruments at the Royal Observatory at Greenwich from stray currents leaking from its electrified lines. In the following years losses became apparent in the inner suburban area following the introduction of electric trams paralleling its own routes and the Committee was also aware of the financial success of its neighbours' suburban electrification programmes after 1909. As mentioned earlier, in 1913 the LBSCR offered to electrify the SER-owned branches from Purley to Caterham and Tattenham Corner using the 6,700V ac overhead system as part of its own electrification programme, provided that it could then lease them for operation. Talks reached the stage of discussing suitable signalling methods, but the plan was deferred with the outbreak of war, only to resurface later. The LBSCR method of electrification was also that preferred by Francis Dent, who had become General Manager of the SECR in 1911 after joining the Managing Committee from the LNWR in 1907.

The SECR Managing Committee finally went into action in 1913 when it commissioned a report from independent consultants Merz and McLellan regarding possible electrification, received in June of that year. This recommended the use of a 1,500V dc system, with current collection from either third rail or overhead wires. Detailed costings were provided for various schemes (both suburban and main line) including a review of the potential for electrically-operated Channel Tunnel traffic. The Committee was still not particularly serious about electrification, however, considering it rather as a possibility for some time in the future rather than an urgent necessity. Before long the European situation and the placing of the railways under direct Government control ensured that no action could be taken anyway.

If anything, wartime constraints made the operation of

steam-worked suburban lines even more difficult and expensive, even though the situation was eased by the closure of certain inner-area routes and stations as a wartime economy measure. These included Crystal Palace (Low Level) – Beckenham Junction from 15th December 1915, and later the Greenwich Park and Crystal Palace branches from Nunhead together with the Woodside – Sanderstead line, all from 1st January 1917. Of these, all were ex-LCDR lines except Woodside – Sanderstead, which had been a joint SER/LBSCR venture. As mentioned earlier, also abandoned were the intermediate stations and service on the ex-LCDR Metropolitan Extension between Victoria and Moorgate Street from 3rd April 1916. The SECR was probably quite happy to jettison these lines and services anyway, as they had become unremunerative at the low fares then in force.

These operating difficulties gave further incentive to pursue a suburban electrification scheme as a means of economising on operating costs, as had the LBSCR before it. The Managing Committee therefore sought further professional opinion regarding its plans, and unsurprisingly contacted Herbert Walker, General Manager of the LSWR, for guidance. Walker recommended Alfred Raworth to the SECR, and by exerting his influence managed to obtain Raworth's early release from RNAS service before the end of the War. Son of the prominent tramway electrical engineer J.S. Raworth, Alfred Raworth had worked under Herbert Jones on the South Western suburban electrification before 1914 and had shown early promise; he was destined to become one of the most important figures in the shaping of the Southern Electric. Appointed by the SECR to the post of Electrical Engineer in March 1918, Raworth went on the regulation fact-finding tour of the United States to look at various electrification systems that November, and presented his report to the Managing Committee in September 1919.

With the confidence of youth, Raworth proposed an electrification system for the SECR which differed substantially from that used on either the LBSCR or LSWR. It was a 'three wire' system involving the use of third and fourth conductor rails in a similar configuration to the London Underground, but with a much higher potential difference of 3,000V dc obtained by having the outside rail at +1,500V above ground potential and that between the running rails at -1,500V. Given the higher voltages the conductor rails would have been protected by continuous boarding and current would have been collected by side-contact, increasing the complexity of both the collector shoes on the trains and the rail mounting itself. (Similar current collection arrangements, albeit with one conductor rail, already existed on the LYR Manchester–Bury route and the Invalides–Issy suburban line in Paris, as well as several systems in the USA.) The high voltage minimised the requirement for substations to one in the inner area and four for the entire scheme, while the two live rails minimised electricity leakage to earth. This latter feature was partly to meet the requirements of the Admiralty (in accordance with the clause in the 1903 powers) regarding Greenwich Observatory, given similar experiences by the LSWR concerning the National Physical Laboratory. Carriage

sidings would have only one conductor rail, while freight yards would be fitted with overhead wiring, but both these arrangements would have increased earth leakage.

Other systems were also considered but promised to be more expensive. A 600V dc third rail power supply (as on the South Western) would have required 26 substations, while increasing the voltage to 1,500 would have reduced this only by eight or nine. A higher-voltage overhead scheme would also have reduced substation numbers but the cost of opening out the necessary clearances on SECR suburban lines, most of which had been built cheaply with sharp curves and a tight loading gauge, would have been prohibitive. However, while cost savings resulting from use of the proposed system were emphasised in the report, its obvious disadvantages were overlooked. In particular the installation of a fourth-rail system with protective boarding over the intricate pointwork at the approaches to the SECR London termini and elsewhere would have been unimaginably complicated.

Raworth's entire proposed electrification scheme was intended to be carried out in three stages, sufficient power for all being generated from a new railway-owned power station to be erected at Angerstein Wharf, Charlton. It was planned that a single substation at Lewisham would distribute current to the entire inner area. This inner 'Zone A' to be electrified as the first stage included routes from the London termini at Charing Cross, Cannon Street, Victoria and Holborn Viaduct to Croydon, Addiscombe, Hayes, Orpington, Dartford, Crystal Palace, Bromley North and Angerstein Wharf, 94 route miles in all. Omitted were the Woodside – Sanderstead and Nunhead – Greenwich Park lines, both of which had been closed and virtually abandoned during the War. The second stage included conversion of 240 miles of middle and outer-suburban routes, extending well into the country area, designated 'Zone B'. Of these, it was intended that Orpington to Tonbridge, Bickley Junction to Gillingham, Dartford to Strood, Swanley Junction to Sevenoaks and the Dunton Green–Westerham branch would be electrified on the 3,000V system, requiring the provision of a further three substations. The remainder of the routes concerned, from Purley to Tattenham Corner, Caterham and Dorking via Redhill, plus South Croydon–Oxted, were to be equipped with 6,700V ac overhead catenary and worked by the LBSCR under a leasing agreement. (As mentioned earlier, this sensible arrangement avoided equipping the lines between Croydon and Redhill with both systems.) The subsequent third stage would involve the haulage of through services from outside the electrified area, plus goods trains, by electric locomotives. For the first stage, Raworth envisaged improvements in both speed and frequency of 30%, while for the second stage figures of 40% and 60% respectively were quoted.

Regarding rolling stock, the 1919 outline proposal included a sketch for a three-coach multiple unit, comprising two driving motor third brakes and a first class trailer. The motor coaches had a combined van and cab area, with a single large access door on each side, and eight compartments. The trailer first also had eight compartments, bringing the total seating capacity to 256. It is likely that these units would have otherwise been similar to the LSWR electric stock but built new with flush panelling on longer 57ft underframes, and would have worked singly or in multiples of two or three. Each motor coach would have been equipped with two 200hp motors and it was intended that half the motor bogies in a train would have been fed at +1,500V and the remainder at -1,500V. No details have survived regarding the proposed electric locomotives for through passenger and freight workings.

Importantly, while formation of the Managing Committee led to common management and a pooling of receipts, the two constituent companies remained separate legal entities and this had implications for the planning of an electrified suburban network covering routes owned by both. The SECR therefore set up an entirely new company to raise finance for the electrification scheme and its power station, this arrangement being chosen to circumvent the legal and financial difficulties caused by the Managing Committee acting for two separate companies. The new concern was known at the start as the SECR Construction and Power Company, and all its directors were members of the SER or LCDR Boards, with Alfred Raworth its Chief Engineer. The new company would also be responsible for construction and installation of all the electrical equipment, after which the completed works would be leased back to the Managing Committee.

As the financial state of both companies remained parlous at this time it was not possible for either to issue shares to fund the work. Instead, it was hoped to raise the necessary monetary assistance from the Government under the provisions of the Trade Facilities Act of 1921. This Act authorised the Treasury to guarantee the payment of loans to be applied towards the carrying out of capital undertakings such as railway electrification, or on the purchase of items manufactured in the United Kingdom required for the purposes of such undertakings, with the aim of reducing unemployment and priming the post-war UK economy. Being a short-term measure, disbursements were to be limited to the twelve months from the commencement of the Act. The Government guaranteed a total of £25 million (£530 million) loan principal and interest which was to be regarded as liquidated by September 1927. Effectively, as far as the railways were concerned, the Treasury was providing an outright grant. The estimated total cost of the SECR electrification project was £6.5 million, and a formal application for this amount under the Act was made in November 1921, following two years of detailed work on the scheme by Raworth and his team.

By this time the rolling stock plans had been altered slightly. It was now intended to use four-coach units, 170 of which would have been enough for the entire electrification of Zones A and B. The motor coaches were similar to what had already been proposed, although longer with nine compartments, but the trailers were now a composite and an all-third. The trailer composites were to be built new on 60ft underframes and their intended design was probably very similar to vehicles 9435-60 eventually provided for the SR

1925 Western section scheme. The trailer third would have been either an existing steam 48ft eight-compartment third (SECR steam numbers in the 697-715, 2305-14 and 3453-56 series) adapted for electric working, or a new flush-panelled ten-compartment vehicle on a 60ft frame. In 1922 a provisional Southern Railway rolling stock working party actually reserved number blocks for all these coaches: these were 8227-8566 for the motor coaches, 9485-9654 for the composite trailers and 8999-9168 for the all-thirds.

Construction of the ten-compartment thirds intended for future electric operation was put in hand in August 1921 and 66, numbered 1372-1437, had been built when construction ceased in June 1923, their cost being met from the Renewals Account. They entered service as steam-hauled vehicles pending electrification, and soon became popular with the operating department due to their high (100-seat) capacity. Soon after construction ended the newly-formed SR changed its plans regarding stock for the Eastern section electrification (basically, Raworth was overruled by Jones and LSWR standards were imposed) and there was no place in the scheme for the 60ft thirds. They therefore remained in steam service throughout their existence, and thus do not form part of the Southern Electric story. (Two have survived, and are preserved in running order on the Bluebell Railway.) An order for a further 45 vehicles of this type was cancelled. Likewise the existing 48ft vehicles remained in steam service for the time being but most of these did eventually find their way into the electric fleet, being formed into trailer sets in the 1121-1167 and 1189-1194 series in 1928-31 and not as Raworth had earlier intended.

Reverting to 1920, in that year Dent resigned following a disagreement with the company Chairman, and his place as General Manager of the SECR Managing Committee was taken by Sir Percy Tempest. Tempest was already Chief Engineer and combined both posts following his promotion. From this time onwards the SECR electrification proposals also became the concern of its neighbouring companies in the run up to the Grouping: the complex problems which had to be addressed and attempts to find solutions are outlined in the next section.

PRELUDE TO GROUPING
The railways emerged from World War One in a run-down condition, with depleted staffs and rolling stock and arrears of maintenance in all departments. Capital renewals and development had been seriously delayed or halted. Even before the housing and other developments which began to pick up pace in the 1920s, the War had reinforced certain trends. It has already been mentioned that a number of lines and stations in the inner area had been closed due to wartime measures or reduced receipts resulting from demographic changes, and such traffic as they had was abandoned to the competing buses and trams. In some cases the lines or stations were never reopened. On the other hand, traffic increased in the middle and outer suburbs for reasons explored in the following chapter, and this put increasing strain on the railways' depleted rolling stock resources with steam operation.

The immediate task after the War was therefore to catch up on arrears of rolling stock, permanent way and equipment maintenance, and this had to be done with depleted workshop staff. The railway rolling stock construction industry had its own problems, with a shortage of skilled staff, a general lack of expertise in electric traction equipment, and high costs in an uncertain economic climate. The limitations of railway workshop capacity, the inability of the railway rolling stock industry to meet the railways' requirements, and the reluctance of railway shareholders to accept heavy capital expenditure which might not secure a reasonable return all contributed to postponement or even abandonment of some of the electrification schemes which the railways had been planning in 1914. We have already seen that the LSWR abandoned the outer-suburban second stage of its electrification scheme for exactly these reasons, the LBSCR seriously curtailed plans for the extension of its 'overhead' system, and the particularly impoverished SECR could only hope to press ahead with Government aid.

For some years prior to World War One the question of railway nationalisation, or at least amalgamation, had been debated. Without going into the arguments for and against, it may be said that by 1914 the idea of amalgamation had been widely accepted. During the War, Government control of the railways was exercised through the Railway Executive Committee, a grouping of senior railway managers with the President of the Board of Trade as titular Chairman and a railway officer as acting Chairman. The acting Chairman of the REC was none other than the hard-working Herbert Walker, and it was for this arduous and largely thankless task that he was knighted in 1915. Government control continued after the War and it was not until August 1921 that the railways became their own masters again. By that time the enthusiasm which the Government had for nationalisation and extensive control (in anticipation of which it had established the Ministry of Transport in September 1919) had waned, but amalgamation – 'the Grouping' as it became known – was about to become a reality. Apart from any other factor, even had they wanted to, the companies were mostly too financially insecure to resist it. The Railways Act, 1921, provided that: 'The railways shall be formed into groups...' and that the railways in each group '...shall be amalgamated...' for '...the more efficient and economical working of the railway system.'.

So far as the south of England was concerned, the Grouping resulted in the amalgamation of the London and South Western Railway, the South Eastern Railway, the London, Chatham and Dover Railway, the London, Brighton and South Coast Railway and their respective subsidiary companies to form a Southern group. Amalgamation of the major constituents was to be complete by 1st July 1923.

One of the main issues the new Southern group had to resolve was that of future electrification, as its constituent companies contained the largest concentration of electrified lines in the country at this time, but on two (and possibly soon, three) incompatible systems. Both the LSWR and LBSCR wished to extend their respective networks when

conditions were right, while the SECR was about to commence installation of a third, untried, system. To consider these matters and to try to recommend a future standard, the newly formed Ministry of Transport set up a Committee to review the Electrification of Railways in March 1920, under the chairmanship of Sir Alexander Kennedy, previously consultant to the LSWR. The conclusions of the Kennedy Report did not, however, help solve any of the future Southern group's problems, and seemed more concerned to avoid upsetting the vested interests involved. Thus the LBSCR was encouraged to extend its ac system to the coast, subject to approval by the new company, while future suburban extensions could be at 750V dc third rail. New schemes should be at 1,500V dc, however, using either third-rail or overhead. Effectively this meant that the proposed SECR scheme was not approved and it was instead referred to a sub-committee chaired by Sir John Aspinall (General Manager of the Lancashire and Yorkshire Railway, which itself had two small electrified systems in the north west, including the Manchester – Bury line mentioned earlier). Although a strong case was put across by Raworth, the sub-committee remained unconvinced and suggested that the matter be further considered by the Board of the newly amalgamated company. It must be remembered that the Kennedy committee was only advisory and the Ministry of Transport had no legal powers to force changes, so the SECR continued to plan suburban electrification on its chosen system.

With Grouping imminent, joint meetings between the companies to be merged began and a committee of officers chaired by E.C. Cox was set up in November 1921. This quickly reached deadlock on the electrification problem as the LBSCR representatives were not even authorised to discuss traction systems. Both the Brighton and SECR Boards endeavoured to establish positions whereby their own management policies might survive or even prevail. The LBSCR Board in particular attempted this, led by their Chairman, Sir William Forbes – the main objective was the survival of its chosen system of electrification, and it did its utmost to commit the new railway in advance to new routes on the 'overhead' system. Likewise the SECR was still determined to press ahead with its 3,000V dc network.

The Chairmen and General Managers met again under the direction of the Ministry of Transport on 18th January 1922, and it was agreed to form yet another committee to consider the SECR proposals, chaired by Sir Philip Nash from the Ministry and formed of consulting engineers of the three companies. Unsurprisingly Sir Philip Dawson represented the LBSCR, but this time Sir Alexander Kennedy was employed by the SECR and the LSWR was represented by Theodore Stevens. The Nash Committee reported on 9th March 1922, it main conclusion being that neither the ac system nor 600V dc were suitable for general use. It did, however, suggest that the LSWR should extend using 750V dc (a fairly insignificant change from what it was already using) and the LBSCR could expand its ac system. Agreement for the LBSCR to proceed was then given by the LSWR and SECR in June/July 1922. Significantly, Nash also recommended that the SECR could proceed with its chosen 3,000V dc system, as it showed considerable cost savings compared to a lower voltage. Stevens disagreed with the findings enough to issue his own, minority report; he was concerned with the use of an untried system with several peculiar and unsuitable features and strongly recommended the use of 750V (presumably using third rail; effectively the LSWR system) instead.

Given that the other three members of the Committee were in agreement, Stevens and the LSWR were forced to withdraw their objections and accept the Report's findings. This would have enabled the Trade Advisory Committee to agree to the SECRs application for £6.5 million finance under the terms of the Trade Facilities Act, had their proposals not then fallen foul of the Electricity Commissioners.

It will be recalled that an important part of the SECR proposals was the construction of a power station at Angerstein Wharf, Charlton to supply the railway with all its electricity requirements, in the same way that Durnsford Road had been built in 1915 to supply the South Western's needs. However, the operating environment had changed during the intervening years and the Electricity Commissioners, given new powers under the 1919 Electricity Act, were keen to discourage the construction of single-user power stations. Instead the preferred arrangements were that the separate electricity supply companies should be encouraged to meet existing and future demand, the idea being that customers such as the railways would provide a heavy base-demand which would justify investment in new power stations which would also enhance the supply to other customers. One of the prospective electricity supply companies involved was the West Kent Electricity Supply Co. Ltd who were proposing to erect a power station at Erith, relatively close to the Charlton site and who, hoping to gain business from the railway electrification, objected to the SECR proposals.

The main SECR argument against the Electricity Commissioners' plans was that it needed to generate electricity at 25Hz rather than 50Hz (which was becoming the national standard, and would be the frequency of 'bought in' electricity) as Raworth insisted that substation rotary-converter equipment worked much more reliably at the lower frequency. The LSWR was in favour of allowing a new power station to be built by the railway (presumably as it might have wanted to build another one itself in the future) but the LBSCR was happy with its supply from an outside company and saw no reason why the SECR should not do likewise. The difference of opinion persisted for some time but the arguments were effectively brought to a close when in October 1922 the Electricity Commissioners tersely insisted that the SECR would have to buy its electricity from an outside source. As a result the loan guarantee requirement was reduced to £5 million and this was finally approved. At this time the SECR were still intending to go ahead with the 3,000V scheme, but work did not immediately commence.

A provisional Board of the new Southern Railway had commenced meeting in 1922 and sought to exercise some control over the LBSCR and SECR electrification plans.

An early result was an agreement that major capital investment required the assent of all three Boards and, as already mentioned, this was grudgingly given in respect of the £300,000 needed to complete the LBSCR's ac extensions to Coulsdon and Wallington (although not to the coast), on which work had started before the War. It was also agreed that contracts could be placed to enable work on the LSWR dc extension to Guildford to commence. The SECR was being more belligerent however, and when the LBSCR directors reminded the South Eastern of the need for joint consultation and approval of capital projects the curt reply was that work was about to start anyway and the provisional Board had no legal powers to prevent this, notwithstanding the earlier agreement. The October meeting of the provisional Board presumably considered this stance unreasonable and yet another independent referee was appointed to report on the proposed scheme. In the meantime the SECR agreed to place no further contracts.

The new referee was George Gibbs, a respected American expert who was consulting engineer to the Pennsylvania Railroad, and his report was received by the provisional SR Board in November 1922. For future dc electrification of LSWR and SECR suburban lines, Gibbs' Report recommended that the upper voltage should be limited to 750, a decision also now ratified by the Ministry of Transport and accepted by the provisional SR Board under a majority vote. He also recommended that extensions of the LBSCR ac system, as well as electrification of SECR main lines outside the suburban area, should eventually use an overhead 11,000V single-phase ac system, as on his own Railroad.

Electrification of the South Eastern and Chatham suburban lines could now be put in hand, largely using the detailed plans drawn up by Raworth but adopting the 600V dc third rail system preferred by the LSWR and Ministry of Transport. (As an aside, objections put up by the West Kent Electricity Supply Co. Ltd did it no favours; the SR instead purchased its electricity from the London Electric Supply Corporation who already supplied the LBSCR electric services and much of London's tramway network, at Raworth's preferred 25Hz. As a result the LESC itself obtained a Trade Facilities Act loan for £1.5 million to extend its power station at Deptford to provide sufficient capacity).

With these machinations over, the main pre-Grouping constituent companies of the Southern Railway ceased to function after 31st December 1922.

2: ELECTRIFICATION AND EXPANSION IN THE SUBURBAN AREA 1923-39

Resulting from the 1921 Railways Act, the Southern Railway came into being on 1st January 1923. For the first six months of its existence the new company was preoccupied with setting up its administration, no easy task in view of the disparate nature of its constituents and the long-standing rivalries between them. In particular the Brighton and South Eastern companies were suspicious of being swallowed up into a greater South Western, and this tended to colour dealings between the newly amalgamated concerns. The new Board at first consisted of 21 Directors (later reduced to eighteen, then sixteen), of whom eight were nominated by the LSWR, five each from the LBSCR and SER, and three from the LCDR. The first Chairman was Sir Hugh Drummond, Bart, CMG, a banker who had been a Director of the LSWR since 1900 and Chairman since 1910, and who was responsible for recruiting Herbert Walker to the position of General Manager of that company.

The SR Board was at first unable to agree on its choice of General Manager, so as an interim measure Sir Herbert Walker, Sir William Forbes from the LBSCR and Sir Percy Tempest from the SECR Managing Committee continued in office jointly, the effective result being that, so far as day-to-day running was concerned, there remained three separate railway concerns each trading under the 'Southern Railway' umbrella. This was a completely unsatisfactory position as Forbes (in particular) and Tempest tended to oppose Walker's ideas for the new company on principle. As they were unable to agree on organisation, Sir Herbert eventually went to Drummond and offered to resign if something was not done. Unwilling to lose his protégé, who had done so much for the good of the South Western, the Chairman saw to it that the Directors were unanimous in nominating Walker as sole General Manager, and it was agreed that Forbes, by then 67 anyway, would retire on 30th June. Sir Percy Tempest also took up his superannuation at the end of 1923, but had in fact proved perfectly willing to co-operate with Sir Herbert once the mischievous Forbes had departed.

Now in control and fully backed by his Directors, Walker was able to announce his choices of senior officers, and his recommendations were approved at the Board meeting of 7th June. The new management positions were filled with effect from 1st July 1923 or shortly afterwards. Although the major appointments were mostly offered on the basis of seniority, it is unsurprising that, as the largest of the Southern Railway's three main constituents, the LSWR, headed by the forceful Walker, became the major influence in the new concern. Only

in respect of rolling stock and operations did former SECR policy have any significant influence in the early years of the company, while the LBSCR was hardly represented at all. Figures who had a direct involvement with the future SR electrification schemes are mentioned here, together with changes in personnel and new appointments in the period up to 1932, mostly due to retirements. Later changes between 1932 and 1939, at which time the company was mainly concerned with the main-line electrification schemes, are covered in Volume 2.

The position of Chief Mechanical Engineer, with overall responsibility for locomotive and carriage design, was given to the Irishman R.E.L. Maunsell, CME of the SECR since December 1913. Surrey Warner from the LSWR was appointed to the post of Assistant Mechanical Engineer in charge of carriages, wagons and road vehicles. Warner had been responsible for the complex but economical conversion of the steam-hauled 'bogie block' sets into electric units, but subsequently had little involvement with SR electric stock other than supervising the conversion of further LSWR steam coaches. With Richard Maunsell from Ashford came his Chief Draughtsman, Lionel Lynes, who set up office at Eastleigh Works which was to become the main SR carriage and wagon establishment. When Warner eventually retired in 1929 Lynes succeeded him as the Southern's chief carriage designer, but his influence had been felt almost from the formation of the new company. The new 1925 suburban electric stock had bodywork based exactly on the final South Eastern suburban coaches, and SR carriage design generally was derived from SECR practice until 1938, with only a faint trace of South Western and none of Brighton at all. Thus Lynes was directly responsible for the external design of all the newly-built suburban and main line electric stock up to the Bognor buffet cars, 2 HALs and the first 'six-a-side' 4 SUBs of 1939-45, in which the new Chief Mechanical Engineer, O.V.S. Bulleid, had a hand. R. Urie (final CME of the South Western) together with L. Billinton and A.H. Panter (CME and carriage assistant respectively on the LBSCR) felt themselves unwanted in the new company and retired. However G.H. Gardener, Panter's deputy, took over the running of Lancing Works and presided over its reorganisation. (Gardener was eventually to succeed Lynes as chief SR carriage designer in 1947, on the eve of nationalisation.)

It is convenient here to review the position of the various carriage and wagon works inherited by the Southern Railway. As mentioned above, the former LSWR plant at Eastleigh became the main coach building shop of the SR. Underframes for steam-hauled stock were made there until 1940, and from 1930 it became responsible for almost all body construction. The bodywork of virtually all the main line electric stock up to 1939 was built there (on Lancing underframes) except those vehicles, mainly all-steel motor coaches and sundry catering vehicles, farmed out to contractors. In April 1924 the Southern decided to reorganise Lancing Works, the erstwhile LBSCR carriage shops, for carriage maintenance and repair and for the construction of coach underframes. Over the next few years Lancing also took over body finishing work (ie trimming and painting) from Brighton Carriage and Wagon Works, Brighton from then on concentrating on electrical installation and repair. The former South Eastern works at Ashford undertook a great deal of body conversion work for the suburban electrifications but, once Lancing's reorganisation had been completed by 1932, was confined to wagons and vans.

Herbert Jones, also from the LSWR, was appointed to the post of Electrical Engineer but, following completion of the 1925 Western section electrification to Guildford and Dorking, was effectively in charge only of day-to-day running and maintenance of the rolling stock and electrification fixed apparatus such as substations. Responsibility for the electrical design of the SR electric rolling stock fleet was given to Alfred Raworth from the SECR, who was also placed in charge of the whole Eastern section suburban electrification scheme with the title Electrical Engineer, New Works. Raworth had actually served under Jones on the LSWR from March 1912 until October 1915, becoming Electrical Engineer for the SECR in February 1918. As such, he was also Engineer to the South Eastern and Chatham Power and Construction Company Ltd from December 1922 until its winding up in June 1925. This division of responsibility, in which Raworth was technically subordinate to Jones but effectively had the greater influence, apparently gave rise to a certain degree of friction between the two men, and it is suggested that Walker placed them in charge of different departments as a means of keeping them apart. Raworth subsequently became heavily involved with the main line schemes of the 1930s and succeeded Jones in 1938, when the electrical running and maintenance and new works departments were at last amalgamated. H. Richards, the LBSCR electric traction engineer, became Assistant Electrical Engineer under Herbert Jones, with special responsibility for the ac overhead system. (Following the demise of this system in 1929 Richards moved to the LNER.)

On the civil engineering side, Alfred W. Szlumper was appointed Chief Engineer, having held the same position on the LSWR since 1914. His deputy was George Ellson, formerly SECR Maintenance Engineer. Ellson succeeded Szlumper in July 1927 and was responsible for the distinctive reinforced-concrete civil engineering structures which characterised the Southern Electric in the inter-war years, such as those on the new Wimbledon–Sutton and Motspur Park–Chessington lines, and the Wimbledon flyover. Signal and Telegraph Superintendent was W.J. Thorrowgood, who had held the same position on the LSWR, and who was notable for introducing four-aspect colour light signals on the busiest electric lines – a world first. Thorrowgood retired in September 1927 and was replaced by Lieutenant-Colonel G.L. Hall, RE, one of the Ministry of Transport's Inspecting Officers.

As important as the engineering and electrification establishments for the smooth running of the railway was the Operating Department, presided over by Edwin C. Cox. Cox had entered railway service on the South Eastern Railway in 1883, having then risen to the post of Superintendent of the Line to the SECR Managing Committee in 1911. In this capacity he had impressed Walker, particularly in his innovative introduction in 1922 of parallel working of peak-hour services out of Charing Cross, London Bridge and Cannon Street to maximise track usage. He was thus an obvious choice to work out and implement intensive regular-interval timetables for the newly-electrified suburban, and later coastal, electrifications. Cox worked closely with his General Manager in an effective partnership which lasted until retirement in 1936. His assistant was Frank Bushrod, who hailed from the LSWR. The Southern Railway was initially split into three operating divisions, electrified lines in existence in 1923 coming within the London West (ex LSWR) and London East (ex LBSCR) divisions. Following the retirement of the Chief Commercial Manager in April 1930 it was decided to amalgamate the Commercial and Operating departments, and they were merged to become the Traffic department. Under the new arrangements Cox became Traffic Manager and Bushrod Superintendent of Operation. Concurrently the system was reorganised into five operating divisions, the sections then electrified coming under London West (former LSWR), London Central (former LBSCR) and London East (former SECR) divisions.

Compared with the London Underground, the Southern Railway often received a bad press in the early years of its existence. In the suburban area, it is unsurprising that electrification-induced shortages of stock and delays due to engineering works greatly annoyed the travelling public, whose views were regularly reflected in the newspaper columns. Although the work being undertaken would greatly ease the lot of long-suffering passengers they were told nothing, Walker preferring not to announce new developments and improvements until he actually had something to show. However, the General Manager was very aware that there was a problem of communication, and to tackle it decided to find someone to liaise between the railway company and the press, a very new thing for a British railway at that time. On the personal recommendation of Lord Ashfield, Chairman and Managing Director of the Underground Group, he gave the job to John Elliot, who had some newspaper experience with the *London Evening Standard*. Appointed for a year on 16th January 1925, as 'Public Relations Consultant' (a title he suggested himself, importing the USA usage), Elliot reported directly to Walker and quickly built a rapport with his boss. Making a success of the job, he was after a year promoted to become Assistant to the General Manager for public relations and advertising. Clearly management material, he was soon being trained in the traffic departments, but his initial work laid the foundations for a much more positive interaction between the company and the press to the benefit of both, something which has now virtually disappeared. Elliot played a significant part in encouraging traffic growth on the newly-electrified suburban lines in the 1920s, although his immortal advertising slogans such as 'Live in Surrey, Free from Worry' and 'Live in Kent and be Content' may seem somewhat naive and unsubtle to modern taste.

Before considering the decisions regarding future electrification which the Southern Railway Board and management had to take, it is convenient to record here that Sir Hugh Drummond died in August 1924. His successor as SR Chairman was Brigadier-General the Hon. Everard Baring, CVO, who had been a Director of the South Eastern Railway from 1908 and a member of the SEC Managing Committee from 1909. Brigadier-General Baring died in May 1932 and was succeeded by Mr Gerald E.W. Loder (from 1934 Lord Wakehurst), who had been a director of the LBSCR from 1896 and who became Chairman of that company in 1922 and Deputy Chairman of the SR in the following year.

Except for a Directors' decision in February 1923 to adopt 600V dc for the sake of uniformity, a consequence of the Gibbs report of November 1922 (see Chapter 1), it was not until after the appointment of officers that SR policy on electrification began to take shape. Due to burgeoning traffic levels and the increasing expense of steam suburban working, Walker considered it imperative that electrification work should be commenced as a matter of urgency, and so it was that by the end of 1923 there were no less than five such schemes under way or authorised. These included the Central section ac overhead electrification to Coulsdon North (renamed from Coulsdon and Smitham Downs earlier that year) and Sutton, restarted by the LBSCR in 1922 and which could be completed without undue capital cost; extension of the Western section (former LSWR) electric network to Dorking North and Guildford, largely using plans already drawn up as the second stage of that company's electrification plans of 1913; and the three phases of conversion of the Eastern section (former SECR) lines, comprising the ex LCDR routes from Victoria and Holborn Viaduct to Orpington and Crystal Palace, the South Eastern lines from Charing Cross and Cannon Street to Bromley North, the Mid-Kent line and Orpington, and finally the routes to Dartford, all again using plans drawn up prior to Grouping. All these latter electrifications utilised the dc third-rail arrangements initially chosen by the LSWR and adopted as standard by the SR Board, leaving the non-standard and incompatible ac *Elevated Electric* network stranded between them. In 1925, with the completion of the initial Western and Central section schemes and with the Eastern section scheme well advanced, there was a further appraisal by the SR's electrical engineers, the inevitable conclusion being that all future SR electrification should be on the 600V dc system. This was confirmed by the SR Board on 29th October 1925, and planning was immediately started for the conversion of Central section suburban lines to dc operation, including those lines already electrified

on the ac system. The Central section dc scheme was authorised by the Directors on 29th July 1926, a decision which effectively signed the death-warrant for the LBSCR high-tension ac system.

One problem facing historians of the Southern Electric concerns rolling stock provision for the suburban electrifications. For the initial Western, Eastern and Central section schemes in the 1925-29 period there is no real difficulty, but after this time the situation becomes rather complex, and units allocated to a particular electrification for accounting purposes were not necessarily intended for that section. In anticipation of traffic increases it was normal to provide more stock than was actually necessary for the planned timetable and maintenance cover, and later units provided for the electrification extensions of 1930-39 were in effect common user over the whole network from the start, wherever they were nominally allocated for financial reasons. Detailed coverage of the rolling stock provided is provided in Chapter 4 for ac stock and Chapter 5 for dc suburban stock, but brief details are mentioned in this chapter for completeness.

For its dc suburban electrification schemes, the SR continued with the headcode system devised by the LSWR, the trains carrying a stencil displaying a prominent letter between the motorman's lookouts, lit from behind at night. By the time the last suburban extension (to Chessington) was completed in 1939, the characters H, I, J, L, N, O, P, S, T, U, V, A (inverted V) and d (inverted P) were in use. In order to cope with the complexity of routes on former SECR (and to a lesser extent LBSCR) lines, it was necessary to qualify these basic letter codes with an additional narrow stencil which fitted above the main headcode. There were three of these; a bar as introduced by the LSWR, a single dot and a double dot. In passenger service the bar was used on all three sections, but the dots only on the Eastern and Central sections. Double dots over a headcode letter on the Western section usually denoted an empty stock movement. These codes continued in use on pre-1939 suburban stock until the last was withdrawn at the start of 1962. The 1925 Coulsdon and Sutton ac scheme continued with the numerical headcode system adopted by the LBSCR in 1911, and the small number of codes used are listed as a table in the section of this chapter which deals with the extensions to Coulsdon and Sutton.

THE AC EXTENSIONS TO COULSDON AND SUTTON AND THE END OF THE SYSTEM

By the end of 1922 and the absorption of the LBSCR into the new Southern Railway, all equipment for the ac extensions to Coulsdon North and most of the way to Sutton was either ready, in the process of being installed (work recommenced in 1922), or on order. Although hostile to the idea of ac extensions, the new SR Board had been prepared to include this scheme in its proposed programme of suburban electrification, but not until yet another reappraisal by departmental committee had taken place to put back completion. With some creative accounting involving transferring the cost of the rolling stock to the Revenue account, it had proved possible to finance completion of the overhead wiring installation from Wallington as far as Beeches Halt, only a short distance from Sutton.

It was left to the SR to finance the final short distance into Sutton station, where the newly-electrified services used the curved Epsom Downs branch platforms, with all thoughts of extending through to Cheam now forgotten. Overhead catenary was also installed on the Down line towards Belmont for a train-length beyond the platform, to enable terminating electric trains to use the crossover at that end of the station. Widening north of Sutton was carried out to fully separate the electrified line towards Wallington from the Carshalton – Epsom route. On the Coulsdon North route four tracks from East Croydon to Purley were wired, the catenary being extended on the through lines a short distance south of Purley station to connect with two electrified reversing sidings and on the local lines through the two terminal platforms at Coulsdon North to serve four electrified berthing sidings beyond. Additionally, an Up bay and adjacent siding were wired at South Croydon. The catenary and supports were generally similar to those on the Crystal Palace routes except at Sutton, where trussed beams were used instead of lattice girders.

As with the Eastern section dc scheme described below and following previous LBSCR practice, power for the ac extensions was purchased from the London Electric Supply Corporation. Supplied at 6,700V single phase, 25Hz, to a main switching station at New Cross Gate, it was first stepped up to 64,000V through two 5,000KVA transformers and then transmitted to a switch cabin at Gloucester Road (south of Selhurst station where the lines to the two Croydon stations diverged) through four 32,000V cables. Here it was stepped down to 6,700V once more and distributed to other switch cabins for supply to the overhead wires.

At Sutton, the station area was resignalled, the re-arranged signalling being controlled from a new cabin on the Up side at the east end of the station and allowing London-bound trains to start from any of the four platforms. The bridge carrying Sutton High Street over the station was rebuilt to give clearance for the catenary and a lofty new single-storey entrance building, in brick with tall windows and a pitched roof, provided on it in 1928. This was designed under the supervision of SR chief architect J. Robb-Scott, who was to be responsible for all new station buildings in the electrified area in the inter-war period.

Beeches Halt was renamed Carshalton Beeches and converted into a station. Here the new platforms, long enough for a ten-coach electric train and constructed partly from prefabricated concrete sections supplied from Exmouth Junction, were ready for the opening day, but the original wooden huts were not replaced until later in 1925. The substantial new platform-level buildings were of brick with steel-framed canopies of a design which would become widespread elsewhere as the Southern Electric system spread. A covered footbridge led to a street-level building, a smaller version of that later provided at Sutton, on the corner of Beeches Avenue and Gordon Road. A new signal box was also provided. The new rolling stock for the scheme comprised twenty five-coach sets formed of four passenger vehicles powered by a motor luggage van marshalled at the centre (there was an additional spare motor van), and was all delivered by early 1924. Some of this new CW stock, which was maintained at existing depots at Selhurst and Peckham Rye, was run-in on Crystal Palace line services.

Although electrification work had been virtually completed by the end of 1924, further delays to the start of electric services were due to negotiations over the supply of electricity. This apparent tardiness on the part of the railway

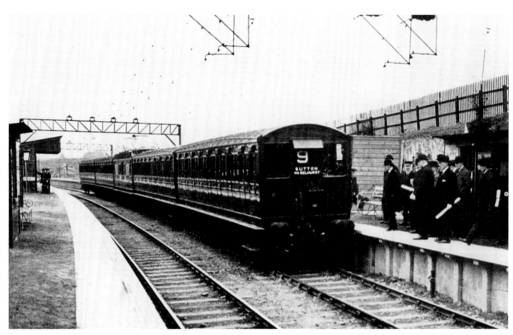

Officials and dignitaries welcome the first ac train, a five-car formation of CW stock, at Carshalton Beeches in April 1925. This former halt was rebuilt as a station with full-length platforms for the new electric service, but the wooden platform buildings had yet to be replaced.

Sutton station frontage, as rebuilt in the late 1920s. *Alan A. Jackson Collection*

company led to increasing irritation from the travelling public, who could see the newly-installed overhead catenary doing nothing. Their complaints were backed up vociferously by a hostile press, and this led the Southern Railway to take the then unusual step of taking full-page advertisements in these papers explaining the problems and announcing future plans for suburban electrification, one of the first tasks for the newly-appointed John Elliot.

The extensions from Balham via Selhurst to Coulsdon North and Sutton finally came into service on 1st April 1925, not long before the first SR dc schemes were due to be completed. The official reason for the delay was that the necessary electricity supply could not be provided before that date. A broken conductor wire near Battersea Park severely disrupted services on the opening morning, but the system soon settled down to reliable operation. In contrast with the earlier schemes where the service on each route, although repeated each hour, ran at irregular times, a proper regular interval timetable of the type favoured by Walker was introduced for the Coulsdon and Sutton services. On weekdays, following the start of service at 6.00am, trains generally ran

every twenty minutes between Victoria and both Coulsdon North and Sutton, except between 11.00am and 1.00pm and after 9.00pm, when it became half-hourly. On Saturdays the twenty-minute interval was maintained until 6.00pm, while after this and on Sundays the service was again half-hourly. Croydon was additionally served on Sundays by Victoria – Crystal Palace trains, two of the three each hour serving East and West Croydon respectively.

The CW stock continued the use of headcodes but additionally carried destination boards underneath, a practice also introduced on the CP stock at the same time. Like the headcode numbers, these were black enamelled plates with white lettering. The headcodes for the new services were as follows:

Headcode	Route
7	Victoria – Selhurst
8	Victoria – West Croydon via Crystal Palace
9	Victoria – Sutton via Selhurst
10	Victoria – East Croydon via Crystal Palace
11	Victoria – Coulsdon North via Selhurst
12	Victoria – Coulsdon North via Crystal Palace

Additionally at this time, the Victoria – London Bridge South London line service was given the headcode SL. This was permanently carried on both ends of the two-coach South London line sets, but without destination boards.

As already mentioned, seven months after the completion and opening of the Coulsdon and Sutton ac electrification, the SR Board firmly decided that all future electrifications should be on the dc system in use on the Western and Eastern sections. It was then but a short step to the decision taken in July 1926 to commence the conversion of the ac lines to third rail operation, made public a month later. Against the short life of the final ac extension were set twenty years' use of the SL stock and up to eighteen years service of the CP stock. This was long enough to approach life-expiry of the traction motors (which could admittedly be replaced without unreasonable expenditure) and much of the other electrical equipment. It had also been found that the maintenance costs of the ac stock considerably exceeded those for the dc motor coaches by then in service. Moreover, every single ac vehicle was converted or altered for further use and some survived – although not as passenger stock – until the mid-1960s. Although no ac line was changed entirely over to dc until 1928, dismantling of the system actually began in 1927, when catenary was removed from the Tulse Hill Junction – Streatham – Streatham Junction section. Although equipped in 1913, this line had never had an ac service, and it seems likely that the wires were never even energised.

Formal dates for the end of ac service were set for each of the various sections of route, but dc trains began to run up to two or more months before so that withdrawal of the ac stock was progressive and for a short period both types of stock were working on the same service. The first *Elevated Electric* routes to go over completely to dc working were the South London line from Victoria to London Bridge via Peckham Rye and from London Bridge to Tulse Hill, Streatham Hill and Crystal Palace, which saw their last ac trains on 16th June 1928. Some of the CP stock made spare was then used to work additional Streatham Hill–Victoria services, which continued until the Victoria–Crystal Palace ac service was withdrawn on 3rd March 1929. CP stock was then used to augment remaining CW stock on additional peak-hour trains on the Victoria to Coulsdon North and Sutton routes. By the summer of 1929 the majority of services on these lines too were worked by dc stock, and the last ac-powered passenger train on the Southern Railway, a five-car set of CW stock, left Victoria for Coulsdon North at 12.10am on Sunday 22nd September 1929. The overhead wiring from Battersea Park to Peckham Rye was kept energised for some months after the end of ac working to enable stock to be worked to Peckham Rye shops for stripping of electrical equipment. After dc electrification of the ac lines arrangements had to be made to dismantle the overhead catenary and supporting structures. The wires themselves were taken down straight away, but the supports not until 1930-33. Most were removed by the quick and cheap method of cutting off near the base with a blowtorch, leaving concrete bases and ends of steelwork to await removal when they got in the way,

and thus a few remain in position to this day. Some gantries and cantilevers were left for use as signal supports. The two last complete examples to remain extant are thought to have been a standard support at Wandsworth Common (across the London end of the local lines adjacent to the road bridge), used as a cable run and a cantilever carrying signals at Pouparts Lane (where the Central lines veer from those of the South Western north of Clapham Junction), dismantled in 1982 as part of the Victoria area resignalling scheme. Some were removed complete and found their way to depots as parts of roof structures or engineering gantries; Nine Elms North goods depot (demolished about 1970) had at least one, while several were used as roof supports for a new engine shed at Ryde on the Isle of Wight, taken down in about 1968. A number of brackets were used as lighting standards in the carriage sidings at Dorking North. As mentioned elsewhere, the sheds at Peckham Rye remained in use after the end of ac working for heavy maintenance of certain classes of dc stock until closed in the early 1960s; houses and flats now occupy the site.

The former paint shop at Selhurst depot, recognisable by its greater height to clear the overhead wires, was the original maintenance shed provided for the Crystal Palace lines electrification in 1911. Taken out of use as late as 1994, it was finally demolished in 1999. Of the other equipment, most of the electrical switch cabins were stripped but left in place as permanent way huts: at least three, at Balham, Norbury and Gloucester Road, remained in situ in 2009, derelict and ivy-covered. A number of other traces of the *Elevated Electric* system still existed eighty years after its abandonment. Between Balham and Victoria and at many other sites, the odd support stump on its concrete base, generally painted white to warn trackside staff, persisted as an impediment to track rearrangement. Similar remains could be seen at the tops of the brick retaining walls in the cuttings between East and South Croydon stations and south of Clapham Junction.

The Suspense Account for the replacement of ac by dc traction stood in the SR's books in 1932 at £1,456,328. It was reduced annually and closed in 1942 by a final write-off figure of £205,473. Although adopted by British Railways in 1955 as an electrification standard for future projects (albeit with rectifiers and dc traction equipment in the trains), high-tension ac overhead electrification did not reappear on the Southern until 1988, when a short section was installed at Selhurst in order to test the dual-voltage class 319 *Thameslink* units allocated there. In 1993 a section of line near Folkestone was also equipped, to enable the *Eurostar* trains via the Channel Tunnel to change from dc third rail at speed.

Overleaf Changeover time on the Central section as ac and dc traction share the sidings at Coulsdon North. On the left is a pair of five-coach ac CW sets, with the leading vehicle sill in LBSCR umber livery. On the right is dc unit 1660, constructed by the SR from existing LSWR coach bodies lengthened on new underframes.

GUILDFORD AND DORKING

Formally approved at the Southern Railway Board meeting on 6th December 1923, by which time contracts had already been placed and work started, the 1925 Western section extension to Guildford and Dorking was the first direct current electrification to be completed under the auspices of the newly-formed company. It was mostly based on stage two of the projected LSWR scheme and covered the routes from Claygate to Guildford via Cobham (known from soon after its opening in 1885 as the Guildford New line), Raynes Park to Effingham Junction via Epsom, and Leatherhead to Dorking. This latter section was an addition by the SR; it had been LBSCR-owned, forming part of that company's main line to Portsmouth. The route mileage of the scheme was 33, total track mileage 67, and estimated cost £833,000. Works involved were very similar in character to the original South Western suburban electrification, and formed the pattern for later schemes: they were carried out under the direction of the Chief Electrical Engineer, Herbert Jones.

The former LSWR generating plant at Durnsford Road provided the electricity for this scheme at 11KV 25Hz three-phase ac. This was carried by lineside cabling to seven substations equipped with rotary converters, which were supplied by British Thomson-Houston. Very similar to the original LSWR examples, these substations were housed in tall brick buildings with a flat or shallow pitched roof and glazed clerestory, and were known by staff as 'cathedrals' in later years. Those at Oxshott, Leatherhead and Clandon were equipped with one 1,250KW converter each while the others, at Epsom, Effingham Junction, Guildford and Dorking, had two. Where possible, substations were given a siding to simplify movement of heavy equipment. Three of the sub-stations were remotely controlled and therefore unmanned in normal operation. That at Oxshott (on the Cobham line) was controlled from the already-existing substation at Hampton Court Junction, while both Leatherhead and Clandon were supervised from Effingham Junction. The substations supplied current at a nominal 600V dc to the conductor rails, rolled from high-conductivity steel and mounted outside the running rails on porcelain insulators.

New bay platforms for terminating electric services were provided on the Down sides at both Guildford and Dorking. Where necessary, platforms at most other stations were extended to the new standard of 520ft which allowed for an eight-coach rush-hour electric train, in some cases using prefabricated concrete platform extensions. For some reason however, platforms at Horsley, Clandon and London Road (Guildford) were not lengthened at this time – this will be mentioned again presently. An entirely new station, opened on the first day of the new electric services, was provided on a green field site at Motspur Park, between Raynes Park and Worcester Park on the Epsom line. This consisted of an island platform of standard length, accessed initially only from the Down side by an open-structured uncovered footbridge fabricated at Wimbledon signal works. The brick platform buildings and steel canopies here were similar to those

provided at Carshalton Beeches. Electrified berthing sidings were provided at Guildford, Leatherhead and Dorking, and a new 520ft seven-road carriage shed replaced a redundant engine shed at Effingham Junction. This was of traditional brick construction and was situated on the Down side just beyond the station platforms: its access sidings included a reversing spur used by terminating trains to and from the Leatherhead line.

26 new three-coach units, numbered 1285-1310, of somewhat slab-sided appearance but otherwise similar to the original LSWR units, were provided to operate the new services, together with thirteen two-coach trailer sets, 1025-1037, adapted from LBSCR steam stock. The South Western practice of using eight coach trains formed motor unit + trailer set + motor unit in the peak hours and a single three-car unit at other times was continued. From the outset this new stock interworked with the original LSWR units, and like them was cleaned and maintained in existing sheds at Wimbledon Park and Strawberry Hill as well as the new facility at Effingham Junction. Due to late design changes insisted-on by Jones as construction was about to commence, and a strike at the carriage builders' works, not all of the motor units were ready for the opening date. Trial running to Guildford began on 24th June 1925.

The London-bound platform of the former LBSCR station at Epsom Town, at the time of closure in 1929. Although conductor rails may be seen, it was never served by electric trains, the new services running through to call instead at the reconstructed ex-LSWR station at the other end of Epsom High Street.
Alan A. Jackson collection

The public commencement of services on 12th July 1925 was preceded by a formal opening ceremony on 9th July, when a special train of the new electric stock was received by civic dignitaries at both Guildford and Dorking. The new regular-interval timetables replaced a motley collection of steam services running to irregular timings. They were designed to make maximum use of the local lines out of Waterloo, and to distribute stops in the inner area in an effort to reduce overcrowding. Originally there was a twenty-minute interval service on both the Cobham and Epsom lines. On the former all trains ran through to Guildford, while on the latter two-per-hour ran to Dorking and one to Effingham Junction, connecting there with Cobham line trains in both directions. These services soon gave rise to public complaint, largely due to inconvenient connections from Epsom line stations to Kingston-bound trains at Raynes Park. Then, as now, Kingston was a major shopping centre for the area and therefore a generator of significant off-peak traffic. As a result of this criticism, the service was entirely rearranged as from 1st December 1925. The Cobham line trains were re-routed onto the through (fast) lines non-stop from Waterloo to Surbiton, giving the first regular operation of suburban electric multiple units at express speeds. This then allowed Epsom line trains to be retimed to give better connections in and out of Shepperton and Kingston loop trains at Raynes Park.

The section between Epsom and Leatherhead was originally jointly owned by the LSWR and LBSCR, and each company had its own fully-staffed stations at both ends of the route. Those at Leatherhead were respectively 23 chains and fifteen chains south of the junction of the Dorking and Effingham Junction lines. At Epsom, trains to and from Sutton had to pass on their own rails through the LSWR station without stopping before or after calling at the LBSCR station (named Epsom Town by the SR) at the other end of the High Street. For the electrification, it was only necessary to equip the LSWR tracks through Epsom with conductor rails, but at Leatherhead the lines through both stations had to be done. These measures were only a short-term expedient

however, as it was clearly necessary to rationalise facilities at both places. Leatherhead was dealt with first, a new spur being constructed from the south end of the former LBSCR Dorking line platforms to the Effingham Junction line, including a new steel bridge over Station Road. This enabled all trains to use the LBSCR station and the former LSWR establishment was closed from 10th July 1927. The lines through it continued to be used as sidings for berthing electric stock, latterly connected at the Ashtead end only and taken out of use in about 1970. Reconstruction at Epsom was destined to wait until the Central section electrification in 1929.

As mentioned above, platforms at Horsley, Clandon and London Road were not originally extended to the standard 520ft, and one result was that the only motor units permitted to operate Waterloo – Guildford via Cobham services were the original LSWR and 1925 Western section types (unit numbers 1201-1310 inclusive). Although only relevant in the peaks, when eight-coach trains were operated, this restriction was because these types were shorter than the 193ft 5in length adopted for the Eastern section and later standardised on. This restriction became increasingly inconvenient as the electric fleet increased, particularly after the programme to rebuild the LSWR units to the standard length was commenced in 1934. The platforms at these three stations were therefore belatedly lengthened in about 1938, after which any suburban unit could be used on the Guildford New line without restriction.

Opposite above Leatherhead (LSWR), showing conductor rails passing through. One of the remaining unconverted LSWR four-coach 'bogie block' sets stands at the platform, c.1926. *Stations UK*

Opposite below The former LSWR Epsom station undergoing reconstruction on 10th February 1929, seen from the temporary footbridge looking towards Ashtead. The Down island platform, partly on the site of the former LBSCR through lines, is under construction on the left, and the new overhead signal box appears substantially complete. The old vaulted canopy remains for the time being on the existing Up platform, which is being widened. *H.C. Casserley*

THE EASTERN SECTION SUBURBAN LINES

The Eastern section electrification programme, completed in three stages in 1925 and 1926, made use of the plans drawn up by the SECR prior to 1923 and discussed in Chapter 1. The scheme remained under the direction of Alfred Raworth, its originator, now appointed Electrical Engineer, New Works by Sir Herbert Walker. Use was also made of the South Eastern and Chatham Power and Construction Company, originally set up by the SECR to obtain the necessary finance and to carry out the electrification in order to circumvent legal problems arising from the constitution of the Managing Committee. It was finally wound up in 1925, after completion of the first stage of the scheme. This covered the ex-LCDR suburban lines from Victoria and Holborn Viaduct to Orpington, via both Herne Hill and the Catford Loop, and also the branch from Nunhead to Crystal Palace (suffixed High Level by the SR, to distinguish it from the former LBSCR station, designated Low Level). The second stage included the ex-SER main line from Charing Cross and Cannon Street to Orpington, including the Grove Park–Bromley North branch and the Mid-Kent line from St John's to Beckenham Junction, Addiscombe and Hayes. The final stage would see electric trains on all routes to Dartford, including the Blackheath–Charlton link, and also included the renewal of the entire platform and track layout at Cannon Street. The scheme involved the conversion of 94 route miles and 250 track miles, and much of the work on the three stages was carried out concurrently.

One change from the Western section scheme, where power came from a railway-owned generating installation, was that electricity for the Eastern section lines was supplied by the London Electric Supply Company from its Deptford Power Station. As explained earlier, this followed the inability of the SECR to gain permission to build its own generating station at Angerstein Wharf (Charlton). Electricity was first sent to a main distribution switching room and substation at Lewisham, and then on to the nineteen other substations which supplied the live rail, all of which were fitted with standard rotary converter equipment. The table shows the substations listed in order of their SR distribution network numbers, and the number of rotary converters in each is shown in brackets.

Eastern Section Suburban Area Substations

1 Lewisham (4)§	11 Grove Park (2)
2 Cannon Street (3)	12 Chislehurst (3)
3 Holborn Viaduct (3)¶	13 Eltham (2)
4 Nunhead (2)§	14 Sidcup (2)
5 Loughborough Junc (3)§	15 Dartford (2)
6 Victoria (2)§	16 Shooters Hill (2)
7 Upper Sydenham (3*)¶	17 Barnhurst (2)
8 Catford (3)¶	18 Charlton (2)
9 Shortlands (3) §	19 Plumstead (2)
10 Elmers End (3)¶	20 Belvedere (2)

*   Upper Sydenham substation served both the Crystal Palace branch and the main line via cables down into Penge Tunnel. The shaft which carried these cables may still be seen.

The substations were variously equipped by BTH(¶), English Electric(§) or Metropolitan-Vickers. Each rotary converter had an output of 1,500KW. Lewisham was additionally equipped with three 400KW transformers to supply 3,300V ac at 75Hz by cable to a transformer at each substation, where it was stepped down to give an auxiliary supply at 220V ac. This was used for station lighting, track-circuiting and signal purposes, including the new colour-light signalling mentioned below, and distributed by local cabling as necessary. (220V was a widely-used domestic voltage at the time, and remained so until the 1950s.) The substation buildings, including the original Lewisham switching room, were based on the LSWR 'cathedral' model. Electrically-operated points had motors operated by direct current from accumulators, which were charged by motor generators supplied with current from the conductor rail. Flat-bottomed rail weighing 150lb per yard was used for conductor rails in areas of intensive usage, but only 100lb/yard elsewhere.

In addition to the normal third rail supplying current to the trains, in some locations a fourth rail was added between the running rails to (according to publicity) amplify the capacity for return current where there were long distances between substations. Unlike the London Transport system, these rails had no contact with the train, being merely spiked to the sleepers and cross-bonded at intervals to the running rails. Locations where these additional rails were laid included the Greenwich line (but not the Blackheath line) at Charlton Junction, and the Hayes branch from Elmers End. It was necessary to run the electric cabling through ducting under water at Deptford Creek, as the railway bridge across it had a lifting section.

For various reasons, including the building of unnecessary rival routes in Kent and of the Metropolitan Extension from Herne Hill to Farringdon Street and Moorgate, both the South Eastern and London, Chatham and Dover Railways had been extremely impoverished in the latter half of the nineteenth century. One result of this was that many of their suburban lines in the London area had been constructed as economically as possible, with sharp curves and minimum clearances. The stations too were cheaply built: all too often they were crude structures with low platforms and mean wooden buildings, unkempt and in a poor state of repair by the 1920s. Nothing was done to raise the height of substandard platforms, but where necessary they were extended to the standard 520ft eight-coach length using brick or prefabricated concrete components, similar to those already used at Carshalton Beeches and elsewhere. Loading gauge restrictions were eased to allow the passage of electric stock on 62ft underframes (considerably longer than any steam-hauled suburban vehicles), involving the reconstruction of a number of bridges, while signal wires and other trackside impedimenta had to be moved at various locations to avoid fouling collector shoes. Such improvement work was probably kept to a necessary minimum to keep costs close to the £5 million Government-guaranteed loan provided under the terms of the 1921 Trade Facilities Advisory Committee (TFAC) scheme to relieve post-war unemployment.

Lewisham main distribution switching room and sub-station, with outgoing feeder cables. *SR Official*

For the initial stage, a new station was provided at Nunhead, resited 200 yards to the west of its predecessor. It consisted of a 520ft wooden island platform on an embankment and was opened for traffic on 3rd May 1925. The island platform on the Herne Hill line at Loughborough Junction was rebuilt to the new standard length and replacement buildings provided, but it was not possible to lengthen the side platforms on the curve to the Catford loop line so they were closed after traffic on 11th July 1925. Platform and track alterations were also carried out at Herne Hill, where the original arrangements dated from the time when nearly all services divided or combined into Victoria and City portions. The platforms and layout were altered to provide two islands, giving cross-platform interchange between Holborn Viaduct/St Pauls and Victoria trains in both directions. Only the tracks serving platforms 2-3 were originally electrified at Holborn Viaduct, as only this platform face could be extended to the necessary 520ft without serious difficulty. At Shortlands, track alterations enabled the Down local platform to be made available for turning Catford loop line services.

The section between Holborn Viaduct and Elephant and Castle was equipped with four-aspect colour-light signalling, the first colour-lights on the Southern and the first four-aspect installation in the world. Designed by the SR signalling engineer W.J. Thorrowgood and under development since 1924, the single red, yellow and green aspects paralleled semaphores, but an additional yellow light enabled a fourth 'double-yellow' aspect between the green 'clear' and yellow 'caution', indicating 'attention – run at medium speed'. This reduced delays on sections where there was insufficient braking distance between signals, as in normal operation a train would always pass a double yellow and yellow indication before reaching a red stop signal. It was particularly useful where electric multiple units with high acceleration rates had to share tracks with slower steam-hauled trains such as, in this case, through transfer freights off the Metropolitan City Widened Lines. The new signalling was manufactured by the Siemens and General Electric Railway Signal Co. Ltd, and came into use on 21st March 1926, eight months after electric services commenced. There were two basic designs, one having the aspects in a vertical line and the other having them in a cluster mounted on a circular backplate. Where necessary, route indicators were liberally provided. The number of signalboxes required to control this section was reduced from seven to two: at Holborn Viaduct a new 86-lever power frame was installed in the existing building, but an entirely new 120-lever box was built at Blackfriars Junction.

Raworth's original SECR plans to use four-coach multiple units were changed (not, it seems, without argument) and three-coach motor units and two-coach trailer sets were specified instead in the interests of standardisation. 29 new motor units, 1496-1524, were initially provided, similar to those for the Western section extension but on longer underframes. They were soon joined by 105 five similar units, 1401-1495 and 1525-1534, but with bodywork converted from SER/SECR steam stock. 67 trailer sets, 1051-1117, to work with them on rush-hour services were also introduced, but for reasons outlined later, sufficient trailer sets were not ready for the inauguration of the first and second stages, and this resulted in the use of temporary four-car formations for about two months.

The major new depot facility provided to service the stock for the Eastern section scheme was at Slades Green, on the North Kent line west of Dartford. The existing steam shed here, dating from 1900 and redundant on electrification, was converted into an eight-road inspection and cleaning shed for the electric stock, each track long enough to hold an eight-coach formation. The layout at each end was altered, and six external sidings were equipped with conductor rails for berthing purposes. Inside, there were no conductor rails, but units could be moved using a flexible electrical connection which ran along ceiling-mounted rails and plugged into the electrical jumper socket on unit ends. For a short period in 1925/26 electric and steam traction shared facilities here, some of the new electric coaches being delivered for storage until their formation into three-car (or, in some cases as a short term arrangement, four-car) units.

East of the existing shed a brand-new repair shop was provided based on that already existing at Wimbledon, comprising a steel framework clad in corrugated asbestos. Although still incomplete, photographs indicate that the new facility was in use by the end of 1925. All six roads could accommodate three coaches, and four had pits. Overhead cranes enabled vehicles to be lifted, necessary as the main work carried out here was bogie and electrical overhaul. Half the shop dealt with 'Eastern section' units with 9ft motor bogies and DK 77 300hp motors, while the other half dealt with South Western and (later) 'Central section' units with Metropolitan-Vickers 339 motors and 8ft 9in motor bogies. Initially, the electric units supplied for the Eastern section were all of the former type, but it was later decided to standardise on the MV 339 (and later, EE 339) motor and, as the three-car units eventually became common-user over the whole suburban network, both types came to Slades Green for overhaul on a regular basis. From 1932 the shops also became responsible for certain electrical and mechanical overhaul work on main-line semi-fast electric stock, which had virtually the same traction equipment, and facilities here were further extended in 1937 when four six-coach-length roads were added.

Other cleaning and inspection sheds were provided at Orpington and Addiscombe. Both had four roads and were also of steel-framed, asbestos-clad construction. That at Orpington was situated on the Down side at the London end of the station and was 1,050ft long, enabling two complete eight-coach trains to be stored under cover on each track. It had the unusual feature of a public footpath passing through the roof on a bridge. Extensive berthing sidings were also laid out on both the Up and Down sides here. Addiscombe shed was only 510ft long and there were also two berthing sidings of the same length parallel with the platform. Other electrified berthing sidings were provided at all the suburban outer-end termini and at sundry other locations. In 1939 a further inspection shed and maintenance shop was provided at Gillingham for the Medway electrification scheme, and this also dealt with suburban stock.

The original timetable drafts had been based on Raworth's dusted-off SECR plans using four-car units which would have divided or combined Victoria and St Pauls/Holborn Viaduct portions at Herne Hill. With the imposition of the new 3-coach standard motor unit + a trailer set + motor unit for rush-hour working, splitting of services en route was not feasible and the timetables had to be replanned to take account of this. Although completion of trailer sets had been delayed, construction of trailers for the motor units was well advanced. To meet the need for eight-coach trains to provide enough capacity, therefore, temporary four-coach motor units were formed and some trains were divided and joined at Herne Hill during the initial trial months of operation.

Crew training and trial running began between Nunhead and Crystal Palace on 1st April 1925, St Pauls and Shortlands via the Catford loop on 8th June, Holborn Viaduct – Herne Hill – Orpington from 22nd June and Victoria to Herne Hill on 1st July, in all cases using the temporary four-car units. A formal opening ceremony for the electrified routes of stage one took place on 9th July and full public services to the new electric timetable on 12th July, the same date as the Western section Guildford and Dorking extensions.

Services on all routes generally ran at twenty-minute intervals off-peak. Trains to Crystal Palace (High Level) and to Shortlands via the Catford loop ran only from St Pauls. The other services were Holborn Viaduct and Victoria to Orpington via Herne Hill. Additional trains in the peaks gave the Holborn Viaduct to Bickley section a ten-minute interval service. It was necessary to 'flight' suburban trains to provide sufficient space for main line services: this was done by running Holborn Viaduct and Victoria to Orpington trains five minutes apart, leaving a fifteen minute gap for other trains. St Pauls to Shortlands/Crystal Palace services were timed similarly, again to provide paths for main line trains routed via Nunhead and the Catford loop. The initial service on Sundays was half-hourly. There were various alterations to the timetable in the first few years, and by June 1928 three trains per hour were operating to Orpington via Herne Hill on Sundays.

Meanwhile, work had been going ahead on the second and third stages. A new station was built to replace the dilapidated wooden SER edifice at Bromley North, and was officially opened on 27th December 1925. Not fully completed until early in 1926, it featured an imposing brick building with a copper-clad cupola, opening onto a single 520ft island platform. There was also a single electrified berthing siding and the then obligatory goods yard. Deptford station, closed from 15th March 1915 as a wartime measure, was reopened on 19th July 1926, served by Greenwich line trains to Dartford. This reopening helped to pacify local interests, who rightly complained that the new electric trains roared across the inner London suburbs without serving them.

The most serious work involved track rearrangements and resignalling at the London end, necessary to facilitate the increased electric services. On the four-track section from Metropolitan Junction through Waterloo to the south end of Hungerford Bridge, the unusual arrangement of having two Down lines between the Up lines had been designed to allow Charing Cross trains to work in and out of Cannon Street.

This practice was planned to cease on electrification, and so the tracks were reorganised into the standard Up-Down-Up-Down arrangement, together with the abolition, replacement or resiting of a number of crossovers during a weekend occupation on 22nd-24th August 1925, with only a skeleton service using a single track working on the Sunday. It is recorded that the work was hindered by heavy rain, and there was much disorganisation and disruption the following morning. Before this, a temporary new platform-level signal cabin had been provided at Charing Cross, enabling the existing overhead mechanical box to be dismantled and replaced by a new power-framed structure in the same position.

More drastic action was required at Cannon Street where the existing track layout was archaic and totally unsuitable for an intensive service, and it was therefore decided to install an entirely new formation at a cost of nearly £110,000. To facilitate this, the station was to be entirely closed for three weeks, during which possession the old track and platforms would be removed and the new installed in an exercise planned with military precision by the Southern's Chief Engineer, Alfred Szlumper, and described in detail by G.T. Moody.[2] Following manufacture the new track layout, including conductor rails, cabling and point machines, was first laid for testing on waste-ground near New Cross Gate, and then carefully dismantled ready to be installed on its new site during the three-week occupation which took place from 3.00pm on 5th June 1926 until 4.00am on 28th June. During that time 1,000 staff were involved in the work, three-quarters of whom worked in three shifts. The new layout at Cannon Street had eight platforms and 77 points (a reduction of 24) and was reopened without ceremony, the first arrival being an electric train.

With the new layout at Cannon Street, a second section of four-aspect colour light signalling came into operation on Sunday 27th June 1926, covering the rearranged lines from Charing Cross and Cannon Street to Borough Market Junction. Two new signalboxes were provided: these were an overhead box across the station throat at Charing Cross containing a 107-lever power frame, and a more conventional box on the west side of the river bridge at Cannon Street with a 143-lever power frame. The actual signals differed only in detail to those installed previously, but were supplied by the Westinghouse Brake and Saxby Signal Company. There were two automatic sections between Waterloo Junction and Metropolitan Junction. Manual working was retained at Metropolitan Junction box, where a new sixty-lever frame was installed. (With the SR's usual eye for economy, the redundant signalbox from Waterloo Junction was shipped to the Isle of Wight and re-erected at Ryde St Johns Road.)

Public services which were used to train motormen began between Elmers End and Hayes on 21st September 1925, a single three-coach unit running to the existing branch timetable with empty stock workings to and from the newly-built Addiscombe Depot. Test running on the Bromley North branch followed from 19th November. It was originally hoped to commence public services on the second stage of the electrification on 1st December and an announcement was made to this effect, but due to power supply difficulties this had to be postponed for three months until 28th February 1926. On that date a limited number of electric trains began running from Charing Cross and Cannon Street to Orpington, Bromley North and the Mid-Kent line. At this stage three platforms of the existing layout at Cannon Street had been temporarily equipped with conductor rails, prior to the total rebuilding and rearrangement mentioned above. Additional electric trains began on these routes from 19th July, but further power supply problems caused by the effects of the coal miners's and resultant General Strikes delayed implementation of the full electric service until 20th September.

The new timetable introduced on this date offered a basic off-peak service of trains every thirty minutes over the SER main line to both Orpington and Bromley North, running alternately from Charing Cross and Cannon Street. A fifteen-minute interval service operated down the Mid-Kent line via Lewisham alternately to Beckenham Junction and Addiscombe, giving each terminus a half-hourly train, again alternating between the two London termini. These Mid-Kent services connected at Elmers End with a half-hourly shuttle to Hayes, starting from the Down bay and returning to the Up bay, therefore involving a shunt between each trip. Additional trains ran in the peaks, including through services to/from the Hayes branch, with a total of nine in and out of Cannon Street and six to Charing Cross in the busiest hour.

On the third stage, a few electric trains had run between Charing Cross and Dartford between 10th-16th May 1926 as a result of the General Strike, but the service then reverted to steam until 6th June. A limited service of electric trains then commenced to a temporary timetable, with about one third terminating or starting at London Bridge while Cannon Street was closed for rebuilding. This demonstrated to staff the ease with which electric multiple units could be terminated and turned back at times of service disruption. More electric trains ran when Cannon Street was reopened on 28th June, but in order to allow staff to get used to the new layout here the full service did not commence until 19th July. However, as on the Orpington and Mid-Kent lines, it was soon necessary to curtail it due to electricity supply restrictions which were a result of the continuing strike in the coal mines, and here too it was not possible to run the full service to the new electric timetable again until 20th September.

Again, the increase in service was massive, with a basic half-hourly headway off-peak on all four routes to Dartford, alternately serving Charing Cross and Cannon Street. These routes were via Greenwich and Woolwich, via Blackheath and Woolwich, via Bexleyheath and via Sidcup. Together with the Mid-Kent, Bromley North and Orpington services, these gave a total of eight suburban trains in and out of both London termini in an average off-peak hour. A twenty-minute interval operated on each route in the peaks with about two-thirds serving Cannon Street, indicating the precedence of the City

2 Moody, G.T.: *Southern Electric 1909-1979*, Fifth Edition, Ian Allan Ltd, ISBN 0 7110 0924 4, 1979. pp31-32

Reconstruction at Bromley North station in the summer of 1925. As well as a new station building, new platforms were provided, using LSWR-designed concrete components made at Exmouth Junction concrete works.

business centre over its West End counterpart at this period. In the rush hours, one service per hour on the Greenwich line turned back at Woolwich Arsenal, while most Bexleyheath line services turned left after Barnehurst to serve Slades Green and return to London via Woolwich and Greenwich or Blackheath.

The provision of headcodes for ex-SER suburban services was considerably more complicated than for stage one of the Eastern section or for the Western section schemes, as there were so many different destinations and permutations of route. For example there were ten route possibilities between London and Dartford and (following electrification to Sanderstead in September 1935) no fewer than sixteen permutations on the Mid-Kent line. The basic method used was to allocate a letter to each country terminus or route, and by using a bar, one dot or two dots above it. Some routes, however, were given different letters for Up and Down services.

There were further new colour light-signalling installations on the Eastern section suburban lines in 1928 and 1929. The lines between through London Bridge station between Borough Market Junction and Spa Road were equipped with four-aspect signals in 1928 as part of the Central section scheme (see page 52). The sections from New Cross to Blackheath, Ladywell and Hither Green were equipped from 30th June 1929, controlled from two new electro-mechanical signal boxes at St Johns and Parks Bridge Junction. The gap between Spa Road and New Cross, together with the Spa Road–Greenwich section, was filled in from 1st December, a new power box being built at North Kent East Junction. It was necessary to spread the introduction of this new form of signalling over a five-year period to make efficient use of the manufacturer's output. These schemes allowed the abolition of no fewer than thirteen existing mechanical signal boxes with consequent staff savings.

The first area of rapid traffic growth as speculative builders moved in was on the Bexleyheath line, which by the autumn of 1930 had an off-peak and late-evening service of four trains per hour (two turning back at Barnehurst). The Hayes branch had received a through service in slack hours by this time, with three per hour, mainly to serve Elmers End and Eden Park. The builders moved into West Wickham in about 1926, and into Hayes around 1931. The Addiscombe off-peak service at the end of 1930 was also three per hour, the Beckenham Junction service having been discontinued outside the rush hours by this time to provide the extra paths for Hayes trains. The Greenwich/Woolwich trains remained half-hourly, but by 1934 the Sidcup line had four off-peak trains per hour. Nearly all of these extra trains were run by more intensive use of the original rolling stock, few new units having been provided. From 1st February 1932 a number of peak-hour services were diverted to serve Charing Cross rather than Cannon Street, in recognition of the gradual spread of London's office area from the City to the West End.

It is convenient to mention here that Waterloo Junction, the first station out of Charing Cross on the Eastern section, was renamed plain Waterloo on Sunday 7th July 1935, its platforms being designated A–D to distinguish them from those at the adjacent Western section terminus. The LT Central line Post Office station was renamed St Pauls on 1st February 1937, and to avoid confusion the SR St Pauls became Blackfriars on the same day. The new name was more appropriate to its location and corresponded to the LT District/Circle Line station below.

Track re-arrangement in progress at Cannon Street station, on 8th June 1926. The new platform faces and track layout on the right appear substantially complete, including colour-light starter signals with route indicators.

CENTRAL SECTION DC ELECTRIFICATION

In August 1926, one year and four months after the last ac extension had gone into full public service, the SR announced that the overhead system was to be abandoned as part of the scheme to convert the Central section suburban lines to dc third rail. 127 overhead-equipped track miles were to be converted and another 105 electrified on the dc system, at an estimated cost of £3.75 million. Contracts for the supply of electrical equipment for the first 116 three-coach motor units and 47 trailer sets from Metropolitan-Vickers, at a cost exceeding £600,000, were announced that December.

The steam-worked lines involved, which included parts of the former SECR system, were Streatham North Junction – Mitcham Junction – Sutton – Epsom Downs, Sutton – Epsom, London Bridge – Forest Hill – Purley – Tattenham Corner/ Caterham, Streatham – Wimbledon via Tooting Junction and Haydons Road and Crystal Palace Low Level to Beckenham Junction. The ac *Elevated Electric* routes to be converted included Victoria – Crystal Palace Low Level – Norwood Junction – Selhurst, Victoria – Streatham Common – Selhurst – Coulsdon North and Sutton, Victoria to London Bridge via Peckham Rye (the South London line), Balham – Tulse Hill – London Bridge, Tulse Hill to West Norwood and Tulse Hill to Streatham Common. Publicity at the time claimed that an annual dc train mileage of 7,636,000 would replace 2,038,556 steam and 2,377,973 ac. Preparing these figures alone must have been a formidable task, when every mile of train journey run was added up manually and the results set up against every last penny of income and expenditure in order to demonstrate to the shareholders the exact state of the company, its performance and its efficiency.

Power for the Central section dc scheme mainly came from an extension of Lewisham distribution station, which served nine new substations. Those at Tulse Hill, Streatham and Norwood Fork and in arches below the South London line at South Bermondsey each had three 1,500KW rotary converters; while Sutton, Forest Hill, Purley, Kingswood and Warlingham had two. More rotary converters were also installed at the existing ex-LSWR installation at Clapham Junction, and this substation also relayed a high-tension supply from Durnsford Road to additional equipment at Victoria. South Bermondsey substation was fed through tappings off the existing cables to Cannon Street. Rotary converters and static transformers were all supplied by the Swedish-owned Asea Electric Ltd, while the new substation buildings were similar to those built previously.

In contrast with the Eastern section scheme, little was done regarding auxiliary power supplies. While the LSWR had on electrification replaced gas and oil station lighting with a comprehensive ac low tension lighting system, the LBSCR had not provided auxiliary power supplies for general station lighting, instead continuing to use the existing gas. This was generally left in situ and functioning by the SR, which was becoming more and more economy conscious as the 1920s became progressively more difficult financially. It is possible that continued use of such outdated lighting on Central suburban stations was connected with long-term

contracts for the supply of gas. Thus thirty years later East Croydon, for example, was converted directly from gas mantles to fluorescent tubes. Some stations, such as Ashtead, were provided with electric lighting powered directly from the traction supply.

The civil engineering works required on the Central section were of a rather different nature to those required on the Eastern section. There were no major rearrangements at Victoria, and track alterations at London Bridge (Central) and its approach lines were less extensive than Charing Cross and Cannon Street had been. The main effect was the need to rebuild South Bermondsey station because track re-arrangements here would have resulted in the original station having Up platforms only. Following representations from local residents, the new station here was located on the South London line two hundred yards south of South Bermondsey junction and consisted of a wooden island platform accessed by steep stairs from Ilderton Road. Opened on 17th June 1928, the platform used space vacated by removal of the third (centre) line on this section. The track layout at Tulse Hill was also modified, and additional platforms provided on the fast lines at Purley Oaks.

Elsewhere the ex-LBSCR lines had been constructed and maintained to 'heavier' standards than those of the SECR. Only the overgrown and derelict line from Crystal Palace (Low Level) to Beckenham Junction, closed to normal traffic since 1st December 1915 as a wartime measure, required attention before it was re-opened on 3rd March 1929. This involved raising track levels between Beckenham Junction and Kent House to ease the gradients over the Mid-Kent line and Chaffinch brook, and widening to provide separate Crystal Palace line tracks for about half a mile at Beckenham Junction. (As a side benefit, these works also enabled the Mid-Kent bridge over the same brook to be raised, reducing but not entirely preventing the incidence of flooding to which the line at this location was frequently subjected.) A new intermediate station at Birkbeck, an unassuming and cheaply-built side-platformed affair, was provided on this section. Opened on 2nd March 1930 for passengers and parcels traffic only, it served an already well built up area and a large cemetery. On the former ac routes, little platform work needed to be done as most platforms had been long enough to accommodate eight coaches of CP stock or two five-coach sets of CW stock. An exception was the South London line, limited to six-coach trains.

An important station rebuilding took place at Epsom. It will be recalled that conductor rails were laid through the existing ex-LSWR station as part of the Western section Guildford and Dorking scheme in 1925, but that Sutton line trains ran through and called at their own station, named Epsom Town by the SR. This nonsense was ended by the rebuilding and enlargement of the former South Western station to serve both routes, and consequent closure of the LBSCR establishment. Reconstruction, which commenced in June 1928, involved lengthening and widening the Up-side embankment and island platform and converting the single Down-side platform into a second island. Both new platforms were 650ft long and 30ft wide, with brick buildings under steel-framed canopies. A distinctive feature was the overhead signal box, with sixty levers. Access to the platforms was through a tiled subway from a concrete-faced entrance hall at street level, one of the first in the Southern's new architectural style, now referred to as *Moderne*. The track layout was altered to provide cross-platform interchange between Waterloo and Sutton line services in the Up direction, and between Effingham Junction/Dorking line and terminating trains in the Down. These rearrangements required the erection of several new steel bridges across the Kingston road just north of the station. While this reconstruction work was going on the station remained open, access to the Up platform being by temporary footbridge. The new station was completed and opened to traffic for the start of electrified services from Sutton on 3rd March 1929; the former LBSCR station closed to passengers on the previous night.

Colour light signalling was extended from Borough Market Junction through London Bridge to Spa Road on the Eastern section, and to Bricklayers Arms and Old Kent Road Junction on the Central section, on which there were fifteen automatic sections. Running line arrangements were altered at London Bridge (Central section) and its approaches. The Central section's signalling was three-aspect but the Eastern section installation was four-aspect as the Charing Cross/Cannon Street resignalling had been. As before, all new equipment was supplied by Westinghouse, Saxby and Farmer. A new 35-lever frame was installed in the existing signal cabin at Borough Market Junction, but an entirely new building was provided at London Bridge, situated at the east end of the station between the SE and Central lines. A brick structure with a steel framework, the equipment was ranged on three floors. The frame had no less than 312 levers and was controlled from the upper floor, but the interlocking was so complex and extensive that the frame actually rested on the middle floor. The new signalling was brought into use on Sunday 17th June 1928, the first day of full dc electric services on Central section routes.

Upon electrification Purley locomotive depot was closed and its site handed over to the Signal Engineers' department, and Battersea loco. depot was also reduced in activity. Peckham Rye ac electric depot, which had been mainly concerned with berthing South London line units and maintaining SL and CP stock, was briefly given the job of de-electrifying withdrawn ac vehicles in readiness for their dispatch to Ashford and Lancing for conversion to dc, before being re-equipped to maintain dc suburban stock. From 1932 onwards it was also concerned with electro-mechanical work on main line electric units, even though its short length and restricted site proved a handicap. (One shed could only handle three coach-lengths, and any EMU with four or more vehicles had to be split.) Selhurst depot, built in 1910/11 for the maintenance and cleaning of CP ac stock, was reorganised and re-equipped to become the maintenance depot for all Central section suburban electric stock. Later it took over Eastern and Western section stock varnishing (intermediate repaint) work from Slades Green and Durnsford Road. Additional

berthing sidings for dc stock were laid at Selhurst and also provided at Epsom, Coulsdon North, Beckenham Junction, Crystal Palace Low Level and Purley.

The rolling stock provision for the Central section scheme included 149 three-coach motor units, 1601-1749, all formed from existing SECR, LSWR or LBSCR wooden bodywork on either new or reconditioned lengthened underframes between 1927 and 1930. Some of the LBSCR-bodied coaches were converted from former ac vehicles. To run with them 58 trailer sets, 1121-1178, were provided, again using coaches of all three origins. Eight two-coach motor units, converted from the 1909 ac motor coaches, were provided for the South London line in 1929. As mentioned earlier, after this time provision of rolling stock for succeeding electrification fill-in and extension schemes becomes very difficult to apportion, and a small number of further units and trailer sets were later added to the fleet, financed from the smaller fill-in electrification schemes described from page 54.

The first part of the Central section scheme to be completed was from London Bridge via Forest Hill to Caterham and Tattenham Corner, and the spur from Sydenham to Crystal Palace Low Level. With its terminus open only on Epsom race days, most steam trains down the Tattenham Corner branch had terminated at Tadworth, and when temporary electric services to the existing steam timings commenced on 25th March 1928 they continued to do so. The acres of racecourse terminus came into daily use on 17th June, when full electric timetables were implemented on the branches and dc trains began running to Coulsdon North (hitherto an ac preserve), Epsom Downs, from London Bridge to Victoria via Tulse Hill, and over the South London line. In rush hours, Caterham/Tattenham Corner line trains were terminated in the Central section platforms at London Bridge, rather than running through to Charing Cross as previously. This avoided the complexities of crossing between Central and Eastern section tracks between London Bridge and Southwark Park, but resulted in heavy public criticism by which the SR remained, then as often since, unpersuaded. Tattenham Corner/Caterham trains divided for the two branches at Purley, and only on race days was it thought necessary to provide self-contained services on either. The platforms on the Tattenham Corner branch were not lengthened to 520ft except at the terminus, as the longest train usually seen was of only six coaches.

It was accepted that the introduction of full electric working, a new and more intensive timetable and new colour-light signalling all on the same day (17th June) was likely to lead to difficulties, and the public were warned. In the event, a failed point motor caused minor delays on the first Monday, but the new services soon bedded down. To help alleviate potential problems a number of trains were diverted to start or end their journeys at Victoria rather than London Bridge, or were terminated short at Crystal Palace (Low Level). They were gradually returned to London Bridge, but the full timetabled service was not running until 4th July.

The remainder of the Central section scheme came into operation on 3rd March 1929, with dc trains running between

London Bridge and Dorking North/Effingham Junction via Tulse Hill, Mitcham Junction and Sutton, Victoria and Epsom via Mitcham Junction, Holborn Viaduct and Wimbledon via Tulse Hill and Haydons Road, and Victoria – West Croydon/Beckenham Junction via Crystal Palace Low Level. The Crystal Palace dc services absorbed the Victoria – Crystal Palace ac service. Although ac rolling stock was still in service interworking with dc stock on the Coulsdon and Sutton routes after this date, its use gradually diminished through 1929 as it was withdrawn for conversion or adaptation to dc operation with a consequent increase in dc stock available. As mentioned earlier, the last ac train eventually ran in passenger service in the small hours of 22nd September.

An interesting deviation from the standard letter headcode arrangement used on dc suburban services occurred on the South London line. On the partial introduction of standard three-coach dc units on this service from 17th June 1928, headcodes H with single dot (London Bridge to Victoria) and H with double dots (Victoria to London Bridge) were used. In May 1929 the original South London ac motor coaches, suitably adapted for dc operation and formed into two-coach units, returned to the line, initially displaying headcodes T (London Bridge to Victoria) and T with single dot (Victoria to London Bridge). In July 1932 these were replaced by the numerical headcode 2, coincident with the opening of the first stage of the Brighton line electrification, on which number codes were also used.

The line between Streatham Junction and Wimbledon, including the loop from Tooting to Wimbledon via Merton Abbey, had closed from 1st January 1917 as yet another wartime cut. As part of the SR's agreement with the Underground Group regarding the proposed Wimbledon and Sutton railway, this section was reopened on 27th August 1923, but served only by a sparse weekdays rush-hour only steam service from Ludgate Hill or London Bridge. On electrification, an all-day service was inaugurated between Holborn Viaduct and Wimbledon, running every twenty minutes in the peaks and half-hourly at other times. The short island platform at Ludgate Hill, sandwiched between St Pauls and Holborn, was closed after 1.50pm on Saturday 2nd March 1929. Also closed from the same date was the Tooting – Merton Park loop, virtually all custom from the intermediate station at Merton Abbey having been abstracted by Colliers Wood station on the 1926 tube extension to Morden. Conversely, the new electric service initially proved popular at all times of day, diverting much traffic from the parallel trams.

At this point, electrification on the 600V dc system of the basic suburban network of the Southern Railway was considered almost complete. Later work, consisting of smaller fill-in and extension schemes, two short new lines, and improvements in areas already electrified, are covered in the remainder of this chapter. At the SR Annual General Meeting of February 1929 the Chairman, Brigadier-General the Hon. Everard Baring CVO, summarised the work carried-out to date, and it is worth repeating a few of his words here together with some additional comments. Up to the start of 1929, 270 route miles and 748 track miles had so far been converted, comprising 13% of the SR's total track mileage. A total of £10.5 million had been spent by the company (or its constituents prior to 1923) on electrification. Of this, only £6 million was charged to Capital, most of the remainder being borne by various Renewal or Reserve Funds and the residue charged to the Revenue Account over a period of years. Thus, apart from the £5 million of Government assistance to finance the Eastern section electrification, the entire cost had been met by the railway company in anticipation of significant traffic growth and reduced operating costs. The minimum expected return on capital for each scheme was usually set at 4% per annum, but in nearly all cases this was exceeded.

COMPLETION OF THE SUBURBAN AREA : WIMBLEDON – WEST CROYDON, GRAVESEND AND WINDSOR

Electrification of the inner and middle-distance suburban lines of the Southern Railway was effectively completed following authorisation of three small schemes covering the Wimbledon to West Croydon, Dartford to Gravesend Central and Feltham Junction/Hounslow Junction to Windsor routes, converted at an overall cost of £600,000. Total route mileage electrified was 49½ and electric services on all three sections commenced on 6th July 1930.

The Wimbledon to West Croydon line was an interesting candidate for electrification as much of it was single-track, and it traversed an almost straight path across an area in places surprisingly rural for inner suburbia. Dating from 1855, its early history is described in detail by Alan A. Jackson,[3] but it is worth mentioning here that part of its route was over the course of the world's first public railway line, the Surrey Iron Railway of 1803. A noteworthy feature at Mitcham, one of only two original intermediate stations on the line, was the booking hall, converted from the former country dwelling of a City merchant. (This historic building still stands in 2009, latterly reconstructed into offices.) From 1868 the LBSCR Peckham Rye to Sutton line crossed on the level by means of a severe S bend and two junctions, between which a new station named Mitcham Junction was constructed. Although passenger traffic was always light in view of the nature of the area served, the line gradually increased in importance for freight, serving new industries developing along the River Wandle. At the Croydon end, a gas works and power station were built adjacent to the line, both with their own internal railway networks.

The main reason for electrifying this seemingly unpromising line was that it filled in a gap in an area otherwise exclusively electrified, and no great electrification-inspired increase in traffic was expected. Authorised by the SR Board on 7th July 1928 it was assumed that the necessary work could be done quickly and cheaply, the original estimated cost

---

3   Jackson, A.J.: *London's Local Railways*, Second Edition, Capital Transport, ISBN 1 85414 209 7, 1999. pp94-101

Waddon Marsh Halt, in the smokey environs of Croydon Gas Works (right) and power stations, was opened on 6th July 1930 with electrification of the Wimbledon–West Croydon Line. 2 WIM unit 1809 is seen departing for Wimbledon on 29th August 1953. The unelectrified track on the left is the additional independent freight line from Croydon to Beddington Lane, added as part of the electrification scheme. In the sidings on the right are two steam locomotives owned by the gas company. *John H. Meredith*

for converting the 6.2 mile route being only £51,700. No new substations would be required, current being fed from existing installations at Raynes Park, Mitcham Junction and West Croydon. However, following a walk-over of the line by Walker and his officers, it was decided to undertake further works which pushed the cost up to £72,000. These included joining a number of existing sidings at the Croydon end to form an independent freight line to serve the factories as far as Beddington Lane, enabling existing and increasing freight traffic to keep clear of the more intensive passenger service proposed. From the junction at West Croydon as far as Waddon Marsh, this track was separately signalled as a single line using independent electric train staffs. The same signalling system was also used throughout the route, staff exchanges being situated at Merton Park, Mitcham, Mitcham Junction, Beddington Lane (not a crossing place), Waddon Marsh and West Croydon box. A new halt was provided at Waddon Marsh, situated on a passing loop just west of where the line passed under the new Purley Way and convenient for staff at the gas works. This consisted of a 170ft island platform accessed by footbridge, both of reinforced concrete, and a signal box. With the separate freight line and another siding, there were no less than four tracks at this point.

Electric services on the route were worked by four two-coach units, initially numbered 1909-1912, specially provided for it. Converted from the 9ft 5in wide centre trailers of the original South London line ac sets, they retained their side-gangway arrangement which made them particularly suitable for conductor-guard operation, where the guard sold tickets from a portable machine while the train was underway. This operation was assisted by doors linking the guard's van and passenger saloons in each vehicle. From the start they carried headcode 2, using a unique full-width stencil similar to the letter stencils used to denote all other suburban services at this time. The similar South London line units also sometimes appeared but these had no side gangways in the first

class section, making the guard's job somewhat more difficult. (In addition to 1909-1912, three three-coach motor units, 1754-1756, were charged to the Wimbledon to West Croydon electrification budget, but were for general Central section suburban use.)

The initial service was basically half-hourly, and required two units which passed on the double track section between Mitcham and Mitcham Junction on their 26-minute run. Despite operating constraints, a 20-minute interval was maintained during rush hours, requiring three units in use, while an hourly service sufficed on Sundays. Due to platform lengths, it was not normal to use more than a single two-coach electric unit on this line, but photographs show that four-car formations (two units coupled) did occasionally operate. Although tickets were issued on the train, to confuse matters they could also be purchased from existing booking offices at the termini and at Mitcham Junction, as well as from the signalman at Waddon Marsh halt.

The shortest of the three routes was the 6.8 miles from Dartford to Gravesend Central, recommended to the Board by Walker in April 1929. This conversion did not take long, as little incidental work was required. It was necessary to provide a new substation at Northfleet, equipped with two rotary converters and supplied from Lewisham feeder station. Swanscombe Halt was rebuilt half a mile east of its original location, nearer to Northfleet, using pre-cast components supplied from Exmouth Junction concrete works. One additional three-coach motor unit (1769) and two trailer sets (1187/88) were funded from the Gravesend electrification budget. The revised timetable on electrification basically involved the extension of three Dartford trains per hour (generally two via Sidcup and one via Greenwich) to Gravesend, with peak extras. Conversion of this route eased terminal congestion problems at Dartford and brought a well-populated area of north Kent into the catchment area of the Southern Electric.

Swanscombe, a new halt built in 1930 for the Dartford–Gravesend third-rail extension. The designs and methods used in platform construction had been devised by LSWR civil engineer William Hamilton Shortt, whose work on precast concrete components had considerable and lasting influence on British railway and road construction. Designs based on his work remained standard on the Southern into BR days. *SR Official*

The Western section Windsor line extension comprised fifteen route miles and was authorised by the SR Board as late as May 1929, taking only fourteen months to complete. Power was supplied from Durnsford Road to new rotary converter substations at Ashford (Middlesex) and Datchet. Two new stations were provided, both situated on the already-electrified section of the route from Waterloo. That at North Sheen, serving an area already built-up, was located between Mortlake and Richmond, and was economically built at a cost of £12,000. It consisted of a 520ft island platform with passimeter booking office, access being from either side of the line by an uncovered concrete footbridge. It was generally similar to the stations provided on the new Wimbledon–Sutton line (see below) and was served by Kingston and Hounslow Loop services. Whitton was rather more substantially constructed, with 520ft side platforms and a covered steel footbridge, but was cheaper at just over £7,000. Of this, £3,000 was offered by local landowners, who were keen to encourage housing development in the area. Located west of Twickenham, it was served by Hounslow loop and Windsor trains. On the newly electrified section, the Down side of the existing station at Staines was also rebuilt. Additional rolling stock funded from the Windsor electrification budget comprised twelve three-coach motor units (1757-1768). Six extra two-coach trailer sets (1181-1186) were also paid for.

The new electric service comprised a half-hourly off-peak frequency between Waterloo and Windsor, non-stop between Waterloo and Richmond and then all stations. This was increased to three per hour in the peaks, one running via Hounslow with Feltham as the first stop out of London. Trailer sets were used on this line, but most trains were formed of one or two three-coach motor units until (probably) the start of the summer 1936 timetable, when they were replaced by two-coach NOL units or multiples thereof. The initial letter headcodes listed in Appendix 3 were replaced by numerical codes when the 2 NOLs took over, these being 17 (later 57) for services via Brentford and 18 (later 58), via Richmond. From 1937, 17 and 18 denoted Windsor/Chertsey-Weybridge services joining or dividing at Staines.

THE WIMBLEDON AND SUTTON RAILWAY

The Wimbledon and Sutton Railway, built in 1929-30, was the first of two entirely new suburban lines built by the Southern Railway. Laid out specifically for electric traction, it abounded in steep gradients, culminating in a fierce incline up to the junction with the Epsom line immediately south of the platforms at Sutton station. The genesis of the line is also described in detail by Alan A. Jackson[4] and others, so only a short summary is given here. Originating as a local initiative before World War One, the fledgeling company was financed and soon absorbed by the District Railway. The District viewed the Wimbledon and Sutton as an appendage to its own Earl's Court–Wimbledon services, giving it access to the very heart of LBSCR suburban territory. Although statutory

---

4 *London's Local Railways*, Second Edition, pp110-113

powers to build the line were obtained in 1910, no significant progress had been made by 1914 when work quickly ceased due to wartime manpower and material shortages. Powers were maintained through the succeeding years but, mainly due to a lack of finance, the scheme was held in abeyance until 1921. In that year the Trade Facilities Act (already mentioned in connection with the SECR's plans and the sub-sequent SR Eastern section electrification scheme) offered Government financial assistance for capital works, and the Underground Group (owners of the District) applied for funding to build the Wimbledon–Sutton line. Additionally, it planned to extend the City and South London tube line from Clapham Common to connect with it at Morden, enabling both District and CSLR trains to be projected through to Sutton. Among proposed incidental works, a large depot was to be built where the two lines met at Morden. A single bill for these works was deposited in 1922, much to the annoyance of the embryonic Southern Railway Board.

Sir Herbert Walker protested to Parliament that the Underground company's plans constituted intrusion on the areas set out by the Grouping Act, and suggested a more modest alternative scheme in which the CSLR could extend to Tooting and then continue over an existing SR line ('mothballed' since 1917) to Wimbledon, where terminal facilities would be made available. In return the Underground Group was to relinquish all powers pertaining to the Wimbledon and Sutton which, of course, it refused to do. The main reason given for this refusal was that more depot space was urgently required, hence the need for both District and CSLR to run at least to Morden. In the face of these arguments, and needing to make a concrete decision, the Lords rejected the entire bill, suggesting instead that the antagonists got together to thrash out a solution, which was finally reached following bitter arbitration. The resulting compromise represented a remarkable concession by the SR, but there was strong political pressure to reach a settlement. In addition, to prevent further territorial disputes, the Southern and Underground companies agreed that there would in future be mutual consultation before competing lines were promoted.

Under the agreed compromise plan, the SR would reopen the Streatham Junction – Tooting – Wimbledon line, while City and South London tracks would be permitted to surface at Morden, but were to have no continuation beyond. At this stage, the Southern would probably have preferred to have buried the Wimbledon and Sutton plans once and for all, but reluctantly agreed to build it as part of its own electrified network following strong local representations. Although initially junctions were to be provided to allow for through-running of District trains, as in the original bill, the MDR was now no longer interested in the proffered running powers to Sutton, and the junction plans at either end of the new line were therefore altered. At Wimbledon the physical junction would be with the West Croydon line, and the widening would take place south of the main lines. At Sutton, the additional terminal station was dropped and a junction was to be made with the existing line from Epsom. This necessitated the long steep incline up from Sutton Common, which quickly led to the line being dubbed by staff the 'Wall of Death', after a popular fairground attraction involving motorcycles. These changes were authorised in the Southern Railway's Act of 1924, but work on the line was deferred. As mentioned above, under the terms of the Act, the Streatham Junction – Wimbledon section was reopened with a steam peak-hour service on 27th January 1923 and electrified as from 3rd March 1929, when an all-day service between Wimbledon and Holborn Viaduct commenced.

Meanwhile, the Underground Group quickly completed the CSLR tube extension to Morden and, renamed the Morden–Edgware Line, it opened for traffic in September 1926, before work on the Wimbledon and Sutton had started. Feeder bus services pierced deep into SR suburban heartlands, mocking Walker's protests regarding intrusion into Southern territory, and within two years were abstracting more than four million journeys per year from competing SR services. The extensive new depot at Morden was ready for the start of service, with the sheds aligned to permit a connection to the Sutton line if eventually required. Services were operated by brand-new tube stock with air-operated sliding doors, somewhat more modern in appearance than the SR converted suburban stock although less comfortable to ride in.

Walker was very aware at this time of moves afoot to amalgamate the various municipal transport concerns in London (an event which finally occurred in 1933). This consolidation would inevitably lead to pooling of the receipts of the main line companies and the body set up to administer London area operation. It was therefore considered desirable in the interests of the shareholders that all possible suburban area developments should be undertaken to maximise the Southern's share of the pool. The Wimbledon–Sutton line definitely came into this category and so, following authority being given to go ahead in June 1927, work on the new line eventually commenced the following October, the long delay probably costing the SR dearly. Although as finally built the route closely followed the original plans, the number of stations was reduced and their locations slightly changed. Starting from the Wimbledon end, they were now to be sited at Wimbledon Chase, South Merton, Morden South, St Helier, Sutton Common and West Sutton. St Helier was a new addition, catering for the large London County Council housing estate of the same name then in the process of being laid out, and most of the land was donated by the LCC. Four additional motor units (1750-1753) and two trailer sets (1179/80) were financed from the Wimbledon–Sutton budget and added to the Central section fleet to provide the two eight-coach trains required.

The route of the Wimbledon and Sutton was sinuous and little was at ground level. There were 24 over and under-bridges, and more than half a million tons of soil were excavated in the course of construction. Gradients were laid out expressly for electric traction and were severe, with only 35 chains of level rail in its whole length. From South Merton to Sutton West Junction was a broken ascent, including stretches at 1 in 60 and culminating in a climb of half-a-mile at 1 in 44 to reach the junction. No new power supply arrange-

ments were necessary, the conductor rails being fed from existing substations at Raynes Park and Sutton. The line was signalled with upper-quadrant semaphores mounted on posts fabricated from old rails, then something of a novelty, controlled from signal cabins at Wimbledon (C box), St Helier and Sutton West Junction.

Construction work proved far from simple, with the embankment near Sutton Common slipping after completion, and a vein of blue clay in the same area requiring extensive drainage. The final climb commenced at West Sutton station, and here the engineers had to cut through much chalk and demolish a number of Victorian villas. With these difficulties and compensation payments, the capital cost was pushed up to just over £1 million. In order to avoid even more expense from land acquisition, this final cutting had almost vertical walls, lined with concrete.

It was originally intended that the entire route should be built by The Housing and Land Development Corporation. However, following a closer look at the plans a different approach was adopted, and construction of the first one and a quarter miles of the line, starting from the Wimbledon end, was carried out by the SR Engineer's Department under the direction of George Ellson. Situated mainly on embankment, this section served the new stations at Wimbledon Chase and South Merton. With work sufficiently advanced, it opened for traffic on 7th July 1929, the existing Holborn Viaduct to Wimbledon trains being extended to South Merton. Although double track had been laid only a single line was at first used, signalled by electric train staff, but from about December 1929 both lines were in use and the trains ran on empty to St Helier for reversal.

Robert McAlpine and Sons were appointed chief contractors for the remainder of the route, commencing operations in July 1928 at the Sutton end. Work continued day and night until September, when a resident secured a restraint on night work from the Vacation Court. This section included a 120ft lattice girder bridge to carry the line over the main London to Worthing road at Morden and a plate girder structure of similar length over the new Sutton by-pass beyond St Helier. Other overline bridges on the route were of steel with concrete floors, while underline bridges were of reinforced concrete. Just into 1930, on 5th January the whole route was opened to traffic, 21 years after the meeting in Merton where it all began. Carrying headcode P with bar in both directions, trains were a further extension of the Holborn Viaduct to South Merton service, running beyond Sutton to West Croydon and then either London Bridge (via Norbury) or Victoria (via Crystal Palace).

The stations were to a common pattern, economically built with 520ft concrete island platforms and wooden platform buildings comprising general waiting room, ladies' and gentlemen's toilets and separate staff accommodation, surmounted by riveted steel and glass canopies similar to those provided at Epsom. Attractive green-and-white glass running-in boards were provided but otherwise they were uninspiring, even ugly. All except Wimbledon Chase and Morden South were adjacent to overbridges, with covered

Above The curved street-level frontage of Wimbledon Chase, a station on the new Wimbledon–Sutton loop opened in 1929-30. This was arguably the only structure on the entire line to show any evidence of architectural thought. *Stations UK*

Below Surrounded by a sea of cheap housing, South Merton was typical of the island platform stations constructed for the new Wimbledon–Sutton line in 1929-30. Post-war 4 SUBs 4285 and 4370, then almost new, pause with a Sutton-bound service on 6th June 1949. *John H. Meredith*

stairs leading down from entrances at road level. Wimbledon Chase, actually situated in Merton and serving an area built-up before 1914, was the only station on the line to be given a road-level entrance hall showing any architectural pretension. The curved facade was covered with white glazed tiles and had shop units at either end; to the rear a stairway led the prospective passenger up to the platform. The other stations were simpler, and only at St Helier and West Sutton were there also roadside buildings. Entrance to South Merton was from Martin Way, where a concrete base was provided for a possible future booking hall. This was never built, and instead a passimeter booking hut was provided at the entrance to the platform. Morden South station was situated on an embankment, and access was via a subway through the north side of it and stairs leading up to the platform where the passimeter booth was situated. Apart from the nearness of the rival tube terminus, its possible catchment area was also denuded by the large acreages of the Underground depot and Morden Hall Park.

At St Helier a basic station entrance hall, executed in concrete blocks, was situated on Green Lane, some distance from the centre of the new community it was intended to serve. As a result it attracted little traffic, most of the new tenants on the estate either working locally or travelling by bus or on foot to the new tube terminus with its much more frequent service. In spite of its unpromising traffic potential, St Helier came to be the most important intermediate station, being equipped with the line's only crossover, signal box and goods yard, the latter having but two sidings and a great deal of spare space. The next station, Sutton Common, was situated at the beginning of a cutting after one mile of embankment from St Helier. It too had a passimeter booking hut, at the entrance to the stairs leading down to the platform. The final station, at West Sutton, was situated at the start of the deep chalk cutting up to the junction with an entrance building in Gander Green Lane. This was another ugly concrete blockhouse, this time with a stubby canopy of the same material.

As elsewhere in the area covered, house-building around the line gave it some traffic, but its proximity to the Morden tube with its cheap fares and feeder bus services put it at a disadvantage from the start. Its usage was not helped by the fact that its entire peak hour service ran to a City terminus, and that over a slow and circuitous route. Southern management was probably right to be unenthusiastic about a line which never really achieved its potential, and with hindsight would undoubtedly have been of more use as an appendage of the London Underground.

SEVENOAKS, SANDERSTEAD AND NUNHEAD – LEWISHAM

The Sevenoaks electrification, covering lines through an area at that time almost entirely rural but ripe for suburban development, was announced to shareholders at the March 1934 Annual General Meeting. At a cost of half a million pounds and involving 24 route miles and fifty track miles, the lines to be converted comprised those from Bickley Junction to Swanley Junction, Otford and Sevenoaks, and from Orpington to Sevenoaks. The loops from Chislehurst Junction to St Mary Cray Junction were also electrified, although no regular electric service was planned to use them. This scheme was authorised at the same time as that of the Eastbourne and Hastings line and was financed from SR internal resources in the expectation of significant traffic growth resulting from the residential development which would inevitably follow electrification. It was originally intended that eleven further three-coach motor units would be required to work Sevenoaks services but the rolling stock eventually officially funded from the Sevenoaks budget was eighteen two-coach 2 NOL units and four trailer sets (1195-1198). The NOLs went directly to the South Coast, releasing ex-LSWR motor units back to the London area suburban pool, helping to make up the required numbers. These convoluted arrangements, basically an exercise to satisfy the company accountants and shareholders at a time of difficult financial circumstances, are explained fully in Volume 2.

By this time unmanned remotely-controlled mercury-arc rectifier substations, supplied with electricity from the National Grid, had been proved on the Brighton line. New electrification schemes planned after 1933 therefore generally made use of this arrangement (described fully in Volume 2), which was considerably cheaper in operation than the manned rotary converters in use elsewhere in the suburban area. 33KV ac electricity at 50Hz was supplied by the Central Electricity Board from feeder stations at Northfleet and Tunbridge Wells and then distributed via lineside cables to six rectifier substations, located at Kelvingtown, Eynsford, Greenhill, Chelsfield, Polhill and Sevenoaks. There were also seven track-paralleling huts, located to reduce voltage-drop between substations. All were remotely-supervised from a new control room at Swanley Junction using a system devised by the SR electrical department under Alfred Raworth and supplied by Asea. Unusually, the feeder cables ran alongside long stretches of unelectrified route; the cable from Northfleet was routed along the Gravesend West branch to Fawkham Junction and thence to Swanley, while that from Tunbridge Wells ran up the Hastings line to Tonbridge and thence to Sevenoaks. The rectifier substations supplied current to the conductor rails at a nominal 660V, slightly higher than elsewhere in the suburban area, but this made little difference other than marginally improving train performance and lighting.

The only major station reconstruction was at Sevenoaks (Tub's Hill), where the layout was altered to provide Up and Down loops off the through lines, served by island platforms with an additional platform serving the outside of the Down loop, making this platform road double-sided. It was normal for services via Bat and Ball to terminate in the Down loop and those via Orpington in the Up loop. Apart from the usual fitting of track circuits, the only signalling alterations were between St Mary Cray and Swanley Junction, where new automatic upper-quadrant semaphore signals were brought into use on 1st July 1934, enabling an intermediate signalbox to be closed.

The original LCDR staggered-platform station at St Mary Cray, on the Chatham main line between Bickley and Swanley Junction electrified in 1934 as part of the Sevenoaks scheme. Recorded in about 1955, this scene would soon change for ever as the station was entirely reconstructed, and the lines through it quadrupled, for Phase 1 of the Kent Coast electrification. *Alan A. Jackson collection*

Work proceeded rapidly, and on 1st May 1934 the Holborn Viaduct – Catford loop – Shortlands service was extended to St Mary Cray. Electric trains reversing at what was then a simple SECR staggered-platform country station had to be slotted in between the heavy main-line traffic to and from Thanet. This service was further extended to Sevenoaks via Swanley Junction and Otford Junction from 6th January 1935, when the Charing Cross/Cannon Street to Orpington services were also projected through to Sevenoaks. The new electric services were lavish: trains via Swanley ran at twenty-minute intervals throughout the day, while those via Orpington ran three times an hour in the peaks and half-hourly at other times. Suburban housing development soon followed the new electric trains, spreading around St Mary Cray, Chelsfield and Sevenoaks. Only where the lines pene-trated the north downs, in the Eynsford, Shoreham and Knockholt areas, did the rural idyll persist.

The short line from Woodside Junction on the SER Addiscombe branch to Selsdon Junction on the LBSCR Oxted line had been jointly owned by the two companies prior to

Grouping. Skirting the eastern edge of the already-populous Croydon conurbation through an area better-served by other stations (Norwood Junction, for example), its sparse passenger service had been entirely withdrawn from 31st December 1916 as a wartime measure. However the line remained open for empty coaching stock, special freight and excursion traffic (indeed the track was relaid in 1927) and its wooden halts at Bingham Road, Coombe Lane and Spencer Road were not demolished, although weeds grew and paint peeled as time went by. Considering Walker's financial acumen, the reason why the Southern Railway decided to resurrect and electrify this moribund stretch of line, on which there was never any great potential for traffic growth, is not altogether clear. Possibly it was considered that another terminating point was needed on the already-busy Mid-Kent line, on which traffic was continuing to grow and, like the Wimbledon–West Croydon line, it filled in a gap in an area otherwise entirely electrified. Finally, a projected Southern Heights Light Railway between Orpington and Sanderstead might have returned electric trains to London via this route, but this scheme had been virtually abandoned by this time. The overall cost of converting the Woodside–Sanderstead line, together with Nunhead–Lewisham (see below) was £232,916, and the entire scheme was authorised in June 1934.

Power for the line was supplied from an impressive new rectifier substation at South Croydon, twice the size of other installations and remotely-supervised from the Brighton line control room at Three Bridges. Bingham Road Halt was converted into a station and Coombe Lane renovated and renamed Coombe Road. In both cases the platforms were extended to the standard 520ft with concrete sections, and new buildings and canopies provided. The erstwhile Spencer Road Halt was demolished, and Selsdon Road station was renamed plain Selsdon. At Sanderstead, electric trains reversed from the Down to the Up platform over a crossover at the country end of the platforms, and the conductor rail was therefore extended a train-length south of the station on the Up line. Oddly, the few yards of line between South Croydon Junction and Selsdon Junction were not equipped with conductor rails at this time, so it was not possible to terminate electric trains via East Croydon at Sanderstead.

Electric services on the Woodside–Sanderstead line commenced on 30th September 1935. From that date there was a lavish half-hourly off-peak service (including Sundays) between Charing Cross and Sanderstead via Lewisham and Elmers End, while in the peaks there were three per hour, most of which ran to or from Cannon Street. Ten additional standard suburban units (1585-1594) were added to the fleet to work these services, and also those using the Lewisham loops described next.

The useful Nunhead–Lewisham link had its origins in the LCDR's short Greenwich Park branch, an unsuccessful incursion by that company into SER territory. Already moribund when closed as a wartime economy from 1st January 1917, it was not reopened after the war, being used solely by freight trains from Nunhead to reach the yard at Brockley Lane and intermittently for carriage storage. In the meantime, freight from the northern railways reaching the Eastern section via the Metropolitan Railway's City Widened Lines and the Farringdon–St Pauls Snow Hill link was becoming heavier. These trains had to be routed via Metropolitan Junction and through London Bridge to reach the marshalling yards at Hither Green, and were difficult to fit into the intensive passenger service, particularly following electrification. The installation of four-aspect colour light signalling in the area helped, but delays still occurred and a more radical solution was needed.

As Alan A. Jackson records, someone in the SR planning department then 'had a bright idea'.[5] It was decided to recondition the branch from Nunhead as far as the first station at Lewisham Road, just before its crossing above the South Eastern main line east of St Johns. From there a new double-track spur, carried across the main line on a massive double-span girder bridge, ran to the London end of Lewisham

station. To complete the connection, a new double-tracked line, the Courthill loop, ran from near the south end of the Mid-Kent platforms at Lewisham and curved sharply to join the Tonbridge line just east of Parks Bridge Junction. Following track relaying on the former branch these sections, equipped with four-aspect colour light signalling but without conductor rails, were brought into use on 30th June 1929, allowing freight trains from the north to be routed from the Snow Hill line via Elephant and Castle, Peckham Rye, Nunhead and Lewisham to Hither Green. The remainder of the Greenwich Park branch was taken up that year. The Courthill loop was also used from its inception for steam excursions to the Kent Coast calling at Lewisham.

It was not long before these routes were being put to regular passenger use. The Courthill loop was electrified from 16th July 1933, enabling Bromley North and Dartford loop (via Sidcup) services to call at Lewisham if required. Two years later conductor rails were also laid on the Nunhead – Lewisham section, and peak-hour services between St Pauls and Dartford commenced on 30th September 1935. There were ten up trains in the morning peak and a corresponding number of down trains in the evening, split roughly evenly between the Dartford Loop and Bexleyheath lines, all non-stop between St Pauls and Lewisham.

WATERLOO AREA RESIGNALLING AND TRACK ALTERATIONS

By the mid 1930s the ever-busier train service out of Waterloo was placing increasing demands on the signalling and track layout in the area, most of which dated from before 1900. In particular the track arrangements inwards from Hampton Court Junction on the SW main line, where the Up and Down local lines ran either side of the through lines, meant that arriving suburban trains had to cross virtually the entire station throat to reach the main suburban platforms 1-6. From Waterloo C box there was an additional Up through relief line into the terminus. On the Windsor lines there were two Up and two Down lines, again paired by direction, as far as C box after which there was one Up and two Down lines into Waterloo. At this time all lines in and out of the terminus had mechanical operation of points and signals using Sykes' Lock and Block system, except in the West London Junction and Clapham Junction area where low-pressure pneumatic operation was used, with track-circuiting. Of the fifteen signal boxes controlling the area, the largest was the 1892 Waterloo A, which had no fewer than 266 levers and spanned the station throat on an overhead gantry.

With suburban traffic growing fast, notably on the Epsom line, and with electrified main line services to Portsmouth plus a new line to Chessington and Leatherhead in prospect to further increase the number of trains entering and leaving the terminus, replacement of the existing signalling and major alterations to the track layout became vitally necessary, and a £500,000 scheme was announced in January 1935. The scheme covered the main line out as far as Hampton Court Junction and the Windsor line as far as Clapham Junction, and work commenced almost immediately.

---

5 *London's Local Railways*, Second Edition, pp16-17

To ease the working of suburban services into Waterloo from Wimbledon and beyond without fouling the main line platforms, it was decided to rearrange the main local and through lines into the terminus in the order Up through, Down through, Up local, Down local. Additionally, an Up through relief line was provided from Vauxhall, and to make room for this the Windsor lines were reduced from this point to one Up and two Down lines. In order to change the arrangement of running lines on the main line into Waterloo from pairing by direction to pairing by use, it was necessary for the Up local line to cross both through lines. The closest to Waterloo that a flyover could easily be provided was in the space between the Gap Road and Durnsford Road overbridges north-east of Wimbledon station. Work started on this 2,174ft steel-framed and concrete-encased structure in September 1935. The line it carried rose at 1 in 60 before passing over both through lines on the skew and falling again at 1 in 45. A siding on the Down side was upgraded and electrified to become the temporary Down local line while the flyover was being constructed.

These alterations to track usage necessitated several platform alterations inwards from Wimbledon. At Earlsfield, the former Up local platform was now on the Up through line and was closed. At Vauxhall, the rearrangements left the Up local (formerly Up through) without a platform. The former main Down slow platform on the eastern edge of the station was therefore demolished, the Down local slewed into the space it had occupied, and a new island platform erected between the lines to serve both Up and Down trains. At the same time, new canopies were erected at both stations.

The entire route out from Waterloo as far as Hampton Court Junction on the main line was equipped with colour-light signalling equipment, supplied by Westinghouse. From Waterloo B box as far as Loco Junction the signals were three-aspect, but west of here, where the freight trains out of Nine Elms yard commenced, they were four-aspect. The new signalling was designed to give a two minute headway on the main through lines out of Waterloo, increased slightly to two and a half on the local and Windsor lines. Ten signal boxes were abolished, including five between Waterloo and Loco. Junction, and eight others retained with lever-frames adapted to control the new signals. The overhead West London Junction and Clapham Junction A boxes were given new electrically-interlocked frames, but pneumatic operation of points was retained. Where necessary, the new signals incorporated route indicators consisting of a diagonal row of three white lights above the main signal, illuminated when the diverging route was set. A novel feature was the mounting of smaller repeat aspects, dubbed 'pig's ears' due to the shape of their shades, lower down the post of some signals to aid sighting when a train was drawn-up tightly at the signal.

The main permanent way alterations between Vauxhall and Waterloo were carried out at weekends with minimum disruption to the timetable, but to enable the new station throat layout to be installed platforms 1-3 at Waterloo were entirely closed from 8th May 1936, followed by platforms 4-6 after 6.00pm on 15th May. As with the Cannon Street re-arrangements ten years before, the new layout was first assembled and tested on spare ground, this time at Mitcham, before disassembly and transport in numbered sections for installation at Waterloo. During this period, many suburban services were terminated at Wimbledon or Clapham Junction. Finally, from 1.00am until 7.00am on Sunday 17th May the entire main line from Surbiton to Waterloo was closed to enable the rearranged lines, flyover and most of the new signalling to be brought into service. At this time the new signalling extended out from Waterloo B box as far as Clapham Junction on the Windsor line and Malden on the main line. The changeover in the Waterloo station area was wisely deferred until the summer train service had ended, although this did require extensive alteration of the existing mechanical installation to control the new layout.

Commissioning of the new signalling from Malden through Surbiton to Hampton Court Junction was deferred for a short time as Surbiton station was being totally reconstructed with a new layout, described fully later in this chapter. It finally came into use on 28th June 1936, controlled from new signal boxes at Hampton Court Junction with 45 levers and Surbiton with 52 levers. The box at Surbiton, situated on the Down side west of the station, was notable as being the first in the distinctive SR 'glasshouse' style, with a long lower storey and a shorter, mainly glazed, upper storey curved in the corners for better all-round vision and with a flat roof. Generally built using facing bricks and with the station name in large letters in relief on a concrete panel, the design was widely used for the main line electrifications of 1937-39 and also for new signal boxes in the immediate post-war period.

The final part of the scheme involved the resignalling of the Waterloo station area itself, the changeover from semaphores to colour lights taking place at about 1.00am on Sunday 18th October. Moody mentions that the change took place smoothly and without ceremony, the 00.35am to Hampton Court being signalled-out by semaphore and the 1.30am to Salisbury by colour-lights.[6] The new Waterloo A signalbox was a rectangular concrete-faced structure situated at the entrance to the south sidings and floodlit at night. It contained 309 levers divided between three miniature lever frames.

The increased number of train paths resulting from the Waterloo alterations enabled a revised weekday service to operate from the start of the 1936 summer timetable on 5th July. The 20-minute interval Waterloo – Epsom – Effingham Junction/Dorking services were altered to run fast to Wimbledon, then Motspur Park and all stations. The inner stations were served by a new all-stations service between Waterloo and Motspur Park, again running every twenty minutes, which reversed using a spur forming the first few chains of the new Chessington and Leatherhead loop then under construction. This service was later extended over the new line when completed to Tolworth and Chessington in 1938/39.

---

6 Moody G.T.: *Southern Electric 1909-79*, p56

THE CHESSINGTON BRANCH

The branch from Motspur Park (on the Raynes Park to Epsom route) to Chessington South was the second new line built by the SR in its suburban area expressly for electric traction. It had a number of features in common with the earlier Wimbledon–Sutton line including steep gradients, use of reinforced concrete for bridge and embankment construction, and stations of unusual design.

Encouraged by convenient transport in the form of trams and the newly electrified suburban services of the SR, new housing had spread the development of continuously built-up London to a distance of about one and a half miles south of the South Western main line out to Surbiton by the late 1920s. The area south remained only slightly touched by developers until 1927, however, when the Kingston by-pass arterial road (now part of the A3) was completed. Alan A. Jackson notes how this 'bright raw concrete strip' almost immediately attracted new small housing, light industry and bus services to the area at its northern end, causing the rapid expansion of the small villages of Hook, Chessington and Old Malden and the surrounding district into further mazes of suburban streets uniformly lined with housing, mainly semi-detached.[7]

These developments were noted by SR management, and in 1929 Walker reported to the Board on the desirability of building a new railway through this expanding area. Resulting from this, a bill was prepared for the 1930 session, proposing a new loop line running from Motspur Park (on the Raynes Park–Epsom route) to Leatherhead, with stations at Malden Manor, Tolworth, Chessington (two), Malden Rushett and Leatherhead North. Apart from exploiting the new area, this new loop would result in the virtual four-tracking of the Motspur Park–Leatherhead line, relieving congestion on this increasingly busy section. The bill aimed to make use of government financial assistance under the terms of the 1929 Development (Loan Guarantee and Grants) Act, which assisted transport companies with schemes likely to help in the relief of unemployment. As the Chessington loop fitted the terms of this Act the bill was given an accelerated passage through Parliament, receiving the Royal Assent on 1st August 1930.

It was a long time before work on the new line could commence, however, due to difficulties in land acquisition. Land in the area was valuable for its building possibilities, ironically made more so by the promise of a new electric railway, and it was hard to coax the many owners into selling at a price the SR considered reasonable. In April 1934, although not all the necessary land had yet been purchased, it was decided to make a start on that already bought. The pattern of housing development suggested to Walker that it would be sensible to start the new loop from the London end, and so the first section would comprise a four-and-one-half mile branch from Motspur Park with four stations and two goods yards, at an estimated cost of £560,700, excluding land

but including the five eight-car trains needed to operate the service. The originally proposed, but rejected, station names for the two southernmost stations on the branch where Chessington Court and Chessington Grange, and these appeared on publicity maps at the time. Walker lobbied unsuccessfully to have 'Chessington' omitted from one of these in order to avoid passenger confusion, and the final station names agreed with the local authorities concerned were Malden Manor, Tolworth, Chessington North and Chessington South. The two goods yards were to be located at Tolworth and Chessington South. Although the original financial aid scheme had lapsed, financing of the new line was helped by making use of yet another Government measure to reduce unemployment. Thus a low-interest loan was granted under the terms of the Railways (Agreement) Act 1935, a scheme which was also used to finance the SR's main line electrification program up to 1939, as recounted in Volume 2. Rolling stock funded from the Chessington budget included twenty 2 NOL units (1863-1882), which actually went to the Waterloo–Windsor service as mentioned earlier. Waterloo–Tolworth/Chessington services were from the outset worked by standard three-coach units, in pairs with trailer sets in the peaks, from the Western section suburban pool.

Contracts were let in May 1935 to Sir Robert McAlpine and Sons and Edmund Nuttall and Sons. Work commenced early in 1936, the contractors working under the supervision of SR Chief Engineer George Ellson. Due to the sticky local clay, construction proved difficult, many earthworks needing concrete reinforcements. Apart from shallow cuttings at the junction, between Malden Manor and Tolworth and at the Chessington terminus, the entire line was on embankment. These used material excavated from the cuttings and transported by narrow-gauge contractor's railway, mixed with dry filling from slum-clearance and other demolition work in London. There were eleven bridges on the line of which only two (near Tolworth and over the south end of the terminus) were overbridges; all were constructed of steel encased in concrete in a misguided attempt to save maintenance, and were supported on concrete piers or abutments. As on the Wimbledon – Sutton line, gradients were specifically designed for electric traction, and the route had an almost 'roller-coaster' profile. Near Malden Manor the line dipped to cross the Hogsmill River on a 140ft bridge, and there were peaks at Tolworth and Chessington North. An interesting constructional feature concerned the formation through the platforms at Chessington South and into the yard beyond, where the track was laid over a 6in deep concrete base with 8 inches of ballast above in an effort to secure long-term stability.

Land had been purchased for much of the remainder of the loop to Leatherhead, with its proposed stations at Malden Rushett and Leatherhead North, by September 1939, but no work other than fencing the alignment was carried out on this section. After World War Two, green belt legislation prevented the housing developments which would have made it worthwhile, and the 1930 powers to build it were finally allowed to lapse in 1961.

---

7 *London's Local Railways*, Second Edition, pp152

The short reinforced concrete span carrying the Chessington branch across the Hogsmill River near Malden Manor. Although the bright off-white finish was attractive and modern when new, pollution and weathering quickly turned the concrete a depressing shade of grey, while the steel girders hidden inside could happily corrode unseen. *SR Official*

The only concrete arched over-line bridge on the Chessington branch, situated between Malden Manor and Tolworth. Although built wide enough for a major thoroughfare, it has only ever carried a quiet access road and the northern carriageway remained grassed-over in 2009. *SR Official*

Malden Manor from street level in about 1939. Its affinity to be the 1929 Wimbledon Chase is clear, and it is certainly the closest attempt by the SR architect J Robb-Scott to emulate Holden's integrated designs for London Transport. The luggage lift tower and steel-framed windows are other points of interest. *Alan A. Jackson Collection*

The ferro-concrete underbridge carrying the Chessington branch over the unimaginatively-named Bridge Road adjacent to Chessington North station, photographed just prior to the opening of the line in May 1939. Also visible in this view are a new bungalow in the *moderne* style and typical SR prefabricated concrete fencing. *SR Official*

A platform view of Chessington North, taken in May 1939 just prior to opening. Details of the reinforced concrete Chisarc canopies may be clearly seen, including the glazed holes to let in daylight and the cold cathode-ray fluorescent lighting tubes. *SR Official*

Overleaf The long underbridge taking the Chessington branch over the new Epsom–Kingston dual-carriageway trunk road (now A240) at Tolworth, whose Up station starting signal can just be seen on the far left. Traffic levels on this road have, of course, risen exponentially since this peaceful view was recorded in 1938. *SR Official*

Although island platforms were originally envisaged for stations on the line, these were changed to 540ft side platforms following an inspection by Walker and his aides. Much of their construction was subcontracted to the building firm of G.T. Crouch, who was among the many erecting new houses in the area. In architectural terms, the four stations on the branch were among the most distinctive examples of J. Robb-Scott's designs in the *Moderne* (or *Odeon cinema*) style of the time. The booking halls were all situated at road level and were fronted by a forecourt with small car park. Similar in layout to the 1929 Wimbledon Chase, each had a single storey curved frontage containing ticket office, toilets and bookstall, with shop units at either end. Those at Malden Manor and Tolworth were constructed of stock bricks faced with concrete, whereas the two Chessington stations had facing bricks. A short subway led to stairs up to each platform at all but the terminus, where the platforms were located in a shallow cutting. Towers for luggage lifts to the platforms were erected, but the lifts themselves were never installed in them. The most unusual feature of the stations were the 200ft canti-levered canopies constructed entirely from pre-cast concrete components: built to the 'Chisarc' design, they arched grace-fully over each platform without any obstructing support columns. Those at the two Chessington stations, built slightly later, had less massive supporting ribs. Lighting was by GEC cold-cathode fluorescent tubes in various colours, and glass lenses were let into the canopies to provide some daylight under them. The platform buildings and draught-screens had Crittall steel-framed windows. Although attractive when new, as elsewhere on the Southern Electric system the almost-white concrete surfaces weathered all too quickly to a depressing mid-grey and the steel window frames were allowed to rust.

Other fitments on the branch were less inspiring, many being re-used from elsewhere on the network. Motspur Park signal box was equipped to operate the branch junction, and there were further boxes situated on the Down platforms at Tolworth and Chessington South. These were given frames and instrumentation recovered from elsewhere and, as on the Wimbledon–Sutton loop, the signals were mechanically-operated upper-quadrant semaphores mounted on posts fabricated from old rails. A single substation, located at Tolworth, was adequate to power the entire branch, and was initially equipped with rotary converter equipment recovered from Leatherhead (which had been given a new rectifier substation as part of the Mid-Sussex main line scheme). Fencing mainly consisted of diamond-patterned steel mesh supported on concrete posts, a new design at the time. The goods yard at Tolworth was on the Down side and initially had four sidings, but an additional three were added in 1940 after which it could accommodate 218 wagons. That at Chessington South was beyond the platforms alongside the alignment of the proposed route to Leatherhead, and had three sidings.

The first section of the Chessington branch, the two and a quarter mile stretch from the junction at Motspur Park to Tolworth, commenced operation on 29th May 1938, with a twenty-minute interval service to Waterloo, seven days a week. This service, which called at all stations, was actually an extension of the Motspur Park–Waterloo service which had run on weekdays from 5th July 1936 following the Waterloo resignalling. Terminating trains reversed in the Down platform at Tolworth, and regained the Up line in the London direction over a crossover at the north end of the bridge where the new line was carried over the Epsom–Kingston Road. While the advanced age of much of the rolling stock used did not match the futuristic stations, the line nevertheless built up a healthy trade, although much of this traffic was extracted from existing nearby stations at Worcester Park and Stoneleigh. In recognition of its new junction status, Motspur Park was improved with a longer canopy, new waiting room and extended footbridge in June 1938.

A year to the day after the first section opened, through services to Chessington North and South commenced on 28th May 1939, the fourteen mile trip from the terminus to Waterloo calling at all stations taking just over half an hour. All three trains per hour were extended, carrying headcode L. At the opening ceremony the Deputy Mayor of Surbiton was photographed exchanging greetings with a baby elephant from the nearby Chessington Zoo, expected to be an impor-tant source of off-peak traffic for the line. At Chessington South only the Down platform, where trains terminated, was completed. Just the basic platform surface and 'Chisarc' canopy were finished on the Up side, and the track was used for carriage stabling outside the rush hours. There was no passenger access to this platform, the intended footbridge never being started. Beyond the station electrified double track was continued through the goods yard and on for a further twenty chains, later extended by another seventeen chains of non-electrified line on the embankment formed of spoil dumped by the contractors. In order to prevent zoo-bound trippers alighting at the wrong station, Chessington North platforms soon carried the prominent signs NEXT STATION FOR THE ZOO. In fact the zoo was a three-quarter mile trudge along the Leatherhead road from the terminus, but even though the rails almost reached it there were never any plans to provide a closer station.

Above right The new station at Tolworth on the Chessington branch, shortly after opening on 28th June 1938 and then acting as temporary terminus prior to completion southwards. Ex-LSWR 'nutcracker' unit 1226 stands in the Down platform under the shadow of the concrete 'Chisarc' canopy, awaiting return to Waterloo. *Stations UK*

Right An elevated view of Chessington South, where only the Down platform was completed and brought into use in 1939 pending completion of the line to Leatherhead, which was subsequently cancelled. The position of the intended footbridge is clearly visible on the wall of the station building immediately to the right of the Chisarc canopy, less substantial than those provided at Tolworth (see previous photograph). The Up line was used for berthing during the day; in this photograph dated 3rd August 1964 it is occupied by post-war all-steel 4 SUB 4688, which has recently gained a small yellow warning panel. *John H. Meredith*

NEW AND REBUILT STATIONS

This section firstly covers, in chronological order, new stations built by the SR on its electrified suburban lines in the period 1928-39 but not provided specifically as part of a particular electrification scheme and, secondly, major and minor station rebuildings not mentioned elsewhere.

Whether the station concerned was new or rebuilt, the components which made it up were highly standardised. Prefabricated platform, footbridge and fencing parts in steel-reinforced concrete came from the SR's own Exmouth Junction concrete works. Canopies were generally steel-framed, glazed, and had riveted-steel or vertically-slatted wooden valances, the latter becoming standard by about 1930. Platform buildings were either brick-built or wooden depending on location, while frontages depended very much on the area served and expected traffic levels. Finish was bare concrete or brick and shades of green and cream in a recognisable house style. Most platform fitments were the responsibility of the engineer's department and, while service-able enough, lacked the originality of Holden's integrated designs for London Underground stations of the period. By the mid 1930s, platforms were being signed with large green enamel running-in boards and small 'bullseye' nameboards typically mounted on lamp posts or suspended from canopies. The average new cost for a small suburban station with island platform in 1930 was about £7,000-£8,000, the side-platform arrangement generally (but not always) being slightly more expensive. It was policy to include retail lettings in all new and rebuilt stations to maximise revenue.

All the new stations came into being to serve already-existing or prospective new housing developments in the areas served, and in most cases at least part of the cost was met by the landowner or estate developer. Those provided in the suburban area between 1928 and 1939, in chronological order of opening, were as follows:

Petts Wood was situated on the South Eastern main line between the Chislehurst junctions and Orpington, and origi-nally consisted of a single 520ft x 30ft island platform located between the local lines, together with a small goods yard. Opened on 9th July 1928, it was served by Orpington trains on both the Victoria (via Bickley) and Charing Cross/Cannon Street (via Chislehurst) routes. Access was via an uncovered public footbridge in steel across the line at the London end, and a substantial wooden booking office and waiting room building was located on the Down side end of this bridge. Speculative building in the area had already begun and the station soon became the hub of a populous suburb. Rush hour traffic quickly built up to an extent that a second island plat-form, between the fast lines, was added in 1931. The railway bisected the new suburb of Petts Wood with only foot access between the two sides in the vicinity of the station.

Hinchley Wood, between Surbiton and Claygate, opened on 20th October 1930 to serve an area already developed. The 520ft island platform was in the form of a vee located where the Up and Down lines parted prior to the former burrowing under the South Western main line to reach Hampton Court Junction. Platform buildings were similar to those at Motspur Park as was the access footbridge, a steel-framed open struc-ture fabricated at Wimbledon signal works. Of the £7,650 cost, £2,500 plus land either side of the line was donated by local landowner Percy Fisher.

Syon Lane was situated on the Hounslow loop line between Brentford and Isleworth, and opened on 5th July 1931. Located near the Syon Park estate, it served a new area of cheap housing and light industry which had arisen to the south-west of Brentford on either side of the new Great West Road (now A4). It was economically-built with short 400ft side platforms, sufficient as six coaches was the maximum train length on the Hounslow loop, accessed down uncovered stairs from an existing road bridge.

Hinchley Wood station, opened on 20th October 1930, was unusually built on a triangular site where the Up and Down tracks of the Cobham line diverged to meet the South Western main line at Hampton Court Junction. This view shows the Up platform in about 1960, although little has changed other than the substitution of BR Southern Region 'hot-dog' nameboards for the earlier 'bullseye' station signs.

Stoneleigh, between Worcester Park and Ewell West, was opened in the midst of fields and copses on 17th July 1932, and was originally an almost exact copy of Motspur Park except that the open footbridge was of concrete. Of the total cost of £7,550, £3,000 was paid by landowners, who also laid access roads either side from Kingston and London Roads respectively. An early intention to name the station 'Stoneleigh Park' after the estate to be built was changed to avoid four consecutive stations on the Raynes Park to Epsom line being suffixed 'Park'. Within five years the whole area within a one mile radius of the station was covered in bricks and mortar, mostly semi-detached chalet-style properties, lining an unusually random layout of streets, crescents and *cul-de-sacs*. As at Petts Wood and elsewhere, the occupiers of these houses were virtually all London commuters and the inevitable result was severe peak-hour overcrowding, leading to vociferous complaints as early as 1934. Minor improvements were made in 1936, but more extensive alterations took place in 1939/40 when the original open footbridge across the centre of the station was replaced by a cavernous covered structure, also executed in concrete. Lacking both glazing and any architectural pretension whatsoever, it incorporated a waiting area and ticket office and was relocated at the southern end of the island platform. The lack of a road crossing the line in the vicinity of the station together with a particularly illogical road pattern mitigated against the introduction of bus services in the area, and Stoneleigh station therefore became the main public transport link in its community in a way not matched by other similar stations.

Woodmansterne was also opened on 17th July 1932. Located on the Tattenham Corner branch between Smitham and Chipstead, it was of the simplest-possible pattern with an island platform accessed from local side-roads by an open footbridge, all executed in prefabricated concrete components. It served a new area of semi-detached and terraced housing in the cheaper price bracket spreading south eastwards from Coulsdon, and the developers provided the land free of charge as well as contributing £1,500 of the £7,500 cost. As Tattenham Corner branch trains were never more than six coaches, the platform was only 400ft long.

Berrylands, opened on 16th October 1933, was situated on a high embankment on the South Western main line between Malden and Surbiton, had wooden platforms on the local lines only, and was served by Waterloo to Hampton Court trains. No fewer than seven building firms donated funds towards its construction, as much as 90% of the £6,257 cost being met in this way. Located in an area in which housing for London office workers was already being erected, the ticket office was situated at ground-level on the Down side and access to the platforms was up long covered stairways from a tunnel through the embankment. If the wind was in a certain direction, waiting passengers could savour the odours emanating from the adjacent sewage works!

Albany Park, built to serve new estates between Sidcup and Bexley on the Dartford loop line, opened on 7th July 1935. Situated in cutting, the stubby brick ticket office was at ground-level and connected to the 520ft side platforms by a covered and glazed steel footbridge.

Falconwood, opened on 1st January 1936, was located in a cutting between Eltham Park and Welling on the Bexleyheath line. Generally similar to Albany Park, it had a simple brick frontage to the booking office with a raised centre section and stubby concrete canopy, leading to a covered steel-plate footbridge with stairs leading down to the two side platforms. Rather more generous canopies and waiting rooms than usual were provided in recognition of the expected traffic levels. Constructed to serve two large new estates going up on either side of the railway at this point, £5,000 of the £12,500 cost was put-up by the estate developers, New Ideal Homesteads.

Next, major station rebuildings not already dealt-with are covered. These took place to modernise antiquated or inadequate facilities, to cope with increasing traffic levels, or where the railway through the station was being widened or otherwise altered, rendering existing accommodation unsuitable. The four most important station rebuildings in the 1929-39 period all took place on the Western section: at Wimbledon, Kingston upon Thames, Richmond and Surbiton.

Wimbledon station, on the main line out of Waterloo, had by the 1920s evolved into three separate parts, each with its own entrance. The main lines were served by side platforms for the local tracks and a central island for the through tracks. To the north were the three terminal bays used by District Railway and SR trains to East Putney and beyond, while to the south were two side platforms serving the former LBSCR lines to Tooting and West Croydon. Total reconstruction took place in 1927-29. The main lines were served by new Up and Down 800ft islands, repositioned to be entirely on the London side of the Wimbledon Hill Road overbridge, while the West Croydon and Tooting lines, soon to be joined by the route to Sutton via St Helier, were given a shorter 520ft island. Two further terminal islands on the north side provided four bays for use by terminating District trains and the residual rush-hour Waterloo via East Putney SR service. All were given new steel-framed and valanced canopies (similar to those provided at Epsom and elsewhere) and the through platforms had brick toilets, waiting rooms and staff accommodation erected on them. Wide covered stairways led from the west end of all platforms to a footbridge leading to the new main station building at one end. The imposing ticket hall, with concrete-faced *Moderne* frontage, faced a small car park and taxi turning area leading into the main road at the bottom of Wimbledon Hill.

Kingston station dated from the construction of the branch from Twickenham in 1863, and had consisted of three low-level terminus bays with an overall roof facing Hampton Wick, and two through high level side platforms added when the line was extended through to Malden Junction to form the Kingston loop in 1869. The terminus platforms had been little-used since electrification, and here as elsewhere the Victorian facilities were inadequate to cope with traffic rises. Apart from a huge increase in season-ticket sales, Kingston had become popular as a retail centre, centred on the Bentalls department store, bringing in shoppers throughout the day from a wide catchment area of south west London and Surrey. The SR decided in 1929 that the time had come to recon-

struct the station, and financial assistance was provided by the local authority. The national economic crisis delayed the start of work, however, and rebuilding did not finally commence until October 1934 when a £40,500 scheme was approved by the Board, with completion by the end of the following year. The low-level platforms were demolished and replaced by a single bay, 522ft long, on the Richmond-bound platform. (A bus station was built on the low-level site after the War.) On the through platforms, completely new buildings in *Moderne* style, with curved glazed end-elevations and faced with glazed tiles, were provided, including a buffet. Notable was the ladies' room on the Up platform, with its *art-deco* stained glass windows. The platforms were linked by a wide subway to an imposing brick booking-office and shop block on a prominent site at the corner of Richmond Road and Wood Street, while a smaller passimeter booking office was added for the benefit of commuters at street level, giving directly onto the Up platform from Richmond Road.

The existing station at *Richmond*, serving an important Thameside town, was opened as an intermediate station when the branch from what is now Clapham Junction to Richmond was extended to Windsor in 1848-49, replacing the original Richmond terminus. The two side platforms were crossed about half-way along by Kew Road, and to the east of this bridge and on the north side of the line a new terminus for the line from Kensington Addison Road was provided in 1869. At the insistence of the LSWR this terminus had no running connection to the Windsor lines and was given entirely separate offices, and by 1930 it was served entirely by intensive Underground District Line and LMS electric services. The duplication of facilities and the usual problem of inadequate accommodation led to proposals for rebuilding, which commenced in November 1935. The Windsor lines side platforms were moved to be completely east of the Kew Road and extended to 600ft. A lofty new station building was provided, with a ticket hall serving both lines (until recently there were separate ticket windows for SR and Underground/North London line services); stairs led down to a concourse behind the terminal bays, and a covered footbridge led to the Windsor lines platforms. New platform-level buildings were provided in a similar style to those at Kingston, and a car park was built on the north side. Although not fully completed until early in 1938, the new station opened on 1st August 1937, and the late G.T. Moody records that 80,000 tickets were collected there on the following day, a bank holiday.[8] Provision was made in the reconstruction for future four-tracking through the Windsor lines platforms, in which case the Down platform would have become an island and the track of the southernmost terminal bay would have been extended westwards.

Surbiton, also on the former South Western main line out of Waterloo, consisted of side platforms serving the local lines and a centre island serving the through lines. This layout, together with the outdated passenger accommodation,

---

8 *Southern Electric 1909-1979*, pp68

The imposing and confident frontage of the reconstructed Richmond station, photographed in 1939. Very much in the *moderne* style, the affinity of its design to contemporary cinema architecture is obvious. *SR Official*

urgently required enlargement by the mid 1930s, sales of season tickets from the station having risen by 100% and those of ordinary tickets by 50% since electrification of the suburban services serving it. The station and the lines through it were therefore entirely reconstructed during 1936-37. The curve through the station was realigned to allow higher speeds on the through lines, and an extra track installed to give a total of five roads though the platforms. Two new 800ft island platforms were provided, the Up platform serving the Up local and Up through lines, and the Down serving the Down local line and a new Down local loop. Thus the Down through line had no platform, but crossovers were provided at either end to allow trains on the through lines to loop into the local platforms. New station entrances and booking-halls were provided at road level on either side, in the concrete-faced *Moderne* style, the larger being on the Up side and incorporating a clock tower. Access to the platforms was by stairs to a covered concrete footbridge which also included luggage lifts. Platform buildings, including waiting rooms, staff offices and toilets, were also concrete-faced brick, and the canopies were of the standard SR steel-framed type with slatted wood valances. The goods yard, on the down side with access from the country end, was enlarged, and new colour-light signalling and signalbox installed as part of the Waterloo area resignalling.

A very large number of other station rebuilding or improvement schemes were carried out during this period, either at individual locations or on entire lines. In all cases the aim was to provide adequate facilities in the wake of vastly increased passenger levels which were the result of electrifi-

cation and speculative house building in the areas concerned. Ever with an eye for economy, such works were generally only authorised by the SR when it became apparent that original Victorian or Edwardian facilities were seriously inadequate. Often, new sections were tacked-on to an original building with little consideration for architectural homogeny, a particularly blatant example being Erith on the North Kent line. No attempt has been made to mention all examples dealt-with in this way, as virtually every station served by the Southern Electric was improved to some degree after the introduction of electric services, even if it was just with better fencing or new station nameplates/running-in boards.

Other stations modernised on the Western section were Raynes Park, Malden, Worcester Park and Strawberry Hill, all of which received new canopies, platform buildings and booking offices. Reconstruction at Twickenham was commenced in 1938, but was incomplete by the time war broke out, when work stopped. The planned new station, east of the then-existing establishment, was to have four through lines served by two island platforms, and a single London-facing bay on the Up side for Rugby traffic. (It was eventually completed, in a slightly altered form, in 1954.)

On the Central section, West Croydon was reconstructed in 1932-33 when the overall roof and street frontage at the south end of the Up-side bay platform, last vestiges of the original 1839 London and Croydon Railway terminus, were demolished. A covered footbridge of glass and steel construction was built to connect the platforms to a booking hall and frontage incorporated in a new row of shops in North End. Like Kingston, Croydon was an important retail centre and

Erith, showing the unsightly extension to the main SER station building added in the 1930s with no consideration of architectural homogeny.

attracted off-peak shopping traffic from a wide area. Banstead, on the Epsom Downs branch and serving the new estates at Nork, was given a new brick booking hall with tiled roof in domestic style together with steel and glass extensions to the platform awnings. The wooden halt at Reedham, which had become totally inadequate to serve the new housing springing-up around the Brighton Road on the Purley/Coulsdon border, was entirely replaced in 1936 at a cost of £8,800, with work completed in July. Extensive use was made of prefabricated reinforced concrete components, including footbridge, fencing and entire 400ft platforms, but the small booking office on the Down side and waiting shelter opposite were of wood. Waddon, the first station south of West Croydon on the Sutton line, was entirely rebuilt in 1936-37 with a new brick booking office, covered footbridge and standard platform canopies. The new running-in boards indicated FOR CROYDON AIRPORT, although the latter was almost a mile away.

As mentioned elsewhere, former SECR lines in particular had suffered from cheaply built and substandard accommodation. Thus in February 1930, for example, it was necessary to allocate £21,000 to reconstruction of the buildings on Bexleyheath line stations at Eltham Well Hall, Welling, Bexleyheath and Barnehurst to cater for the vastly increased traffic resulting from the extensive new estates then being erected in its catchment area. The new main buildings were single-storey brick with tiled pitched roofs, fitting-in well with the housing they served, and another improvement was the installation of electric lighting. Most were finished in 1931 but at Barnehurst, where the pace of building was slower, work was not completed until 1935. The terminus of the Hayes branch was rebuilt at a cost of £14,000 during 1934-35 for the same reason; a new 520ft island platform and 200ft canopy were fronted by a booking hall and shop units (badly mutilated in World War Two).

MISCELLANEOUS DEVELOPMENTS 1926-39

This section covers a small number of miscellaneous developments and happenings which took place after the lines concerned had been electrified or otherwise do not conveniently fit into other sections of this chapter.

The 1926 General Strike. Already mentioned in connection with the electrification of the Eastern section suburban lines, what became known as the General Strike was called by the Trades Union Congress as from 4th May 1926 in support of a wages and hours dispute in the coal mining industry. Although its effects were considerable, the strike was hardly 'general' on the Southern Railway as 12,000 staff either did not strike or were allowed to resume work. On the first day electric services operated on the Waterloo–Hampton Court and Victoria–Coulsdon North routes and were gradually added to as the strike went on, so that by the time it was called off on 14th May most electrified lines were served. The normal timetable was resumed on 17th May with some exceptions. On the Western section, rush hour services between Waterloo and Shepperton via Richmond and between Waterloo and Wimbledon via East Putney did not run. On the Central section East Brixton, Clapham and Wandsworth Road stations remained closed, the South London line service which called at them was suspended, and there were no Sunday trains between London Bridge and Crystal Palace via Tulse Hill. On the Eastern section, trains between Holborn Viaduct/St Pauls and Shortlands/Crystal Palace High Level were withdrawn completely. Services were once more reduced substantially from 20th May in order to economise on coal as the miners continued to strike. Normal working resumed on 20th September, after which time rush-hour trains between London Bridge and Victoria were reduced to four coaches only in recognition of declining patronage, not helped by the enforced closure through the summer.

The London Passenger Transport Board. As had been expected for some years previously, the passenger transport undertakings (excluding the Southern Railway and the other three main line railway companies) providing services in the London area were amalgamated as the London Passenger Transport Board from 1st July 1933. These included the Metropolitan Railway, the Underground Group of companies (including the District and tube lines) and various tram and bus undertakings. Four members of the Board of the LPTB together with the General Managers of the four main line railways formed a Standing Joint Committee to coordinate suburban services in the Board's area. Once operating expenses had been taken into account, the receipts from that area were to be pooled and divided pro rata between the Board and the main line companies. As recounted elsewhere, one of the justifications for the building of the Wimbledon–Sutton line was that it would increase the SR share of this pool. In 1933 this was set at 25½%, easily the largest received by any main line company. It was increased slightly when the Nunhead–Lewisham and Woodside–Sanderstead lines were electrified in 1935.

Track Alterations and Resignalling Schemes. The centre track from Old Kent Road Junction to Peckham Rye Junction, unnecessary and seldom used after the introduction of dc services on the South London line, was officially taken out of use from 18th July 1933. It was later removed, together with the short and narrow wooden platforms serving it at Queens Road and Peckham Rye, leaving a wide space between the Up and Down lines. Resignalling between St Margarets and Twickenham was commenced in 1938 but had not been completed by September 1939, when installation stopped. Work might have continued into 1940, as indeed it did on some other projects (see Volume 2), but the lever frame constructed for the new 'glasshouse' signal box was sent to the LMS at Derby to replace one lost in a fire.

Two more resignalling schemes were completed during this period. New three-aspect colour-light signalling was brought into use between Streatham Common and Thornton Heath on Sunday 16th February 1936, resulting in the closure of two signal boxes. Further up the Central section main line, resignalling was put in hand between Victoria and Battersea Park, and also in the Victoria (Eastern) station area, in 1937. Although already planned, this scheme was carried forward with some urgency following the Investigating Officer's report into the serious collision at Battersea Park in April 1937, referred-to below. Existing signalling on the Central side was mainly mechanical using Sykes' Lock and Block system, dating from 1908, but electrically-worked semaphores had been installed by the SECR on the Eastern side in 1919. The general arrangements of this scheme were similar to those in the Waterloo area (see above), but all new colour-light signals were three-aspect except the intermediate platform signals under the roof over the double-length platforms 9-17 at Victoria, where two-aspect (red/yellow) sufficed. The new signalling came into use on 16th October 1938 from a point south of the terminus through Battersea Park to Pouparts Junction, with the abolition of Grosvenor Road A box. A new power-operated lever frame was installed in the existing overhead cabin at Battersea Park. On 3rd-4th June the Victoria (Central) station area was changed over, controlled from a new signal cabin, flat-roofed and brick faced, situated on the Up side adjacent to the end of platform 17 in the shadow of the new Imperial Airways building. This contained 220 levers, separated into three frames, and its commissioning resulted in the abolition of three old boxes. The final changeover on the Eastern section side took place on 24th-25th June, although the conversion had gradually been taking place for some months. Here the existing A signal box and electric point motors were adapted to work with the new signalling, and three more existing boxes were superseded.

UNFULFILLED SCHEMES

Three schemes affecting the suburban area were proposed but never carried through, the first two of which were put forward early in the history of the Southern Electric.

In 1925, while the Eastern section suburban lines were being electrified, there was a proposal to run Mid-Kent line electric trains from Addiscombe over the East London Railway from New Cross to Whitechapel or Shoreditch. The freehold of this short line, which made use of Marc Brunel's 1843 Thames Tunnel between Wapping and Rotherhithe, was acquired that year by the Southern Railway. Electrified on the fourth-rail dc system in 1913, the service was operated by the Metropolitan Railway using saloon stock of the types which also operated on the Hammersmith and City and Circle lines. (Indeed at this time East London trains continued via the St Mary's curve over the north side of the Inner Circle and on to Hammersmith, but whether it was proposed that any Addiscombe trains should work through this far is not known.) Various problems of compatibility soon put an end to the proposal. The Metropolitan stock was insufficiently powered to interwork with SR trains, while the SR slam-door trains did not meet operating requirements on the Metropolitan Railway (although the Met had slam-door stock of its own) and moreover were out-of-gauge for the East London line. A further problem was that, although the Metropolitan originated the idea, it was far more interested in developing its traffic out to 'Metro-land', and disinclined to spend money on this insignificant corner of its empire.

The Southern Heights Light Railway scheme was a proposal for a line to run through, and open up for housing development, the sparsely populated area along the ridge of the North Downs on the Surrey/Kent border south-east of Croydon. Due to the nature of its terrain, which to the south rose above the 800ft contour, no railway had penetrated this area to serve the villages on its slopes by the turn of the century. However following the passage of the Light Railways Act in 1896, which allowed for the construction of more lightly-engineered (and hence cheaper) railways subject to certain stringent operating conditions, there was a proposal for a light railway branch from Orpington to Tatsfield. In spite of interest from the South Eastern Railway this scheme failed, but in the meantime low-density housing development on very cheap land began to spread to the villages of Tatsfield,

ALL through the day the services are good. It takes a woman no longer to run up to town for a couple of hours' shopping than it would for her to travel from a crowded suburb to the great stores. Houses can be obtained quite close to the stations. In fact, the new electric services of the Southern Railway make possible all the joys of the country with all the facilities of town.

A frequent service of new electric trains

Brings the garden counties to your office door!

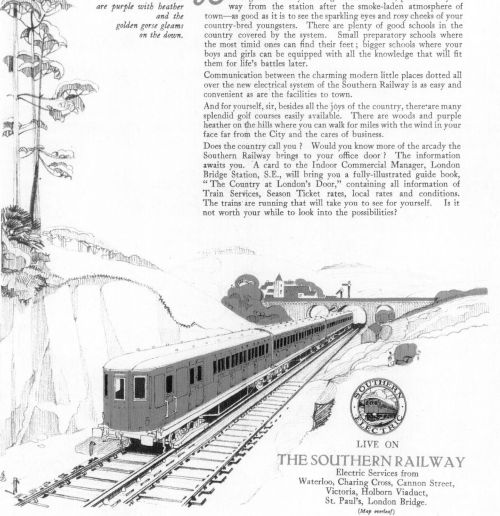

Come and live in the country far from the smoke of the town, where the hills are purple with heather and the golden gorse gleams on the down.

BEFORE you have digested the news in your evening paper, the Southern electric trains take you from the gloom of the City and the cares of business back into the country of your home. It is good to fill your lungs with the clean, pure air on your way from the station after the smoke-laden atmosphere of town—as good as it is to see the sparkling eyes and rosy cheeks of your country-bred youngsters. There are plenty of good schools in the country covered by the system. Small preparatory schools where the most timid ones can find their feet; bigger schools where your boys and girls can be equipped with all the knowledge that will fit them for life's battles later.

Communication between the charming modern little places dotted all over the new electrical system of the Southern Railway is as easy and convenient as are the facilities to town.

And for yourself, sir, besides all the joys of the country, there are many splendid golf courses easily available. There are woods and purple heather on the hills where you can walk for miles with the wind in your face far from the City and the cares of business.

Does the country call you? Would you know more of the arcady the Southern Railway brings to your office door? The information awaits you. A card to the Indoor Commercial Manager, London Bridge Station, S.E., will bring you a fully-illustrated guide book, "The Country at London's Door," containing all information of Train Services, Season Ticket rates, local rates and conditions. The trains are running that will take you to see for yourself. Is it not worth your while to look into the possibilities?

LIVE ON
THE SOUTHERN RAILWAY
Electric Services from
Waterloo, Charing Cross, Cannon Street,
Victoria, Holborn Viaduct,
St. Paul's, London Bridge.

(Map overleaf)

A page from the Southern Railway's promotional booklet of 1926-27 extolling the nearness of the countryside to the new electric services. The artwork was apparently inspired by Cannon Hill Common, which was within walking distance of Motspur Park station, built for the Guildford and Dorking electrification in 1925.

Biggin Hill and Downe. From 1913 a bus service linked these communities with Bromley, and after World War One development gradually continued.

This housing activity, together with the SR suburban electrification to nearby Orpington, attracted the attention of Lieutenant Colonel Holman Fred Stephens, the well-known promoter and constructor of light railways in Britain. Stephens basically resurrected the earlier scheme, although on a slightly different alignment, but proposed extending it beyond Tatsfield to Sanderstead to form a 15.75 mile loop connecting with the Southern Railway at either end. Romantically titled the 'Southern Heights Light Railway', application for a Light Railway Order was made in November 1925. From the start, SR interest in the scheme was strong, and Walker recommended to the Board early in 1926 that the company should become involved financially and work the line electrically. By 1928 plans had further developed, and a new Light Railway Order obtained at the end of that year approved a slightly revised sixteen mile route. Most of the improvements were at the insistence of the SR who, in return for providing much of the financial backing and working the line, imposed its own standards and wanted it constructed to virtually main line specification. This was contrary to the ideas of the promoter, who was renowned for building at minimum cost and operating ramshackle lines with lightly-laid track on the surface of the ground, and with ancient rolling stock.

In the late 1920s, the Southern Heights Light Railway was shown on route maps inside the compartments of electric stock and elsewhere (see pages 8 and 9). At Orpington, the new line would connect with the SR on the Down side and then descend to cross under the main line. Station sites along the route agreed between Walker and Stephens were at Green Street Green for Farnborough, Downe and Keston, Cudham and Biggin Hill, Westerham Hill, Tatsfield, Chelsham for Woldingham, Hamsey Green, and Mitchley Wood. At Sanderstead a flat junction was proposed half a mile south of the Oxted line station. The entire route was to be single, with passing loops at Westerham Hill, Tatsfield and Hamsey Green; these were to have permanent island-platform stations on the pattern of Woodmansterne. Elsewhere, temporary structures would be used which could be replaced without undue expense if traffic levels made doubling necessary.

No progress was made as Stephens was having difficulty raising the remainder of the unsecured capital for the scheme, and he died in 1931 just before an intended trip to the USA to raise the money. Stephens was undoubtedly the main force behind the project, and with his death SR interest quickly evaporated. With the intended pooling of receipts within the London Transport area (mentioned earlier in the chapter) the Southern did not want to be saddled with a new line of doubtful traffic potential and, while it could probably have found the cash to fund it, it is doubtful whether it would have generated enough building development in its vicinity before World War Two to make it profitable. After 1945, of course, green belt legislation effectively precluded any further suburban development on the 'Southern Heights'.

A third proposed scheme, recorded by the late Charles Klapper, was to electrify the West London line from Clapham Junction to Kensington Addison Road on the third-rail system, and run a twenty-minute interval service of SR suburban units between Wimbledon and Willesden Junction via East Putney and Clapham Junction.[9] (The northern section of the West London line was already electrified on the LT/LMS fourth-rail system for use by the infrequent LMS Earl's Court – Willesden Junction service.) Although the idea was considered feasible and plans were drawn up in about 1938 (not particularly seriously, one suspects), the scheme got no further due to objections by the LMS and GWR that a frequent passenger service would hinder freight movement over this important artery. Ironically, LMS freights bound for Norwood Yard had at this time to slot between no fewer than eleven electric trains per hour on the Southern!

ACCIDENTS

Two serious accidents involving electric stock in the suburban area occured in the period 1925-1939.

The first took place at London Bridge on the evening of 9th July 1928, only three weeks after the start of Central section dc services. Already the day had been unfortunate for the operating department, with an earlier power fault and points failure, and traffic was only just recovering from the disruption. The driver of a light engine engaged to do some shunting misunderstood instructions, ignored a ground signal and ran into the side of the leading vehicle of the 7.22pm London Bridge–Epsom Downs just after the latter had passed the north side of the signal box. As it had been behind the box, the passenger train was invisible to the locomotive crew until seconds before the collision. The resulting impact derailed the first two coaches of the passenger train and the locomotive, and the casualties included one dead and ten injured. Of these, six were seriously hurt, one subsequently dying in hospital. The collision caused much damage to permanent way and signalling equipment, and the lines concerned were not restored to normal until late the following morning. At the ensuing Ministry of Transport enquiry, it was alleged that the new colour-light signalling was difficult to understand, but no recommendations were made by the Inspecting Officer. One of the coaches concerned (trailer 9702 in unit 1702) was a write-off and was replaced, while the others were subsequently repaired and returned to service.

The second occurred on 2nd April 1937 at Battersea Park during the morning peak at about 8.02am. The 7.30am from London Bridge via Tulse Hill was waiting in the Up local platform for the 7.37 South London line service from London Bridge to precede it, when it was run into from behind by the 7.31 from Coulsdon North, not booked to stop at Battersea Park, at about 35mph. The collision was severe, with the wooden bodywork of the two colliding motor coaches being ripped from their underframes and smashed to matchwood.

---

9 Klapper, C.F.: *London's Lost Railways*, Routledge and Kegan Paul, ISBN 0 7100 8378 5, 1976. p14

Ten people were killed, including the guard of the 7.30, and 59 others injured. Miraculously, the motorman of the train from Coulsdon North was uninjured despite the carnage, but suffered severely from shock. Although the lines were busy at the time, prompt steps were taken to stop further trains, cut off traction current and summon help. The lines were cleared and reopened for normal traffic at about 4.30pm the same afternoon. At the subsequent enquiry it was found that the signalman on duty was inexperienced and had become confused regarding the train standing in the platform. He had therefore overridden the safety system of the Lock and Block apparatus to allow the Coulsdon North train into the same block section and hence the collision occurred. The main recommendation of the Inquiring Officer was that the area should be resignalled with colour lights as soon as possible to relieve the workload for signal staff on this congested section, and this was put into motion without delay. Only one vehicle, motor third brake 8523 from unit 1615, was entirely written off as a result of the collision, and was replaced by a new vehicle with LSWR bodywork. The body of the other motor coach which took the brunt of the collision, 8371 from 1473, was also destroyed, but in this case it was possible to salvage the original underframe and new body-work, again of LSWR origin, was provided.

SOCIAL AND ECONOMIC EFFECTS OF SUBURBAN ELECTRIFICATION

The LSWR, LBSCR and SECR London-area suburban routes electrified, or proposed for electrification, in the period 1909-25 had run through two types of traffic area. In the inner suburban area, development was mostly continuous. This area ran from the London termini outwards to, roughly, Hounslow, Norbiton on the Kingston loop via Richmond, Wimbledon on the LSWR main line, Streatham Common on the LBSCR main line, the Norwood area, Bromley, Hither Green, Blackheath and Abbey Wood. The outer suburban area comprised a number of towns and villages with open land in-between. In the 1920s the gaps between these towns and villages, as well as odd unfilled gaps in the inner area, began to fill up with new housing estates and, in some places, light industry. As we have seen, the visible changes on the railways were the rebuilding or enlargement of a number of stations, and at some points the construction of additional stations or halts to serve the new developments.

The effect of these housing developments, and the population shift which resulted, was to substantially increase traffic at all times of the day in the outer suburban areas, while reducing it – albeit to a lesser extent – in the inner suburban areas. Prior to Grouping, it is recorded that traffic on the lines electrified by the LBSCR and LSWR increased by 26% between 1913 and 1923. In spite of periodic national financial problems which were in themselves serious, economic conditions in the south east remained relatively favourable in comparison with the rest of Britain. The younger generation of professional and clerical workers in particular, and to a lesser extent industrial workers as well, took advantage of these economic conditions to obtain homes of their own.

Existing houses, mostly built before 1900, were fully occupied by a still-active older generation. The demand was therefore met by speculative building firms which, in favourable economic and financial conditions for the supply of new housing, sprang up to meet it with new out-of-town estates which could be reached not only by rail but also by the new and expanding motor-bus services. By the mid 1920s the development trend was firmly under way and the Southern Railway positively encouraged it with estate-orientated publicity handbooks, advertisements for household removals by railway-owned container, more frequent services and cheap fares. The process was still in full swing in 1939, when the start of World War Two brought it all abruptly to a halt.

Investigation of the electoral registers of London boroughs during this period, undertaken by L.A. Mack, reveals that the new houses tended to be occupied not by people from the nearest old suburb, but from the one beyond it. This was particularly the case in the areas served by the Central and Eastern section lines. Thus, for example, Purley residents tended to come from Thornton Heath and Streatham rather than from Croydon, while many people who moved into Hayes and West Wickham came not from Bromley but from Lewisham or Brockley. Likewise, people brought up in New Cross and Deptford migrated to Eltham and beyond. This 'hopover' movement resulted in a dramatic increase in passenger traffic from outer-suburban stations and a significant increase in revenue as commuters increased their weekday journey lengths three or five-fold, and travelled back to their old homes at weekends to visit relatives. Conversely, the average length of the working day was reduced, resulting in a concentration of peak-hour traffic into shorter periods, increasing congestion and operating problems at and near the London termini.

Most of the new owner-occupiers of the suburban estates could not afford both the mortgage and hire-purchase payments on a car, so travel for both business and pleasure was overwhelmingly by public transport. Services were expanded to absorb this increasing traffic, but in many suburbs the very rapid population increase resulted in the maximum train capacity being unable to cope in the morning and evening peaks, quickly leading to severe overcrowding. This in turn resulted in vociferous complaints from newly-formed rail user groups and residents' associations who were sometimes, but not invariably, able to persuade the SR to provide service and/or station improvements. In many cases, however, saturation point was being reached by 1939.

A case in point was the Waterloo–Epsom line, on which two new stations were provided and all others except Ewell West provided with improved facilities following electrification in 1925 and building-over of the surrounding land. The new suburb of Stoneleigh, in particular, suffered from severe congestion and, prior to the 1939-40 improvements (see above), it was virtually impossible to get onto the station in the evening peak via the narrow concrete footbridge, due to the sheer weight of home-going commuters disgorged from arriving trains. Following the Waterloo resignalling the service was increased to the maximum possible but over-

crowding persisted, and hence one of the intended purposes of the planned Motspur Park – Chessington – Leatherhead loop was to provide additional paths for outer-suburban Dorking and Guildford services to help relieve overcrowding.

Further complaints resulted from the inconsistent seating capacity of peak-hour trains, formed of two three-car motor units sandwiching a two-coach trailer set. This was because the original LSWR and 1925 SR motor units largely used on the Epsom – Waterloo route were shorter and had fewer seats than the later, more standardised, suburban stock. Alan A. Jackson mentions that a seat count carried out in June 1934 showed that on four consecutive days the same train had 78, 60, 65 and 78 first class seats and 540, 470, 480 and 540 third.[10] Furthermore, the eight-seat first class compartments carried on average only three passengers each in the peaks, while fifteen squeezed into the cramped ten-seater thirds. This latter problem was also commonplace on other parts of the network, particularly on routes to Dartford. These complaints were ameliorated firstly by the lengthening of most of the 'short' (former LSWR) units to give additional seating from 1934 onwards, the conversion of additional two-coach trailer sets from steam-hauled coaches and the rearrangement of some of the existing sets by the conversion of yet more steam vehicles. First class in the suburban area was then abolished in 1941. Finally there was the introduc-

tion of new 'six-a-side' steel-bodied 4 SUB units from 1944, some all-new and some with new bodies on rebuilt underframes, and the augmentation of three-coach units to four coaches, many of which them formed with new vehicles of greater capacity.

Finally, although this book does not purport to be a financial history, a brief mention of the financial results of the Southern Railway's suburban electrification policy is in order. Although Britain (and indeed most of the western World) was going through a difficult economic period in the late 1920s and early 1930s, as mentioned above this affected south east England much less than elsewhere. The massive expansion of the housing stock through these years, encouraged by railway electrification, increased the number of passengers using the Southern's trains many times. For example, to consider Stoneleigh once again, the number of passengers per annum rose from 256,209 in 1932 (the year it opened) to almost one million by 1937, while the number of season ticket holders (virtually all to Waterloo) rose fivefold from 5,671 to 30,127 in the same period. Corresponding receipts were £12,987 in 1932 and £57,110 in 1937. This one example, repeated many times over the system, shows that electrification and the provision of new stations was extremely successful in purely financial terms, quite apart from, as the late Charles Klapper records, enabling '…many thousands of its users to live in more congenial surroundings'[11].

10 Jackson A.J.: *Semi-Detached London*, Second Edition, Wild Swan Publications, ISBN 1 874103 01 1, 1991 p233

11 Klapper C.F.: *Sir Herbert Walker's Southern Railway*, Ian Allan Ltd, ISBN 0 7110 0478 1, 1973. p196.

3: SOME GENERAL MATTERS RELATING TO ROLLING STOCK

SR DC ELECTRIC MULTIPLE UNIT CLASS CODES

A distinctive and idiosyncratic feature of the Southern Electric as it developed was the use of class codes, such as 4 LAV and 6 PUL, to distinguish the various different types of dc electric multiple unit introduced from the time of the 1932-33 Brighton line electrification onwards. This section briefly explains how they were arrived at.

Before 1932 all SR dc electric rolling stock was suburban and there was no requirement to differentiate between the various varieties although, as has already been noted in Chapter 2, they were not at this time necessarily interchangeable across the entire electrified suburban network. Carriage Working notices simply referred to electric stock by the number of vehicles in the train as follows:

2: A single two-coach motor unit on the South London or Wimbledon–West Croydon line.

3: A single three-coach motor unit.

4: Two two-coach motor units coupled.

6: Two three-coach motor units coupled. This was the longest train formation allowed on certain ex-LSWR routes such as the Hounslow Loop.

8: Two three-coach motor units with an intermediate unpowered trailer set (3+2+3). This was the usual peak-hour formation on most suburban routes.

9: Three three-coach motor units. This was the formation of rush-hour London Bridge–Caterham/Tattenham Corner services between London Bridge and Purley, where they split or combined. Six cars generally ran to/from Caterham and three to/from Tattenham Corner.

With the introduction of different EMU classes for specific types of service or with different facilities from 1932, it was necessary to devise a system of codes to differentiate the various types in operating documents etc. The new codes comprised a number indicating how many vehicles the unit possessed, followed by three letters related in some way to its use or facilities. The codes were not given to suburban stock until the introduction of four-car suburban units. Although some unofficial publications described three-coach suburban units as '3 SUB', they were in error and this code was never used officially. Similarly, the codes 2 SL and 2 WIM for the two-coach units 1801-12, although convenient, were never

officially recognised. One two-letter code, however, was officially used: 4 DD was the code for the experimental double-decker units 4001 and 4002, introduced in 1949.

Some changes were made during the early years of EMU code use; in particular the codes originally allocated to the Brighton line express EMU classes in 1932 were changed to reduce ambiguity when the Eastbourne express stock was introduced in 1935.

For non-gangwayed stock intended for semi-fast and stopping services on the electrified main lines, described in detail in Volume 2, the class code generally made reference to the lavatory facilities provided. For example, 4 LAV referred to a four-coach unit in which one vehicle had LAVatory facilities, while a 2 NOL referred to a two-coach unit with NO Lavatories. The origins of other codes used are given in the appropriate sections.

For through-gangwayed stock intended for express services, also described in detail in Volume 2, the class codes generally made reference to the catering facilities provided. For example, 6 PAN referred to a six-coach unit including a PANtry car (basically a six-compartment side-corridor first with a short kitchenette and pantry area at one end from which limited light refreshments could be served). One exception was the 4 COR class, a four-coach CORridor unit with no catering facility. Again, the origins of other codes used are given in the appropriate sections.

These EMU class codes were mainly for the benefit of the operating departments, and it did not necessarily follow that all units with the same classification had exactly the same seating capacity or mechanical design, although it is generally true that all within a class were equivalent for stock diagramming purposes. For example, after 1948 there were two distinct types of 2 HAL unit with different bodywork design and third class seating capacity. Furthermore, reformations (the swapping of vehicles between units) following accident or war damage, together with a reduction in first class seating and catering facilities to reflect reduced demand in the post-1945 period, meant that after a time most classes included several units that were non-standard in some way. A notorious example was 4 LAV 2926 which, having had the appropriate coach replaced by a suburban compartment vehicle in 1963 following a mishap, was actually bereft of toilet facilities.

Carriage Working Notices for the electrified main lines continued the same system as for the suburban area, except that the number of vehicles in the train was suffixed by the three-letter class code (or codes, where two classes were coupled in the same train). For example 12 COR referred to three 4 COR units together. Further abbreviations were also used, such as CBC for a 4 COR+4 BUF+4 COR formation.

This system of codes was continued and expanded when new classes of electric unit were introduced by what was now the Southern Region of British Railways from 1951 onwards. The new codes were indeed derived from previous practice; for example a 2 HAP had passenger accommodation similar to a 2 HAL but was fitted with electro-pneumatic brakes. The system really petered out in the 1970s, being superseded by three-digit class codes, and the last new EMU type officially allocated an SR-style code was the 4 VEP class built between 1967 and 1974[12].

In SR (and BR) engineering and operating documents it was usual (although by no means universal) to refer to the unit class codes using lower case for the last two letters. eg 4 Lav, 6 Pul. In some texts, the figure has been closed up to the letters or – in error – a hyphen has been inserted. After some consideration, it has been decided in this book to use upper case throughout. eg 4 LAV, 6 PUL. This is entirely for practical purposes, as otherwise the codes tend to become lost within the text.

SR CARRIAGE DIAGRAM NUMBERS

All Southern Railway carriages, vans and wagons were issued with a diagram number by the Carriage and Wagon Department. These diagram numbers were related to the layout plan of the vehicle concerned by reference to its exact dimensions and function, and sometimes (in the case of electric stock) to couplings and electrical connections. If a vehicle was modified at some point during its life it would generally be given a revised diagram number. Virtually all diagram numbers are known (subject to the odd anomaly) and are mentioned extensively in the following chapters which cover the SR electric suburban rolling stock in detail.

The SR diagram number list started at 1. Low numbers up to about 600 were reserved for designs of pre-Grouping origin.

Diagram numbers from 660 up to 795 were first-generation suburban electric stock vehicles, including the 2 NOLs. Diagram 660 were the original LSWR motor third brakes in un-lengthened condition, while diagram 795 were the 2 NOL driving trailer composites. Coulsdon/Wallington AC electric coaches were to diagrams 676, 677, 738, 761-763, 770 and 790-92 (number 738 was used again for DC stock).

Diagram numbers in the 8xx series included oddments such as Waterloo & City tube cars (diagrams 840, 841, 842, 845 and 846), Coulsdon and Sutton ac motor vans (dia. 830) and Ryde pier trams (dia. 848, 849 and 850).

Vehicles built to 'standard' SR carriage designs were given diagram numbers from 2000 upwards, with blocks for thirds,

third brakes etc. In each block, electric and steam-hauled vehicles were placed in the same series. Peculiarly, individual diagram numbers within these blocks were not necessarily in order of date of introduction of the vehicle types concerned as might be expected, suggesting that the series from 2000 was a late introduction or was altered at some time. The SR-designed electric stock diagrams were as listed below. The list records the position circa 1960, after the completion of the last Southern Region-designed multiple units. Subsequent alterations are not included.

Diagram numbers for SR-designed electric stock.

Trailer thirds (seconds)

2006	6 PUL 10001-20
2009	4 COR 10055-10112 and replacement 10039
2010	6 PAN 10021-54
2012	4 SUB 10419-28
2013	4 SUB 10230-10400
2014	4 SUB 10429-38, 10449-71 4 EPB ten-compartment trailer (with SR bodywork)
2015	4 SUB 10439-48
2016	6 PUL 10113-10115 derated City Limited firsts from 2504
2018	4-SUB 10-bay saloon 4 EPB saloon (with SR bodywork)
2020	4 DD (A)
2021	4 DD (B) (difference between A and B believed to be in couplings)

Motor third (second) brakes:

2106	4 LAV
2107	6 PUL 11003-46
2108	6 PUL 11001 (ex-6 CIT)
2109	6 PUL 11002 (ex-6 CIT)
2111	2 BIL 10567-76
2112	6 PAN 11047-80
2114	4 COR 11081-11254
2115	2 BIL 10577-10718
2116	2 HAL 10719-10810 (two periscopes in guard's compartment)
2117	4 LAV 10497-10500; as 2116 but single periscope in guard's compartment, for units 2954/55
2118	4 SUB 10941-60
2119	4 SUB 10895-10940, 10961-80
2120	4 SUB semi-saloons (2x4 bays)
2126	4 SUB
2126A	4 SUB saloon 12664 after transfer to 2 HAL 2700 and fitting with two periscopes

---

12 Old habits die hard, however. The class 460 units for the *Gatwick Express* service, introduced in 2000-01, were referred to as 8 GAT in some operating documents, and some blocks of units reformed as late as 2003 were given semi-official, ad hoc, class codes.

2127   2 HAL 10811-10817 as 2119 but 7 comps for units 2693-99

2128   4 DD

2129   4 EPB

2130   2 HAP 5651-36 and 2 EPB 5651-84

Composites:

2305   4 LAV 11501-33 The downrating of these from 5F4T to 2F7T in the late 40s-early 50s was listed in SR documents as "2305/AMD"

2306   4 LAV 12001-33

2307   6 PUL 11751-80

2309   4 COR 11791-11860

2310   4 LAV 11999, 12000

2311   4 LAV 11534/5

2312   4 SUB 11471-80

2313   4 COR composite 11861 derated from diner first dia. 2571

2314   4 SUB 11448-70/81-11500

2319   6-PUL 11862-67, derated City Limited firsts from dia. 2504

2321   This number was given to the driving trailer lavatory composites 12847–53 intended for 2693-99 – probably in error, because DTLCs should be in 27xx; 2705, last of the DTLC nos., was assigned to them at a later date.

Firsts and catering vehicles:

2504   6 CIT firsts 12251-59 (prior to derating)

2505   4 RES kitchen thirds 12601-19

2506   6 PAN firsts 12260-76

2571   4 RES diner saloon/compartment firsts 12232-50

2572   4 GRI griddle cars 12602/5/9 (converted from dia. 2505)

2600   6 PAN pantry cars 12501-17

2601   4 BUF buffet cars 12518-30

2602   4 RES buffet car 12613 converted from dia. 2505

Driving trailers:

2700   2 BIL 12100-10

2701   2 BIL 12034-12100/11-85

2702   2 HAL 12186-12231, 12801-46

2703   2 HAP 16001-36

2704   2 EPB 16101-34

2705   2 HAL 12847-53

HEAD OFFICE ORDER NUMBERS

Throughout this book, and particularly in the chapters which cover electric rolling stock to Southern Railway design, frequent mention is made of Head Office (HO) order numbers. These were issued whenever the SR Board, or a Head Office committee (such as the Rolling Stock Committee) with authority delegated to it by the Board, authorised a specific order involving capital expenditure. These numbers were noted in the SR committee minutes now held at the National Archives, Kew and elsewhere, and are of interest as they give an insight as to exactly what was ordered and when. Their use commenced late in 1922 just prior to Grouping and they were issued in roughly chronological order starting at 1, although there were sometimes delays in implementation for various reasons. For the first three years some jobs, particularly those inherited from the pre-Grouping companies, were not given HO numbers. They reached four figures before 1939, and their use continued into the BR Southern Region era, ending in 1966. As far as rolling stock was concerned, HO numbers were issued to cover anything from new construction and rebuilds to minor modifications, whether carried out at works or depot level. They were generally not issued for individual repairs, nor for work carried out by outside contractors, but there were exceptions. We have quoted HO numbers wherever these are known.

PERIODS OF MAUNSELL COACHING STOCK DESIGN

With a few exceptions, the bodywork of the main-line electric stock built for the Southern Railway's electrification schemes of the 1932-39 period was designed under the overall direction of R.E.L. Maunsell, Chief Mechanical Engineer from 1923 until 1937. His assistant in charge of carriage design was Surrey Warner from the LSWR and the chief draughtsman was Lionel Lynes who, like Maunsell, came from the South Eastern and Chatham Railway. Lynes succeeded Warner in 1929 but, as explained in Chapter 2, SECR carriage design influence had been strong from the beginning.

SR main-line coaches of the Maunsell era, both steam and electric, can be conveniently divided into six distinguishing periods according to their dates of ordering and various salient design features. These periods are summarised below, although electric stock is included only in periods 3, 4 and 6 (Note that some period 4 electric coaches had certain period 5 features to confuse matters). Characteristic features introduced in a particular period were continued through each succeeding period unless mentioned otherwise. Readers particularly interested in the development of Maunsell steam stock are referred to Mike King's definitive work on the subject listed in the bibliography, and a number of restored examples may be sampled on the Bluebell and Kent and East Sussex Railways.

Period 1: These first Maunsell coach designs, ordered in April 1925, were largely an amalgam of existing SECR and LSWR practice. Their main distinguishing features were a thick wooden cornice rail at cantrail height and external wooden window mouldings of complex curved cross-section, known as bolection mouldings. All compartments had an external door and quarterlights. On the corridor side were wide windows the same height as the droplights, while doors were opposite compartments and alternated with additional body side droplights. Droplights were wood-framed and secured by leather straps. All droplights and toilet windows were surmounted by a single ventilator bonnet.

Period 2: Ordered from April 1926 and largely similar to period 1, the main external differences in these vehicles were simple external window fillets and a much thinner cornice rail. Droplights were now secured internally by a sprung garnish-rail strip and were opened/closed using a small leather tab.

Period 3: These were the first SR coaches to have the characteristic high corridor windows reaching to the eaves. The first vehicles to these designs were ordered in April 1928 and construction took place between 1929 and 1932. Fixed windows had simple external wooden fillets. Corridor windows reached to the eaves, except at coach ends to allow space for destination boards. External doors and lavatory windows again had a single ventilator bonnet. Corridor internal panelling was painted an ivory shade. Saloon windows had a single large droplight (which lowered about 7in) surmounted by a single ventilator bonnet. 4 LAV electric units 1921-1953, ordered in May 1930, belonged to period 3 by virtue of the single ventilator bonnet above the toilet windows on their side-corridor trailer.

Period 4: The most numerous pattern of Maunsell coach design, this period covered 1932-35. Designs were mainly similar to period 3 except that lavatory windows had two ventilator louvres above them. Main-line electric stock of this pattern included the 6 PUL, 6 CIT and 6 PAN types plus the first ten 2 BIL units 1890-1899 (later 2010/01-09) On 6 PAN and 2 BIL units, corridor sides had narrow fixed panes replacing intermediate droplights (similar to period 4ii). The PAN units had 'Alpax' aluminium window frames on the motor coaches (as in period 5), 'Airstream' window ventilators on the motor coaches and pantry cars, and frameless door droplights (as in periods 4ii/5).

Period 4ii: This period covered a small number of 9ft wide steam-hauled coaches built in 1934-35, superficially similar to period 4. The body sides had a large number of protruding screw heads, but fixed windows were flush-fitted with corners rounded off to a large radius (reminiscent of the later 2 HAL electric units of 1939). Corridor windows reached to the eaves and narrow fixed windows replaced intermediate droplights. Passenger doors had ventilator bonnets and 'Beclawat' frameless droplights with a lever-locking device on the garnish rail, with the exception of inset end doors on saloon thirds which retained wood-framed droplights. Large saloon windows had glazed 'Airstream' sliding ventilators with external glass deflector plates. Interiors were varnished wood without the ivory-painted corridor panels. A diagram 2007 open third (No.1309) and a diagram 2403 composite brake (No.6686) from this period are preserved in running order on the Bluebell Railway.

Period 5: These were the final Maunsell/Lynes coach designs, produced during the 1936-38 period. Fixed windows were fitted externally with 'Alpax' aluminium frames and had almost square corners. Corridor windows reached to the eaves but could be wider than before, and there were no intermediate droplights or narrow windows. External doors lacked ventilator bonnets, and those on the corridor side were positioned between compartments, rather than opposite them. Saloon windows were again topped with 'Airstream' glazed sliding ventilators with external glass deflector plates, but were incorporated into the main window frame. Interior finish was varnished wood or 'Rexine' synthetic leathercloth. This period covered the major proportion of main-line electric stock, including 2 BIL (2011 upwards), 4 COR, 4 RES and 4 BUF (the latter having buffet cars with interiors designed by O.V.S. Bulleid, Maunsell's successor).

AN INTRODUCTION TO CONTROL SYSTEMS AND AUXILIARIES ON THE DC ELECTRIC STOCK

Very basic details of the three types of main control system, and associated auxiliaries, used in LSWR and Southern Railway-design dc electric multiple units introduced between 1914 and the end of 1951, are given here. This is not intended to be a technical treatise, but will hopefully give the interested reader some idea of what is involved.

Simply, an electric train is powered by electric motors, often termed traction motors, whose speed and torque are controlled by varying the voltage and current available to them. In the earliest systems, this was achieved by placing resistances in the circuit between the power supply (eg the conductor rail) and the motors to limit the starting current. As the train accelerated from a stand, the resistances were gradually switched out of the circuit manually using a controller, a process known as 'notching up'. An early advance was the introduction of a 'multiple unit' control system, enabling the motor circuits in two or more motor coaches coupled in the same train to be controlled simultaneously from one master controller. This involved passing electrical signals, which could be at a lower voltage than that picked-up by the motors, along wires connecting the control circuits in each motor coach. The system originated in the USA just before 1900 and was subsequently developed by the various railway electrical equipment suppliers; for example, the Sprague Thomson-Houston system equipped much of the first generation of the London Underground fleet, while British Westinghouse designed the system used by the LSWR electric stock and subsequently adopted by the Southern Railway. A major advance of the British Westinghouse equipment was that it incorporated automatic notching-up, so that the train could be made to accelerate automatically at a controlled rate until the balancing speed (or a slower speed if selected on the controller) was reached. The balancing speed was a theoretical maximum attainable on level tangential track while carrying a specified load. This system used electro-magnetic relays which gradually switched out the resistances or re-connected the motors from series to parallel as the train accelerated and the current draw decreased.

The control system used in all SR suburban and semi-fast electric units (the latter including LAVs 1921-1953, NOLs 1813-1882 and BILs 1890-1899) built between 1924 and 1936 was supplied by Metropolitan-Vickers (Metrovick), successors to British Westinghouse, and was based on that designed for the original LSWR stock. Electricity at a nominal 600V was picked up from the conductor rail and passed along a power line which ran the length of the train, from whence circuits were separated out though potential dividers to supply traction current to the motors and to the control system, air compressor, heating and lighting, all at line voltage. Current return to earth was through the wheels and running rails, and there was significant leakage of current into the surrounding ground (which, as explained in Chapter 1, could cause problems). The contactors and resistances were located in a cupboard at the rear of the cab, but the compressor was underframe-mounted. (In the original LSWR units before their 1934-40 reconstruction, virtually all equipment had been in a separate compartment between the motorman and guard.) Heating and lighting were at line-voltage, the two carriage lighting circuits each having about 7-10 70V dc lamps (ie one on each circuit per compartment) connected in series along each side of the vehicle.

Although robust, easy to maintain and supremely reliable, the Metrovick system in use on SR suburban stock had some disadvantages, such as the control lines operating at high voltage and the lack of a back-up emergency lighting supply. For the express stock provided for the 1933 Brighton line electrification, which was to be kept entirely separate from the suburban and semi-fast fleet, an improved control system was therefore developed by the SR Electrical Department under Alfred Raworth in conjunction with the equipment suppliers. The revised system operated at 70V dc rather than at line-voltage, and was supplied from a motor-generator rather than directly from the traction supply. Furthermore, the motor-generator also charged emergency batteries, which could then supply carriage lighting in the event of power failure. Actuation of the system was now electro-pneumatic, whereby the low-voltage control signals activated solenoid valves which admitted compressed air (supplied by the brake compressor) into cylinders which acted against pistons to operate the main contactor switches. As well as the original Brighton line stock, express units for the Eastbourne and two Portsmouth electrifications were equipped with this system, although there were some configuration changes in the latter case which are explained in Volume 2. One other development was that virtually all equipment was now underframe mounted, only the automatic acceleration relays remaining at the rear of the cab.

After 1935 Raworth became concerned with increasing standardisation in the SR electric stock fleet, and in 1936 the Southern Railway negotiated the first of three ten-year contracts with English Electric for the exclusive future supply of rolling stock electrical equipment, including traction motors. Although it was necessary for the equipment supplied by EE for suburban and semi-fast stock to be compatible with the existing Metrovick eight-wire control gear which worked at line-voltage, changes were made to increase standardisation of parts with the express stock system. In particular, electro-pneumatic actuation of the contactor switches was adopted with the solenoid valves working at 70V, supplied from the 600V supply via the control potentiometer (a device to step-down line voltage). As on the express stock, most equipment was now mounted on the underframe, allowing motor coach cabs to be shorter. Units fitted with this system, which included three-coach suburban units 1579-1584, BILs 2011-2152, NOLs 1883-1890 LAVs 2954/55 and the entire fleet of HALs and second-generation SUBs, were collectively known as 1936 stock. It was not possible to use motor-generators and batteries to supply current for the control system and lighting, as on the express stock, as such an arrangement would have made the system incompatible with older stock. Thus it was that, until the end of 1951 when the final 4 SUB was outshopped, new units were being built whose control system still allowed them to operate in multiple with the original LSWR stock of 1914.

BRAKING SYSTEMS ON ELECTRIC STOCK
A further important feature retained from those earliest electrifications until 1951 was use of the Westinghouse automatic air brake, standard on both the express and suburban/semi-fast fleets. As early as 1875 the LBSCR had adopted this brake as standard, as its power and relative quickness of application and release gave shorter stopping distances and smarter operation in comparison to the rival vacuum brake. These factors were particularly important on its suburban routes, where closely-spaced stations resulted in a high stopping frequency. It was also a proven product, already widely used on US railroads. Against this, the air brake was more complex and expensive in comparison to the vacuum brake, which was adopted by the majority of railway companies in Britain, including the LSWR and SER. By the time that continuous automatic brakes became a legal requirement on passenger trains in 1889, in the London area only the Great Eastern and London, Chatham and Dover Railways (who operated similarly dense suburban networks with closely-spaced stops) had joined the LBSCR in adopting the air brake. With this background the Westinghouse brake was inevitably adopted for the LBSCR ac electrics which took over a significant proportion of steam suburban services between 1909 and 1912, while its advantages also made it the obvious choice for the suburban electric units of the LSWR, an otherwise vacuum-braked system.

With LSWR standards being mostly continued for SR electrifications, the Westinghouse therefore became the standard service brake on all Southern Electric suburban, semi-fast and express stock until the general adoption of the electro-pneumatic (EP) brake on the SR after 1951. Although other railways had introduced the EP brake on electric stock before 1930, the Southern persisted with the Westinghouse brake throughout its existence, driven mainly by compatibility considerations. The last units to be so-equipped were the 257-strong second-generation 4 SUB fleet constructed in the 1941-51 period (see Chapter 6).

The Westinghouse Automatic Air Brake (usually referred to as an Automatic Air Brake) uses compressed air, held in auxiliary reservoirs on each vehicle, to operate pistons which press cast iron (or composition) brake blocks against the treads of all wheels on the train. The resulting friction converts the movement of the train into heat, thus reducing its speed. The brake is continuous (it can be fitted to all vehicles of the train and operated by the driver) and automatic (it automatically self-applies on all parts of the train should it become divided). On electric units, the compressed air is produced by electrically-driven compressors which supply main reservoirs located on the motor coaches. The main reservoirs supply the brake (or train) pipe which runs the entire length of the train, and hence the auxiliary reservoirs. A second pipe, known as the main reservoir equalising pipe, connects all the main reservoirs in the train together, thus maintaining an equal pressure in each. The pressure in the train pipe is normally maintained at around 70 lbs per square inch (psi) when the brakes are released, and a governor automatically activates the compressor(s) when the pressure drops significantly below this figure.

The driver (motorman) causes the brakes to apply by placing the brake handle in the application position which lowers the air pressure in the brake pipe. This actuates a complex valve in each coach, known as a triple valve, which allows compressed air from the auxiliary reservoir to pass into the brake cylinder so applying the brakes. It is this system of having a pressurised brake pipe along the length of the train which provides the automatic feature as, if the train divides, the brake-pipe pressure will fall to zero and the brakes will be fully-applied throughout the train independently of the driver. The same process is involved when a passenger pulls the 'communication cord', a valve being opened in the brake pipe. The driver can lower the brake-pipe pressure, and hence apply the brake, in stages, and therefore the brake is described as being graduable in application.

However, to retain a selected braking rate the handle must be returned to a holding or 'lap' position, and hence the brake is said to be non self-lapping.

To release the brake, the handle is placed in the release/running position and air from the main reservoir system enters the brake pipe and raises the pressure to 70 psi, causing the triple valves to exhaust the brake cylinder and to begin charging the auxiliary reservoirs in preparation for the next application. It is important to note that the brake cannot be released in gradual stages (an arrangement also known as direct or single release) and that the auxiliary reservoirs only commence recharging with compressed air, a process which takes between seven and ten seconds to complete, after the brake is released. If the driver attempts to re-apply the brake before the auxiliary reservoirs are fully recharged, the brake will react more slowly than usual and only a reduced braking force will be available. It is therefore evident that handling of the air brake required a certain skill, particularly when drawing to a halt at tight terminal platforms such as those at Holborn Viaduct.

With the aim of improving braking performance, experiments were carried out with the more technically advanced electro-pneumatic brake in 1947. In this system the individual brake cylinders were activated by electrically-operated valves controlled by signals along a wire instead of by air passing along a pipe through the train, enabling all the brakes in the train to be applied or released simultaneously rather than progressively. Other major advantages included the ability to release the brake gradually, and to make frequent small brake applications without exhausting the air supply. As related in Volume 2, the successful outcome of these trials resulted in the EP brake, together with a revised control system sharing many features of the pre-war express stock, being adopted as standard by the Southern Region of British Railways for all new electric units from the end of 1951.

Corridor third 10083 was completed in April 1937 for four-car unit 3129. Bodywork and livery features of the fine Maunsell/Lynes ('Period 5') designs, with 'Alpax' aluminium window frames and external doors without ventilation bonnets. Livery was olive green, lined out (by this time along the waist only) in yellow and black. As well as roof board brackets, the standard SR destination board brackets can be seen above the windows; these were picked out in yellow. All nine compartments were labelled as 'smoking'. *SR Official*

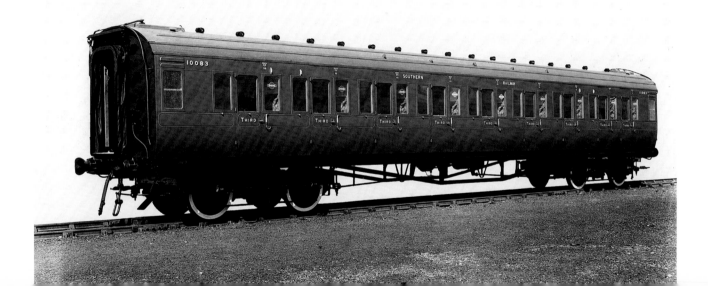

4: THE LBSCR AND SR ELEVATED ELECTRIC STOCK 1909-29

This chapter covers in detail the rolling stock provided for the London, Brighton and South Coast Railway's *Elevated Electric* ac overhead lines converted in 1909-12 and for the final extensions to Coulsdon and Sutton completed by the Southern Railway in 1925. Their story forms a discrete episode in the history of the Southern Electric although, as will be seen later, all vehicles were re-used in one form or another when the system was abandoned in 1929. A short section describing the four petrol railcars used for inspection and maintenance is included at the end.

THE SOUTH LONDON LINE (SR 'SL') STOCK

The electric trains provided by the London, Brighton and South Coast Railway for the South London line from Victoria to London Bridge via Peckham Rye, which commenced operation in 1909, were the first to be built by any of the main line companies which would later group to form the Southern Railway. Tenders for the South London stock were invited in March 1907, and the contract, won by the Metropolitan Amalgamated Carriage and Wagon Company (MACW), was dated 31st December 1908. However, construction must have actually commenced some time before this as the first set was delivered in the same month. Built by MACW at their works in Saltley, Birmingham, eight three-coach sets were provided, designed under the supervision of Albert Panter, LBSCR Carriage and Wagon Superintendent and deputy to Douglas Earle Marsh, Locomotive and Carriage Engineer. Electrical equipment was the responsibility of Philip Dawson and was supplied by AEG. The second set was delivered in April 1909, four more in May or June, and the remaining two probably in July or August. (The situation is unclear because the LBSCR instigated a half-yearly booking system in 1909 and thus stock could in reality have been delivered up to six months before the recorded date. 'Official' delivery dates are June for sets 3-6 and December for sets 7-8.)

Each three-coach set was loose-coupled (that is, with standard side-buffers and screw couplings between intermediate vehicles) and comprised two motor third brakes with a trailer first between them. The motor coaches were to LBSCR carriage diagram number 280, but the original diagram number of the trailer firsts is unknown. All vehicles were 60ft long over headstocks and had a greater than standard width and height of 9ft 5in (9ft 1in at cantrail height) and 12ft 3in respectively. The motor coaches contained a brake compartment with a small half-width cubicle partitioned off for the motorman, and seating accommodation was initially for 66 third class passengers, while the trailers had 56 first class seats. By 1910 the motor coaches were rated at 82 seats. Externally the vehicles were conventional with a hinged door to each compartment but the internal arrangements (described in greater detail later) were unusual, with a side-gangway connecting the compartments within each. No second class seats were provided, the Brighton company (in common with the LSWR) using the introduction of electric stock as justification to do away with this anachronism. The bodies were mounted on underframes with steel-plate sole-bars and trussing, an unusual feature in this country perpetuated on later *Elevated Electric* motor coaches. The quoted weight of the South London motor third brakes was 54 tons and of the trailer firsts, thirty tons.

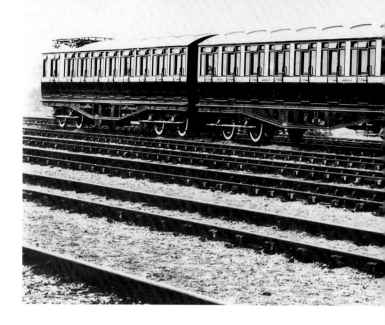

The first three-coach LBSCR South London Line set as built, with motor third brake 3203 leading, almost certainly photographed in the Metropolitan Amalagamated CW works yard at Saltley, Birmingham, and probably just prior to delivery in December 1908.

The vehicles in each set were numbered consecutively from 3201 upwards (ie the first was formed Motor Third Brake 3201 + Trailer First 3202 + Motor Third Brake 3203, the next was formed MThB 3204 + TF 3205 + MThB 3206 etc.). Following delivery but before entering passenger service the sets themselves were numbered 1E–8E in order of coach numbers (thus 1E was formed 3201/2/3 etc) but these numbers, in large white figures between the windscreens on the cab fronts, were only used for the short period that three-coach sets were in operation.

In view of the inner-suburban nature of this route it might seem surprising that compartment-type stock, albeit with side gangways, was chosen when other railways such as the District and North Eastern were providing saloon stock with sliding doors for similar newly-electrified urban lines. The reason is purely that, as the new trains were built by a contractor, a cheaper price was quoted for compartment vehicles. In the event, the LBSCR seems to have made the right choice as, whereas the MDR and NER saloon stock was soon suffering from structural defects due to poor workmanship (probably due as much as anything to unfamiliarity on the part of the builders), most vehicles of the South London line electric stock survived in largely original condition for 45 years, latterly working on the third rail dc system. It seems that the generous maximum width of 9ft 5in was quoted in the specification to the manufacturers when sliding door stock was being considered, as this allowed room for internal door pockets without reducing passenger space too much. When a slam-door layout was finalised, no-one saw fit to reduce the width to a more conventional dimension. This was acceptable because the South London line had a more generous loading gauge than other LBSCR suburban lines, but it limited the stock's use as the electrified network spread. This also suggests that much of the detailed design work was carried out by MACW, and only 'rubber stamped' by Panter.

The wooden bodywork of these vehicles had the usual LBSCR cross-section of the period with a sharp angle at cantrail height and arc-profile roof, but in other respects there were a number of detail differences when compared to other Brighton coaches, aside from the larger-than-normal dimensions. The panelling corners were squared off, and the compartment quarterlights (windows to either side of each external door) were surmounted by opening frosted-glass toplights. Bodywork was of conventional wooden construction with mahogany side panels and deal roof boards, floorboards and ends. Other woods used for various parts as specified in the contract document included ash, oak and pine. Some attempt was made to produce an attractive frontal appearance for these trains, each cab end being slightly bowed and the flattened roof above tapering down to meet it. In order to prevent electrical leakage from the current collector bows, all external wooden surfaces were covered with aluminium sheet, 12swg thickness being specified for the sides and 21swg for the roofs. The roofs also had external

wooden cross-ribs to help avoid damage in the event of a sagging or broken contact wire. Again, for safety reasons, there were no roof vents on these, or any other ac vehicles. The floors were particularly well-insulated, being formed of a sandwich of slag wool between two layers of wood, below which there was a layer of Uralite insulating material and finally aluminium sheeting which was, like the body, earthed to the underframe.

Electricity at a nominal 6,700V, 25Hz ac, was collected from the overhead wires through bow collectors mounted on each motor coach, and to accommodate these the roof above the cab and van was flattened as mentioned earlier. Although simpler than pantographs, bows could only trail along the contact wire, and therefore separate ones were required for each direction of travel. They folded flat along the vehicle roof when not in use, one being slightly narrower to fit when both were lowered. The horizontal section of the bow collector in contact with the overhead wire consisted of a U-shaped aluminium channel section collector-strip, filled with a mixture of black-lead and Vaseline for lubrication purposes. This arrangement gave a collector-strip life of about 5,000-6,000 miles (four to five weeks in normal service) between renewals. As built, each bow had a trailing extension arm to ensure continuous contact with the overhead wire, but these were soon found to be unnecessary and were removed. The area containing the bow collector fittings, on which all equipment was live, was originally unprotected, but a wire-mesh 'basket' guard was provided before the sets entered passenger service. The bow appropriate to the direction of travel on each motor coach was raised by compressed air.

The motor coach driving ends had one lookout for the motorman, (the offside window, behind which electrical equipment was situated, being obscured with paint), and were originally devoid of any kind of route indicator. The motorman's cubicle had a droplight (that on the offside again being painted over) but no external door, access being gained through the brake compartment. Cab instruments included volt, amp and watt meters and a brake pressure gauge, but no speedometer, while the master controller included a simple 'deadman's' safety device which had to be held down continuously by the motorman to prevent current being disconnected and the brakes applied. The unusual head and tail indication arrangements comprised a rotating horizontal rail across the cab front just below the lookouts. On the motorman's end this had a red glass, and on the other a plate which was red on one side (stencilled LV) and white on the other. In the upright position the red glass covered a white oil lamp and the red side of the plate showed, denoting 'last vehicle' for the benefit of signalmen. However, the rail could be rotated to move the red glass down away from the lamp and display the white side of the plate, to show the front of the train. This apparatus could be operated from inside the cab. Westinghouse air brakes, standard on LBSCR coaching stock, were used. Driving ends had connecting hoses for the train air pipe and bow collector air pipe, but between vehicles there was also a main reservoir equalising pipe connection. A compressor, powered by a 6hp two-pole motor, was mounted on each motor

coach underframe to supply air both for the brakes and for raising the bow collectors.

These trains were true multiple units, signals from the controller in the leading cab passing to all controllers in the train through low-voltage (300V) cables running below the coach floors, obviating the need for a high-tension power (bus) line between vehicles. From some (not particularly clear) drawings published by Dawson, it appears that these cables contained eleven wires. To connect them between coaches, two multiple-unit jumper sockets were located below the headstocks inboard of the buffers, loose jumper cables (not attached permanently to any vehicle) being utilised. Motor and trailer bogies were all of pressed-steel construction and had a wheelbase of 8ft. Both bogies of the driving motor coaches were motored, each being equipped with a pair of 120hp (one hour rating) single-phase compensated repulsion motors, eight motors giving a total rating of 960hp for a three-car set. This repulsion motor design was invented and designed by a Dr Eichberg and patented by electrical engineers Winter Eichberg, but the motors were actually manufactured in Berlin by AEG. They were geared to the driving wheels at a ratio of 25:83. Two 220KW main transformers, each serving a pair of motors, were mounted on the underframe of each motor coach to step-down the voltage from 6,700 to 750. Electricity could then be supplied to the motors at 450, 580, 640 or 750V through contactors, which had to be 'notched up' manually by the motorman, there being no automatic acceleration relays. 450V was the minimum necessary to provide sufficient torque to start the motors turning on a gradient, but it caused these units to have a characteristically severe jolt on starting. Power for the control circuits, brake compressor and lighting was supplied at 300V from an auxiliary transformer. The high-tension switches, fuses and auxiliary transformer were located in a fire-proofed steel compartment to the right of the motorman's cubicle, accessed through a cylindrical access door concentric with the handbrake column. This door was interlocked so that the high-tension circuits were automatically disconnected and earthed, and the bow collector lowered, when it was opened.

As originally outshopped, the South London sets were painted in an approximation of the official 'main line' LBSCR livery of the time, which had been introduced in 1906. The basic scheme consisted of umber (a shade of brown) below the waist and on door and window frames, and ivory white on the fascia panels. For some reason, however, the carriage builders used the wrong shade of ivory paint. Vehicle ends, including the cabs, were black, as were underframes and bogies, while the roofs were originally white. Lining-out consisted of a thin gold line over a thicker black band, while numbers and lettering, all at waist level, were also in gold, shaded black. Class was indicated by the words FIRST or THIRD on appropriate compartment doors, while the smoking sections had SMOKING etched into the quarterlights.

The internal arrangements in these vehicles were distinctly unusual, being designed to give the loading and unloading benefits of a side door to each compartment, combined with the improved internal circulation of the sliding door saloon stock mentioned above. There was a side gangway, like a side corridor but without the partition between seats and passageway, to help passengers find seats at busy times. The seating in the motor coaches was arranged in eight bays, the gangway swapping sides from the offside to the nearside in the fifth bay back from the cab to even-out weight distribution. Each seating bay accommodated four passengers each side (re-rated to five by 1910), except at the ends where the seats occupied the width of the coach and had room for one more. The trailers had nine bays, each seating three-a-side, with the gangway swapping from the offside to the nearside at the centre of the coach. Again, there was an extra seat at each end of the coach. In both cases, there was a swing door across the gangway approximately half-way along each vehicle, separating the smoking and non-smoking sections. The distance between partitions in the motor coaches was 6ft and that in the first class trailers 6in more. Internal fittings were both lavish and ornate, with two carbon-filament lamps and double luggage racks being provided in all compartments. There was, however, no heating provided on this or any other LBSCR electric stock. Upholstery was originally red in third class, brown in first.

The internal opulence of what was basically short-distance suburban stock possibly had something to do with the main line aspirations of the company regarding its electrification system, and hence the need to demonstrate on this experimental line that electric trains could be built to a standard suitable for longer-distance operation.

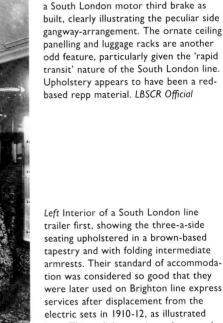

Above The passenger accommodation in a South London motor third brake as built, clearly illustrating the peculiar side gangway-arrangement. The ornate ceiling panelling and luggage racks are another odd feature, particularly given the 'rapid transit' nature of the South London line. Upholstery appears to have been a red-based repp material. *LBSCR Official*

Left Interior of a South London line trailer first, showing the three-a-side seating upholstered in a brown-based tapestry and with folding intermediate armrests. Their standard of accommodation was considered so good that they were later used on Brighton line express services after displacement from the electric sets in 1910-12, as illustrated later. This and the previous photograph were taken in November 1908 at Saltley, when the vehicles had just been completed. *LBSCR Official*

Although the electrification stimulated the looked-for rise in traffic, it soon became clear that the three-coach formation provided as a result of pre-electrification traffic surveys was not ideal, as it gave an inadequate number of seats in the rush-hours and too many at other times. In addition, most of the traffic growth had been in third class, while first class custom dropped. Not only were fewer first class tickets being sold, but these were spread over a larger number of trains and, as a result, the sets had a disproportionately large number of first class seats. The chosen solution was to reform the motor coaches with 'new' driving trailers to produce two-coach sets with a smaller proportion of first class accommodation, this work being carried out between 1910 and 1912. The first two-coach set ran in October 1910 and the last three-coach in about April 1912.

Apart from the requirement to produce a shorter set for off-peak operation however, it is quite possible that there was more to these rearrangements than merely the need to correct an imbalance in accommodation, which could have been met more simply purely by downclassing some of the first class seats. It has been suggested that the LBSCR wished to abolish the intermediate trailers because, being without handbrakes, they were an operational liability.[13] It was quickly found that the motor coaches required a considerably longer maintenance period than the trailers, and it was therefore frequently necessary to uncouple individual coaches at Peckham Rye. An uncoupled trailer was effectively unbraked and had to be 'scotched' (fitted with wooden wedges between wheel and rail) to prevent movement, an inherently unsafe practice. By substituting driving trailers with hand-brakes the problem no longer existed. Correlating evidence for this is that the next batch of ac stock, ordered for the Crystal Palace lines before the South London reformations, consisted entirely of driving coaches with handbrakes.

13 Comments by 'SCWS' from article in *Live Rail* 148, December 1995, p313.

The only ac vehicles to be adapted from former steam-hauled stock rather than being built new, the fourteen South London line driving trailer composites were converted at Lancing from suburban seven-compartment third brakes formerly working in seven-coach 'bogie block' suburban sets. Dating from 1898-1901 and built at Brighton or by Birmingham RCW, they were of entirely conventional LBSCR design, lacking the plate frames, side-gangways and ornate interiors of the motor coaches. They were also shorter, narrower and less tall, being only 48ft long over body, 8ft wide and just over 11ft 9in high – this gave the reformed two-car sets a very mismatched appearance. Body alterations consisted of replacing the former van space and one third class compartment adjacent to it with two new first class compartments and a motorman's cab. Following conversion there were thus six third and two first class compartments, the latter being situated at the outer end of the coaches behind the cab, which had its own external doors. The third class compartments were narrow and straight-backed, just under 5ft 3in between partitions, and alternate partitions only reached to the tops of the quarterlights. The first class compartments were almost identical to the thirds, with only slightly greater leg room and a complete lack of armrests, only the upholstery cloth being significantly different. First class compartments seated four each side and third class compartments five, giving a seating capacity of sixty third and sixteen first. No attempt was made to design a distinctive cab front, two windscreens being merely superimposed upon a standard coach end, that on the offside having a slightly thicker frame. All subsequent ac stock driving vehicles were given exactly the same uninspiring front-end arrangements, and contrasted unfavourably with the bullet-nosed LSWR electric units which ran beside them through Clapham Junction from 1915.

These converted driving trailer composites, to LBSCR diagram number 281, were numbered 3225-30, 4057-60 and 4065-68. Although there were sixteen South London motor

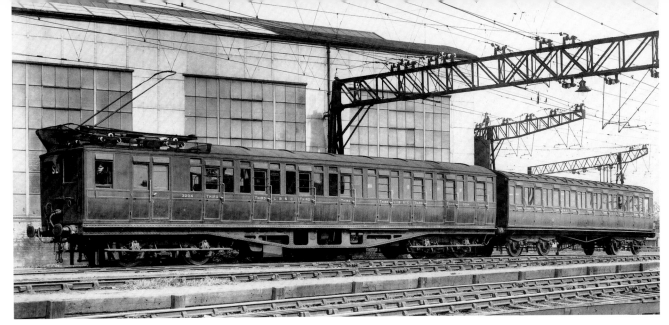

coaches only fourteen driving trailers were provided because it was found that the trailers required less maintenance cover, and as a result formations were continually changing. For this reason set numbers were no longer carried. Trains were formed of one set in slack hours and up to three in the peaks. The total seating capacity of one set was now 126 third and sixteen first. From photographs it would appear that all the motor coaches faced Victoria, so half must have been turned. The origins of the converted driving trailer composites are listed below:

ac DTC No.	Converted from 3rd Bk	Builder /Date*		Conversion Date*
3225	594	LBSCR	12/00	6/10
3226	1236	LBSCR	-/96	6/10
3227	1240	LBSCR	6/97	6/10
3228	1270	LBSCR	6/99	6/10
3229	1271	LBSCR	6/99	6/10
3230	1284	BRCW	12/00	6/10
4057	1268	LBSCR	12/98	6/11
4058	1320	LBSCR	6/00	6/11
4059	710	LBSCR	6/01	6/11
4060	718	LBSCR	6/01	6/11
4065	708	LBSCR	12/00	12/12
4066	1321	LBSCR	6/00	12/12
4067	1302	BRCW	6/01	12/12
4068	1303	BRCW	6/01	12/12

* Dates shown are the official book dates; see earlier comments regarding the LBSCR's six-monthly booking system. Actual outshopping dates could be up to five months previously.

These 'new' driving trailers were painted in a revised body side livery of overall umber with plain yellow lining-out and block lettering, and this became standard for all the ac stock prior to 1923. The motor coaches were initially altered to conform merely by painting over the upper panels in umber, but were later repainted properly on overhaul circa 1917-19. The front and rear indications were also altered, the plate on the offside being removed, the rotating rod shortened and the lamp position lowered so that the red glass covered it in the 'down' position. The driving trailers had this revised arrangement from the start. A third control jumper socket was fitted to vehicle ends, situated slightly to the right of centre about 18in above the buffer beams, and cab ends also gained brake main reservoir equalising pipe hoses. There were now therefore no fewer than six jumper hoses between vehicles (two brake, the bow collector air supply and three control), which must have made coupling and uncoupling something of a chore. These revised brake and control jumper arrangements were continued exactly for the CP and CW ac stock. Finally, it was evidently decided that the limited clearances created by the 9ft 5in width of the motor coaches posed a safety hazard and horizontal bars were provided over the passenger door droplights.

The Southern Railway knew these sets as SL stock, although there is considerable doubt as to how official it was as a rolling stock designation; even after conversion to DC operation, they were listed in Carriage Working Appendices only as 'two-coach motor set'. In April 1925 they were given route indicators of the same type as those fitted to the CP and CW driving cars, situated between the motorman's lookouts: these permanently showed SL at both ends. New SR numbers for the SL stock were 8601-16 (motor coaches, to diagram 677) and 9811-24 (trailers, dia. 790).

From 1924 onwards all vehicles except (probably) MThB 3204 were repainted in lined olive green livery and renumbered during overhauls at Lancing, and at the same time some toplights on the motor coaches were blanked-off to enable SOUTHERN RAILWAY lettering and the new numbers

LBSCR Baltic tank No. 329 *Stephenson* departs from Victoria with a Brighton fast service in about 1920. The first two coaches in the train are former ac South London line trailer firsts, modified for steam working in 1913. The centre seating bay in each has been converted into a toilet compartment with the external door sealed, handles removed and windows obscured. These vehicles later returned to suburban electric service on the Wimbledon – West Croydon line in 1930.

to be applied in their standard positions below the cantrail. The SR painted driving ends unlined green rather than black. The South London line ac stock was withdrawn in one go on 17th June 1928, and all vehicles were re-used in dc stock.

The fate of the eight redundant trailer firsts, for which no work could be found on electric services, should be mentioned here. Following a short period of storage, they were converted for steam haulage in 1913, with the central compartment converted into a pair of lavatories, one serving each half of the vehicle. Renumbered 167-174 in the steam series in order of their original electric numbers, they were then put to work on Brighton main line services, their width normally limiting route availability to services via the Quarry line. The fact that they were used on some of the fastest and most important business expresses for a time gives some idea of their superiority over most other LBSCR rolling stock of the period. They later returned to electrified suburban duties when they were rebuilt into four two-coach dc units for the Wimbledon to West Croydon line in 1930.

THE CRYSTAL PALACE LINES (SR 'CP') STOCK

Once the financial success of the South London line electrification was assured, no time was lost in getting conversion of the Crystal Palace lines underway. Due to clearance problems in Crystal Palace tunnel, the rolling stock built for these extensions was of more conventional LBSCR carriage dimensions and styling, all vehicles being 54ft long over body and only 8ft wide. With operating experience it had been decided to alter the stock arrangements so that all vehicles had driving cabs and formations could more easily be tailored to suit demand. 34 motor coaches (numbered 3231-64, to LBSCR carriage diagram 282) and 68 driving trailer composites (4001-56, 4061-64, 4069-76, dia. 283) were eventually provided. The gaps in the DTC numbering series were filled by the contemporary South London line driving trailers.

The initial contracts were with MACW for the first thirty motor third brakes (3231-60), dated 3rd August 1910, and for thirty driving trailers (4001-30) dated 9th October. At the same time 26 driving trailers (4031-56) were ordered from

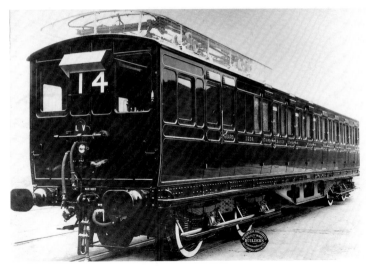

Left Crystal Palace motor third brake 3236 photographed when new outside the Saltley Works of its builder, MACW Co. in 1911. It is unlikely that the SMOKING plates on the cantrail above the first, second and third compartments lasted long after entering service.

Below CP driving trailer composite 4022 still looked relatively pristine in LBSCR umber brown livery when photographed in Selhurst depot in 1928. This was one of the few CP stock vehicles not to be overhauled and repainted at Lancing in the 1924-27 period prior to being withdrawn and then rebuilt for dc use. *O.J. Morris*

Bottom A pair of Crystal Palace three-coach sets in original condition at Streatham Hill in 1911. This photograph shows the sets as first formed, with a motor third brake on the end. The working shown is a test trip. Neither steam headcode discs nor the spurious headcode 91 were ever carried in passenger service.

A three-coach set of CP stock, showing the later formation with motor coach at centre, between Wandsworth Common and Clapham Junction with a Crystal Palace – Victoria service on 17th March 1928. The leading driving trailer composite is in its final condition, carrying SR green livery and a destination plate (showing Victoria) beneath the headcode panel. *H.C. Casserley*

Lancing, but Orders to Lancing took the form of a letter from the General Manager to the Works Manager, starting 'Dear Sir' and signed 'Yours faithfully', with no other references – not unlike ordering stock items off the shop shelf. Not surprisingly, some details have been lost. With 4031-56 went a contract with AEG for trailer electrical equipment, but no motor coach equipment contract can now be identified in the Rail Archives. A further contract with MACW dated 20th December 1911 covered a further four motor coaches (3261-64), four driving trailers (4061-64) and four spare motor bogies, electrical equipment for all these being covered by an order to AEG dated 29th August 1912. Finally Lancing constructed a further eight driving trailer composites (4069-76) to alleviate stock shortages in 1913 – the first four of these were ordered in January as 'urgently required and to be put in hand at once' and the remainder in May, by which time there seems to have been less of a hurry.

The layout of motor third brakes 3231-64, all built by Metropolitan, comprised a motorman's cubicle (again without its own external doors), guard's and seven third class compartments. This gave a seating capacity of seventy. These vehicles, which weighed 51 tons, were again given plate-frame underframe trussing and ran on 8ft wheelbase motor bogies. Electrical equipment included four Eichberg-type repulsion motors; these were similar to those fitted to the South London motor third brakes and interchangeable with them, but were described in contemporary reports as having a higher rating of 175hp (1 hour) and 100hp (continuous). Bow collectors were mounted on a flattened section of roof above the brake van, surrounded by a wire-mesh cage, and were similar to those on the earlier stock. However, the offside cab lookout and side droplight were of clear glass, suggesting that the internal

electrical equipment was differently positioned. The first thirty motor coaches were delivered in 1911 and the remaining four the following year.

The driving trailer composites had five third and three first class compartments, followed by a motorman's cab, giving a seating capacity of fifty third and 24 first. These vehicles had conventional underframe trussing, again with 8ft bogies, and weighed 26 tons. It is possible that a few of these driving trailers ran temporarily with the South London line motor coaches until all their own 'converted' driving trailers were ready. The first 56 (4001-56) entered service in 1911, four more (4061-64) came from MACW with the additional motor coaches in 1912, and the remaining eight (4069-78) from Lancing by the end of 1913. Following this there were still stock shortages so two further DTCs, 4084/5, were also added to the fleet in 1914, but these had originally been intended for projected electrification extensions and had a revised layout with four first and four third class compartments.

The cab ends were all fitted with similar head and tail-lighting arrangements to the reformed South London sets, but now mounted centrally below the headcode panel. Unlike the earlier stock, however, both ends of all vehicles, including the driving cabs, had two brake pipes from new as all were driving coaches and formations varied. Vehicle bodies were once more plated with thin aluminium sheet and the roofs had pronounced transverse ribbing. Numerical headcodes were introduced for the Crystal Palace line services, as related earlier; these were fitted to a panel between the motorman's lookouts. The interchangeable headcode numbers were on enamelled plates, white on a black background, and were illuminated from above at night by a hooded bulb.

Internally, the Crystal Palace stock lacked side gangways, conventional compartments being used; and although less well-appointed than the South London motor coaches, they were still apparently above-average for LBSCR suburban stock. Third class compartments were about 5ft 10in between partitions, seated five each side and were upholstered in red and black tapestry, with small armrests below the quarter-lights. First class seating was covered in blue cloth, and the four seats each side were separated by armrests (as already noted, a feature by no means universal in LBSCR first class compartments). The width between partitions in the firsts was 6ft 6½in. In their later years enamelled iron advertise-ment plates were affixed to the internal door panels, while many of the compartment partitions featured views of an LBSCR steamer en route from Newhaven to Dieppe, or of Old Shoreham Bridge. Smoking compartments were given box-type ventilators above the door droplights, rather than louvres. Externally, the coach body sides were again painted umber with yellow lining and lettering in the same style as on the reformed South London stock, while ends and under-frames were black.

The Crystal Palace stock vehicles were loose-coupled into three-coach sets, giving a seating capacity of 48 first and 170 third, but formations were not constant. Originally they were formed with a motor coach followed by two driving trailers, but this was soon changed so that the MThB was running between the DTCs. Six-coach trains were run in the peaks, and some eight-car formations were made up by adding another motor coach and driving trailer. The presence of a driving cab in every vehicle made for flexibility in set forma-tion, provided that the driving trailer was facing the correct way, of course.

After entering into Southern Railway ownership most vehicles were overhauled at Lancing between 1924 and 1927, where they were repainted olive green, including cab ends, and given SR numbers. Designated by the SR as CP stock, new coach numbers were 8567-8600 (motor coaches, SR diagram 676) and 9825-92 (trailers, dia. 791). The two CW DTCs (dia. 792) 4084/5 in the CP fleet became 9893/4. In 1925, concurrent with the opening of the final ac extension that April, brackets for destination plates were fitted directly below the headcode panel. Like the headcodes, these plates were of enamelled steel with white lettering on a black back-ground. From this date CP stock worked a few rush-hour services to East Croydon and Coulsdon North, and to both East and West Croydon via Crystal Palace on Sundays.

One three-coach CP set was temporarily fitted with exper-imental electro-pneumatic braking in 1927, a system in which the brake valves were electrically activated rather than relying on a drop in air pressure (See Chapter 3 for a fuller explanation.) Tests proved unsuccessful as the system required a constant electrical supply which could not be provided due to gaps in the overhead wiring and the lack of a motor-generator on the train, and the equipment was there-fore removed after a very short period.

All CP stock coaches were withdrawn between late 1928 and the middle of 1929 for conversion to dc stock.

THE COULSDON AND SUTTON 'CW' STOCK

The last section of the *Elevated Electric* system to open, down the main line from Balham to Selhurst and then on to Coulsdon North and Sutton via East and West Croydon respectively, did not come into operation until 1st April 1925. By this time the LBSCR had become part of the Southern Railway and, as recounted elsewhere, the writing was on the wall for the ac overhead system. Nevertheless the stock built for this extension was once again different, having features never before (or since) seen on the Southern Electric system. Planned by the LBSCR well before Grouping, the basic unit length was five coaches, but with all electrical equipment and luggage van space being concentrated in the short centre vehicle, officially known as a 'motor brake coach'. The passenger vehicles were similar to those of the CP stock, and their history is somewhat complicated because some were built prior to 1923 in anticipation of electrification and were temporarily used as steam-hauled coaches; indeed, some were never used for ac electric working. The Coulsdon and Sutton ac stock was classified CW by the Southern Railway, for 'Coulsdon and Wallington'.

There were three types of trailer coach in the CW fleet, which numbered eighty vehicles excluding the motor vans. Forty (SR numbers 9169-9208) were driving trailer thirds with motorman's and eight third class compartments. Twenty (9895-9914) were driving trailer composites, having motor-man's, four first and four third class compartments. The remaining twenty (9655-74) were trailer composites without driving cabs, and these also had four first and four third class compartments. Perversely, the non-driving coaches were without handbrakes once more, despite the problems appar-ently encountered with the original South London stock. Not all of these vehicles ever carried their allocated SR numbers. Due to the intervention of World War One, their history is very complex, and 42 vehicles intended for electric services were built prior to the 1923 Grouping.

The concept of the motor vans appears to date from 1921 when, as recounted in Chapter 1, the LBSCR had just with-drawn from a 1913 contract for 200 more motor coaches similar to the CP type ordered for the electrification exten-sions aborted due to the War. The contractors, who had been renamed Metropolitan Carriage, Wagon and Finance Co. Ltd (MCWF) in 1912, agreed this provided that twelve motor coaches were purchased anyway. At this time the railway was keen to continue limited suburban electrification, at least to West Croydon, as much work had already been carried out. To work these new services, the LBSCR now opted for a new type of 'motor brake coach', to all intents and purposes an electric locomotive with luggage van space, because the oper-ators considered that operational advantages would accrue from a 'more versatile power unit'; in other words one which could be used for shunting in carriage sidings. In fulfilment of the 1921 agreement, the first twelve were ordered for the West Croydon line from MCWF in February 1922, and a further nine in July, after completion of the Coulsdon and Wallington extensions had been agreed by the provisional SR Board and to pre-empt objections from dc supporters in the

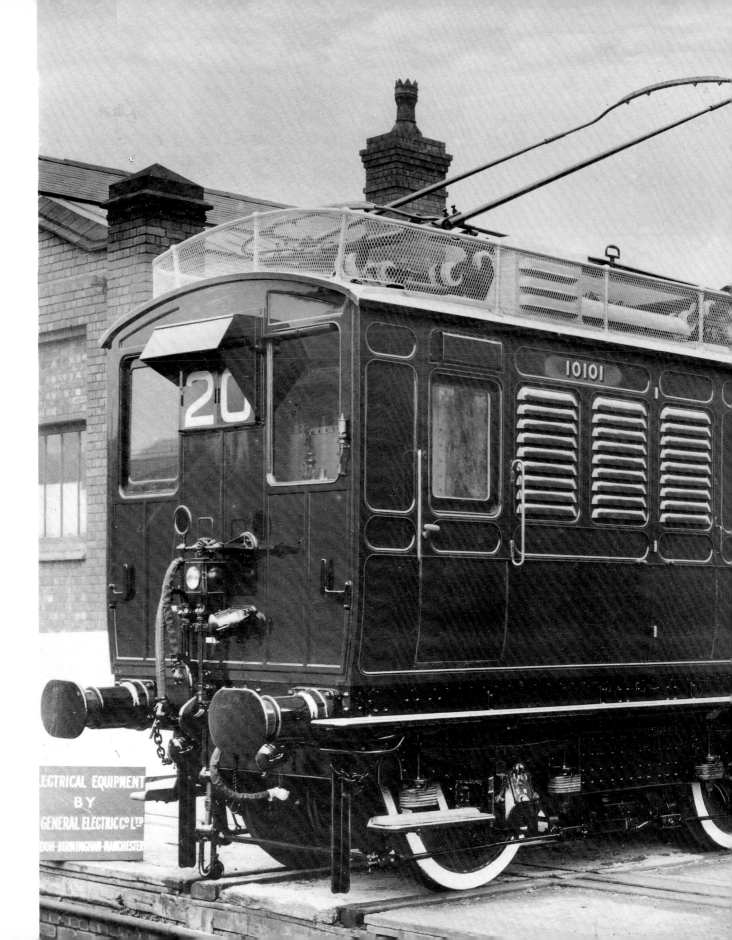

20

10101

ELECTRICAL EQUIPMENT
BY
GENERAL ELECTRIC Cº LTD
DON·BIRMINGHAM·MANCHESTER

A carriage builder's photograph of the first CW motor luggage van, 10101, outside Saltley Works in 1924. Livery is the original SR sage green, including the driving ends.
C.J. Marsden Collection

Steam push-pull driving trailer composite brake 6941 at Lancing in 1949. This vehicle, originally numbered 4117, was built as an ac driving trailer composite in 1921 for projected electrification extensions, but remained steam-hauled throughout its life. It was converted into its final configuration by replacement of one first class compartment and the cab by a driving/luggage area in 1931, and was withdrawn in 1958. *R.C. Riley*

LSWR and SECR camps. The official contract document was not in fact signed until December 1922, as one of the last acts of the pre-Grouping LBSCR.

The 21 motor vans were constructed at Saltley by MCWF in 1924 and were to SR diagram number 830. Built in the same style as the coaches with which they were to run, they were only 38ft 5in long and had driving cabs at each end. These cabs were rarely used except for shunting, the motorman's controls including two slow-speed notches for this purpose. Much of the internal space was taken up by electrical equipment, but there was a guard's and luggage compartment at the centre with a floor area of seventy square feet. The roof had four bow collectors, two for each direction of travel, raised and lowered by compressed air supplied from tanks on the roof. It is recalled that this system operated with a distinctive 'hiss'. Electrical equipment was of entirely British manufacture supplied by General Electric, and included four Oerlikon-type series-wound 250hp ac traction motors, main and auxiliary transformers and motor-driven cooling fans. The fans were supplied with air through prominent louvres on the vehicle sides, and made these vehicles relatively noisy when compared with previous ac electric stock. The bogies were again of pressed-steel construction

and had 3ft 7in diameter wheels, a wheelbase of 8ft 9in (the same as on the first third-rail units), and LBSCR-designed brake rigging. This was soon found to be simpler and superior to that fitted to dc suburban stock already in service, and was to become standard, possibly the only lasting design feature these unfortunate vehicles had. Overall weight of the motor vans, quickly dubbed 'milk vans' by the staff, was 62 tons. Southern Railway numbers were 10101-21, and all were delivered in SR olive green livery, lined except at the driving ends.

An initial batch of sixty driving trailer composites for the LBSCR's major suburban scheme had been ordered from Lancing works in November 1913; termed in the contract 'extension stock', they were intended to run with the Metropolitan-built motor coaches ordered at the same time. They differed from the otherwise similar Crystal Palace DTCs in having an additional first class compartment (and consequently one fewer third) as it was expected that there would be a greater demand for first class accommodation in the outer suburbs. Twelve vehicles (LBSCR numbers 4077-88) were built in 1914, and two, 4084/85, were completed and allocated to the Crystal Palace stock fleet where they remained until withdrawal. As the electrification for which they were intended could not be completed due to the war situation, the remaining ten were for the time being stored minus control equipment. Fifteen more (4089-4103) were completed by the end of 1915, again without controls, together with approximately 23 underframes, and were also placed into store. Notwithstanding a further order from Head Office for an additional seventy coaches by October 1916, work on electric stock then ceased due to a wartime-induced shortage of craftsmen at Lancing. Although firm evidence is lacking, it seems likely that at least some of these underframes were used under ambulance coaches then under construction. Electrification work recommenced on a small scale in October 1919, and nine further DTCs (4104-12) were completed early in 1920 utilising existing frames. These were followed by a July 1920 order for a further six (4113-18), completed early in 1921. Of these post-1918 vehicles, 4107-12 were built to the CP configuration with only three first and five third class compartments, reflecting a reduced demand for first class after the war.

Between September 1920 and April 1921 stored coaches 4077-83/86-98 were fitted-up for steam haulage and placed into traffic, 4099-4118 being dealt-with similarly in March and April 1921. The redundant cab became a small luggage area with its windows obscured by white paint. Of these, 4099-4118 were never converted for working in ac trains and remained steam-hauled, some being later adapted for use as push-pull driving cars. Four of them (4099/4104/13/14) were later converted into motor coaches and four (4107-09/12) into centre trailers in dc electric suburban units. Disregarding the two vehicles allocated to the CP ac fleet and the twenty remaining as steam stock, this gave twenty DTCs to be inherited by the Southern Railway in 1923. By now already

ten years old, they were belatedly equipped for ac electric working in 1923-24. Most remained in umber and only seven were repainted in olive green and given SR numbers prior to their withdrawal as ac vehicles.

The remainder of the Coulsdon and Wallington trailer coaches, a further sixty vehicles, were ordered in December 1922, another final act of the LBSCR. With the exception of three composite trailers and three driving trailer thirds built by MCWF in 1923, they were constructed at Southern Railway company workshops in 1923-24. Lancing was responsible for thirty complete coaches and for the underframes of the remaining 24. Surprisingly, all the wholly Lancing-built vehicles were all turned out in umber livery with LBSCR numbers; these included twenty driving trailer thirds numbered 3267-87 and ten trailer composites numbered 4119-28 (SR allocated numbers were 9189-9208 and 9659/60/64-71 respectively). The other underframes were hauled over to Eastleigh where the bodies were constructed in the former LSWR carriage workshops. This was because Lancing could not cope with the orders given to it due to a continuing shortage of skilled labour. All of these were turned out in olive green with SR numbering, and consisted of seventeen driving trailer thirds 9172-88 and seven trailer composites 9655-58/61-63. The MCWF-built vehicles were also turned out in green with SR numbers, these being DTThs 9169-71 and TCs 9672-74. Driving trailers painted in SR livery had unlined green cab ends, but on those in LBSCR umber they remained black. The CW driving trailer thirds were given SR diagram number 738, the trailer composites 768 and the driving trailer composites 792. A summary of all the trailer coaches which formed part of the CW fleet is shown in the table below.

A Summary of CW Trailer Coaches

Coach (dia.)	LBSCR Nos.	SR Nos.	Builder	Date Built	Livery
DTTh (738)	---------	9169-71	MCWF	1923-24	Green
DTTh (738)	---------	9172-88	Eastleigh¶	1923-24	Green
DTTh (738)	3268-87	9189-9208*	Lancing	1923-24	Umber
TC (768)**	---------	9655-58/61-63	Eastleigh¶	1923-24	Green
TC (768)	4119-28	9659/60/64-71*	Lancing	1923-24	Umber
TC (768)	---------	9672-74	MCWF	1923-24	Green
DTC (792)	4077-83/86-88	9895-9904§	Lancing	1914	Umber§
DTC (792)	4089-4098	9905-14§	Lancing	1915	Umber§

Notes:

*   SR number not carried

** according to Ashford works register, but 792 in other documents.

¶   Bodywork built at Eastleigh on Lancing underframes

§   Most retained LBSCR livery and numbers; only seven painted green and given SR number.

The driving trailer composites had a length over body of 54ft, the other two types being 6ft shorter. Both types of composite weighed 24 tons and the driving trailer thirds were one ton lighter. All had conventional underframe trussing and built-up 8ft wheelbase bogies, reported as giving an excellent ride. Dimensions, styling, construction details and interiors were virtually identical to the earlier CP stock, with straight cab fronts, two motorman's lookouts with a headcode panel between them, and the unusual head/tail light with swinging red glass. They carried destination plates below the headcode panels from new. Internally, the third class compartments in the driving trailer thirds were only 5ft 2in between partitions, but those in both types of composite trailer were 6 inches wider. Shortly after entering service, the smoking accommodation in forty CW trailers was reduced by one compartment, involving the replacement of 160 quarterlights etched SMOKING with plain glass. This work was covered by SR Head Office (HO) order number 92 (dated circa May 1925).

The CW stock was made up into loose-coupled five-coach sets, formed driving trailer third + driving trailer composite + motor van + trailer composite + driving trailer composite. This gave a total length of 254ft 4in and seating accommodation for 64 first and 240 third class passengers. As all the motor vans were painted Southern green but the trailers varied, with many coaches remaining in umber (including all but seven of the pre-1923 driving trailer composites), virtually all the sets must have presented a rather piebald appearance. Sets were run in pairs in the rush hours. The CW stock did not normally venture onto other sections of the *Elevated Electric* network, but the motor vans were additionally used for marshalling electric stock in Selhurst depot. The entire CW fleet was taken out of passenger service between March and September 1929, but the official withdrawal date for the motor vans was not until 31st December. This suggests that they were used for shunting withdrawn ac coaches destined for stripping at Peckham Rye shops after overhead services had ended.

Opposite top CW driving trailer third 9171, one of three built by Metropolitan and delivered in SR green, poses for its official photograph at Saltley, also in 1924. The very cramped dimensions of the eight compartments, only 5ft 2in between partitions, are obvious.

Left A pair of five-coach CW sets stand in Coulsdon North carriage sidings on 28th May 1927, waiting to form a service to Victoria. The leading vehicle is driving trailer third 3284 (LBSCR number) in umber brown with black driving end, followed by an unidentified driving trailer composite in Southern green. Note the baffle on the right of the headcode panel, presumably to prevent the headcode illumination affecting the motorman's vision at night.

A rare photograph of bogie brake van DS 56273 at Lancing in 1961, having just been withdrawn from departmental service. Converted from CW motor luggage van 10102 in July 1934, its body profile clearly indicates its LBSCR lineage and distinguishes it from later SR-built examples. *L.A. Mack*

EPITAPH

Soon after the Coulsdon and Sutton scheme had been completed it was decided to convert the ac network to third-rail dc in the interests of standardisation and compatibility, and it is worth here summarising the fate of the ac stock following abandonment of the system, although virtually all of it appears again later in this history. The SL motor coaches were converted to become the eight third-rail South London line units, most surviving in this form until 1954, while the driving trailer bodies were lengthened for use in other dc electric units. The CP motor coaches were converted for use in dc trailer sets numbered between 1168 and 1187, and remained easily identifiable by their underframes with characteristic plate-fame trussing. The remaining passenger vehicles from the CP and CW classes were also converted for use in dc stock. However, due to the relative youth of their underframes, these were not scrapped (as was done with other converted pre-Grouping stock) but instead most were lengthened to the standard SR 62ft length and re-used. A combination of circumstances resulting from this accounted for the fact that coaches with these underframes were to be the final SR electric vehicles with bodywork of pre-1923 design to meet their demise, the last of the 4 SUBs containing them (4501-4518) not being withdrawn from passenger service until 1960.

The most ignominious fate befell the 21 CW stock motor vans. Following withdrawal they were assembled in Selhurst yard, and then worked to Peckham Rye shops to be stripped of their electrical equipment, the last ac stock to be dealt with. There followed a period when they were dumped in Streatham Hill sidings for more than two years, their dereliction increasing while somebody decided what to do with them. Eventually 10108, presumably at one end of the scrap line, was sent to Eastleigh in about July 1933 for experimental conversion into a bogie goods brake van (HO 773 of 11th July

1933). The rebuilding proved very successful and the rest were therefore converted similarly between March 1934 and January 1935 (HO 790, 24th November 1933). As well as underframe and bogies, the central section of the body with its typical LBSCR profile was retained on conversion, although some flush-panelling was done. Original motor van numbers, 'new' brake numbers and conversion dates are as follows.

ac Motor Van	Goods Brake No.	Conversion Date
10101	56272	August 1934
10102	56273	July 1934
10103	56274	December 1934
10104	56275	July 1934
10105	56276	October 1934
10106	56261	March 1934
10107	56262	May 1934
10108	56263	September 1933 (Prototype)
10109	56264	June 1934
10110	56277	August 1934
10111	56278	January 1935
10112	56265	March 1934
10113	56266	April 1934
10114	56267	March 1934
10115	56268	April 1934
10116	56279	July 1934
10117	56269	May 1934
10118	56270	September 1934
10119	56280	October 1934
11020	56271	March 1934
11021	56281	August 1934

Most of these goods brakes were withdrawn in the 1950s, but about four were transferred to Departmental stock for use in engineer's trains and survived until about 1969.

DEPARTMENTAL STOCK ON THE AC NETWORK

Four self-propelled railcars, all petrol-engined with mechanical gearboxes, were acquired by the LBSCR Electrical Department between 1908 and 1915 for maintenance of the ac overhead fixed equipment and structures. Being self-propelled, they could operate when the current was discharged. Two were purpose-built and the others adapted from vehicles which had previously been in passenger service. They are described here in the order in which they appeared as service stock.

The first was supplied by Dick, Kerr and Co. in May 1908 at a cost of £2,261. It had a four-wheel chassis and the two engines, gearbox and controls were probably by Daimler. Its

Still carrying LBSCR numbers and livery, Dick, Kerr/Daimler overhead inspection and maintenance petrol railcars 1 (right) and 4 stand outside Peckham Rye shed sometime in 1927. Although of superficially similar design, No.1 was built for the purpose but No.4 was converted from a passenger-carrying vehicle. *JSM collection*

Below The peculiar Drewry overhead maintenance car No.2, again pictured outside Peckham Rye shed, on an unknown date. Note the two large toolboxes and winch mounted on the roof. *O.J. Morris*

box-like body had side-doors at each end, was painted overall in umber and lettered ELECTRICAL DEPARTMENT No.1. It was fully-equipped internally for wiring repairs, and the roof carried a platform, totally without handrails, on which maintenance staff stood while working on the overhead wiring. As with the later vehicles, large warning horns were fitted at either end, as the petrol engines were virtually silent compared to a steam locomotive. No.1 was used in the later stages of overhead catenary erection on the South London line.

Two petrol railcars, of broadly similar design to No.1 but with passenger seating, had been purchased by the LBSCR in August and September 1905 respectively, and used on the lightly-loaded service between Eastbourne and St Leonards. (The Board of Trade Inspector would not allow them to run through the tunnels to Hastings for some reason.) Again of Dick, Kerr manufacture with Daimler mechanical equipment, they proved unsuccessful and were withdrawn from capital stock in 1911. With extension of the electrified network, it was decided to adapt them for use as further overhead maintenance and repair vehicles. The first, No.3, was altered at Lancing, being ready in November 1911. Again painted umber, the interior was stripped, the centre-doors removed and the roof strengthened and provided with an inspection platform. The other was converted similarly at Brighton and became No.4, but retained its centre doors. It suffered a broken crankshaft while on trial following rebuilding, and was therefore not available for service until September 1912.

A final overhead inspection vehicle, No.2, was acquired from Drewry in 1915 at a cost of £560. This was fitted with a Baguley 20hp four-cylinder petrol engine, giving a (reputed) maximum speed of 31mph. Although also on a four-wheeled chassis it bore no resemblance to the other three, being both shorter and lower, and it weighed only 1 ton 12 cwt. Its

three-door superstructure was vaguely reminiscent of an eighteenth-century horse-drawn road coach. Given the numbering sequence, No.2 was probably ordered before it was decided to use the former passenger railcars.

All four service railcars lasted into Southern Railway ownership, although No.3 was withdrawn in June 1923 without ever carrying an SR service stock number. The others however all survived long enough to carry their new numbers, although as far as is known they remained in umber livery. No.1 became 342s and No.4 345s, both surviving beyond the end of ac passenger services to help with the dismantling of the overhead catenary. They were finally taken out of service in December and August 1931 respectively. No.2 became 343s and was lettered CROYDON ENGINEER. Following the demise of the ac system it was transferred to the Chief Mechanical Engineer's department at Eastleigh in April 1931. 343s was apparently still at Eastleigh in 1946, albeit with replacement bodywork, but its scrapping date is unknown.

5: LSWR AND SR DC SUBURBAN STOCK INTRODUCED 1914-38

It is now nearly fifty years since the last of the Southern Railway's first generation suburban electric stock was withdrawn from passenger service, and over twenty five since the last of the de-icing units converted from it was finally scrapped. Only one 1925-built motor coach, preserved as part of the National Collection at the National Railway Museum, York, remains as a physical reminder of the ubiquitous green trains with their distinctive domed ends which scurried past the back gardens of new semi-detached houses in the expanding south London suburbs between the wars. However, we can be grateful that their complex story was documented at the time by a number of dedicated contemporary observers, all the more so as many official records no longer exist. Their observations and notes form the basis for what follows in this chapter, which is thought to be the fullest overall description of the pre-World War Two SR electric suburban stock yet published in one book. The author makes no apologies for the variable amount of detail, as it is felt important to put into print that information which is available. Most of the coaches being discussed had bodies rebuilt from former steam-hauled suburban stock, often in a complicated (if ingenious) manner, and no attempt has been made to reconcile every steam-stock (or LBSCR ac electric) vehicle used with a particular suburban unit or trailer set coach. SR carriage diagram numbers are given where known, although the odd uncertainty persists. Extensive reference is also made to Head Office (HO) order numbers and an explanation of these is given in Chapter 3. The order in which the various types of dc suburban electric unit and trailer set came into service is summarised in Appendices 1 and 2 of this book. Coach numbers for all the units and trailer sets, as originally formed, are given in Appendix 2.

THE LSWR ELECTRIC UNITS

At the time when electric traction was first being contemplated for the suburban lines of the London and South Western Railway, in 1912, many of the services on these routes had just been equipped with new coaching stock. Formed into close-coupled four-vehicle 'bogie block' sets, which could be used in pairs at busy periods, these coaches had been in production at Eastleigh Works from 1902 until 1912, when the building programme was halted in anticipation of electrification. They were wooden-bodied with a semi-elliptical roof and, as was the custom on the LSWR at the time, compartments were provided for all three classes of accommodation within each set. Their designer was William Panter, who had been Carriage and Wagon Superintendent of the LSWR from 1885 until 1906. Father of Albert Panter, who designed the LBSCR South London line and Crystal Palace stock described earlier, he was largely responsible for the gradual improvement in LSWR coaching stock which took place from the turn of the century onwards. Hauled by smart new class M7 0-4-4 suburban tank locomotives out to the leafy south western suburbs at Epsom, Hampton Court, Shepperton and Hounslow, these trains were a great improvement on the collection of hard-riding four and six-wheeled coaches they replaced, even if speed and service frequency still left something to be desired.

Most other railways in Britain which had gone in for suburban electrification in the early years of the twentieth century followed American practice by building new rolling stock with saloon accommodation for their electric services. Apart from the North Eastern Railway's Tyneside lines and London's District Railway, already mentioned, railways where this type of stock was already used included the Liverpool–Southport and Manchester–Bury lines of the Lancashire & Yorkshire Railway, the Metropolitan Railway, and the tube lines of the Underground Group. Vehicles of this type provided plenty of standing room in the peaks and adequate seating capacity for slack periods, but were really designed for short distance 'rapid transit'-type operations, and were considered less suitable for middle distance suburban services such as those provided by the LSWR. At this time only the neighbouring LBSCR had constructed new electric stock with compartments, some albeit with side gangways, and specific reasons for this have already been given. A few railways, such as the Metropolitan, had used existing compartment coaches, suitably modified, as a small part of their electric fleet.

Given that one of the chief aims of the LSWR electrification scheme was to reduce operating costs, it would have been uneconomic to scrap steam-hauled suburban coaches, all of which had been in service for less than ten years at the time. Accordingly, Herbert Walker planned to have 'bogie block' sets converted to electric multiple-unit working, in which the coaches would be permanently coupled together in groups of three, with driving controls and a motor bogie at each end of

A typical eight-coach suburban electric train of the type used by the SR almost throughout its existence, and based on LSWR practice. The leading three-coach motor unit is 1790, built by the SR in 1931 using bodywork from LSWR six-wheelers spliced together and mounted on new underframes. It is followed by a two-coach trailer set made up of former LBSCR vehicles, followed by another three-coach motor unit comprising LBSCR bodywork on new or lengthened underframes. The ensemble was photographed in 1935 between Sydenham and Forest Hill, forming a London Bridge 'roundabout' working via Norwood Junction, Selhurst and Tulse Hill. *SR Official*

the unit. Two, three or even four units could be coupled together and driven from the leading cab if a longer train was required, although two units (six coaches) was the maximum originally intended, and on which the projected rolling stock requirement was based. Apart from the financial advantages of conversion, compartment stock provided more seats in a given vehicle length, an important consideration as some LSWR suburban routes were quite long.

The decision to go for units of three-coach length was based on passenger surveys but, even with two units coupled, severe overcrowding in third class occurred as peak loadings increased dramatically in the immediate post-World War One period. (As we shall see, this would later lead to the introduction of two-coach trailer sets, enabling rush-hour trains on the busiest routes to be lengthened to eight coaches.) Notwithstanding this, the three-coach motor unit remained the standard for electrified suburban routes of the LSWR, and later the Southern Railway, until 1942. A final point in favour of conversion was that the work neatly coincided with the first major overhauls for many of the vehicles concerned.

It was calculated that 84 three-coach units would be required for stage one of the electrification scheme, and these were to be provided by converting 63 of the 'bogie block' sets. A minimum specification for the traction equipment was drawn up by the LSWR electrical engineer Herbert Jones, and the contract for its design, manufacture and installation

was won by the British Westinghouse Electric and Manufacturing Company Limited of Trafford Park, Manchester, in March 1913. There were also to be eight spare traction motors with gears and cases. Surrey Warner, who had succeeded Panter as Carriage and Wagon Superintendent in 1906, was responsible for the bodywork and mechanical alterations required. In practice, however, much of this work was also carried out by British Westinghouse, who were given shop-floor space at Eastleigh for installation purposes. British Westinghouse became Metropolitan-Vickers Electric Company Limited (Metrovick) late in 1919 following its financial collapse and subsequent rescue.

Each unit was composed of two motor coaches with driving controls and a brake van, flanking a non-powered trailer coach. Each motor coach was equipped with a single motor bogie at the cab end, fitted with a pair of 275hp traction motors fixed to brackets supported by the driving wheel axles, an arrangement generally termed 'axle hung'. (The motors were also quoted as 280hp in some contemporary technical literature, but rating electrical machines was then, as now, a somewhat inexact science.) The motors were designed to the largest dimensions possible given the track gauge and wheel diameter, giving maximum power for rapid acceleration away from station stops and high speeds where appropriate. Fully-enclosed, with a thick casing and fan to ensure adequate heat dissipation, they were geared 59:21 to driving wheels of nominal 3ft 6in diameter. The motor bogie wheelbase was 8ft 9in and the leading wheels were fronted by guard irons of T-section. Power was collected from the upper surface of the conductor rail by cast iron pick-ups, generally known as collector shoes, mounted on wooden beams which were suspended between the axle boxes on both sides of the motor bogies. These collector shoes were five inches wide and the length of shoe in contact with the rail was nine inches. They had a small amount of vertical play, and contact with the live rail was maintained purely by gravity. The connecting cable from each shoe ran through a substantial copper fuse, mounted in a spark-arrester box (known as an arc-chute) suspended on brackets below the solebar, and then entered the coach body through a slot in the lower side panel above the footboard. A power (bus) line ran externally along the roof of each coach and was joined by flexible cables between vehicles throughout the length of the train, connecting all its collector shoes together.

The electrical equipment installed in these units proved very successful in service once early problems had been ironed-out and, with detail alterations, was adopted by the SR as standard for suburban stock up to 1936. The driving controls were designed to require a minimum of skill to operate, so consistent schedules were not dependent on the ability of the motorman. The multiple unit control system was electro-magnetic and featured automatic acceleration using current limiting relays, a new feature at the time. The track-side coasting marks which indicated to the motorman where to cut off power have already been mentioned. The master controller incorporated a 'deadman's handle'; downward pressure had to be applied to this at all times while the train was moving, or the brakes would automatically be applied. The master controller positions were as follows:

(A) *Switching*: In this position, the motors were connected in series, with all resistances in the circuit. As the train accelerated, the current drawn by the motors decreased, and this caused a system of current limiting relays to gradually switch out the resistances.

(B) *Full Series*: In this position the motors remained connected in series, but with all resistances switched out.

(C) *Parallel*: In this position, the motors were reconnected from series to parallel, and the resistances were switched back into the circuit. As the train continued to accelerate, the resistances were once again gradually switched out.

(D) *Full Parallel*: In this position, the motors remained connected in parallel, but with all resistances switched out. This position allowed the train to reach its maximum speed.

In normal service, the master controller could be turned straight to the Full Parallel position, and the control system 'notched up' through the sequence automatically until the balancing speed of about 55mph was reached. This was rarely attained in practice, however, because of the short distances between station stops. Although a continuous maximum speed of 57 mph was prescribed for performance, the LSWR specified a maximum free-running speed of 52mph on level track, with an availability of 20 hours a day, on two types of service: (i) stopping: average 1.3 miles between stations,

schedule speed 25mph, and (ii) semifast: average 2.75 miles between stations, schedule speed 34mph. For both types of service, a 25-second stop was to be allowed at each station.

The units were officially limited to 40mph anyway, due to rough riding at speeds greater than this, and the timetables were based on an average scheduled speed of 25mph. The manual control notches were used merely for shunting, or to prevent slipping and wheel-spin on wet and greasy rails – there is no evidence to suggest that this stock was any less prone to wheel flats than modern EMUs. Incidentally, the acceleration relays in each motor coach operated independently of those in the other motor coach(es) in the train.

An eight-core control cable, also routed along the roof and linked between vehicles in each unit by flexible jumpers, connected the control equipments in each motor coach. When the master controller was moved to activate the control system in one cab, the control wires were energised in sequence to send electrical signals at line voltage (600V dc) to activate the control system at the other end of the unit in an equivalent manner. Furthermore, by means of a jumper cable and associated socket on the cab ends, the control cable could be connected throughout the train when two or more units were coupled, enabling all the equipments in the train to be controlled from one cab. The system was developed by electrical contractors British Westinghouse and was based on that originally invented in the USA by Frank Sprague for tramway operation. First used in Britain in the Central London Railway motor coaches of 1903, it was the Sprague system that was really responsible for the successful adoption of multiple unit operation on electrified railways.

The switchgear, resistances and associated apparatus were housed in a compartment behind the driving cab. It had been decided to locate them here rather than on the underframe partly for ease of access for maintenance, but also because having their mass directly over the motor bogie increased the available adhesion. A further advantage was that most of the cabling could then be neatly routed through the cab. The resistances generated significant heat, and cooling air was provided through ventilating louvres, with horizontal slatting, in the coach sides. The control gear operated with a loud and ringing series of clicks, quickly giving rise to the epithet 'nutcrackers' being bestowed upon these units. Mica sheet was extensively used for insulation in the cab and electrical equipment areas.

Adding to the noise in the equipment compartment was the air compressor for the Westinghouse quick-acting air brake, one of which was situated in each motor coach. These compressors operated with a high-pitched 'ping-ping' sound; they were activated by brake application and exhaustion of the air in the system, and could therefore often be heard while the train was standing in a station. The Westinghouse air brake was used rather than the vacuum brake, previously standard on LSWR suburban stock, because it allowed faster station stops, necessary given the frequent and tightly-timed services planned. The brake and main reservoir pipes were situated at buffer-beam height, while the brake control in each cab was to the left of the master controller.

Other controls in the cab included a whistle, supplied with air from the brake compressor, and a hand-operated wind-screen wiper on the motorman's lookout. A brake pressure gauge and ammeter were also provided but, as with the LBSCR ac stock, no speedometer. (This latter feature was not provided in suburban EMU cabs until the EPB stock built from 1951.) Although the cabs of these units would appear spartan to modern eyes, working conditions in them were far better than on the footplate of a steam locomotive – they were draught-free, dry and clean. Trade Union concern was later expressed regarding the close proximity to the motorman of sparsely protected high-voltage cables, and in later SR units the power lines were re-routed outside the cab.

The two flexible jumper cables and their associated receptacles (sockets), enabling the power and control circuits of two or more units to be coupled together for multiple unit operation, were located on the cab fronts just below waist level. Underneath the motorman's lookout on the nearside was the power jumper, connecting the 600V dc bus lines running through each unit, and thus the current collector shoes through the entire train. This prevented an interruption to supply when one or more collector shoes passed over a gap in the conductor rail at points and crossings. Its equivalent receptacle on the opposite side was mounted on a thick wooden plate, to insulate the bodywork from stray current, sparks or heat. The control jumper, situated on the left, had eight cores to connect the control lines of each unit together. Both power and control receptacles had spring-hinged covers to prevent the ingress of water when not in use and which also acted to lock in the jumper cable plugs when correctly located, preventing them being shaken free by train vibrations. Similar arrangements connected the power and control cables between vehicles in each unit, but situated at roof height as they were not normally uncoupled in everyday service. With the brake cables at buffer-beam height but the jumper connections three feet higher, it was necessary for staff to have access at both track and platform-level to couple or uncouple units.

Externally, the most striking feature of the new trains was the driving ends of the motor coaches, which were heavily rounded to give a blunt 'torpedo' shape in plan view, with a domed roof above. The vehicles all retained their original panelled appearance, with the raised panelling now being extended around the nose ends. The basic bodywork was wooden, but steel sheeting was used for the driving cabs and equipment compartments. Typical LSWR styling features included the louvres above the droplight on each door, the door and commode handles, and the deep solebars. The underframes were of composite construction, with steel channel solebars and oak stretchers. Where the stretchers carried the bogie pivots, however, they were reinforced or substituted with steel channel to better withstand the increased drawbar pull and acceleration of electric traction. The buffer beams below the cab ends were straight, and therefore the corners of the underframe jutted out below the bodywork. The tip of the 'nose', however was 1ft in front of the bufferbeam, and later photographs show a small section

removed to provide adequate clearance for the coupling. Conventional round side buffers and screw couplings were provided at unit ends, but simple pivot blocks, retained from the 'bogie block' sets, coupled individual vehicles within each unit. The width over body of all the vehicles was 8ft 0¾in, increased by 10in by the step-boards and commode-handles. Unpowered bogies at the inner ends of the motor coaches and on the centre trailer were of the Fox pressed-steel type with an 8ft wheelbase, and were also inherited.

As delivered, the first few units had two equal-sized lookout windows on the nose ends, with plain panelling between, and it was in this condition that they appeared in early publicity photographs. By the time that public services commenced, however, the headcode system had been devised and put into operation. On the trains, this consisted of a rectangular opal-glass plate, illuminated from behind at night, mounted on a protruding metal frame replacing the panel between the motorman's lookouts. An interchangeable iron stencil plate, painted black and showing a particular headcode letter, was attached to this by means of brackets and a clip. A full set of headcode stencils was carried in a rack inside each cab and, as they sometimes dropped-off en route, a stock of spares was kept at principal terminal stations.

A plain plate, or a stencilled bar plate could be pushed into a slot above the main panel so that the headcode could be modified (e.g. S and S with bar above). Brackets for destination boards were fitted below the cantrail on the sides of the motor coaches in front of the guard's doors. The boards themselves, however, were only used when an unfamiliar service was operating, such as to Kempton Park on race days. The rear headcode panel was left plain and acted as an unofficial 'last vehicle' indication to signalling staff, although the statutory red oil lamp also had to be carried. The headcode stencil plates could be changed from inside the cab, the offside lookout being made to open outwards for this purpose. The heavy framing it then acquired gave an asymmetric appearance to the cab end which was a familiar feature of much SR electric stock built subsequently. A large ventilator hood was added above the headcode panel, and the unit number painted on this.

In order to give the electric services a new and modern image, the three-coach units were painted in a different livery from the salmon pink and brown of the steam trains they superseded. It is probable that the choice of shade was influenced by Herbert Jones' visit to the USA in 1912. The basic colour was sage green, lined out in black and yellow and with mid-brown window mouldings. This livery was carried around the cab noses but inner carriage ends, underframes and bogies were black. The roofs were off-white lead, which very quickly weathered to mid-grey in service. The class of accommodation was indicated by 1 or 3 as appropriate on the narrow waist panel directly below the droplight on each compartment door. The letters LSWR and the coach number appeared in gilt transfers, shaded black, at waist level on the two panels nearest to the centre of the coach.

The electric units were numbered from E1 to E84. They were not all identical, this being a consequence of the make-up of the original 'bogie-block' sets from which they were converted. The main variations concerned overall length and the layout of the seating accommodation. Few modifications were carried out to the bodywork and passenger areas of the vehicles concerned, mainly for reasons of economy. These units were, incidentally, the first trains on the LSWR not to have three classes of seating accommodation, second class being an anachronism which Walker was keen to end. The War conveniently enabled him to do away with it completely in 1918. The whole rebuilding exercise must have involved some very creative planning by staff in Surrey Warner's design offices at Eastleigh.

Before conversion, the LSWR 'bogie block' sets were formed of two 51ft third brake vehicles with seven compartments, flanking a 49ft tri-composite arranged 11122233 (i.e. three first class, three second and two third) and a 51ft tri-composite. In most of the sets used – i.e. those built from September 1905 onwards – the compartments were arranged 11112223. In sets built prior to September 1905, this vehicle was a bi-composite arranged 11111222. Sets were admitted into Eastleigh Carriage Works in groups of three (twelve coaches) or six (24 coaches) and converted to form four or eight electric units respectively. In each group of three sets, one was of the earlier type incorporating a 51ft bi-composite. The method of conversion from three sets is shown below, and the conversion from six was similar except that twice the number of vehicles was produced. Batches of electric units produced from groups of six 'bogie block' sets were E1-E8, E25-E32, E33-E40 and E65-E72.

The third brakes were all converted into six-compartment driving motor third brakes, the driving cab, equipment compartment and guard's van occupying the former van space and the compartment adjacent to it. After conversion, these vehicles were numbered from 6701 upwards. The two 51ft tri-composites were converted into five-compartment driving motor composite brakes, the cab, equipment and van replacing two second class compartments and the one third. The inner first class compartment and the remaining second class compartment next to it were both downclassed to third, the resulting vehicle therefore having three first class compartments and two thirds. Rather meanly, the former first was reduced from 6ft 6in to 6ft by increasing the thickness of both partitions by 3in. These vehicles were numbered from 7201 upwards. The tare weight of all the motor coaches was quoted as 36 tons nominal, plus or minus 2cwt. An unusual feature was the additional quarterlight for the guard, located between the van doors and the first compartment.

There were three types of trailer composite used in the electric units. The 51ft bi-composite merely had its three second class compartments downgraded to third, giving a vehicle with three third and five first class compartments. The first to be altered was numbered 7551, subsequent conversions being numbered 7555, 7559 and upwards in sequence to 7631. Of the three 49ft tri-composites, one was altered by opening out the three second class compartments to form a first class saloon, and after conversion contained two third class compartments, the first class saloon and three

ordinary first class compartments. The first of these vehicles was numbered 7552, subsequent conversions being 7556, 7560 and upwards in sequence to 7632. The other two had their former second class compartments downgraded to third class, thus giving a vehicle with three firsts and five thirds. The first two were numbered 7553 and 7554, subsequent conversions following on 7557/58 and upwards in sequence to 7633/34. This type of trailer ran between a motor third brake and a motor composite brake. The tare weights of trailers were quoted as 22 tons (7552/3 etc) or 23 tons (7551 etc). From these conversions, three types of electric unit were formed:

Unit Numbers E1, E5, E9 etc. to E81 (Total 21 units) In these units, two 67xx motor third brakes flanked a 7551-type 51ft composite trailer. This gave an overall length of 159ft 5in and a total seating capacity of forty first and 150 third.

Unit Numbers E2, E6, E10 etc. to E82 (Total 21 units) In these, two 67xx motor third brakes flanked a 7552-type 49ft composite trailer (with saloon). This gave a length of 157ft 5in and seating of 42 first and 140 third.

Unit Numbers E3, E4, E7, E8 etc. to E83, E84 (Total 42 units) In these, a 67xx motor third brake was followed by a 7553-type 49ft trailer composite and a 72xx motor composite brake. The unit was marshalled so that the first class compartments in adjacent vehicles were together. Their overall length was also 157ft 5in, and they seated 48 first and 130 third.

Conversion work started at the end of 1913, and was in full swing when World War One broke out the following August. This obviously created supply and manpower difficulties at Eastleigh Works, but at least the consequent traffic reductions enabled enough of the 'bogie block' sets to be withdrawn for conversion into electric trains without causing an acute stock shortage. As a result of the supply problems, units were completed with minor differences in various fittings, such as roof ventilators and upholstery. The four roof ventilators above the equipment compartment on the motor coaches, for example, were either of the 'shell' type or one of two sizes of the 'torpedo' pattern, so it appears that Eastleigh was using up spares.

Third class compartments seated five each side and were 5ft 6in between partitions, except those downgraded from first or second which had an extra four or six inches of legroom, the former being those in the 7553-type 49ft trailers. The seats were of the bench type with fixed wire-framed cushions, and (unlike the 1925 SR contractor-built stock, described later) the upright cushions had headrests. Most were upholstered with red and black tapestry, but a few units had a shiny black 'American cloth', while others had rattan – these variations were again probably due to wartime supply difficulties. First class compartments were 6ft 6in between partitions, seated four each side with end and three intermediate armrests, and were upholstered in blue cloth with loose 'lift-out' cushions. In the saloons, opened out from three second class compartments, the centre door on each side was sealed, and a five-seat divan (without headrests to obstruct the view through the windows) was positioned along each

LSWR three-coach electric unit E7 shortly after entering traffic. *R.N. Coombes collection*

side. The idea of these saloons was allegedly to impart a 'club'-style atmosphere to first class suburban travel, an idea which never caught on. (This seems obvious in retrospect as, with only one quarter of the units having saloons, the odds of one appearing regularly on a particular service were not high.) In contrast to contemporary LBSCR electric stock, heaters were fitted, located under the seats. Each compartment was illuminated by two series-wired 75V 40W lamps in opal-glass bowls, the pattern differing in the two classes. Both heating and lighting worked at line-voltage, and the lighting circuits were originally controlled independently in each vehicle. There was no cab lighting, so at night the motorman had to open the rear of the illuminated headcode box to read his notices.

Delivery of the electrical equipment commenced in September 1913 but the first unit, later numbered E4, was not released from Eastleigh works until the following June. It was tested on the Wimbledon–East Putney line where several problems came to light – in particular, the automatic relay control failed to function properly, apparently as a result of voltage drop. British Westinghouse claimed that the problem was not their responsibility, but Jones insisted otherwise. In due course these trial difficulties were overcome, but they did cause delay to the delivery of electrical equipment. The second unit appeared in November 1914 and the rest then came steadily, if not exactly quickly.

Following the completion of Unit E4 in June 1914, E1-E3 and E5-E45 followed in November 1914 continuously to September 1915; E46-E48 in December 1915; E49-E54 in February and March 1916. E55-E80 and E83 were completed between June 1916 and April 1917, with no completions in some months. E81, E82 and E84 were completed in August 1917.

On delivery, the electric units were allocated to the new running and repair sheds erected adjacent to the power house at Durnsford Road, Wimbledon. Final preparation for service carried out here included the fitting of collector shoes. With the trial problems solved a nucleus of motormen was trained, and public services on the Waterloo–Wimbledon via East Putney route commenced on 25th October 1915, with units E20, E28 and E41 being noted in service on the first day. The other services commenced during the following year (as related previously) and, as listed above, the final units of the 84 were delivered in August 1917. Other early problems included a number of instances of burnt-out compressors, and on one occasion it is reported that equipment in unit E42 'fused' and caught fire, burning a large hole in the roof of one motor coach. However, the electric stock soon settled down to relatively reliable operation, with few mishaps being attributable to their propulsion system.

On 1st January 1923 Grouping took place, the LSWR becoming (both in size and influence) the major component of the new Southern Railway. Comparatively little changed on the suburban lines at first, the electric trains retaining their green livery with yellow and black lining. Renumbering soon took effect, E1-E84 becoming 1201-1284. Individual vehicles also took revised numbers, the new SR scheme being somewhat tidier than that of the LSWR which preceded it. The renumbering was as follows (carriage Diagram numbers in the SR series were also allocated):

(a) Motor third brakes 6701-6826 became 8001-8126 (Diagram 660)

(b) Motor composite brakes 7201-7242 became 8751-8792 (Diagram 690), in units 1203/04, 1207/08 and every third and fourth unit upwards to 1283/84.

(c) 51ft trailer composites 7551/55/59 etc to 7631 became 9414-9434 (Diagram 752), in units 1201/05 and each fourth unit upwards to 1281.

(d) 49ft trailer composites with saloon 7552/56/60 etc to 7632 became 9351-9371 (Diagram 750) in 1202/06 and each fourth unit to 1282.

(e) 49ft trailer composites 7553/54/57/58 etc to 7633/34 became 9372-9413 (Diagram 751) in 1203/04, 1207/08 and each third and fourth unit to 1283/84.

Unit renumbering was carried out promptly, as the figures were hand-painted and it was a job which could easily be done at a maintenance depot. Individual coaches took rather longer. Here renumbering was only carried out on repaint following general overhaul as the transfers were inaccessible under layers of varnish, and it was not until about 1929 that the last was done. The new carriage livery adopted by the SR was very similar to that of the LSWR, the sage green base colour remaining identical to start with. The words SOUTHERN RAILWAY in gilt with black shading appeared at the centre of each vehicle below the cantrail, with coach numbers at the same height at either end, and the complex lining-out was retained.

Following representations from guards as early as 1924, possibly after hearing that the new 1925 stock was to have them, the motor coaches of 1201-1284 were eventually fitted with guard's duckets (projecting side lookouts on the left hand side only, as used by the guard when facing the running direction; for most stations, this was the guard's 'platform side') in the latter half of 1928. Situated in place of the quarterlight between the guard's door and the first compartment, they increased the nominal overall width of the units to 9ft. This work, together with various other very minor alterations, was authorised as part of HO 335 (dated 2nd June 1928) and was carried out at Eastleigh. Modifications to the Fox trailer bogies, involving replacement of the original fixed bolsters with moving bolsters, were carried out between August 1929 and August 1933 (HO 391, issued 8th November 1928) in an unsuccessful attempt to improve their riding.

In the suburban area, 1201-1284 were confined to the routes for which they were originally intended (including the 1925 extension to Dorking and Guildford) until about 1938, due to clearance problems on some ex-LBSCR and SECR routes which had been electrified. It was not until after rebuilding and lengthening from 1934 onwards, and after the reconstruction of Crystal Palace tunnel, that they could be worked over all suburban routes. At the end of 1932, however, several of them were banished from suburban territory to Brighton, to work stopping services on the newly-electrified

line from there to West Worthing. This was because the suburban electric units authorised for this service (units 1797-1801, converted from ex-LBSCR steam stock) were considered to be of too low a standard; moreover, the new Brighton – West Worthing service was an economy measure to reduce the 4 LAV requirement by seven units (see Volume 2). The units concerned were all of the '1203' type including a motor composite brake, and the first class compartments in these vehicles were downclassed to third, giving new seating totals of 24 first and 160 third. This was done properly, at Selhurst depot, the first class seating actually being taken out and replaced by third class. Eight units were dealt with in this way, these being 1211/12, 1223/24, 1235/36, 1247 and 1259. The downclassed coaches were renumbered 8596-8602/04 in the motor third brake series as shown below. (Note that the number 8603 was not used.)

Renumbering of Downclassed Motor Brake Composites in ex-LSWR Suburban Units Transferred to Brighton – West Worthing Services

Unit No.	MCB	Renumbered as MThB	Conversion Date
1211	8755	8596	12/32
1212	8756	8597	11/32
1223	8761	8598	11/32
1224	8762	8599	11/32
1235	8767	8600	11/32
1236	8768	8601	11/32
1247	8773	8602	12/32
1259	8779	8604	4/33

The Carriage Working Notice for October 1934 shows that eleven units were required in traffic at peak times, and units 1220/48/60/71, in unmodified condition, were also reported to have been working on the coastal service at this time. In December 1934 all '1201' class units working on the south coast, modified and unmodified, were returned to the London area. Their coastal duties were taken over by 'new' 2 NOL units, but passengers would have noticed little difference as these were also converted from LSWR steam stock.

On return to suburban duties, those units which had been working on the coast had their downclassed seating and original coach numbers restored. By this time, work had just commenced on rebuilding the entire class on standard 62ft underframes to provide approximately the same seating and electrical layout as in later units. This lengthening work is covered later in this chapter. In the meantime, in spite of the modifications mentioned above, deterioration of the original trailer bogies led to their replacement by the standard SR (SECR) 8ft wheelbase type, this substitution taking place in many instances before the unit concerned was rebuilt. These new bogies, which also went to the LSWR trailer sets, were ordered from Lancing in two batches of 100 to HO 809 (23rd March 1934) and HO 854 (29th March 1935).

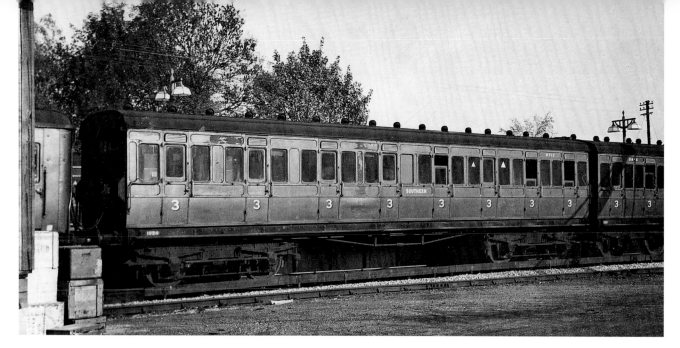

Showing the inevitable signs of war-damage repairs, LSWR trailer set 1024 (originally T24) stands at Hayes in 1946. The leading vehicle, 8912, is a 49ft diagram 720 vehicle originally altered from a 'bogie block' composite. *H.C. Hughes*

THE LSWR TRAILER SETS

The immediate post-war period saw significant peak-hour traffic increases on the electrified suburban lines of the LSWR, leading to severe overcrowding in third class at these times. The solution of lengthening the motor units to four coaches was resisted partly because the company did not want to spend money hauling empty coaches around off-peak when the extra capacity was not needed, and partly because parts of the network were limited to 6-coach trains, and the use of two different EMU formations would not have been operationally practicable. Instead, Jones hit upon the idea of using two-coach trailer sets which could be marshalled between a pair of motor units to lengthen peak-hour services from six to eight cars, and left in sidings at other times. On 29th May 1919 the decision was therefore taken by the LSWR Locomotive and Carriage Committee to add twelve of these trailer sets to the electric fleet, and a further twelve were authorised two months later. Cheaply converted from twelve more of the 'bogie-block' sets at a cost averaging just £500 per vehicle, the trailer sets were originally numbered from T1 to T24.

The brake vehicles were all converted into nine-compartment thirds by the simple expedient of converting the luggage van into two more compartments. The buffers and drawgear were left at the ex-brake end, and here also was fitted a horizontal box at waist level on which were situated the jumper cables and associated sockets. Vacuum cylinders and batteries were removed from the underframe, these being unnecessary for electric working, and rather feeble electric heaters were installed beneath the seats. These alterations reduced the tare weight to about 22 tons. Carriage numbers were 7401/04/05/08/09/12/13/16/17/20/21/23 and odd numbers up to 7447.

The 51ft composites had their first class compartments downgraded to third (the ex-seconds had already had this done on abolition of this class in 1918) to produce a vehicle with eight third class compartments. Other changes were the same as above, the end of the coach with wide compartments being equipped with side buffers, screw couplings and jumper cables. Carriage numbers were 7402/06/10/14/18/24/28/30/36/38/40/46. The 49ft composites were dealt with in the same manner, again to produce a vehicle with eight compartments. The outer end was again that with the wider compartments. Numbers were 7403/07/11/15/19/22/26/32/34/42/44/48.

These converted vehicles were then used to form two variations of trailer set, each type making use of one former third brake and one former composite, The twelve sets numbered T1,3,5,7,9,11,14,15,18,19,20 and 23 had 51ft nine-compartment (7401 type) and 51ft eight-compartment (7402 type) vehicles, giving a length of 107ft. The remainder, numbered T2,4,6,8,10,12,13,16,17,21,22 and 24, were formed of 51ft nine-compartment and 49ft eight-compartment (7403 type) coaches, and were 2ft shorter. All sets therefore had seventeen compartments, seating 170 third class passengers. The coaches in each set were close-coupled with bar-couplers inherited from the 'bogie-block' sets, and in width and height were the same as the motor units. Livery was also the same, but the outer ends were painted black.

Conversion took place over a period of three years, from January 1920 until December 1922, and completion dates for each set were:

T1, T2, T6 – 1/20; T3-T5, T7 – 4/20; T8-T10 – 5/20; T11, T12 – 10/20; T13-T18 – 12/21; T19 – 11/22; T20-T24 – 12/22.

The first trailer sets into traffic were allocated to trains on which overcrowding was particularly severe, such as those on the Kingston Roundabout route. They were soon found to be a cheap and effective way of relieving congestion, although their lack of driving cabs posed operating problems. In particular, the need to remove them from the middle of an eight-coach train at the end of the rush-hour meant that a certain amount of blind-ended shunting was required. This involved a pilot man leaning out from the leading compartment of the trailer set and giving hand signals (flags by day, hand lamps after dark) to the motorman in the cab of the motor unit pushing it, a somewhat risky practice. In spite of these problems, however, the 3+2+3 motor unit + trailer set + motor unit formation became standard on most SR electrified suburban routes until 1942. They could not operate on Hounslow loop services because the platforms at Barnes Bridge were too short. Further details regarding the operating arrangements involved in berthing trailer sets appear later in this chapter.

The trailer sets were renumbered 1001-1024 in 1923, and as with the motor units all were eventually given SR livery on overhaul. In the new coach numbering scheme, LSWR 7401-type 51ft nine-compartment vehicles became 8925-48, to SR carriage diagram number 722. Of the eight-compartment coaches, the 51ft 7402-type (to SR diagram 721) became 8913-24, formed in sets 1001/03/05/07/09/11/14/15/18/19/20 /23, while the 49ft 7403-type (dia. 720) became 8901-12 in sets 1002/04/06/08/10/12 /13/16/17/21/22/24. As time went on they could be seen all over the system, coupled between pairs of motor units of any origin. The only major modification in SR days was the replacement of the original Fox pressed-steel bogies (which had already been subjected to the same unsuccessful alterations as those under 1201-1284) with the standard SR type used on other electric stock; replacement began in 1934 and was completed about 1936. At about this time consideration was given to lengthening the coaches on new 62ft underframes in a similar manner to the motor units, but this was never carried out.

GENERAL COMMENTS ON THE SR DC SUBURBAN STOCK

The rolling stock arrangements of the pioneer LSWR electrification were continued by the Southern Railway, dominated as it was by former South Western management and electrical engineering staff. The reasons why the low-voltage direct current third-rail system was adopted have been discussed in previous chapters. The stock of 84 LSWR three-car units inherited by the SR on its formation had been increased to no less than 466, all of the same basic layout, by the time the last of the suburban electrification schemes (the new line from Motspur Park to Chessington) was completed in 1939. Up until this time, any vehicles written-off by accident were replaced as a matter of course. The basic arrangements of the units were the responsibility of Herbert Jones, now SR Chief Electrical Engineer, who also expanded the unwieldy LSWR practice of using two-coach trailer sets coupled between pairs of the electric units to make eight-car trains for the rush hours. Hence the fleet of trailer sets was also enlarged from 24 to 212 in the same period. While the more practical solution of using four-coach motor units as

proposed for the SECR by Alfred Raworth was postponed for the time being, it will become clear that in other respects Raworth's influence increased as the electrified network grew.

As the various suburban electrification schemes got under way, so an ongoing programme of rolling stock production was organised. Although for financial and publicity purposes each batch of units was authorised for a particular group of newly-electrified lines or as a result of traffic increases, all had many features in common and as time went on they became mixed up. However it was not until 1939, with the completion of clearance work on former SECR routes, that all varieties became completely interchangeable over the whole third-rail suburban network. The formation comprised two motor coaches, each including motorman's cab and guard's van, flanking a trailer. Between vehicles the units were close-coupled, and had side buffers and conventional screw couplings only at the cab ends. Except for the series built new for the Guildford and Dorking electrification of 1925 (1285-1310), which for reasons given later were shorter, all new or reconstructed underframes for the suburban units were 62ft long, somewhat longer than most steam stock. Nearly all the units on these frames had eighteen third class compartments seating 180, and seven first class seating 56, although there were variations in the arrangement of the compartments and their distribution between vehicles. Overall length of units was 193ft 5in (with the exception of the '1285' class). All underframes were of entirely steel construction. As explained in Chapter 3, the three-coach suburban electric units were not given any special class designation, being indicated on working notices simply as 3, 6, 8 or 9 (depending on the number of units coupled in the train). Although the main line stock was given codes to distinguish the different types for operating purposes (eg 4 LAV) the standard suburban units remained just 3 until their 'augmentation' into four coaches commenced in 1942, after which the lengthened units became 4 SUB.

A numbering scheme for the dc electric units and trailer sets, using four-figure numbers intended to be in a block from 1001 upwards, was worked out by an officers' joint rolling stock working party just prior to Grouping. (The SR also formed much of its steam stock into semi-indivisible sets of two or more coaches, each set being given a one, two or three-figure number.) Initially, Western section motor units were numbered from 1201, starting with the original LSWR examples, Eastern section units from 1401 and Central section dc units from 1601. It was later necessary to fill up available gaps in these series with additional units converted after 1930, but by this time the suburban electric stock was gradually becoming common-user throughout the network anyway. The trailer sets were initially numbered upwards from 1001, 1051 and 1121 for Western, Eastern and Central section examples respectively. Again, once the main schemes had been completed, the need for additional sets in the 1930s was met by filling the gaps, and when the 1001-1200 series ran out it became necessary to invade the steam series downwards as far as 989. The trailer-pairs were defined as sets rather than units because they had no multiple unit control equipment. SR official documents used both terms interchangeably for powered formations, but trailer sets were always 'Sets'.

The carriage numbering scheme worked out for the SR provided blocks of numbers for the dc stock: MThB from 8001, MCB from 8751, Th from 8901, TC from 9301; ac stock was given ad hoc blocks of numbers in these ranges: 8567-8616, 9169-9208, 9655-9674, 9895-9914. After the ac stock was withdrawn, its numbers were used for dc conversion stock, and the range 9751-9999 was then used for all classes of carriage.

With the same careful husbandry practised by its LSWR predecessor, the Southern Railway utilised bodywork of existing compartment (mostly suburban) stock of its constituents as the basis of all but 55 of the new motor units and all of the trailer sets. Steam-hauled vehicles from all three constituent companies were converted, as well as LBSCR-design SL, CP and CW ac electric stock. Apart from being far less costly than building completely new trains, these arrangements gave further life to hundreds of otherwise obsolete coaches which were in many cases less than half-way through their designed life span. However, as we shall see later, by the mid 1930s the rolling stock engineers were having to scrape around for suitable vehicles. On the negative side, the converted bodies continued to appear old-fashioned and, more importantly, had virtually no structural integrity in the event of a collision.

The bodies used for conversion were all of traditional wooden construction with joints covered by raised panelling, and until 1936 this was generally perpetuated when new sections of bodywork were incorporated to make up the required length, in order to give a uniform appearance. When the original LSWR '1201' series units were lengthened to fit on standard-length frames between 1934 and 1940, however, some vehicles had new or replacement sections panelled with plain steel sheet, giving a rather less tidy appearance readily apparent in photographs. A much neater look resulted when the entire lower body panelling was dealt with in this way, such as later '1201' class rebuilds and 24 coaches of the final trailer set conversions (vehicles 9825-30 and 10401-18).

On the motor coaches of units with converted wooden bodywork of all three origins, the cab and van sides were constructed of steel sheet on teak framing as far back as the leading van door (or to the first compartment on SR conversions with LSWR bodywork), while the domed roof above was also of steel panels. A guard's ducket was generally situated between the rear van door and the first compartment on the left only, but a few SECR-bodied conversions originally lacked them; more will be said about this presently. The cab fronts continued the LSWR arrangement of two windscreens with a headcode panel between them. There was a deep gutter above the windscreens, emptied through two downpipes, one at each corner of the cab. These splayed outwards at the bottom, giving the units concerned a somewhat 'bottom-heavy' appearance from the front, particularly characteristic of LBSCR and later LSWR conversions.

Unless otherwise mentioned, all units were fitted with Metropolitan-Vickers (Metrovick) electrical equipment, including automatic acceleration control using electro-magnetic relays situated in a cupboard at the rear of the motorman's compartment. This was basically the same as that installed in the LSWR units, but a refinement was the fitting of an additional control circuit which lowered the setting at which the current limiting relays were activated, thus slowing down automatic acceleration with the aim of reducing slipping in adverse weather conditions. Activated by a separate switch in the cab, it seems that this facility was little-used. With it went an additional three-wire jumper cable and socket located under the headcode box. Only one wire was required for the variable acceleration control, the other two being utilised to enable all compartment lights in the train to be switched from one cab. Like the original LSWR units, 1285-1310 lacked this feature when new but gained it later. Control and power cables were again routed along the roofs of vehicles, but the brake compressors were mounted externally on motor coach underframes.

Motor bogies, each fitted with two axle-hung, nose-suspended traction motors, were situated at the cab end of each motor coach. Apart from Eastern section 1401-1534, which had a different design, motors were the same as those on the earlier units but by now supplied by Metropolitan-Vickers and classified MV 339. With the same exceptions, units had motor bogies of 8ft 9in wheelbase, similar to those under the LSWR units 1201-1284 and designed by Surrey Warner. However, apart from those under coaches with lengthened ac underframes, they were fitted with the simpler LBSCR brake rigging originally designed for the 1924 ac motor vans of the Coulsdon and Sutton electrification. This hybrid bogie was known as the 'central' type, and could be recognised by straight guard-irons in front of the leading wheels; virtually all survived to be used under post-war 4 SUB and EPB units.

The exterior painting processes specified for new and rebuilt coaching stock were extremely complex, with the aim of producing a smooth, waterproof and long-lasting finish in the days before synthetic paints. The main exterior side panels of wooden bodies received the most attention. They were first rubbed down with turpentine substitute (white spirit) and pumice stone, and then given successive coats of red lead, lead colour and filler, after which these coats were stopped with hard stopping. There followed another coat of filler, another of stopping, three more coats of filler and then a rub-down with artificial pumice stone and water. After this, further coats of red lead, stopping, facing, and red lead were applied. This was followed by two coats of SR green, lining and transfers, and three coats of varnish. The panelling was then flatted, window glass and brasswork cleaned, and one coat of finishing varnish applied. The painting of steel-panelled areas was simpler, with some of the early filler coats omitted or substituted by primer. Window frames, including droplight frames, were painted dark buff with lighter streaks to resemble teak wood grain, while roofs were given four coats of white lead. Underframes, bogies and ends (other than driving cabs) were black. These processes were standard for both suburban and main line electric stock until 1939, although lining and lettering were gradually simplified.

The coaches of all suburban units built or converted up to 1939 had bodies and underframes constructed separately, and it was the practice to paint bodywork of a new or rebuilt vehicle before mounting it on its underframe. Likewise, it was usual during general overhaul to separate a body from its underframe prior to repair and repainting. When uniting (or reuniting) the two parts, the underside supports of the body were painted with a thick compound and then lowered onto the underframe while still wet, thus ensuring a weatherproof paint seal with none being chipped away by the impact of several tons of body mass on the underframe girders. Only with the introduction of the first entirely new 4 SUB in 1941, which had steel body framework permanently attached to the underframe solebars, did this practice cease.

Between the ten-yearly general overhauls, suburban stock received what was known as a 'revarnish' about every two years (in practice, the interval could vary from 21 to thirty months). Until 1940 the original paint finish was of such high quality that this merely involved a scour to remove ingrained dirt, touching-in of chipped or worn areas, and finally a new coat of varnish, hence the term. Although in the first years of electrification Durnsford Road and Slades Green also carried out this work, by the early 1930s revarnishing of the suburban stock of all three sections had been concentrated at Selhurst. By 1935 revarnishes were recorded on vehicle sole-bars or ends as SV (for Selhurst Varnish) followed by the date, in 2in-high stencilled figures. eg SV11.35 noted on the solebar of unrebuilt LSWR unit 1225.

The original sage green body colour adopted by the SR was, as mentioned above, identical to the LSWR electric stock livery. This was replaced by a darker shade, sometimes termed 'Maunsell green' from 1929, chosen because it withstood the effects of weather better than the original hue. Initially, body sides were fully lined-out in black and yellow, to the extent that flush steel sections on the cab and van sides were lined to resemble raised wooden beading. Apart from the motor coaches of 1925 contractor-built units 1285-1310 and 1496-1524, driving ends on suburban stock were never lined. From about 1935 lining was limited to the waist line only and was gradually simplified until by 1938 units were being outshopped following overhaul with none at all. Various brighter greens also appeared from 1938, but the definitive malachite shade was not adopted until 1942. This colour was continued by the Southern Region of British Railways after 1948 with minimal change, and was carried by virtually all remaining suburban stock of pre-war origin until withdrawal. Numbering and lettering were originally as for the SR repaints of the LSWR units, described above. From 1939 the lettering was changed to a sans-serif style in yellow, and the words SOUTHERN RAILWAY were moved to the waist. Further changes are described towards the end of this chapter.

Although internal repainting, revarnishing and reupholstering took place to give an 'as new' appearance following conversion, little was done to alter the physical appearance of the seating accommodation in the units converted from steam stock. Characteristic fittings of the constituent companies such as door locks and luggage-rack brackets were generally retained, as were the ornate lincrusta ceilings in some former first or second class compartments, even where these were downclassed to thirds. The woodwork in third class compartments was generally varnished oak, and that in first class polished walnut with sycamore panels, although there were obviously variations. Successive coats of SR toffee-coloured varnish tended to darken the woodwork as the years passed. All vehicles were non-gangwayed, the third class compartments seating five passengers each side, the first class compartments four. In the thirds seating could be either 'half-back' in which the backrests reached only to shoulder height, 'full-back' in which there was also a headrest, or an intermediate height between these two extremes. Fixed or folding armrests generally subdivided the seating in the first class compartments, the most common arrangement being a single central armrest dividing the seats into two groups of two. However in some units each individual seat was separated by armrests (like the original LSWR units) and in a number of LBSCR conversions there were none at all. First class seating almost invariably had loose hammock-slung seat cushions, usually two across the width of the coach, but those in third class could be loose or of the fixed wire-framed bench type. In both cases they were stuffed with horsehair, an almost indestructible padding material which was washed and recycled when ten-year-old cushions were 'scrapped'. Floors were covered with linoleum, first class compartments also having rugs.

Upholstery patterns varied over the years, particularly in third class. Initially a black, orange and red velvet moquette of SECR origin was used, but in about 1934 this gave way to two 'jazz' patterns, one predominantly green/fawn and the other blue/fawn. These in turn were superseded by a pair of much brighter and bolder patterns in about 1935, again in green and blue. From 1936, at the time when many units introduced for the initial electrifications of 1925-29 were being reupholstered as part of their ten-yearly general overhaul, the upper parts of the back cushions were sometimes covered in green or blue 'Rexine' (a synthetic leathercloth with an embossed pattern manufactured by ICI, much used for carriage trimming by the SR during this period), probably to make it easier to clean off hair-oil stains. In some cases other internal surfaces were also covered with rexine at this time, including door panels and a narrow strip above the back cushions. It was common practice to trim the seating at one end of a unit in one pattern and the other end in another. In 1939 the brown and beige Medway pattern, introduced by Bulleid, started to appear – this was very drab in comparison with earlier designs, especially when dirty or worn. From the start of the SR era first class seating was generally trimmed in a predominantly red, green and gold multi-coloured floral tapestry of Edwardian taste known as Saladin. Other styles were introduced from 1939, including a plain light green with a ribbed surface and a pattern of black and orange birds and foliage on an apple green background.

A typical third class compartment interior in an SR suburban unit, in this case motor third brake 8076 from LSWR unit 1250 following rebuilding on standard-length underframes in 1937. The cushions are upholstered in the later blue-based 'jazz' moquette. *SR Official*

A standard suburban first class compartment seating four each side, showing the rug, central folding armrests, and floral Saladin tapestry upholstery. This view illustrates a compartment in trailer composite 9363, again from unit 1250. *SR Official*

It was necessary to construct 55 entirely new units in order to avoid having to take too many vehicles out of service for conversion prior to the completion of the first electrification schemes, with the consequent reduction in service, and therefore passenger complaints (which nevertheless happened, anyway). This total included the 26 units for the 1925 Western section Guildford and Dorking scheme, and 29 for the first stages of the enormous Eastern section conversion, on which electric services commenced at the same time.

These two batches will be described first, followed by the units formed by conversions from steam stock. Note that vehicles of a particular constituent company did not necessarily return to work on the same lines; for example 1655-1701 were converted from LSWR stock for the 1928 Central section scheme. For convenience, in the account which follows the batches of units are grouped together according to the origin of their vehicle bodies rather than in strict chronological order of introduction.

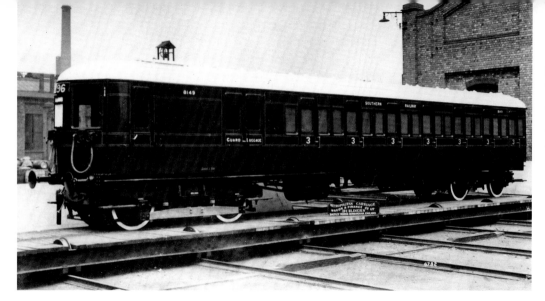

THE NEW 1925 STEEL-PANELLED STOCK

The Western and Eastern section suburban electrification schemes (see Chapter 2) were authorised by the provisional SR Board in November 1922, just prior to Grouping, in order that work on them could commence without delay. Of the 55 entirely new electric units required, it was originally intended that all would be to a common design based on the Raworth/Lynes plans for the SECR electrification, modified to suit the adoption of the 600V dc system. Although similar in concept to the original LSWR units and with the same Metrovick automatic series-parallel control system, the vehicles would be on long 62ft underframes to maximise capacity, while traction motors, bogies and couplings between vehicles would also be to a different design. The 26 Western section units were to be of three-coach formation to interwork with the earlier units and with trailer sets, but the 29 Eastern section examples would have been made up to four coaches with one of the 60ft 100-seat thirds already in production and intended for just this purpose. In the event Jones, who as Chief Electrical Engineer was nominally senior to Raworth, insisted that three-coach motor units and LSWR-style trailer sets were to be used on the Eastern section as well in the interests of standardisation, no doubt much to Raworth's annoyance. These original orders were ratified by the SR Board in June 1923.

A second opportunity for standardisation was then lost as Jones raised objections to the use of the proposed Raworth/Lynes design for the Western section extension, just as construction was about to commence at the contractors in 1924. In particular, he protested that the motor coaches would be 'too heavy' (at 41 tons) for bridges on the Guildford New line, a reason which seems somewhat flimsy in retrospect. Jones instead told the other officers that he and Warner would produce a revised design, more in keeping with the original LSWR units, for the Guildford and Dorking electrification, and in due course they did. Hence two different types of unit were subsequently built, the 26 for the Western section being on shorter underframes and with cab ends, electrical equipment and motor bogies similar to existing LSWR units.

In other respects Jones and Warner seemed happy to allow Ashford standards to prevail, or perhaps the combined engineering weight of Maunsell, Raworth and Lynes just proved too much for them, so all 55 units had SECR-type bodywork with flush-panelled sides and distinctive Ashford-style commode handles and ventilator hoods exactly resembling the final SECR 60ft 100-seat suburban coaches. It appears that detailed design of the mechanical parts took place at Ashford during 1924 under the direction of Lynes who, as mentioned earlier, had come from the SECR as Maunsell's assistant and was given the SR title Chief Draughtsman. Body construction was of galvanised steel sheet on a teak framework with deal partitions, while roofs comprised ash boards covered in canvas, except that steel plates were used for the cab roofs, which were domed. The units had a somewhat slab-sided appearance due to a complete lack of raised panelling, unusual at that time.

The 26 motor units ordered for the 1925 Western Section electrification to Guildford and Dorking to Jones' revised specification were numbered 1285-1310 and were basically a modernised version of the earlier LSWR units with which they were designed to interwork. They were thus shorter and carried fewer passengers than the standardised stock built subsequently, but unlike the '1201' class were never lengthened. With the Southern's own carriage shops being tied up with the construction of much-needed main line coaches, it was necessary to order the vehicles for these units from contractors. Metropolitan Carriage, Wagon and Finance Co were responsible for the motor coaches. The trailers were ordered from Cammell Laird, who built the main body structure and underframes, but the finishing work was carried out by the Midland Railway Carriage and Wagon Co, whose works plates appeared on the solebars of the completed coaches. The electrical equipment, including type 339 275hp motors, was ordered from Metropolitan-Vickers in March 1924, and arrangements were made for it to be installed in the carriage builder's workshops.

The driving motor third brakes, to SR carriage diagram 661 and numbered 8127-78, were built on 57ft frames and had seven third class compartments behind the motorman's cab and guard's van. They weighed 39 tons (only two tons lighter than the Eastern section motor coaches to which Jones had objected). Their cab ends were heavily bowed in a similar manner to the LSWR units although they looked, if anything, even more pointed. Inside the cab, the front of this 'nose' accommodated no more than a rack for the headcode stencils. The trailer composites (diagram 753, 9435-60) had six first and three third class compartments arranged 331111113, and were 60ft long. Weighing 27 tons, these were on the same type of underframe as the SECR all-thirds described above. Livery was the green originally chosen for SR passenger stock, fully lined-out in yellow and black. Unusually, this lining originally had square corners. The class appeared on each door as 1 or 3 directly below the droplights. The units were formed up in strict numerical order of coach numbers, thus 1285 was formed 8127+9435+8128, and so on in sequence. Overall unit length was 181ft 8in – still appreciably greater than the original LSWR units.

Mechanical and electrical equipment closely followed LSWR practice, but the electrical equipment was ventilated through roof-mounted air ducts rather than louvres in the coach sides. The 8ft 9in wheelbase motor bogies were the same too, but the 8ft 6in trailer bogies were of a unique design, not used on any other SR electric stock. Many of the axleboxes were lettered LSWR. Coupling between vehicles within a unit was also different. Instead of the simple bar-couplers used on 1201-1284, cast steel automatic 'buckeye' couplings, to the American MCB specification, were initially fitted instead. (MCB stood for Master Car Builders, a North American railway manufacturers' standards association.) They were also used on 1401-1534. As related below, they did not prove a success in this application and, following several break-aways, were replaced in 1926 by the Southern's own design of screw-coupling with central buffer. (Buckeye couplings would not reappear on SR electric stock until the prototype 4 EPB unit of 1951.) The buffers at the cab ends had round heads and shafts, again similar to the South Western units but unlike any subsequent SR stock.

Internally, third class accommodation was rather austere, and the best impression of this can be gained from a peep into a compartment of motor coach 8143 from unit 1293 (later 4308) of this class preserved in the National Railway Museum. Notice the planked ceiling with projecting light fittings, the droplights with leather straps, and 'half-back' seating which came only to shoulder height. First class accommodation was rather better and fitted the description given in the general notes above, with end and folding centre armrests dividing the seat two+two across the carriage, full-height back cushions and rugs. The lights were originally enclosed in elliptical shades, but these were later replaced by open reflectors.

Regarding delivery of 1285-1310, it was planned that the first four units would be ready for service by the end of March 1925, with the rest being delivered at the rate of about six per month. 22 were to be available when the Guildford and Dorking scheme was inaugurated on 12th July, and the last four by the end of that month. Possibly due to the redesign insisted on by Jones, and certainly as the result of a strike at the contractors' works early in 1925, production was badly delayed and only seven or eight units had actually arrived on the SR by the middle of June. It was therefore necessary to draft in some of the dozen or so spare ex-LSWR '1201' class units to provide enough stock for the opening day, and it appears that the last few were not delivered until August. From this time the two classes were completely interchangeable over electrified Western section suburban routes, to which they were nominally restricted until about 1938.

For the extensive Eastern Section inner-suburban electrification schemes of 1925-26, covering routes from Holborn Viaduct/Victoria to Orpington and Crystal Palace (High Level), and from Charing Cross/Cannon Street to the Mid-Kent line, Bromley North, Orpington and Dartford, no fewer than 134 three-coach suburban units were constructed. These were all to the new SR standard with 62ft underframes, and 105 of them made use of former SECR coach bodies, as described in the next section. The remaining 29 units, 1496-1524, were built new, and are discussed here. They were numbered in the middle of the series because it was originally intended to provide only 124 units for the entire Eastern section scheme and these entirely new units would have been at the upper end of the number block – for reasons discussed below 'converted' 1525-1534 were only ordered after unit numbers had been allocated.

As with the Western section units, it was necessary to contract-out construction. Metropolitan CWF Co were again responsible for the motor coaches, but this time the Birmingham Railway Carriage and Wagon Co built the trailers. The driving motor third brakes weighed 41 tons and were to diagram 670. Numbered 8417-74, they had motorman's, guard's and eight third class compartments. The trailers were to diagram 758, weighed 27 tons, had seven firsts and two thirds arranged 311111113, and were numbered 9580-9608. Although external styling was very similar to the '1285' class, the driving ends were considerably flatter, being only slightly bowed. Both cab lookouts had thick frames to give a more symmetrical appearance, but only the offside one opened. The livery again featured squared-off panel lines, but the class designations were lower down on the doors. This latter position became standard for electric suburban stock until 1939, but the panel lines on both the '1285' and '1496' classes were later repainted with radiused corners. Internal design and decor was similar to the Western section units except that the lights were originally enclosed in glass bowls; again these were later replaced by standard open reflectors. There were slight external differences between vehicles from the two contractors – for example the motor coaches were delivered with white roof ventilators but the trailers had black ones.

The major differences involved the bogies and traction equipment. As specified by Raworth, who as the former Chief Electrical Engineer of the SECR had been placed in charge of the Eastern section suburban electrification by Walker, 9ft wheelbase bogies of SECR design were used, equipped with 300hp motors classified DK 77, supplied by English Electric and built at the Dick, Kerr works at Preston. Although there was nothing at all wrong with these motors, it was later decided to standardise on the MV 339 type for suburban and semi-fast electric stock, and they were all eventually scrapped between 1949 and 1953. The motor bogies themselves survived, however, virtually all seeing further service under 4 SUB and 4 EPB units. They were known as the 'eastern' type, and were recognisable by their kinked guard irons, necessary to clear the brake rigging. The 8ft wheelbase trailer bogies were also of SECR design, and this type then became standard for subsequent builds of suburban EMUs. (The design was, incidentally, also used on the majority of main-line electric stock.)

It is interesting that contractors' publicity photographs carried misleading numbers to confuse future railway historians. One of the motor coaches pictured at Crystal Palace HL carried the obviously touched-in unit number '1401' on its front and a works photograph of trailer 9600 carried unit number '1421' on its solebar – in both cases these unit numbers were actually allocated to units with converted SECR bodywork. (As an aside, the motor coach numbered '1401' was 8418 which was actually formed in the first unit of its class (1496), while trailer 9600 for '1421' was indeed the twenty-first trailer, so at least the misleading examples were consistent!)

Although the motor coaches were formed into 1496-1524 in consecutively-numbered pairs, the trailer composites were allocated at random. This seems to have been because the trailers were delivered first and parked in sidings to await the motor coaches (which the SR apparently had to chase the contractors for) and then formed up into units as the motor coach pairs were delivered on a grab-the-nearest basis without regard for coach numbers.

To further complicate matters, the first eleven units to be formed were temporarily made up to four coaches with an additional trailer composite, and ran in this state for about two months, from July to September 1925. (37 units with converted SECR bodywork were also initially formed with two trailers, as described below.) This was to compensate for the late delivery of the first Eastern section trailer sets, which were delayed for reasons discussed later. Operating pairs of four-coach units in the peaks theoretically provided the required capacity without trailer sets, although in practice the number of extra third class seats in each unit (twenty, in two compartments) was not great and it is unlikely that any of the first class compartments were downgraded. These arrangements also helped motormen to get used to handling eight-coach trains. (Some Eastern section trains also ran as nine-coach trains composed of three three-coach motor units during this period.) Afterwards, the extra trailers were reformed with other motor coaches, but no-one seems to have been able to face the business of sorting them all out into their correct numerical sequence. Units of the '1496' class formed with four coaches from new were 1496/97 and 1499-1507, and their temporary formations are shown below. Note that 1497 lost *both* its original trailers to later units when reduced to three coaches, and was instead given 9595 out of the original four-coach 1505.

Temporary four-car formations:

Unit	MThB	TC	TC	MThB	
1496	8417	9583	**9582**	8418	(9582 to 1512)
1497	8419	**9592**	9594	8420	(9592 to 1514, 9594 to 1513)
1499	8423	**9581**	9584	8424	(9581 to 1519)
1500	8425	**9601**	9603	8426	(9601 to 1521)
1501	8427	**9600**	9604	8428	(9600 to 1509)
1502	8429	**9602**	9598	8430	(9602 to 1522)
1503	8431	**9608**	9606	8432	(9608 to 1515)
1504	8433	**9605**	9607	8434	(9605 to 1524)
1505	8435	9597	**9595**	8436	(9595 to 1497)
1506	8437	**9586**	9588	8438	(9586 to 1516)
1507*	8439	**9580**	9587	8440	(9580 to 1518)

1496-1524 were originally devoid of gutter downpipes in front of the cab doors, as fitted to the Western section units, but they were added in about 1927 when the gutter around the cab front at its junction with the roof was also made deeper on both these and 1285-1310. Both batches were equipped with guard's duckets from new, but it was found that these caused clearance problems on certain sections of route and from late 1928 they were removed and replaced by roof periscopes. Motorman's cabs were fitted with new hinged seats at the same time. These latter modifications were carried out at depots; the Western section '1285' class at Wimbledon (HO 368) and the Eastern section '1496' class at Grosvenor Road, Victoria (HO 370). Although units with pre-Grouping bodywork were never given periscopes, they became standard on the main line electric stock built in the 1930s and later on the replacement suburban 4 SUB and EPB units. (It is ironic that duckets were being removed from the 1925 units at roughly the same time as they were being fitted to 1201-1284; indeed, as some of these latter were given the earlier style of ducket with slit-shaped lookouts it is all too likely that they were the same ones.)

SR CONVERSIONS FROM SECR STEAM STOCK

There were two main batches of units produced by mounting ex-SECR bodies on new 62ft underframes, totalling 135. These were 1401-1495 plus 1525-1534 (105 units) provided for the Eastern section electrifications of 1925-26, and 1601-1630 for the 1928 Central section scheme. In fact, only ex-South Eastern Railway coaches proved suitable for conversion and no ex-LCDR vehicles were used at all. SER coaches had distinctive panelling with only one line of horizontal beading below the quarterlights and this was retained on the electric conversions. The vehicles chosen were from close-coupled suburban sets, and were either four or six-wheeled, with lengths of around 27ft and 33ft respectively. The bodies from a total of 730 steam coaches were used. The conversion arrangements were not as tidy as for the LSWR sets, no fewer than twelve different SR carriage diagrams being required to cover all the slight variations in compartment spacing, due to the hotch-potch mixture of bodies used. The former SECR Carriage Works at Ashford was responsible for the construction of most underframes and bogies, all basic bodywork conversion, some interior trimming and external painting, and the fitting of traction motors. Painting and trimming was also carried out at Lancing; all the trailers for 1401-1495 and 24 of the motor coaches were dealt with there, to HO orders 62 and 63 respectively. The coaches were then hauled to Brighton for other electrical equipment to be installed and for general finishing off, including the fitting of headcode panels. This work was carried out in the former LBSCR carriage painting shop at Lovers Walk, which was to become an electric running shed in 1932.

The timetables of Raworth's original scheme, as initially adopted by the SR for the first stage of the Eastern section suburban electrification, envisaged combined Holborn Viaduct/St Pauls and Victoria services dividing and joining at Herne Hill. It was calculated that 136 four-coach units would be required to operate the entire timetable including maintenance spares, but the Grouping preparation Joint Committee would agree to only 124. The 95 SECR-bodied conversions were placed at the beginning of the number series starting at 1401 and the 29 entirely new units (see above) at the end. 1401-1495 were ordered in November 1922 at the same time as 1496-1524. Almost immediately it was decreed that the LSWR arrangements with three-coach motor units and two-coach trailer sets were to be adopted instead. With the 3+2+3 formation it would not be possible to divide and combine en route, and so a revised timetable with separate City and West End services was necessary. The timetables required the use of 118 motor units in traffic for the whole Eastern section scheme (to make up, with trailer sets, a total of 59 eight-coach trains for the peaks), and it was initially hoped that the 124 units ordered would still prove sufficient, although this left only six units for maintenance cover.

In fact, as mentioned elsewhere, the service on the first stage of the Eastern section electrification commenced using 48 temporary four-coach units (only 45 had originally been intended), and it soon became very clear that the rolling stock requirement had been underestimated. Officers' committee notes from this time reflect concern that some peak hour trains were formed of four (instead of eight) coaches, and that passengers were complaining about it. A further ten motor units with converted bodywork were therefore ordered on 8th September 1925, to HO 135, in order to provide an adequate float for maintenance. (Twelve were requested, but ten were as many as the Board would authorise.) As the earlier unit numbers had already been allocated they were added on at the end of the number series after the new-build stock, and this accounts for 1496-1524 being sandwiched numerically between two batches of wooden-bodied 'converted' units. The thirty underframes for 1525-1534 were built in 1925 by Birmingham RCW. With an operating requirement for 118 motor units, the final total of

134 allowed for approximately one in seven being out of traffic undergoing maintenance at any time, a ratio found by experience to be workable with almost all classes of unit during the period covered by this book.

The formation and seating capacity of all these units was the same as that of the newly-built '1496' class units, with two eight-compartment motor third brakes and a composite trailer with a third class compartment at either end of seven firsts. Like the '1496' class, there were window frames on both cab lookouts, but no gutter downpipes at the cab ends. (These were retrospectively fitted in about 1927, together with a deeper gutter around the cab front.) They were also equipped with exactly the same electrical equipment, including 300hp DK 77 traction motors and 9ft wheelbase 'eastern' motor bogies. The first few units outshopped were initially devoid of guards duckets, but soon after construction commenced it was agreed to fit them as on 1496-1524. Most were therefore given them on conversion, and the earliest examples were equipped retrospectively. Internally little was altered, the compartments retaining their characteristic South Eastern Railway fittings, including luggage-rack supports lettered 'SER Co'. Work started on the conversions in about April 1924, and the first five were ready for traffic at Slades Green depot by the end of February 1925. Units up to 1441 had been delivered by the end of May 1925 and all the initial 95 were in traffic by early 1926. Additional units 1525-1531 were ready for service by June 1926, and 1532-1534 the following month.

When original carriage bodies (or sections of them) were joined to form a new longer body, it was usual, where possible, to retain and butt together the existing coach ends to avoid having to build a new partition from scratch. However, this method meant that the partition between the two former end compartments was 5in thicker than usual, and the resulting wider panel between the adjacent quarterlights at this position was very noticeable in side views of these coaches.

The motor third brakes of the '1401' and '1525' types were to diagrams 662 (130 vehicles, numbers 8227-46, 8327-8416, 8475-94), 665 (41 vehicles, 8247-58, 8298-8326) and 666 (39 vehicles, 8259-97). Diagram 662 made use of the bodies of six-wheeled six-compartment thirds, originally built in 1890-97. At Ashford these were grouped in threes, one being cut in half. One complete body was mounted on the inner end of an underframe, followed by one of the halves. A new 8ft 10in driving cab went on the outer end, and the intervening space was filled by the guards compartment, including the 'unused' outer compartment from the half-body (only two compartments being required from this). The extra 5in length where the ends of the original bodies were butt-joined together was therefore located between the second and third compartments (from the driving end). Some of 8475-94 (formed in additional units 1525-34) were, however, assembled from a complete third brake body joined to part of an all-third, rather than as above. Four-wheeled 27ft five-compartment thirds dating from 1897-1901 were the basis of diagram 665, two bodies being mounted on the underframe with the two compartments nearest the cab being converted into van area.

The extra space where the original bodies were joined was therefore between the third and fourth compartments. Not only this but, because the compartments themselves were shorter (5ft 3in between partitions, rather than about 5ft 7in), the luggage space was approximately three feet longer. Finally, diagram 666 was similar, but this time one 27ft third was combined with a three-compartment third brake of similar vintage. The ex-brake body went in the centre, its van space continuing in use as such, but as its compartments were about 5ft 7in wide, this area was reduced in length by about 1ft compared to diagram 665. Interestingly, the first twelve coaches to both these latter diagrams had the van doors in the same position as diagram 662, giving the additional space between the doors and the first compartment, whereas the others had them further back, putting all the extra length directly behind the cab. Thus there were variations even between coaches officially to the same diagram number. All these converted coaches weighed 40 tons except for 8395-8416, which were 41 tons.

A peculiar feature of four motor coaches from this batch (8355/62/78 and 8405, all to diagram 662) was the vertical matchboarding on the lower body sides, including the doors. The SECR introduced matchboarded sides on its boat train stock in 1921, and also adopted it as a means of repairing rotten or otherwise damaged lower panelling. Its appearance on electric stock conversions was probably due to the use of coaches which had suffered damage in World War One (probably due to war use rather than enemy action) and were subsequently rebuilt in this style.

The trailer composites were formed by mounting part of an existing body at either end of a new underframe, and filling in the space between with the requisite number of new compartments. Only two diagrams were needed for these. 75 vehicles were to diagram 754 (coach numbers 9485-9504/19/24-44/56/58-79, 9609-18) and were formed fairly simply using two 27ft bi-composites (arranged 2112) of 1898-1900 vintage, deleting the inner second class compartment from each and filling the intermediate space with three new first class compartments. The ex-seconds at the ends became third class and were 6ft 2in wide (nearly a foot more leg-room than in some of the motor coaches), while the firsts were just under 7ft. Diagram 755 (9505-18/20-23/45-55/57) covered the remaining thirty vehicles, this time making use of 33ft five-compartment seconds dating from 1893-99. Three compartments were used from one and four from the other, the remaining space being filled up with two new 7ft compartments. As the width of the other compartments was only 6ft 5in, this left a gap of 1ft 7in, inserted between the two new compartments. Presumably this was to avoid making the two centre compartments too large. As with the contractor-built '1496' class, trailers were marshalled into these units at random, in this case probably entirely as a result of formation of the temporary four-coach units referred to below. Additional units 1525-1534 were formed with trailers 9609-18 built specifically for them, although not in order.

Like the new '1285' and '1496' class units, 1401-1495 and 1525-1534 were originally fitted with MCB buckeye couplers

between vehicles, and this is an opportune moment to relate the rest of their unhappy story on SR suburban stock. They proved unreliable and there were a number of instances of breakages causing vehicles to separate in traffic, often resulting in severe service disruption. The problems were attributed to lack of synchronisation between the motors at each end of the unit, which resulted in jerking and hence serious wear to the couplings leading to eventual fractures. It was decided to replace them with a centre-buffer and drawbar coupler, designed to minimise the time for which each unit had to be withdrawn from traffic for conversion. It comprised a 2in square drawbar with turnbuckle, located 2in below the centre of the 12in headstock, on the same centre line as the MCB coupler previously fitted. A sprung buffer with a 12in diameter face was fixed at each end of the trailer coach, with its centre line $^3/_8$in above the top of the headstock and bearing on a rubbing block on the inner end of each motor coach. Both buffer and rubbing block were carried on brackets projecting above the headstock. This work was authorised by HO 150 of 27th March 1926 and completed by June 1926. It seems probable therefore that at least some of the 1525-1534 batch never ran in traffic with MCB couplers.

Following a buffer stop collision at Charing Cross on 19th September 1928, in which over-riding and telescoping took place, the Inspecting Officer, John Pringle, criticised the design of the buffer. As a result, the coupling was redesigned. The buffers and rubbing blocks were relocated to the centre of the headstock and the drawbars replaced by three-link chains located 3½in below it. This new arrangement also enabled the gap between headstocks to be reduced from 2ft 2⅛in to 1ft 10in, the minimum allowed by the curves over which the stock was to run. It proved capable of standing up well to rough shunts and buffer stop collisions, and was adopted as standard on all SR non-corridor electric stock, right up to the final BR Standard 4 EPB units of 1963.

Due to initial non-availability of trailer sets when electric services commenced, as mentioned above some of the 1925 Eastern section units ran in four-car formations as a stop-gap measure for about two months, using an extra trailer composite. 37 SECR-bodied units, 1402-07/09-27/29/30/32-38/40/44/45, were involved in this exercise, and their temporary formations are shown below. In three units, 1411, 1432 and 1444, *both* original trailers were reformed into other units and a different trailer was transferred from another unit. Note that, as with the contractor-built stock, trailers were formed up with motor coach pairs (probably at Slades Green) entirely randomly, presumably as they arrived from Lancing. Furthermore, analysis of coach numbers reveal that some units were formed with two diagram 754 trailers, others had two of diagram 755 and the remainder had one of each. After the four-coach formations were disbanded, some trailers were temporarily stored. 9491/94 and 9510/25/30, from units 1418/25/14/32/13, were parked at Streatham Hill sidings, afterwards going to units 1488/89/92/87/91. Again, the enormity of the process probably ensured that no-one was prepared to sort the trailers out into their proper numerical order afterwards.

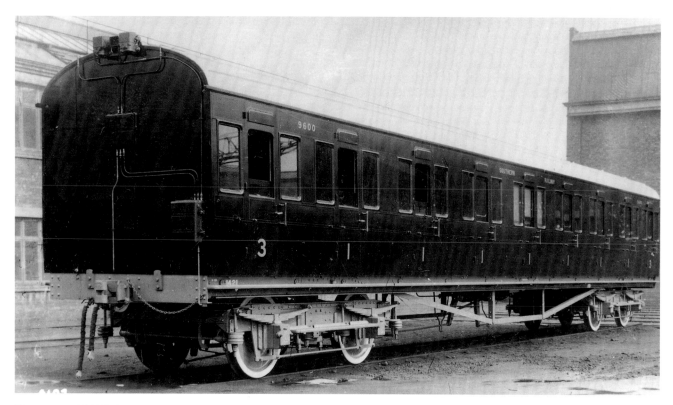

The unsuccessful MCB buckeye coupler can be clearly seen in this view of diagram 758 long-framed 1925 trailer composite 9600, photographed outside the Smethwick works of its builder, Birmingham RCW Co. In spite of the misleading unit number on the solebar, this vehicle was originally temporarily formed in four-coach 1501, then permanently in three-coach 1509.

Ex-works unit 1415, constructed from SER bodywork on new underframes for the 1925 Eastern section electrification, awaits the fitting of jumper cables at Brighton, probably in the latter half of 1924. This unit was one of the few delivered without guards' duckets behind the offside van doors, these being fitted later.

Formations of Eastern Section '1401' Class Units Temporarily Reformed as Four-Coach Units on Entry into Service in 1925. In all cases, the TC shown in bold type was later reformed into another unit as shown in brackets at the end of each row. Units were formed with vehicles in the order shown, except that in those marked * the orientation of motor coaches to trailers is not known and might have been the opposite of that printed.

Unit	MThB	TC	TC	MThB	
1402	8229	9518	**9521**	8230	(9521 to 1490)
1403*	8231	**9499**	9501	8232	(9499 to 1455)
1404	8233	9517	**9519**	8234	(9519 to 1465)
1405*	8235	9502	**9504**	8236	(9504 to 1469)
1406	8237	9498	**9500**	8238	(9500 to 1478)
1407	8239	9524	**9520**	8240	(9520 to 1484)
1409	8243	**9495**	9513	8244	(9495 to 1443)
1410	8245	**9549**	9546	8246	(9549 to 1479)
1411	8247	**9508**	**9512**	8248	(9508 to 1483, 9512 to 1433)
1412*	8249	**9507**	9509	8250	(5907 to 1466)
1413	8251	**9530**	9534	8252	(9530 to 1491)
1414	8253	**9510**	9506	8254	(9510 to 1492)
1415	8255	**9511**	9505	8256	(9511 to 1461)
1416*	8257	9532	**9533**	8258	(9533 to 1481)
1417	8259	**9527**	9528	8260	(9527 to 1474)
1418	8261	**9491**	9552	8262	(9491 to 1488)
1419*	8263	**9522**	9523	8264	(9522 to 1442)
1420*	8265	9526	**9529**	8266	(9529 to 1475)
1421	8267	**9559**	9564	8268	(9559 to 1459)
1422*	8269	**9486**	9493	8270	(9486 to 1432)
1423*	8271	9514	**9515**	8272	(9515 to 1480)
1424*	8273	**9485**	9487	8274	(9485 to 1467)
1425*	8275	9488	**9494**	8276	(9494 to 1489)
1426	8277	**9574**	9573	8278	(9574 to 1453)
1427	8279	**9489**	9490	8280	(9489 to 1473)
1429	8283	9548	**9554**	8284	(9554 to 1438)
1430*	8285	9545	**9547**	8286	(9547 to 1456)
1432*	8289	**9492**	9525	8290	(9492 to 1464, 9525 to 1487)
1433*	8291	9512	**9569**	8292	(9569 to 1486)
1434*	8293	**9567**	9571	8294	(9567 to 1482)
1435	8295	**9561**	9563	8296	(9561 to 1468)
1436	8297	9560	**9558**	8298	(9558 to 1471)
1437	8299	9550	**9570**	8300	(9570 to 1441)
1438*	8301	**9516**	9566	8302	(9516 to 1485)
1440*	8305	**9540**	9542	8306	(9540 to 1470)
1444*	8313	**9556**	**9557**	8314	(9556 to 1477, 9557 to 1472)
1445*	8315	**9555**	9562	8316	(9555 to 1444)

For the first stages of the dc electrification of the Central section suburban lines 116 three-coach units, numbered 1601-1716, were ordered on 3rd September 1926 to HO 206. Between them these units made use of bodywork designs from all three constituent companies. (1631-1657/1702-1716 and 1658-1701, which had LBSCR and LSWR bodywork respectively, are dealt with in subsequent sections.) Units 1601-1630, which formed the first part of this stock order, were generally similar to the '1401' type. However, they were fitted with 8ft 9in wheelbase 'central' motor bogies, based on the original LSWR design but with the superior LBSCR-type brake rigging. These bogies had MV 339 275hp motors, which became the standard for all subsequent suburban units until 1936. The revised design of centre-buffer and coupling was fitted between vehicles from new, and the cab front design reverted to a large motorman's windscreen and a smaller, framed, outwardly-opening offside window, as on the '1201' and '1285' types. The 600V power cables connecting the roof-mounted bus line to the cab end jumper and associated socket were moved to an external position, running vertically in conduit to the left of the motorman's and offside windscreens respectively. These changes, which were also standard for future builds of suburban and semi-fast stock with Metrovick equipment, gave the ends a less tidy appearance. By the time that 1601-1630 were authorised some Works reorganisation had occurred, so although bodywork conversion and motor bogie construction was still carried out at Ashford, the underframes and trailer bogies were now fabricated at Lancing.

The ninety coaches for these units were built to seven diagrams, no fewer than five covering motor coach variations. The thirty coaches to diagram 663 (numbers 8495-8524) had the same bodywork origins as diagram 662. Diagram 664 covered one coach only (8554), which used a six-compartment six-wheel third (as in diagrams 662/3) and a 27ft four-wheel two-compartment third brake. The fourteen coaches to diagram 667 (8525-38) were similar to diagram 666 above, but instead of a four-wheel third brake they utilised a six-wheeled 31ft four-compartment third brake of 1896-97 vintage, utilising only three of the 5ft 6¾in compartments. There were ten vehicles to diagram 669 (8539-48): these made use of two of the same six-wheeled four-compartment brakes as in diagram 667, but in order to preserve the join in the same place as before, it was necessary to fabricate a new compartment in one body (to give five compartments) and discard the rest of the brake section.

Finally, diagram 668 (8549-53) covered five motor coaches which made use of two 27ft third brakes, one with three compartments and one with two. It was necessary to build three extra compartments into the existing van areas, and the join was between the fourth and fifth compartments. It seems that by now the supply of suitable vehicles was drying up, and the staff at Ashford had to be more inventive.

Only two diagrams were necessary to cover the trailer composites of the 1928 stock: 25 (9619-24/29-31/3-48) were to diagram 756, in which the bodies were formed from six-wheeled vehicles of 1893-99. Three compartments of a 33ft

A later '1401' series unit, 1470, at an unidentified location, possibly Slades Green, in 1925. Although the motor coaches are clearly just outshopped, the condition of the paintwork on the trailer composite shows that it has already been in service, being temporarily formed in four-coach unit 1440. This photograph gives a good view of the 9' wheelbase 'eastern' motor bogie, with its kinked guard irons ahead of the leading wheels.

SER-bodied motor coach 8405 from unit 1490, one of four diagram 662 vehicles with matchboarded lower bodysides, stands at Balham on 27th September 1947. *K.G. Carr*

five-compartment second were joined to a 30ft four-compartment first, and a third class compartment built onto each end to give the requisite 62ft total. The remaining five (9625-8/32) were to diagram 757, made up from pairs of 27ft four-wheeled four-compartment firsts, with an identical compartment inserted in the gap. To make up the required length it was necessary to incorporate a 1ft 7³/₈in gap next to the new compartment. Motor coaches and trailers were allocated to 1601-1630 in sequence.

1601-1630 were delivered between November 1927 and March 1928, with 1601 and 1603-1606 noted in storage at Streatham Hill that November, and 1610/11 and 1622/29 running trial trips out of London Bridge by early March. They entered passenger service from 25th March 1928, at first operating certain trains on the London Bridge to Caterham/Tadworth and London Bridge – Sydenham – Crystal Palace LL lines to existing steam timetables. They worked full services on the first stages of the Central section suburban electrification from 17th June 1928.

SR CONVERSIONS FROM LBSCR STEAM AND AC ELECTRIC STOCK

The SR made-up 103 three-coach units (309 vehicles) utilising the bodywork, and in many cases underframes and bogies also, of former LBSCR vehicles, including steam suburban and ac types. (As described in Chapter 4, some ac vehicles were actually constructed to LBSCR designs after Grouping, although all had been ordered prior to the end of 1922.) Numbers 1631-1657 and 1702-1716 were further units for the 1928-29 Central section dc electrification. 1717-1772 also went mainly to the Central section, but a minority were ordered to cover traffic increases and for the Gravesend, Windsor and Wimbledon–Sutton extensions of 1928-30. 1795-1801 were additional units converted in 1931/32 to make use of spare underframes and electrical equipment already delivered and were charged to the Brighton and Worthing electrification scheme (see Volume 2). 1801 was renumbered 1600 in 1934, to make way for the renumbering of the two-car South London line units at the same time.

Unit 1618, one of thirty constructed using SER bodywork for the 1928 Central section dc electrification, poses for an official photograph on leaving Tadworth for Tattenham Corner shortly before the official start of electrified services. The leading MThB, 8529, is to diagram 667; differences from equivalent Eastern section vehicles include use of the 'central' motor bogie with straight guard irons, a thick frame on only the offside (opening) cab windscreen, and re-routeing of power cables externally up the cab front. *SR Official*

Features common to all were standard Metrovick control gear and 8ft 9in wheelbase motor bogies with MV 339 motors. Externally, apart from the cab and van, panelled in sheet steel, all units retained their original panelling and box or louvre door ventilators. The arc roofs gave them a particularly vintage appearance, even when newly converted. As on 1201-1310 and 1601-1630 only the opening offside cab windscreen had a thick frame, and this became the standard pattern for subsequent suburban conversions as well as for main line semi-fast stock (to be covered in Volume 2) built or converted between 1931 and 1938.

Units 1631-1657 and 1702-1716 were the first to be converted from former LBSCR stock. They were ordered on 3rd September 1926 as part of HO 206 for the first stages of the Central section suburban electrification, and entered

service between April and December 1928. 1631-1657 followed the layout of the SECR conversions exactly, having two eight-compartment motor third brakes flanking a trailer composite with seven firsts and two thirds arranged 311111113, giving the standard seating capacity of 56 first and 180 third. However 1702-1716 had a revised formation of motor third brake + trailer composite + motor composite brake. The MThB was the same as above, but the TC had six thirds and four firsts arranged 3333331111, and the MCB three firsts and four thirds arranged 1113333, followed by the guard's and motorman's compartments. The coaches were arranged so that the first class compartments in the TC and MCB were adjacent, and capacity remained the same as before. As with the original LSWR stock, this layout was chosen to make best use of existing coach bodies with the minimum of new work.

The 'raw material' for these units was from former seven-coach close-coupled 'bogie block' suburban bodies designed by Robert Billinton and dating from 1898-1901. Most of the 28 sets had been built by Birmingham Railway Carriage and Wagon Co., but four were constructed at Brighton. They were generally made up of a seven-compartment third brake, an eight-compartment third, an eight-compartment composite arranged 33331111, a seven-compartment first, another composite, another third and another third brake, although there were some variations. The third class compartments in the composites and four compartments in the all-thirds had originally been seconds before abolition of that class in 1911, and were slightly wider than the original thirds. Some sets were disbanded over the years – in particular between 1910 and 1912 fourteen third brakes were converted into ac driving trailer composites to run with the South London line motor coaches, other vehicles were fitted with long buffers and normal couplings for use on main line services, and twelve all-thirds were incorporated in dc electric trailer sets 1111-1113 and 1115-1117 from 1926 (see page 138). By 1927 only seventeen sets remained intact (SR set numbers 941-957) and all but two vehicles from these were utilised in the electric units. In addition one long-buffered all-third and eight long-buffered all-firsts from sets previously disbanded were used to provide the requisite 126 coaches for 42 units.

LBSCR-bodied '1631/1702' type unit 1642 at London Bridge Low Level on a Caterham/Tattenham Corner train circa 1948, with 'British Railways' on the carriage side and 'S' prefix to the unit number. 'British Railways' was soon discarded in favour of the 'lion-and-cartwheel' logo, and S prefixes for unit numbers became intermittent.

The Caterham/Tattenham Corner services, which divided at Purley, were formed from three 3-car units until 1948. This rare view shows a 9-car train near Windmill Bridge junction, Croydon, on 9th April 1928. The leading unit is from the 1601-30 series with SECR bodywork.

The 'bogie block' sets were taken out of service between September 1927 and November 1928 and sent to Ashford for conversion in groups of three, 21 vehicles providing enough material for seven three-coach units. Bodies used were removed from their existing underframes and then lengthened or modified for mounting on new 62ft underframes from Lancing. Although standard SECR-pattern 8ft trailer bogies, also constructed at Lancing, were used, these were fitted with recovered LBSCR-pattern axle boxes. The 'central'-type motor bogies were fabricated at Ashford and, as with the SECR conversions, finishing-off was carried out at Brighton. The first set to be used, 951, provided the bodies for 'prototype' electric units of each type, 1631 and 1702, with one all-third left over for use in a future unit. A particular feature of electric vehicles with LBSCR 'bogie-block' bodywork was that the glazed toplights between the tops of the windows and the cantrail were replaced with plain sheeting.

Thirty-four of the driving motor third brakes (odd numbers 8617-39, 8645-51 and 8657-61, and all 8671-85) were to diagram 672 and used the bodies of all the 48ft third brakes. A new compartment was built on at one end and the existing brake compartment converted and lengthened to form steel-panelled motorman's and guard's compartments at the other. The remaining 35 motor third brakes (even numbers 8618-40, all 8641-44, even numbers 8646-50 and all 8652-56, 8658, 8660, 8662-70), to diagram 673, were adapted from the 50ft eight-compartment thirds with a driving cab and guard's van

added. All of the 1702-16 series had a diagram 672 motor third brake (8671-85), but nineteen of the 1631-1657 series (1631-1642, 1645-1648, 1651-1653) had one motor coach each of diagrams 672 and 673, while the remaining eight had two diagram 673 vehicles; while this made absolutely no difference to the accommodation provided; as the units were formed-up in strict order of coach numbers it accounts for the peculiar number sequences noted above. The fifteen motor composite brakes for units 1702-1716 (8837-51) were to diagram 692 and made use of an equivalent number of the 50ft composites. The requisite accommodation was arrived at by downgrading the first class compartment adjacent to the thirds, abolishing the outer third class compartment and replacing it with 18ft of luggage van and cab. All the motor coaches had a tare weight of 39 tons.

Of the trailer composites for these units, all of which weighed 26 tons, those in 1631-1657 (coach numbers 9675-9701) were to diagram 762 and utilised the bodies of the 48ft seven-compartment firsts, two additional compartments of first class dimensions being added at one end to make up the requisite length. Thus, as with the SECR conversions, the knowledgeable third class traveller could head for particular compartments to have a sensible amount of leg room (or, indeed, standing space!). Those in 1702-1716 (9702-16) were lengthened from fifteen of the 50ft composites with two additional compartments added to the third class end; these were to diagram 763.

Internally, the compartments in the motor third brakes of these units were very narrow and straight-backed, only 5ft 2⅝in across, and alternate partitions only reached to the tops of the seats. Other than (in most cases) greater legroom, different moquette and the provision of rugs, the first class compartments differed little in their appointments from the thirds, there being a complete absence of armrests. Internal fittings were left virtually unaltered, except that some compartments were given lights in glass bowls (as with the '1496' class) and others had open reflectors: these latter became the standard fitting on later units. Aside from their particularly spartan accommodation, these units also soon gained a reputation for being the roughest riding of the pre-1939 suburban fleet and were most uncomfortable to travel in, particularly during rush hours.

Not long after entering service unit 1702 was involved in the London Bridge collision of 9th July 1928 (see Chapter 2), resulting in trailer composite 9702 being written off. Two LBSCR six-wheeled gas-lit coaches and a new underframe were then used to provide a replacement vehicle, with the same number, in December 1928. Under Southern Railway procedure, replacements of accident losses such as this were regarded as the same as repairs and given the number of the lost vehicle. The cost was covered by internal 'insurance' with no capital expenditure being involved, and hence such replacements did not appear in HO order lists. This arrangement was changed some time in the 1940s, probably when the railways were nationalised.

The intended purpose and ordering details of units 1717-1772, converted in 1929-30 are as shown in this table:-

Unit Nos.	HO (Date Ordered)	Into Traffic	Intended Use
1717-1736	373 (25.8.28)	1929	Central section suburban
1737-1749	374 (25.8.28)	1929	Central section suburban
1750-1753	398 (14.11.28)	By 1.30	Wimbledon–Sutton new line
1754-1756	396 (10.11.28)	By 12.29	Additional to suburban pool (a)
1757-1768	480 (28.6.29)	1930	Windsor electrification
1769	515 (5.9.29)	1930	Gravesend electrification
1770-1772	553 (1.2.30)	6-8.30	Additional to suburban pool (b)

Notes:

(a) 1754-1756 charged to budget for Wimbledon–West Croydon electrification, but added to suburban pool.

(b) 1770-1772 formed part of HO 553 (thirteen units) which also included LSWR-bodied 1773-1782.

Most of 1717-1772 were converted at Ashford, but a few (1737-1749) were assembled at Eastleigh following reorganisation of SR workshop facilities (referred to in Chapter 2), these changes also causing delays to the delivery of 1750-1756. Formation was the same as 1702-1716, with an eight-compartment motor third brake, a trailer composite arranged 333331111 and a motor composite brake arranged 1113333-van-cab. All but two of the 168 vehicles needed came from former ac trailers and driving trailers, including eight vehicles built for electric services but not so used until now. As part of the conversion process, it was necessary to strip the aluminium sheeting from the bodies of these coaches. A total of 148 of the underframes also came from the *Elevated Electric* stock, as they were considered far too new to dispose of. Being originally either 48ft or 54ft long over headstocks, these needed to be extended to the standard SR 62ft length, and this was done by splicing in new sections to the original solebars and trussing. After conversion they could still easily be identified by the fact that whereas the standard ones had channel-section solebars with the webs pointing outwards ([>), the ex-ac examples were the opposite way round ( ] >), thus presenting a flat surface to the outside. This also meant that the underframe trussing was fixed to the outer surface of the solebars. The ac-framed vehicles were also given LBSCR-type built-up trailer bogies from the CP and CW stock. (Seven of these underframes and ten bogies were also used in LSWR-bodied units 1780-1782.) The motor bogies of vehicles with these underframes had slightly different brake gear to the standard 'central' type, somewhat resembling that fitted to the 9ft 'eastern' bogies under units 1401-1534.

Use of existing trailer bogies made these units rather better-riding than earlier conversions from Brighton stock. Construction of the necessary new underframes and bogies, as well as modifications to existing frames, was undertaken at Lancing. Vehicle weights were similar to the earlier LBSCR conversions, but there were minor variations depending on particular bodywork and underframe origins.

The motor third brakes in this group of units were numbered 8686-8722 and 8731-49 (the gap being filled by the eight South London line MThBs – see later). 8686-96 and 8706-08, to SR diagram number 675, were converted from the fourteen SL driving trailers by downgrading the two first class compartments and lengthening the original motorman's compartment to include a van space. With the exception of two others, all the rest were to diagram 678 and were obtained by adding a lengthened cab and van to former CW driving trailer thirds, which also already had the requisite eight compartments. The exceptions were 8747 and 8748 to diagram 679 – these had been loco-hauled 50ft nine-compartment former 'bogie block' thirds (downgraded from composite before conversion) which had one compartment abolished and cab and van added. 8693-8722 and 8731-46 weighed 39 tons, but 8747-49 tared one ton more. A note in an SR carriage register states that 8700/13/18 were converted, not by the SR itself, but by a contractor, BRCW. The reason may have been that at this time the SR was undertaking a heavy programme of new corridor steam stock construction.

The motor composite brakes in these units were numbered 8852-8900 and 9801-07 and were of three types. 8852-62 and 8872-74 were to diagram 693 and were formed from CP driving trailer composites with the cab removed and a new cab and van added to the opposite end, one third class compartment being deleted. Former CW trailer composites formed the material for a further twenty, 8863-71, 8875-84 and 8889, to diagram 694, with the outer first class compartment removed and a cab and van added at the third class end. CW driving trailer composites, including four which had never actually been used on electric services, were altered in a similar manner (except that the original cab was also removed, of course) to provide the remaining 22 vehicles, numbered 8885-88, 8890-8900 and 9801-07, which were to diagram 695. Finally, the intermediate trailer composites were of two types. Diagram 761 covered fifty-three vehicles numbered 9717-49 and 9461-80, and were converted from the rest of the CP driving trailer composites by removing the cab, adding an additional first class compartment at one end and an additional third at the other. The remaining three were to diagram 768, converted in the same manner from driving trailers built for ac services but which had remained steam-hauled; numbered 9481-83, they were formed in the final units of the type, 1770-1772.

The units in these batches were again formed-up in strict numerical coach number order except that, as shown above, the first 33 trailers (formed in units 1717-1749) were numbered 9717-49 and the remainder upwards from 9461. Other than the vehicles of Billinton 'bogie block' origin, which included the former SL driving trailers, the accommodation in the 1717-1749 series units was better than in other LBSCR conversions, as the third class compartments had proper partitions and armrests graced the first class seating. Moody notes that units 1738-1748 had 'full-back' seating in third class; presumably lower backs were fitted in other units.

The 148 vehicles in units from the 1717-1772 series mounted on former ac underframes lengthened to the standard 62ft were as shown below. 42 units (1724-1765) had all three vehicles on lengthened ex-ac underframes while only three units (1770-1772) were entirely on new underframes. Vehicles to diagram numbers 678, 693, 694 and 761 were exclusively on ex-ac underframes, but diagrams 675, 695 and 768 included coaches with both types of underframe. This is not really surprising because, as noted in Chapter 3, diagram numbers normally only related to bodywork design, dimensions and accommodation, and not to running gear. Lancing works stamped serial numbers on the lengthened underframes, prefixed AT ('altered trailer') or CM ('converted motor'). The vehicles from units 1717-1772 mounted on lengthened former ac underframes were:

Coach Nos.	Type	Diagram No.	Formed in Units	Total
8693-96	MThB	675	1724-1727	4
8697-8705	MThB	678	1728-1736	9
8706-08	MThB	675	1737-1739	3
8709-22	MThB	678	1740-1753	14
8731-46	MThB	678	1754-1769	16
8852-62	MCB	693	1717-1727	11
8863-71	MCB	694	1728-1736	9
8872-74	MCB	693	1737-1739	3
8875-84	MCB	694	1740-1749	10
8885-88	MCB	695	1750-1753	4
8889	MCB	694	1754	1
8890-8900	MCB	695	1755-1765	11
9461-80	TC	761	1750-1769	19
9481-83	TC	768	1770-72	1
9717-49	TC	761	1717-1749	33

Units 1797-1801, delivered between November 1931 and January 1932, were the final units to be constructed with LBSCR bodywork, and reverted to the same layout as 1631-1657 with two eight-compartment motor third brakes and a nine compartment trailer composite arranged 311111113. They formed part of a batch of seven units, 1795-1801, ordered on 12th June 1931 to HO 663 and intended for 'Brighton – Worthing services'. Their origin was slightly unusual as they made use of underframes, bogies and electrical equipment which had been delivered as part of an order for forty 4 LAV semi-fast units for the 1932 Brighton line electrification (see Volume 2), the last seven of the order subsequently being cancelled. 21 of the underframes, fourteen motor bogies and five sets of electrical equipment were used instead for these additional suburban units, all of which were converted at Ashford as one of the last jobs of this type carried out there. 1795 and 1796 had LSWR bodywork and are dealt with below.

The bodywork for 1797-1801 came from most of the remaining Billinton 'bogie block' vehicles still in steam-hauled service, by now already thirty years old. The motor third brakes in all five units were to diagram 674. Those in 1797-1798 utilised four 50ft eight-compartment thirds with the cab and van added and were numbered 8586-89. Those in 1799-1801 were numbered 8590-95 and utilised six 48ft third brakes with an additional compartment, cab and van added. The trailer composites made use of firsts, lengthened with a third class compartment added to each end, and were to diagram 762, numbered 9666-70. 1797-1801 were formed up in strict numerical order and were virtually identical in all respects to the '1631' series, suffering from the same narrow compartments and poor riding qualities of the motor coaches.

As the Brighton–Worthing electrification was not ready for a year after their completion, 1797-1801 were put to work in the London area, although due to their underframe origins they were known among staff as 'Brighton' units for some time. When the time came to provide stock for the coastal services, ex-LSWR '1201' class units, which had much more comfortable seating, went there instead. 1797-1801 remained on suburban services not only because their standard of accommodation was considered too poor for coastal duties but also due to their greater capacity. In any case neither type was exactly 'fresh from the workshops' by this time, so the Brighton operating department were probably quite happy to have the ex-LSWR units for whatever reason.

1600 (originally 1801), the last of five units constructed to HO 663 in November 1931–January 1932 utilising ex-LBSCR 'bogie-block' bodywork on underframes and bogies originally intended for main-line 4 LAV stock, stands at New Beckenham with a Charing Cross–Hayes working in 1946.
H.C. Hughes

FURTHER CONVERSIONS FROM LSWR STEAM STOCK

LSWR bodywork was used for seven further batches of three-coach motor units, totalling 89 (267 vehicles), but these could easily be distinguished from the original '1201' class by their flush steel-panelled brake van sides, as well as driving cabs with much flatter fronts. (A batch of two-coach units of similar origin, classified 2 NOL, was also built, but these were mainly for outer-suburban and coastal services, and so are dealt with in Volume 2.) As with other conversions, the vehicles kept most of their original body panelling as well as internal and external fittings. The first 44 units were converted for the 1928-29 Central section electrification, but the remainder came into existence mainly as additional stock to cover traffic increases and also for the few suburban extensions completed after 1930. A summary of the orders for these units is shown below:-

Unit Nos	HO (Date Ordered)	Into Traffic	Authorised Use
1658-1701	206 (3.9.26)	1928	Central section suburban (a)
1773-1782	553 (1.2.30)	6-8.30	Additional to suburban pool (b)
1783-1794	584 (5.6.30)	11.30-1.31	Additional to suburban pool
1795-1796	663 (12.6.31)	11.31-1/32	Additional to suburban pool (c)
1595-1599	803 (23.3.34)	7-8.34	Additional to suburban pool (d)
1585-1594	842 (13.2.35)	9-11.35	Additional to suburban pool (e)
1579-1584	900 (8.1.37)	8-12.37	Additional to suburban pool (f)

(a) 1658-1701 formed part of HO 206 which covered 116 units for the 1928 Central section electrification and also included 1601-1630 1631-1657, 1702-1716.

(b) 1773-1782 formed part of HO 553 which also included 1770-1772.

(c) 1795-1801 of which 1797-1801 had LBSCR bodywork, formed under HO663. They were charged to the Brighton electrification budget but allocated to the London suburban pool in exchange for 12xx series LSWR units sent to the Brighton area.

(d) To cover additional services to Motspur Park and hence on hand for the Chessington branch scheme. They may have been charged to Revenue Account.

(e) Charged to the Portsmouth No.1 electrification budget.

(f) Charged to the Lewisham loop and Sanderstead electrification budget. HO 842 also included lengthening original LSWR unit 1232.

To further complicate matters, there were no fewer than five variations of compartment arrangement within SR converted units with LSWR bodywork, and these did not necessarily coincide with the number blocks and HO order numbers listed above. The various arrangements are summarised in the following table, in unit number order as far as possible, and further information is provided in the detailed descriptions which follow.

Unit Nos	MThB	TC	MThB or MCB*
1579-1584	cab-van-33333333	311111113	33333333-van-cab
1585-1599	cab-van--½ 3333333	311111113	3333333½ van-cab (a)
1658-1694, 1696-1701, 1783	cab-van-33333333	3333311111	1133333-van-cab*
1695, 1773-1782, 1784/85	cab-van-33333333	3333331111	1113333-van-cab*
1786-1796	cab-van-33333333	111111133	33333333-van-cab

(a) '½' refers to third class 'coupé' or half-compartment, seating five.

Units 1658-1701 were ordered as part of HO 206 for the Central section suburban electrification completed in 1928-29, and were delivered between about March and July 1928. As with other units to the same HO number, conversion work was carried out at Ashford using underframes and trailer bogies from Lancing. Their bodies came from 44 more of the four-coach 'bogie block' sets of the type which had been utilised for the original LSWR conversions, although this time only three vehicles were used from each. (The remaining third brakes were used to produce coaches 9209-55 in trailer sets 1121-1167.)

With one exception these units were formed with an eight-compartment MThB, a trailer composite with five thirds and five firsts, and a MCB with two firsts at the inner end and five thirds. The oddity was 1695, whose TC 9344 and MCB 8830 were arranged 3333331111 and 1113333-van-cab respectively, as in 1702-1772. The reason for this inconsistency is that the 'bogie block' 51ft composite body used for TC 9344 was from a set built after August 1905, and so had one fewer first class compartment than those in earlier sets used for the other units in this order. All had the standard seating capacity of 180 third and 56 first class seats. Original features retained in all units included 'torpedo' ventilators, door locks and coloured views of places of interest served by the LSWR. Third class compartments which had originally been seconds in both types of composite retained their lincrusta ceilings.

The motor third brakes, numbered 8179-8222, were to SR diagram 671. They were converted from the 51ft seven-compartment third brakes by adding another compartment and converting the van area to include a cab. The 49ft

The only known photograph of an eight-compartment diagram 689 motor third brake with LSWR bodywork and English Electric 1936-type electrical equipment. The shorter brake van and power cable conduit looped over the headcode panel (rather than onto the roof) are distinguishing features. Coach 9798 was originally part of unit 1583, but augmented with an extra trailer to become 4 SUB 4428 by the time this photograph was taken at Forest Hill on 6th August 1950. *John H. Meredith*

composites were used to make the new motor composite brakes 8793-8836. All but one of these had a first class compartment removed from one end and cab and van added at the other to give the requisite five third and two first class compartments, and were to diagram 691. The exception was 8830 to diagram 697, whose three firsts and five thirds were arrived at by removing one third class compartment and adding the cab and van at the same end. All these vehicles had a tare weight of approximately forty tons. The trailer composites came from 51ft composites lengthened with the addition of two third class compartments and weighed just under 28 tons. They were numbered 9307-50 and with one exception were to diagram 759 with five compartments of each class. The oddity was coach 9344, which had six thirds and four firsts and was to diagram 760; as mentioned above, this is because the body used originally had only four first class compartments.

The thirteen units constructed between June 1930 and January 1931, 1773-1782 (part of HO 553) and 1783-1785 (part of HO 584), made use of yet more of the 'bogie-block'

sets, this time all but one being of the later type built from September 1905. Again only three vehicles were used from each of the steam-hauled sets, and some of the surplus third brakes were once more used in trailer sets, this time in the 1188-1194 batch. The conversion work was once more carried out at Ashford, using underframes fabricated or (in the case of seven vehicles) lengthened at Lancing. With one exception, all had the same formation as the formerly unique LSWR-bodied unit 1695, with which they were virtually identical in all respects, consisting of an eight compartment MThB, a TC arranged 3333331111 and a MCB arranged 1113333-van-cab. The different unit in this batch was 1783, which had the same compartment arrangement as 1658 etc because the body used for the trailer composite came from a 'bogie block' set built prior to September 1905. Similar comments to those above regarding fixtures and decor apply to these units also, which for some reason were being quoted as being two tons heavier. By now, vehicles were being allocated number blocks in available gaps in the 8xxx/9xxx series, but within these blocks units were formed up in numerical order.

The motor third brakes (8555-64 and 8223-25, diagram 671) had the same origin and were identical to those in the previous batch. Motor composite brakes 9808-17, 9823/24, to diagram 697, were again converted from 49ft composites in the same manner as 8830, while odd vehicle 9822 in unit 1783 was to diagram 691, having the same origins as 8793 etc. described above. The trailer composites in these units (9649-58, 9301-03) were to diagram 760, with the exception of 9301 in 1783 which was to diagram 759, and all were again lengthened from 51ft composites by the addition of two compartments.

Seven vehicles in the 1773-1782 batch had LSWR bodies mounted on lengthened LBSCR-design ac underframes, surplus after all ex-ac carriage bodies had been rebuilt. These were MThB 8564 (unit 1782), TCs 9656-58 (units 1780-1782) and MCBs 9815-17 (units 1780-1782). The only LSWR-bodied unit entirely on ac frames was therefore 1782, which later became Instruction Unit S10. Three other vehicles, 9656/7 and 9815, were retained in passenger service until 1959, again some years after the remainder of LSWR-bodied stock had become extinct. The reasons for all these survivals is that their non-standard underframes were not suitable for reuse in new EPB stock.

The nine units 1786-1794, delivered in January and February 1931 as additional stock, were again assembled at Ashford but all had new 62ft underframes. Unlike the remainder of HO 584 however, these units were formed with two eight-compartment motor third brakes (numbers 8226, 8565-81) and a trailer composite (9304-06, 9484, 9659-63) with seven firsts and two thirds, but arranged 111111133 with both third class compartments at one end of the coach. Again, although it will be seen that the number series of these coaches was not entirely consecutive (by this time the tidy number blocks allocated in 1922 had been filled, and odd spare spaces were being used), these units were made up in strict order. Thus 1786 was formed 8226+9304+8565 etc. Vehicle weights were roughly similar to those in previous LSWR-bodied units, typically 40 tons for the motor brakes.

The bodies of the 27 vehicles in units 1786-1794 came from LWSR six-wheeled coaches dating from 1898-1900, cropped and spliced together in a similar manner to the '1401' class. Three diagrams were necessary for the motor third brakes to cover the different compartment spacings, resulting from the variety of coaches utilised. 8565/67/69/71 were to diagram 680; of these 8565 utilised all six compartments of a 34ft third brake plus the two first class compartments from a 31ft five-compartment composite, while the remainder used a six-compartment third instead of the third brake but were otherwise similar. 8226 and 8566/68/70 were to diagram 682; these also used a six-compartment third but this time the two additional compartments came from a third brake. Finally, diagram 683 covered vehicles 8572-81 which once more utilised a six-compartment third but now made up to length with two compartments from a five-compartment third, except for 8581 where they came from a third brake. Motor coach 8572 in unit 1790 was badly damaged in a collision while berthed at London Bridge (Central) on 19th April 1934

and the following month was given a new body with seven compartments and a coupe (probably to diagram 687), altered from an LSWR eight-compartment 48ft third, SR (steam) no. 232.

The trailer composites of 1786-1794 were also covered by three diagrams. 9304-06 were to diagram 765, apparently made up using a five-compartment composite arranged 11333 and a five compartment third (built as a first). (This is unclear as the only official dimensioned layout diagram of these vehicles in the author's possession mysteriously omits the distances between compartment partitions, which are present in all the other drawings!) 9484 and 9659-61 were to diagram 766. 9659-61 utilised a five-compartment first with two new first class compartments built onto one end and two thirds from a six-compartment body onto the other. 9484 was from part of a 2F3Th plus a 5F, giving 7F2Th. 9662 and 9663 were both assigned to diagram 767 but differed in their origins. Both were basically lengthened five-compartment firsts, the additional compartments in 9662 coming from a 2F3Th composite with one third class compartment removed. The origin of 9663 was somewhat more complex, the two extra first class compartments coming from another all-first and the two thirds being added from scratch using either entirely new wood or parts left over. (The official record lists only the two first class vehicles used.)

1795 and 1796, assembled at Ashford and delivered in November 1931, had the same formation and bodywork origins as 1786-1794, being made up with two diagram 683 eight-compartment motor third brakes (8582-85) and a diagram 767 trailer composite (9664/65) formed in the same way as 9663. However they constituted part of seven-unit order HO 663 (also including 1797-1801) and were built using spare underframes and equipment intended for Brighton main line 4 LAV units which had been cancelled. Although known therefore as 'Brighton' units, as related earlier they remained in the London area due to their greater seating capacity.

1585-1599 were converted at Eastleigh in two batches. 1595-1599 to HO 803 entered service in reverse numerical order between July and August 1934, followed by 1585-1594 to HO 842, again in reverse order, between September and November 1935. The origins of 1595-1599 seem somewhat more complex than the term 'additional stock' might suggest, and provide a good example of SR creative accounting. Although not budgeted for any particular scheme, they were almost certainly intended for the 1935 extensions to Sevenoaks. However, the stock actually charged to the Sevenoaks budget included seventeen two-coach 2 NOLs (see Volume 2) which were really intended for coastal duties, but no three-coach units. This peculiar accounting exercise was probably to keep the cost of the Eastbourne electrification scheme down, whereas additional suburban units could be more easily justified to a sceptical Board. (On Brighton–West Worthing services these NOLs also replaced the ex-LSWR units which could then be returned to the London area, thus providing sufficient additional stock for the Sevenoaks services.) 1585-1594 were more straightforward, being intended to provide the extra units necessary for the Sanderstead and Nunhead–Lewisham electrifications.

1585-1599 all made use of former LSWR main line non-corridor bogie coaches which had slightly wider third class compartments than the 'bogie block' sets, so it was not possible to fit eight on to the standard 62ft frame and still leave enough length for the van and cab. Thus the motor third brakes of this batch (numbers 9831-60, to diagram 687), adapted from eight-compartment 48ft thirds dating from 1895-1900, had only seven and one half compartments giving a reduced seating capacity of 75. Thus there were ten fewer third class seats than usual in each unit. The 4ft half compartment, or 'coupé', was positioned next to the brake van and had one row of five seats, facing backwards from it – passengers looking up from their newspapers encountered a blank wall. The trailer composites (9761-9775, dia. 770) were of the standard pattern, with a third class compartment at either end of seven firsts. They were converted from 46ft seven-compartment firsts, dating from 1895/96, with a new third class compartment added at each end. Unusually, there was a 6in void between the third and fourth first class compartments which had been incorporated when the coaches were new. Again, vehicles were formed into units in numerical order. Tare weights of the motor coaches and trailers were 42 and 28 tons respectively.

Internally 1585-1599 all had comfortable 'full back' seating in third class. In the first three units of the 1934 batch this was trimmed in the standard red, orange and black moquette, but the remainder were outshopped with the new 'jazz' patterns introduced that year. The 1935 batch had a narrow rexine-covered panel between the seat tops and fascia, and in the motor coaches the partition separating the coupe from the adjacent compartment reached only to luggage rack height. It seems that these low partitions were filled-in on first overhaul, and certainly none remained by 1950.

The intended purpose of 1579-1584, to HO 900 and delivered from Eastleigh between August and December 1937, was also not straightforward. Budgeted out of the Portsmouth No.1 electrification account, they entered the suburban pool to help provide sufficient stock for the extensions to Holmwood/Horsham and to Chessington South. (Stock actually budgeted to the 'Motspur Park–Leatherhead' [i.e. Chessington South] account was nominally twenty more 2 NOLs, but these were allocated to Waterloo–Windsor/Weybridge services, displacing further three-coach units to other suburban duties.) It is possible that 1579-1584 were also intended to work the summer Woking–Alton shuttles but it is likely that NOLs were actually used for this as well.

1579-1584 were the final six three-coach suburban units to be introduced, and while mechanically virtually identical to their predecessors, they differed significantly in their electrical equipment. As mentioned in Chapter 3, in 1936 the SR entered into an exclusive ten-year contract with English Electric for the supply of EMU electrical equipment, and the control system was redesigned mainly to increase the number of components in common with the express stock. The new system, although fully compatible for multiple working with the existing Metrovick equipment, featured electro-pneumatic (rather than electro-magnetic) contactors. Units so fitted, which would eventually include examples of 2 NOL, 2 BIL, 2 HAL, 4 LAV and 4 SUB types, were classified 1936 Stock. The motors were also supplied by English Electric, but were of standard type and classified EE 339. Externally the 1936 Stock units were easily recognisable because the cable conduits from the power jumpers no longer ran up the cab front on to the roof, but were merely looped over the headcode box, giving a much cleaner appearance.

A further advance relevant here was that, unlike the Metrovick equipment it superseded, the English Electric system was fitted entirely below underframe level. This freed body space for more seating accommodation, and it was therefore possible to return to an eight-compartment layout in the motor coaches, even though the bodies came from the same source as 1585-1599. They were to diagram 689, were numbered 9789-9800 and weighed 42 tons. A result of the additional seating in the motor coaches was that these units reverted to the standard third class capacity of 180. The trailers were identical to those in the previous batch, to the same diagram, and were numbered 9671-74 and 9759-60. These units were also formed up in the vehicles' numerical order. Interiors were similar to the earlier LSWR conversions, but internal metal fittings had an 'oxydised' copper finish, third class seats had loose cushions, and in at least some units the door ventilators were blanked off internally.

Two further coaches in motor units were given LSWR bodywork in the period up to 1939. These were motor third brakes 8371 and 8523 from units 1473 and 1615 respectively, which were the colliding vehicles in the Battersea Park accident of 2nd April 1937 (see Chapter 2.) In the case of 8371 the existing SECR wooden bodywork was smashed beyond repair but the underframe was salvageable, whereas 8523 was a complete write-off. A new underframe was provided for 8523 and both were given replacement bodies with seven compartments and a coupé, converted from 48ft eight-compartment thirds, identical to those in 1585-1599 and also to diagram 687. Presumably this was done because there were no more suitable coaches of SECR origin which could be used. It is thought that 8371 retained its 9ft motor bogie and DK 77 motors, making it unique as the only LSWR-bodied motor coach with this equipment, but there is now no clear evidence as it was a war casualty.

THE SR TWO-COACH TRAILER SETS

As explained earlier, Herbert Jones' LSWR electric rolling stock arrangements were continued by the Southern Railway, including the adaptation of further existing steam-hauled vehicles to form two-coach trailer sets. These trailer sets operated on most routes only during the peaks, marshalled between pairs of three-coach motor units to form eight-car trains which provided (in theory, if not always in practice) sufficient capacity at these times. This formation had its problems, particularly regarding the 'blind shunting' necessary at the beginning and end of the rush hours, but it survived until the last trailer set was withdrawn at the end of September 1948.

Alterations to convert the former steam-hauled vehicles for electric use were somewhat less extensive than those for the motor units, and only for conversions of ex-LSWR stock by the SR were new underframes built. Otherwise, the modifications generally consisted of adding through control and power cables along the roofs, with jumper cables and their associated receptacles mounted on a raised box at waist-height at the outer ends of each set. Other than on ex-LBSCR vehicles which already had them, Westinghouse quick-acting air brakes were fitted. The coaches in the majority of the sets were originally only loose-coupled, but the close-coupling/centre-buffer arrangements were used in some of the later conversions and subsequent reformations. Except in the cases where bodies were lengthened on new frames, interiors were generally not touched except for the fitting of inadequate electric heaters under the seats and series-wired lighting. All were third class only, each compartment seating ten passengers. Until 1932 electrical installation and bodywork alterations were carried out at Lancing, but some later conversions were done at Eastleigh.

The various batches are described below in order of introduction, rather than by bodywork origin, although in many cases the vehicle numbers were not in order. The first eighty sets for the initial Western and Eastern section schemes used LBSCR vehicles, but when this source was exhausted it was necessary to utilise SECR and LSWR coaches to provide the 47 sets for the Central section dc scheme, the LSWR bodywork being lengthened and mounted on new 62ft frames as on the motor units. Following this a small quantity of redundant LBSCR ac stock (either not required or unsuitable for use in dc motor units) was used to form twenty sets, and a further seven SECR/LSWR pairs were turned out. The remaining 68 trailer set coaches were lengthened from former LSWR main line non-corridor stock in 1934-37, but in a complex reformation exercise these were eventually all paired with LBSCR vehicles from earlier sets.

Sets 1025-1037 (Coaches 8949-74) Authorised on 9th October 1924 to HO order 67 for the Western section Guildford/Dorking extension, these sets were made up from pairs of LBSCR 54ft nine-compartment thirds, originally built at Lancing in 1921 and adapted for dc electric working there in April and May 1925. Ex-LBSCR coaches were chosen because they were already fitted with the necessary Westinghouse air brake. Compartments retained their original red and black tapestry upholstery. The vehicles, given SR diagram number 723, were loose-coupled with end and intermediate side buffers. The overall length of each set was 115ft and tare weight was 48 tons.

Sets 1051-1117 (Coaches 8999-9132) For the 1925-26 Eastern section electrification, 59 sets numbered 1051-1109 were initially ordered from Lancing on 11th July 1924 to HO 53. These were also to be modified from pairs of nine-compartment LBSCR coaches, planned to be redundant following the Coulsdon and Sutton electrification, and it was intended that work on them should start in the autumn of 1924. However,

opening of the Coulsdon/Sutton ac scheme was delayed, and in the meantime Central section operators protested that withdrawal of steam coaches would lead to insufficient stock for rush-hour services, particularly as autumn was the busiest time for City business traffic. It was therefore not possible to release vehicles for conversion until April 1925, so there were insufficient trailer sets available for the start of electric services on the Eastern section in July, leading to the interim formation of some motor units with four coaches for the first few weeks of service, as mentioned earlier. The inadequate maintenance cover which became apparent soon after services started was rectified by providing a further ten motor units and eight trailer sets. The additional trailer sets were authorised on 11th September 1925 to HO 136, and records indicate that they were funded from the Revenue account, rather than from the Eastern section electrification budget which had probably all been apportioned. This could be done by assigning the cost of adaptation to the overhauls and repairs budget. Numbered 1110-1117, they were converted at Lancing in February and March 1926 from more nine-compartment LBSCR vehicles. The initial HO 53 batch was officially completed by January 1926 but not all were ready for traffic until June. Note that, although within each batch the coaches were allocated into sets in a somewhat random manner, there was no overlap of vehicles between the two batches, the 1111-1117 batch being formed of coaches 9117-32.

The 122 vehicles which made up 1051-1110 and 1114 were of two basic types, both on 54ft underframes. 8999/9001/10/11/13/14/20/22/25-34 and 9060-9120 (78 coaches) had been built new at Lancing or by contractors in 1910-13 and were also to diagram 723. 9000/02-09/12/15-19/21/23/24/35-59 (44 coaches) were from former six-compartment six-wheeled vehicles which had been lengthened with three new compartments and placed on bogie underframes in 1910-11; these had slightly different compartment spacings and on conversion became diagram 724. The two types were distributed at random among these sets, which were loose-coupled with an overall length of 115ft and a tare weight of 46 tons. The twelve coaches formed in 1111-1113 and 1115-1117, 9121-32, were former 'bogie block' vehicles dating from 1899-1901, and were to diagram 726. Being only 50ft long over body, these had narrower compartments and, like the motor units of similar origin, were cramped and uncomfortable. Again loose-coupled, overall set length was 108ft and tare weight 48 tons. Many sets of the '1051' type and all six of the '1111' type were reformed from 1934 by substituting an LSWR-bodied vehicle for one of the LBSCR ones.

Sets 1121-1167 (Coaches 8975-98, 9133-55 and 9209-55) For the 1928/29 dc electrification of the Central section, 47 trailer sets were initially provided. Authorised on 30th September 1926 to HO 214, the original order was for 52 sets, the last five subsequently being cancelled. Comprising one coach of South Eastern origin and one of South Western, these sets had a somewhat peculiar appearance. 8975-98 and 9133-55 were 46ft SECR eight-compartment thirds, which had been built between 1900 and 1906 (and subsequently

Diagram 725 ex-SER 46ft third 8991, formed in trailer set 1137, berthed at Hayes in about 1946. Note the quarterlight replaced by boarding, a common repair in the immediate post-war period. *H.C. Hughes*

earmarked by Raworth for use in four-coach motor units as part of the SECR electrification scheme). On conversion, they were given diagram number 725. Coach 8981 was unusual in having matchboarded lower bodysides. 9209-55, to diagram 727, had new 62ft underframes on which were mounted bodies from LSWR seven-compartment 'bogie-block' third brakes with the van removed and four extra compartments added. Converted at Lancing between December 1927 and February 1929, these sets were 114ft long, with a tare weight of 49 tons. Unlike earlier sets, 1121-1167 were close-coupled using the standard SR centre-buffer arrangement, the centre buffer being fitted to the SECR coach and the rubbing block to the LSWR-bodied coach at the opposite end to the new compartments.

Sets 1168-1180 (Coaches 9256-81) 1168-1178 were ordered on 25th August 1928 (HO 375), and 1179-1180 followed on 14th November (HO 399), the former being additional stock for the Central section, the latter being charged to the Wimbledon–Sutton budget. These sets were formed of two identical nine-compartment vehicles (to diagram 728) converted in the latter half of 1929 from LBSCR ac CP stock motor coaches by replacing the former motorman's and guard's section with two new compartments. They retained their underframes with distinctive plate-frame trussing, but the former motor bogies were replaced by ex-ac trailer bogies. Loose-coupled, their length was 115ft; their weight 50 tons.

Sets 1181-1186 (Coaches 9282-93) These sets were covered by HO 455 of 7th May 1929, and were formed between February and August 1930. Although charged to the Windsor electrification account, they were really intended for general suburban use. A number of peak hour Windsor duties required eight-car trains, so some of these sets probably did eventually run on the Windsor branch. Each was made up of one nine-compartment vehicle (odd numbers 9283-93, diagram 728) identical to those in 1168-1180 and converted from a former ac CP motor coach with plate frames, and one eight and one-

Diagram 728 trailer third 9272, formed in trailer set 1176, was converted from LBSCR CP ac motor coach 8586 in 1929 for the Central section dc electrification, retaining its original distinctive underframe with plate frame trussing. It is seen here berthed at Hayes in 1946. *H.C. Hughes*

half compartment coach (even numbers 9282-92), originally built as a driving trailer composite for ac working but with the former driving compartment now converted into a coupé. 9282/88/90 were former CW coaches (with four ex-firsts) and were to diagram 730, while 9284/86/92 were former CP vehicles (with three ex-firsts) to diagram 729. Length of these loose-coupled sets was 115ft and their weight, 49 tons.

Sets 1187-1188 (Coaches 9294-97) These two sets were ordered on 5th September 1929 to HO 516, charged to the Dartford–Gravesend budget, and completed by July 1930. 1187 was identical to 1168-1180, vehicles 9294-95 being to diagram 728 and converted from the two remaining CP motor coaches. 1188 had the same formation and origins as 1121-1167, 9296 being the former SECR vehicle and 9297 an eleven-compartment LSWR body on a new 62ft underframe. Diagram numbers were the same as for similar vehicles in earlier sets.

Sets 1189-1194 (Coaches 9156-67) These were ordered to HO 585 (5th June 1930) and were converted between February and March 1931. They were identical to 1121-1167 and 1188, having one 46ft eight-compartment coach of SECR origin (even numbers 9156-66, dia. 725) and one 62ft LSWR-bodied eleven-compartment vehicle (odd numbers 9157-67, diagram 727).

Sets 1195-1198 (Coaches 9168-75) These four sets were ordered to HO 791 of 25th November 1933, charged to the Sevenoaks electrification budget. Converted at Lancing, all were completed between September and November 1934.

They were formed of pairs of ten-compartment vehicles, close coupled, on new 62ft underframes. The coaches were to diagrams 731 and 732, the former having a centre buffer and the latter a rubbing block. The bodywork was of LSWR origin, and made use of eight-compartment bogie thirds dating from 1895-1900, with two additional compartments added at the inner end. To make up the required length, the additional compartments had a width of 6ft 11in, virtually a foot more than the others in the coach, Internally, these sets were given 'full-back' seating with loose cushions, and the additional compartments were separated by a low partition which reached only to the luggage racks. Overall length was 129ft with a tare weight of approximately 54 tons. 1195-1198 ran in traffic for only about a year in their original formations.

Following accident damage, LBSCR 9078 in set 1078 was condemned and replaced late in 1935 by a ten-compartment LSWR-bodied vehicle given the same number. This utilised the body of a 48ft eight-compartment third as in 1195-1198, but was mounted on an SR 61ft underframe recovered from 1927 loco-hauled 'continental' corridor third 779 which had burnt out at Dover Marine in July 1935, rather than a standard 62ft frame. The two additional compartments were therefore only 6ft 5in (rather than 6ft 11in) between partitions, and the non-standard dimensions required a new diagram number, 739. Coach 9140 was an accident loss at Epsom Downs in 1937, and was replaced in set 1152 by an LBSCR 54ft nine-compartment vehicle with the same number to diagram 737.

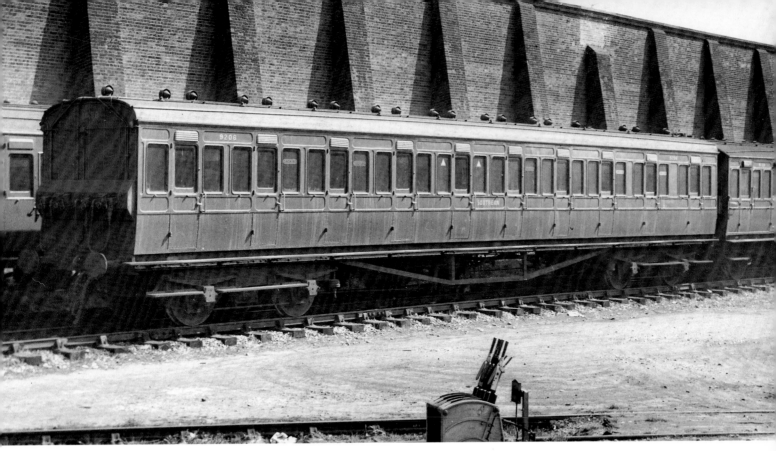

The trailer set story now becomes extremely complicated. A further five small batches, totalling thirty sets, were ordered from Lancing or Eastleigh between February 1935 and April 1937, to make up eight-coach peak-hour trains with the additional motor units ordered during this period. Numbered 989-1000, 1038-1050, 1118-1120 and 1199-1200, all had but a fleeting existence in their original formations, and it is doubtful whether any worked in passenger service before being reformed. All were of the same origin and layout as 1195-1198, with LSWR bodywork on (with one exception) new 62ft frames and bogies built at Lancing. Internally they resembled the final LSWR-bodied motor unit conversions, with some having rexine-covered panelling and 'oxydised' brass fittings. The later sets were outshopped in a simplified livery with much-reduced lining along the waist only. Original formations are not all known with certainty. Details of these sets are as follows:

Sets 1043-1050 (Coaches 9176-91) These eight sets were ordered to HO 844 (13th February 1935), charged to the Lewisham loop and Sanderstead electrification budget. Converted at Eastleigh, all had been outshopped in their original form by September 1935.

Sets 1039-1042 (Coaches 9192-99) These four sets were ordered to HO 853 (29th March 1935) from Lancing as additional stock, and were completed in their original formation during the latter half of 1935.

Sets 1038, 1118-1120, 1199 (Coaches 9200-08, 9298) These five sets were ordered from Eastleigh (as were succeeding batches) to HO 901 dated 8th January 1936, charged to the Portsmouth No.1 electrification budget. 1038 appeared in June 1936 and 1118-20/99 followed in the first three months of 1937. They were intended to provide additional stock for extensions to Holmwood/Horsham/Chessington etc. 9298 made use of the spare 61ft underframe from 'continental' corridor first 7372 (also destroyed in the fire at Dover Marine in August 1935) and was in consequence identical to accident replacement 9078 (see above), its two additional compartments being 6in narrower than standard. This vehicle was therefore to diagram 739.

Sets 998-1000, 1200 (Coaches 9299-9300, 9825-30) These four sets were ordered to HO 929 (28th May 1936) as additional stock, and all were outshopped by September 1937. Vehicles 9825-30 had the lower half of their bodysides flush-panelled in steel, with only a single narrow beading strip below the windows.

Sets 989-997 (Coaches 10401-18) These final nine sets were ordered from Eastleigh to HO 965 (16th April 1937) and were completed as additional stock between about January and May 1938. All vehicles were given steel lower bodyside panelling, as on 9825-30.

Above Reformed trailer set 1068 is seen parked at Crystal Palace (Low Level) in about 1947. The leading vehicle, 9206, was constructed using lengthened LSWR bodywork on a new 62ft underframe; the extra width of the two additional compartments at the far end is clearly visible. In 1948 this coach was used to augment motor unit 1660 to 4 SUB 4193. *H.C. Hughes*

In 1934 it was decided to reform some wholly LBSCR-bodied trailer sets with converted LSWR steam coaches, taking advantage of the need for additional stock to even out seating capacities. (Mention has already been made of passenger complaints regarding inconsistent seating capacity on a particular service from day to day.) As explained earlier, between 1934 and 1938, 34 additional sets, nominally formed of two LSWR coaches, were turned out, and as they became available, LBSCR-bodied sets from the 1051-1117 series were split, each vehicle then being paired with a ten-compartment LSWR-bodied vehicle, mostly from one of those 34 sets which had been given numbers 989-1000, 1038-1050, 1118-1120 and 1195-1200. This gave a seating capacity of 190 in an overall length of 117ft 6in or 121ft 6in and a tare weight of approximately 51 tons. Note that although all the set numbers were reused, in many cases in the 1051-1117 group neither of the vehicles in a reformed set came from the original set of that number. The reformed sets were close-coupled, so modifications were necessary to the LBSCR vehicles; apart from the removal of side buffers at the inner end, half were given a rubbing block and paired with a centre buffer-equipped diagram 731 vehicle, while the remainder were given a centre buffer and paired with a diagram 732 vehicle with rubbing block. They were also outshopped in a simplified livery to match their new LSWR-bodied partner, and many were also refurbished internally with loose seat cushions.

The sets involved in these reformations are listed below, with the HO authority date for reforming.

Trailer Sets involved in Reformations, 1935-37

HO (Date)	LSWR-bodied Sets	LBSCR Sets	Total	Dates to traffic
848 (18.3.35)	1195-1198	1087, 1115-1117	8	1935
849 (18.3.35)	1043-1050	1064/70/71/92/97 1111-1113	16	1936
878 (15.8.35)	1039-1042	1055/59/73/96	8	1936
913 (3.4.36)	1038, 1118-20, 1199	1067/68/72/98, 1103	10	1937
933 (18.6.36)	998-1000, 1200	1081/84/85/95	8	1937
996 (7.9.37)	989-997	1051/61/82/86/90, 1093/99, 1104/08	18	1938

Following these reformations there were 77 sets composed of one LSWR-bodied and one LBSCR-bodied vehicle, and 56 with two LBSCR coaches.

The first of the trailer sets to be withdrawn were both original LSWR examples. 1013 was written-off following an accident at Hampton Court on 19th November 1937, while 1003 was condemned after an incident at Effingham Junction on 29th June 1938.

By about 1938, and possibly as early as 1935, the trailer sets were assigned type numbers related to their compartment arrangement, seating capacity and overall dimensions.

In the descriptions which follow, overall lengths are quoted to the nearest foot. These type descriptions also provide a summary of the 210 trailer sets in traffic at the height of their use, just before withdrawals commenced.

Type 1: 11 sets 1002/04/06/08/10/12/13/16/17/21/22/24 These were the original LSWR sets with nine-compartment 51ft and eight-compartment 49ft (8901-type) vehicles. They had a seating capacity of 170 and an overall length of 105ft.

Type 2: 11 sets 1001/03/05/07/09/11/14/15/18/19/20/23 These were the original LSWR sets with nine-compartment 51ft and eight compartment 51ft (8913-type) vehicles. They had a seating capacity of 170 and an overall length of 107ft.

Type 3: 56 sets 1025-1037,1052-54/56/58/60/62/63/65/69/74 -76/77/79/80/83/88/89 1091/94, 1100-02/05-07/10/14, 1168-1180, 1187 These were the remaining sets formed with two 54ft LBSCR vehicles following the reformation exercise. All had two nine-compartment coaches seating 180. Loose-coupled, their overall length was 115ft.

Type 4: Six sets 1181-1186 These were made up of one nine-compartment coach and one eight-and-a-half compartment coach loose-coupled, again both with LBSCR bodywork. Their seating capacity was 175 and their overall length 115ft.

Type 5: 52 sets 1121-1151, 1153-1167, 1189-1194 These were formed of an eight-compartment ex-SECR third and an eleven-compartment coach with LSWR bodywork on a standard 62ft underframe, close-coupled. Their seating capacity was 190 and their overall length 114ft.

Type 6: Twelve sets 1049/50/97, 1111-1113/15-17, 1195-1197 These were the reformed sets composed of a LSWR-bodied ten-compartment coach on a new underframe, and 50ft LBSCR vehicle with nine compartments originally from sets 1111-1113 and 1115-17. They were close-coupled and seated 190 in an overall length of 117ft.

Type 7: One set 1152 This unique set included an LBSCR nine-compartment 54ft third (provided as an accident replacement for a SECR coach) and an eleven-compartment LSWR-bodied coach identical to those in the 1121 series. Seating capacity was therefore 200 and overall length 121ft.

Type 8: 52 sets 989-1000, 1038-1048/55/59/64/68/70-73/87/92/96, 1103/18-20, 1198-1200 These were the 'standard' reformed sets comprising a 54ft LBSCR nine-compartment coach close-coupled to an LSWR-bodied ten-compartment coach on a 62ft underframe. Seating capacity was 190 and overall length 121ft.

Type 9: Two sets 1078, 1098 Almost identical to Type 8, the LSWR-bodied coaches in these sets were on 61ft underframes recovered from withdrawn corridor stock. They seated 190 in an overall length of 120ft.

The subsequent history of the trailer sets, leading up to their abolition in 1948, is dealt with later in the chapter.

THE SOUTH LONDON LINE AND WIMBLEDON–WEST CROYDON TWO-CAR UNITS

Twelve two-coach units were converted from the vehicles of the original 1909 South London line ac sets. As recorded above, in 1910-12 the sixteen motor coaches of this stock had been reformed with narrower 8ft wide driving trailers (converted from steam stock) to produce two-coach sets, while the original centre trailers had been put to work on the Brighton main line following a short period in storage. On conversion of the South London line to the third rail system in 1928, the overhead sets were withdrawn, the service being taken over by standard three-coach dc units. While the driving trailers of the displaced stock could be incorporated into the ongoing dc suburban unit construction programme, the motor coaches were unsuitable for this, being 9ft 6in wide overall.

It was decided to adapt these sixteen former ac motor coaches to form eight two-coach loose-coupled dc units which would then return to service on the South London line. The conversion work (to HO 372 dated 25th August 1928) was carried out at Lancing during late 1928 and early 1929, the completed units emerging in April ready to return to traffic the following month. Eight of the vehicles concerned remained as motor third brakes, the others becoming driving trailer composite brakes. Initially numbered 1901-1908, the overall length of each unit was 127ft 2in and weight was 78 tons, with the MThB accounting for 45 tons. Coach numbers were 8723-30 (MThB, SR diagram No. 681) and 9751-58 (DTCB, dia. 793). These units have often been quoted as 2 SL, but this designation never appeared in operating documents.

8723-30 were converted from ac MThB Nos. 8604/06/08/10/13-16, and 9751-58 from MThB Nos. 8601/02/05/07/09/11/12/03 respectively. All were allocated to units 1901-08 in numerical order.

Photographs of the dc South London line units in the later SR period are rare. In this view a pair, led by 1803, stands outside the former ac shed at Selhurst having just been outshopped in about 1946. Driving trailer third (formerly composite) 9753 is nearest the camera; its cab, with side droplights, has been little altered externally since its former existence as an ac motor coach. *A.T.H. Tayler*

Following conversion, the motor coaches consisted of motorman's and guard's compartments, followed by seven third class seating bays connected by side-gangway. The full-width cab was new and had its own external doors, and to provide enough space for the guard's van it was necessary to abolish the original first seating bay. Fewer modifications were needed to produce the driving trailers, the original van space and half-width cubicle for the motorman remaining in situ. Two first class compartments without a side gangway, each seating eight, were partitioned off at the non-driving end, resulting in this vehicle having six third class bays. Apart from this, the interiors of both coaches remained largely unchanged, the swing doors and side gangways remaining in their original positions. Following these re-arrangements, seating was provided for sixteen first class and 108 third class passengers.

Externally, few changes were made to the unusual square panelling and opening toplights (some of the latter had already been plated over before conversion), but the motor third brakes were given plain steel panelling around the cab and van area in the same manner as the three-coach suburban unit conversions. The original louvres above the door drop-lights were replaced by rectangular box-shaped 'tin' ventilators. Also retained were the distinctive depressed roofs at the driving ends, where the ac bow-collectors had originally been mounted. The driving ends were given the standard

Above In final condition with 'Monarch' ventilators on the flattened roofs of the driving cabs, South London line unit 1803 stands at Wandsworth Road with a Victoria–London Bridge service. *R.C. Riley*

Left Interior of a third class section of a South London line two-coach unit, not long before withdrawal. Relatively little has changed since the vehicle was built in 1908-09, but the well-worn upholstery moquette is one of the green 'jazz' patterns introduced in about 1935. *Lens of Sutton*

2 WIM unit 1812 stands at Wimbledon on 29th June 1953, waiting to depart with the 3.48pm to West Croydon. Note the full-width 2 headcode stencil, unique to this route. The leading vehicle is driving trailer third 9954 with half-width driving compartment, hence the offside droplight is actually part of the guard's van. *J.H. Aston*

centre headcode panel and EMU jumpers, and the bus lines and control cables were routed along the coach roofs. The coaches retained their original underframes with plate-steel trussing and side buffers at both ends. Thus the usual intermediate centre buffer was not fitted, connection between coaches being by normal screw coupling. New motor and trailer bogies were fitted, the former being the 8ft 9in wheel-base 'central' type and the two inner trailer bogies the normal 8ft suburban variety. The unpowered bogie at the driving end of the DTCB had 8ft 9in frames and was fitted with collector shoes, the first trailer bogies on SR electric stock to be so equipped. Electrical equipment included the usual Metropolitan-Vickers MV 339 motors and the same manufacturer was also responsible for the other electrical equipment, which was identical to that on the standard three-coach suburban units.

For service on the peculiar Wimbledon to West Croydon line (a largely single-track route through sparsely-populated marshland in South London, electrified in 1930 for reasons outlined in Chapter 2) the eight aforementioned first class trailers, then numbered 7644-51 in the SR steam stock list, were rebuilt at Lancing and Brighton in 1930 to HO 530 dated 4th November 1929. Four vehicles became motor composite brakes and the other four driving trailer third brakes, and these were made up into four loose-coupled units, initially numbered 1909-1912.

As with the SL stock, conversion was planned to involve the minimum of internal rearrangement. In both cases the centre lavatories which had been installed for the main line were removed. The motor coaches were converted by replacing three seating bays with new steel-panelled motorman's and guard's compartments. The two bays adjacent to the van had first class seating and the gangway changed sides in the second, allowing the use of an existing partition and swing door to separate the two classes of accommodation. The remaining four bays were downclassed to third, giving a vehicle with twelve first and 33 third class seats. The driving trailers were arrived at by replacing two seating bays at one end by a van with a half-width cubicle for the motorman. This cubicle had droplights but no external doors, as on the South London driving trailers, and it seems likely that Lancing Works made use of parts discarded when the SL motor coaches were rebuilt. These changes gave a vehicle with seven third class seating bays, accommodating 57. In both vehicles a door was fitted between the guard's van and passenger accommodation; in conjunction with the side gangways this enabled issue and collection of tickets to take place en route, although there was no gangway between the coaches.

1909-1912 had the standard SR domed cab roofs grafted onto the LBSCR body profile, giving them a pleasing appearance similar to the semi-fast 2 BILs which appeared five years later. Otherwise they were similar externally to the SL units, and had exactly the same bogies and traction equipment. Overall length was 127ft 4in and tare weights of the motor coaches and trailers were 44 and 32 tons respectively. Total seating was originally twelve first and 91 third. Coach numbers were 9818-21 (MCB, diagram 696) and 9951-54 (DTThB, dia. 794). As with the South London line units, the convenient classification 2 WIM, sometimes quoted, seems to have been entirely unofficial. 9818-9821, allocated to units 1909-12, were converted from steam firsts (SR nos.) 7651/44/49/47, and 9951-54 from steam firsts 7645/46/48/50.

Note that in the period 1909 to 1930, each coach carried no fewer than *four* numbers; these being original ac centre trailer, LBSCR steam stock, SR steam stock and SR dc electric.

Once outshopped, the WIM units were run-in on South London line services from March 1930, taking up their duties on the Wimbledon–West Croydon section from 6th July.

As both the SL and WIM units were 9ft 6in wide overall, they were restricted to the South London and Wimbledon–West Croydon lines, with access to Selhurst Depot from Peckham Rye via Streatham and from West Croydon. 1909-1912 were often berthed on the Down side at Wimbledon, and both types were also permitted down the Brighton main line via Quarry tunnel for overhaul at Lancing Works. On both routes they usually ran as single units, but peak-hour workings on the South London line were of four cars. There is plenty of photographic evidence to show that South London units frequently worked on the Wimbledon–West Croydon line (particularly in their later years), but the use of WIM units between London Bridge and Victoria was less frequent. The equipment on both types was identical to that of three-coach suburban units and coupled working was possible in theory, but because of the exceptional route restrictions on the remainder of the suburban network, no SL or WIM unit ever worked 'passenger' with a three-coach unit.

Further changes to these units were few, and as they were not involved with the 4 SUB reformations from 1942 it is convenient to relate their later history until withdrawal here. Some SR operating documents used the greater width of this stock to quote an increased third class seating capacity, as had LBSCR management in earlier years. Revised third class totals were 134 for the SL units and 112 for the WIMs. The full-width seats across the ends of the coaches officially seated six, several years before the first 'six-a-side' Bulleid 4 SUB unit of 1941. It is unlikely that this hypothetical additional accommodation was regularly required, particularly on the Wimbledon–West Croydon run. In April 1934 the units were renumbered 1801-1812 and all received a general overhaul in about 1939 when they were outshopped in unlined green. It appears that 1809-1812 were equipped with guard's periscopes at this time. Both classes survived intact until 1940, when 1807 was destroyed by enemy action at Peckham Rye. As they worked purely local services in the London area, their first class seats were downclassed on the abolition of suburban first class in October 1941.

After 1948 both types were repainted into the early BR malachite green livery with 'cycling lion' badges on the motor coaches. Between June 1950 and March 1951 the remaining seven South London line units were each fitted with six 'monarch' ventilators (vaguely resembling inverted soup-plates in profile but square in plan-view) on the flattened cab roofs of their motor coaches. This modification, authorised by HO 3699 and carried out at Peckham Rye, followed complaints from motormen regarding overheating cabs. 1802 was withdrawn in about May 1951 but the remainder lasted until 1954, with 1809 going in January and the rest following between August and November. By the time they were withdrawn these last survivors were 47 years old. All but 1802 were broken up at Newhaven, which in 1953 had become the main location on the SR for the scrapping of wooden-bodied coaches.

MODERNISATION AND LENGTHENING OF THE ORIGINAL LSWR UNITS

Being the pioneers, the original LSWR three-coach units 1201-1284 differed in many respects from their more standardised successors, particularly in that their shorter length gave a decreased seating capacity. In 1933 it was therefore decided to modernise these units by lengthening their bodies (some of which were already 30 years old) and mounting them on new 62ft underframes of the standard suburban pattern. At the same time their bogies were replaced and electrical equipment updated. The work took place in stages between 1934 and 1940 by which time 82 of the units had been converted, with 1203/07 the first to be done (February 1934) and 1230 the last (May 1940). The remaining two, 1202 and 1210, were due to be rebuilt as part of HO 1050 but instead the HO order was amended and they were withdrawn at the end of 1939 to provide a source of spare parts. The rebuilding work was split between Lancing and Eastleigh Carriage Works, Ashford having ceased carriage conversion in 1932, while the new underframes and bogies also came from Lancing. The orders for rebuilding were allocated as shown opposite.

2 SL DTC 9756 from unit 1806 on the scrap line at Newhaven sidings in about December 1954. Note that the jumper cable fittings and stepboards have already been removed. *Lens of Sutton*

HO Order	Units	Works
771 (4.7.33)	1203/07/27/28/31/56/59/60/79/84	Lancing
808 (23.3.34)	1208/11/51/63/68	Lancing
842 (13.2.35)	1232	Eastleigh
	(charged to Woodside–Sanderstead electrification)	
863 (18.4.35)	1215/39/40/43/44/48/52/55/64/67	Eastleigh
930 (28.5.36)	1205/06/19/22/34/37/41/46/58/61/ 62/65,1269/71/80/83	Eastleigh
966 (16.4.37)	1201/09/17/23-25/33/45/49/72/ 75-77	Lancing
967 (16.4.37)	1226/38/42/50/54/66/70/82	Lancing
	(some work on these was transferred to Eastleigh)	
1050 (3.10.38)	1204/12-14/16/18/20/21/29/30/ 35/36/47/53/73/74/78/81	Eastleigh

It will be noted that the first four batches of these conversions, covering 26 units, were entirely composed of the '1203' type with a motor composite brake. The likely explanation for this is that these units had the fewest third class seats (only 130 as against 180 in a standard unit) and therefore the need to increase their capacity was considered the most urgent.

The motor third brakes (SR diagram 660 in original form) were altered in two ways. In those units which had them at both ends (1201, 1205/6 etc), each was given an additional one and one-half compartments inserted between the slightly-enlarged luggage space and the first compartment, giving a seating capacity of 75. The half-compartment (coupé) had its single row of seats facing backwards, abutting the van space. The revised diagram number of these vehicles as rebuilt was 676. In units 1203/4, 1207/8 etc, which had a composite motor coach at the other end, the motor third brake was given two whole additional compartments, again spliced in behind the van space. These vehicles were also given a revised diagram number (685) and now seated eighty. The motor composite brakes (originally diagram 690) also had two new third class compartments inserted between the luggage space and first compartment, and another of the original firsts was downgraded to third. This left only two first class compartments at the inner end of the coach seating sixteen, the third class capacity being fifty. Their new diagram number was 698. As lengthened, the motor third brakes weighed 42 tons while the motor composite brakes were half a ton lighter.

Below Diagram 772 trailer composite 9418 from rebuilt LSWR unit 1217. Although photographed post-war after having been downgraded to all-third, the large window and the door and quarterlights to the left of it indicate the position of the former first class saloon compartment, inserted when the body was lengthened on a 62ft underframe. Being from the HO 966 batch altered in 1937, the lower panelling on both new and existing body sections have been panelled with steel sheet, and the door ventilator louvres have been removed. *Pamlin Prints*

The original diagram 752 51ft trailers in units 1201, 1205 etc were lengthened by inserting a new 11ft long first class saloon between the existing first and third class sections. This was asymmetric, having a row of four seats across the compartment on the side adjacent to the other first class compartments and longitudinal divans, without headrests, seating three against the carriage sides on the other side of the door. There were the usual quarterlights on either side of the door, and an additional larger fixed window and quarter-light above the longitudinal seating. The new diagram number for the conversion was 772, and the revised seating was fifty first and thirty third. The 49ft trailers in units 1206, 1210 etc (diagram 750), which originally had a saloon, had this reduced in size by converting the part of it at the third class end into an additional third class compartment. Two new first class compartments were added at the other end of the coach. The remaining saloon was of similar layout to that in the 51ft trailers, but had four-seat divans, and thus had two additional first class seats. The new diagram number for these vehicles was 771. Both types of trailer with saloon had a tare weight of 28 tons. Finally, the 49ft composites in 1203/04 etc. (dia. 751) were simply lengthened by the addition of a further two first class compartments to the end, becoming diagram 769 with forty first and thirty third class seats in a weight of 29 tons. The revised seating totals of all these unit types are given below:

1201, 1205 and every fourth unit up to 1281: Motor Third Brake (dia. 676) + Trailer Composite (dia. 772) + Motor Third Brake (dia. 676). Seats: First fifty, Third 180.

1206, 1214 and every fourth unit up to 1282: Motor Third Brake (dia. 676) + Trailer Composite (dia. 771) + Motor Third Brake (dia. 676) Seats: First 52, Third 180.

1203, 1204, 1207, 1208 and every third and fourth unit up to 1283, 1284: Motor Third Brake (dia. 685) + Trailer Composite (dia. 769) + Motor Composite Brake (dia. 698) Seats: First 56, Third 180.

Apart from the lengthening work, many other alterations were carried out to the units in the course of conversion to increase standardisation with the rest of the fleet. Although the original electro-magnetic control equipment was retained, the cab-side ventilation grilles were plated over and replaced by roof vents and ducting. New compressors were fitted and their location moved from the equipment compartment to the standard position on the underframe. These alterations apparently made the units much quieter. The additional three-wire lighting/variable acceleration cables were fitted, with their associated jumpers beneath the headcode panels, and the power lines re-routed externally up the cab fronts. They were given replacement MV 339 or (from 1936) EE 339 motors mounted in new 8ft 9in wheelbase 'central' type motor bogies, although some original motor bogie parts were retained, including axle box castings lettered LSWR. (These bogies later found their way under new 4 EPB units in the 1950s, and hence a few LSWR axleboxes survived until 1993.) New trailer bogies of the standard SECR pattern replaced the Fox pressed-steel originals although, as already mentioned, in some cases this had occurred before rebuilding due to their poor condition. The couplings between intermediate vehicles were changed to the centre-buffer arrangement. On many units the prominent ventilator hood above the headcode panel was removed and the hole plated over, and deeper guttering was fitted around the junction of roof and cab front.

In 1937 the standard Lancing 62ft suburban underframe was redesigned with additional strengthening cross-braces to increase end-loading from ninety to 120 tons, and the final forty '1201' series units rebuilt from that year onwards to HO orders 966, 967 and 1050 were given these heavier frames, together with the self-contained Spencer-Moulton buffers (as fitted to express stock) at the driving ends. Nine of the sixteen units from the HO 930 batch, 1205/06/34/37/41/58/62/65/69, had the new body sections panelled in plain steel sheet rather than wood, and this had the effect of making the raised waist panelling 'disappear' along part of the coach, only to re-appear further along. On all but six of the forty units with heavier frames however, all the lower panelling was thus dealt with, leaving only a single beading line directly below the windows and giving a much tidier appearance. The exceptions were 1223/24/66/72/76/82, which had steel panelling only on the added sections, as on 1205 etc. It seems likely that these variations depended on the state of the original body-work of the unit concerned. Conversely, the steel panelling with its decorative raised beading around the cabs and vans was left largely untouched. Virtually all units given the heavier underframes also had the door ventilators above the droplights removed and plated over, excepting one which kept them on two vehicles. The uneven appearance of many of the body side alterations was ameliorated by the abolition of most (then all) lining from the late 1930s, the overall plain green tending to hide such irregularities.

The earlier conversions were largely unchanged internally. Later on, many of the hard third class bench-type seats were replaced by much softer loose hammock-slung cushions, and wider luggage racks were fitted. There seems to have been little standardisation regarding interior fittings on modernisation, even amongst units in the same batch of rebuilds.

Finally, although 1202 and 1210 were withdrawn from service for spares in December 1939, two sets of new under-frames, possibly for entirely new replacement units, were ordered from Eastleigh, not Lancing, in January 1941 (HO 1393). The order was eventually cancelled. The body of motor coach 8003 from unit 1202 was rebuilt and used in October 1940 as a replacement for the body of 8581 in unit 1794, which had been wrecked in an unrecorded accident.

SUBURBAN ELECTRIC STOCK: CHRONOLOGY OF ORDERING AND ENTRY INTO SERVICE.

The list below shows the chronological order in which the various batches of motor units and trailer sets for succeeding suburban electrification schemes, and later as additional stock to cover traffic increases, were ordered by the Southern Railway and entered service. In a few cases the HO order sequence and dates of entry into service do not exactly coincide. In some instances dates of entry into service are approximate. Reference has been made to paint dates actually noted at the time by the late G.T. Moody.

Note that, following completion of the initial schemes of the 1925-28 period, all additional rolling stock built (excepting units 1901-1912) was effectively common user over the entire network from its introduction. Only where the financing arrangements for a particular batch of stock were peculiar are additional notes given; reasons for these odd accounting arrangements are given in Chapters 2 and 5.

Following their introduction, trailer sets 1095-1098 only ran in traffic for about one year in their original formations, while 989-1000, 1038-1050, 1118-1120 and 1199-1200 were almost certainly reformed prior to entering service. In all cases, coaches were swapped with a vehicle from a set in the 1051-1117 series.

HO Number (Date)	Units or Sets	Purpose	Dates to Traffic
Not applicable (a)	1285-1310	Western Section	6.25-c.8.25
Not applicable (a)	1025-1037	Western Section	4.25
Not applicable (a)	1401-1495	Eastern Section	c.2.25-12.25
Not applicable (a)	1496-1524	Eastern Section	c.4.25-10.25
Not applicable (a)	1051-1109	Eastern Section	8.25-1.26
HO 135 (8.9.25)	1525-1534	Eastern section (b)	By 6.26
HO 136 (11.9.25)	1110-1117	Eastern section (b)	2.26-4.26
HO 206 (3.9.26)	1601-1716	Central section	11.27-3.28
HO 214 (30.9.26)	1121-1167	Central section	12.27-1.29
HO 372 (25.8.28)	1901-1908	South London line	By 4.29
HO 373 (25.8.28)	1717-1736	Central section	1929
HO 374 (25.8.28)	1737-1749	Central section	1929
HO 375 (25.8.28)	1168-1178	Central section	6.29-8.29
HO 396 (10.11.28)	1754-1756	General suburban (c)	By 12.29
HO 398 (14.11.28)	1750-1753	Wimbledon–Sutton new line	By 1.30
HO 399 (14.11.28)	1179-1180	Wimbledon–Sutton new line	11.29
HO 455 (7.5.29)	1181-1186	General suburban (d)	2.30-8.30
HO 480 (28.6.29)	1757-1768	Windsor	2.30-4.30
HO 515 (5.9.29)	1769	Dartford–Gravesend	6.30
HO 516 (5.9.29)	1187-1188	Dartford–Gravesend	By 7.30
HO 530 (4.11.29)	1909-1912	Wimbledon–W. Croydon	3.30
HO 553 (1.2.30)	1770-1782	General suburban (additional)	6.30-8.30
HO 584 (5.6.30)	1783-1794	General suburban (additional)	11.30-1.31
HO 585 (5.6.30)	1189-1194	General suburban (additional)	2.31-3.31
HO 663 (12.6.31)	1795-1801	General suburban (e)	11.31-1.32
HO 791 (25.11.33)	1195-1198	Sevenoaks	9.34-11.34
HO 803 (23.3.34)	1595-1599	General suburban (additional)	7.34-8.34
HO 842 (13.2.35)	1585-1594	Lewisham loops and Sanderstead	9.35-11.35
HO 844 (13.2.35)	1043-1050	Lewisham Loops and Sanderstead	7.35
HO 853 (29.3.35)	1039-1042	General suburban (additional)	By 12.35
HO 900 (8.1.36)	1579-1584	General suburban (f)	8.37-12.37
HO 901 (8.1.36)	1038, 1118 1120, 1199	General suburban (f)	7.36-8.37 -
HO 929 (28.5.36)	998-1000, 1200	General suburban (additional)	7.37
HO 965 (16.4.37)	989-997	General suburban (additional)	1.38-5.38

Notes:

(a) Some early orders authorised prior to Grouping, as well as stock ordered from contractors, were not allocated HO numbers.

(b) Additional maintenance spares for Eastern section.

(c) Charged to Wimbledon–West Croydon electrification budget, but added to general suburban pool.

(d) Charged to Windsor electrification budget, but added to general suburban pool.

(e) Charged to Brighton electrification budget, using underframes and bogies supplied for aborted 4 LAV order (HO 570). Sent directly to London area suburban pool, ex LSWR '1201' class units initially being used instead on Brighton–West Worthing services from 1.1.33.

(f) Charged to Portsmouth No.1 electrification budget, but added to general suburban pool. Probably intended for Chessington and Dorking–Horsham extensions, and (1579-1584 only) possibly for summer Woking–Alton shuttles.

ORIGINAL FORMATIONS OF SUBURBAN STOCK AND SUBSEQUENT ALTERATIONS

No motor units were withdrawn between 1914 and the end of 1939, and the few vehicles destroyed in accidents during this period were replaced like-for-like (although bodywork origins may have differed). Likewise, only four unit reformations took place, all involving trailer composite swaps. No trailer sets were withdrawn until 1937 and then only four in the period up to December 1939. Extensive trailer set reorganisation took place between 1935 and 1938.

As mentioned earlier, the original formations of trailer sets 989-1000, 1038-1050, 1118-1120 and 1195-1200 were not documented at the time, probably because most never went into traffic in this state, but were immediately reformed with existing vehicles. (Alternatively, it is possible that the records have simply been lost).

From 1940 until the end of World War Two a significant number of suburban unit and trailer set vehicles were destroyed as a result of enemy action or due to accidents. This resulted in numerous ad-hoc reformations taking place in an attempt to keep all serviceable vehicles in traffic. The sixty or so suburban coaches destroyed as a result of enemy action in the 1940-44 period are listed in Appendix 2. Space considerations preclude a full list of the original formations and the dozens of other reformations that took place. Planned withdrawal of trailer sets and augmentation of motor units to four coaches (4 SUB) using trailer set vehicles commenced in 1942, and this further complicates matters. These processes continued after 1945 until all three-coach motor units had either been withdrawn or augmented, and all trailer sets withdrawn. During the immediate post-war period a number of serious accidents occurred which resulted in further depletions and reformations.

OPERATING ARRANGEMENTS AND DIAGRAMMING

Operating arrangements on the SR's electrified suburban lines were generally the same as those of the LSWR although, as the network grew, there were exceptions. Off-peak and weekend services were mainly worked by single three-coach motor units, and most rush hour services were of eight coaches formed motor unit + trailer set + motor unit. The rolling stock requirement for each succeeding suburban electrification scheme was based around the number of trains needed to operate the peak-hour service, with a relatively generous surplus to cover for stock in works for maintenance or overhaul. This resulted in there being roughly twice as many motor units as trailer sets, so when a trailer set was berthed in the off-peak period, there was always also a motor unit to which it could remain attached. The effective split was thus three + five, with the five-coach part (motor unit + trailer set) only working in the peaks. Due to their lack of a handbrake, it was necessary for a trailer set to be attached to a motor unit at all times other than in non-electrified sidings or in works. It was not possible to scotch trailer sets (hammering a wooden wedge between wheel and rail surface to prevent movement) due to the possibility of the scotching hammer coming into contact with the live rail.

On the Eastern section, the only exception to these arrangements was the Charing Cross/Cannon Street to Sevenoaks service, where an eight-coach formation worked as far as Orpington all day, but with only three cars continuing to Sevenoaks. On the Central section Tattenham Corner and Caterham combined service, which divided at Purley, rush hour trains were composed of nine coaches (three motor units), with six running to Caterham and three to Tattenham Corner. This was due to a larger than normal number of first class season ticket holders travelling from this prosperous part of Surrey. On the Western section, trailer sets were used on only one duty in each direction on the Hounslow loop, the maximum train length for stopping services being six coaches. The limitation on this line was the short 400ft platforms at Barnes Bridge which were only designed for six-coach trains, the longest envisaged when it opened in 1915.

A single three-car unit was enough at any time of the day on the Waterloo–Wimbledon via East Putney service. Three-coach units worked on Windsor services only from electrification in July 1930 until 3rd January 1937, with peak hour trains (eight Up am, nine Down pm) made up to eight cars with a trailer set. From this latter date combined Waterloo–Windsor/Weybridge services were operated, dividing and combining at Staines, and for these, the two-coach 2 NOL units (described in Volume 2) were used.

A major operating difficulty was the handling of the trailer sets, which had to be removed from service at the end of the morning peak and reformed into trains for the start of the evening (or Saturday lunchtime) rush hour. As trailer sets had neither handbrakes nor driving controls, any movement with the trailer set leading involved a member of the crew leaning out of the front compartment and waving flag signals (or hand-lamps by night) to the motorman in the rear cab of the motor unit attached to it. Between 1935 and 1939, this seemingly hazardous operation was carried out virtually every hour during the day at Orpington where, as mentioned above, the leading unit of an eight-coach train from Charing Cross was detached to run on to Sevenoaks. The remaining five coaches were then shunted from the Down to the Up line, ready to be coupled to the next three-coach unit arriving from Sevenoaks. Similar detachments took place at the end of the morning peak at country termini such as Hayes and Bromley North, where 'blind-ended' five-coach trailer set + motor unit formations were berthed, the remaining three coach unit continuing in service through the day. On the Western section, trailer sets were removed from Kingston loop trains at Strawberry Hill. Following uncoupling of the leading motor unit which continued in traffic, a trailer set was hauled out of the station by the rear unit and then propelled back through the platforms and over complex pointwork into the depot sidings beyond.

A number of these five-coach formations were also berthed through the off-peak hours against the buffer stops at London termini, again following the detachment of a single unit which continued in service. Where the platform remained in use, it was necessary for passengers to walk the length of these coaches before boarding their train, which 'topped' the berthed vehicles. As an example, in the summer of 1939 the situation at the Eastern section London termini was as follows. At Cannon Street three services detached five cars which were then 'topped' by several successive independent three-coach services, prior to coupling up to a unit to form an eight-car train at the start of the evening peak. On Mondays there was also a shunt of five cars between platforms. At Charing Cross two five-car trains berthed, one of which was 'topped' by various three-car services, but in this case the berthing was for under an hour. There was no such berthing at Victoria, but at Holborn Viaduct one five coach train berthed, but without being 'topped'.

Following the coastal electrifications of 1933-38, suburban stock was regularly used for weekend and bank holiday extras and excursions. Such trains were sometimes made up of three units and a trailer set, the resulting eleven-coach formation seating roughly 900 day trippers. However, the complete lack of toilets could make the return trip something of a strain, and extended stops at intermediate stations sometimes resulted.

WARTIME, REFORMATION AND WITHDRAWAL

During 1938 plans were drawn up to reform and renew the SR electric suburban fleet. Basically, so far as existing stock was concerned, the scheme involved lengthening the 1925 contractor-built three-coach units 1285-1310 and 1496-1524 to four coaches by adding a new trailer, complete abolition of the trailer sets, and gradual rebuilding of those wooden-bodied vehicles on standard SR 62ft underframes with new wider all-steel bodywork, coincidentally providing a much-needed increase in seating capacity. Eight-coach peak hour trains could then be formed of two four-coach motor units, and the inconvenience of trailer set shunting would be eliminated. The first part of this suburban renewal programme, on which work commenced during 1939, actually involved the construction of new motor units and trailers, and none of the planned alterations to existing stock had been carried out when war was declared that September. The complete programme, as planned and as eventually executed, is covered in detail in Chapter 6 and in Volume 2. However, as the changeover from three to four-coach formations was a long and extremely untidy process, made all the more so by the intervention of World War Two and problems in its aftermath, some explanation here is necessary to provide a coherent story of the three-coach motor units and two-coach trailer sets up until their final demise.

The entire fleet of 466 dc three-coach suburban units constructed or converted between 1914 and 1937 remained intact until the end of 1939, when two units (1202 and 1210) were withdrawn, probably for spares. Likewise all but four of the trailer sets still existed, only 989, 1003, 1013 and 1197 having been disbanded or condemned, all as a result of accident damage. In the period 1914-39, reformations involving motor units were virtually unknown, with only two instances traced by the author. (Both were trailer composite swaps, one involving units 1206/1262, probably on rebuilding in 1937/38, and the other involving 1211/1695 in July 1938.) As we have seen, it was SR policy to replace individual coaches written off in accidents, the new vehicle being given the number of the coach it replaced. Furthermore, after about 1930 there was a general over-provision of rolling stock on the suburban lines anyway, so there were ample spare units and sets to cover for those undergoing repair, and there was therefore no pressing need to reform units in order to keep serviceable coaches in traffic.

All this changed from 1940. The effects of wartime aerial bombardment, mainly in the 'blitz' between September 1940 and May 1941, and of the V1 and V2 missiles between June 1944 and March 1945, accounted for the destruction of 56 electric suburban coaches, while a number of others were wrecked in accidents or depot collisions, inevitably made more commonplace by blackout conditions. A list of SR suburban electric vehicles destroyed by enemy action during World War Two, together with resulting reformations, is shown in Appendix 2. Apart from vehicles totally destroyed, many others were damaged. A lack of necessary materials caused coaches to remain out of service for long periods before repair, and an acute shortage of glass led to many broken windows being replaced by plywood or hardboard. In the circumstances, rolling stock shortages meant that reformations became commonplace in order to keep operable vehicles in service when part of a unit was damaged. To complicate matters further, as mentioned below, a start was made in 1942 on augmenting existing ex-LSWR units to 4 SUB, using standard underframed coaches from trailer sets, while a few other four-coach units were made up using intact vehicles from bomb-damaged units. In one or two cases, it proved possible to recover the underframes from wrecked coaches for rebuilding with new all-steel bodywork, as part of the post-war 4 SUB construction programme.

Original LSWR unit 1283 and its involvement with units 1259, 1305 and (indirectly) 1697 provides a typical, and complicated, case study. Damaged in October 1940 during the 'blitz', motor third brake 8125 was a complete write-off and the unit was disbanded. Following a period in store, trailer 9412 went to 1925 short-framed unit 1305, replacing TC 9455 which had been destroyed at Lancing in April 1941. Motor coach 8791 went to unit 1259 in place of 8779, which had itself been reformed in unit 1697 following destruction of 8832 in October 1940. There were a number of other similarly complex examples.

A general survey of alterations to SR electric rolling stock in order to comply with blackout regulations, and to help protect staff and passengers as far as possible, will be given in Volume 2. However, an early problem with the blackout, specifically affecting suburban services, was the difficulty first class ticket holders had in identifying the accommodation for which they had paid. Experiments were therefore undertaken in an attempt to make first class compartments more conspicuous. Unit 1679 was noted outside Peckham Rye shops on 12th February 1940 with the entire body side of two first class compartments painted yellow with a black 1, shaded green, in the usual position on the doors. The two compartments adjacent had their doors only painted in the same style. This scheme was evidently considered unsuccessful, as by 12th June the same unit had been outshopped in plain green, with first class accommodation now having 1 in white, shaded black, next to the handle on the waist panelling of each compartment door. A number of other units also had their first class compartments identified in the same way, but the problem was shortly to disappear anyway as train services in the suburban area became third class only as from 6th October 1941. The difficulty in identifying first class compartments during the blackout was one of the reasons given to justify this change.

The abolition of first class in the suburban area was initially intended to be a temporary measure only. Where possible folding armrests in the former first class accommodation were secured in the 'up' position to allow five passengers to sit across the width of the coach but otherwise, apart from removal of rugs, the seating remained unchanged. Understandably, the former first class compartments soon became the most popular part of the train, and after a short time this popularity caused a marked deterioration in their condition. After the war it was decided not to reintroduce first class in the inner suburban area and many of the compartments concerned were eventually retrimmed to third class standards.

Withdrawal of trailer sets as part of the revised programme commenced in 1942, justified partly because wartime service cuts allowed a reduction in stock anyway, and partly because the abolition of trailer set shunting promised staff savings. The first to be withdrawn were those with one LSWR-bodied coach on a standard 62ft underframe, and one 50/54ft LBSCR or 46ft SECR vehicle on its original underframe (which still contained wooden spacers in many cases). Following the necessary alterations, the 62ft vehicle was then formed into a three-car motor unit and the other coach was withdrawn. The bodies of many of these redundant vehicles were not immediately scrapped, but instead were grounded for use as huts by the ARP or Home Guard at various locations all over the Southern Railway area. Due to service cuts the withdrawal of other trailer sets, formed entirely of vehicles of LBSCR origin on non-standard underframes, was also put in motion. Many bodies from these also became hutments for wartime purposes, the furthest travelled arguably being 9004 (from set 1066) which was withdrawn in July 1943 and ended up at Halwill Junction in North Devon.

Concurrent with the first trailer set withdrawals in 1942, the lengthening or 'augmentation' of existing three-coach units to four coaches commenced. Of these, approximately 330 were eventually augmented to four coaches between 1942 and 1949, at which point they became 4 SUB and their subsequent history is dealt with in Chapter 6. An exact total is difficult to quote because in some instances a unit was withdrawn shortly after being augmented and its additional trailer was then used to lengthen yet another three-coach unit. The first to be dealt with were 81 of the original LSWR units of the '1201' class, augmented between 1942 and 1948 with a ten or eleven-compartment LSWR-bodied coach on a standard 62ft underframe from a disbanded trailer set, as mentioned above. A further 38 units built by the SR with LSWR bodywork were also lengthened in the same way in 1947-49, while eight more were made up from spare vehicles of varied origin following war damage or accidents. All the rest were augmented using a new 'six-a-side' trailer constructed in the 1945-48 period, and included all 55 of the 1925 SR contractor-built units, 35 more with LSWR bodywork, 85 of SECR origin and the remainder LBSCR. As far as the wooden-bodied units went, those in the best condition were generally selected for augmentation but, as detailed later, it was not quite as simple as this.

By 1945 it became clear that remaining trailer sets, many of which had been allowed to fall into a dreadful state due to wartime conditions and in expectation of early withdrawal, were being taken out of service too rapidly, resulting in stock shortages. This was countered by running a number of 2 NOL units as substitutes for trailer sets, with shoebeams, leads and fuses removed. There is a suspicion that controlgear parts and motors from these may also have been cannibalised to keep SUBs in service, or even to enable brand new units from the 4355-4377 batch to enter traffic. (The NOLs were all reinstated as motor units on overhaul in 1947-48, concurrent with the introduction of further new 4 SUBs.)

After the war, withdrawal of the remaining trailer sets continued gradually as new and augmented 4 SUBs entered service. Virtually all coaches not on standard 62ft underframes were condemned, but ten former LBSCR 54ft vehicles were converted into de-icing vehicles in 1946-48, being renumbered 351-356S and 396-399S. Withdrawn sets were dumped at various points around the system prior to being broken up; for example at the beginning of August 1948 four were noted at Horsted Keynes and seven at Tattenham

Corner. It was reported that many sets were scrapped at Lancing. Remaining sets were by this time in a sorry state, as none had been overhauled since 1939. The pre-war dark olive had weathered and faded to an almost blue shade, many had nearly all their windows replaced by boarding, and a few ex-LBSCR vehicles even retained pre-Grouping upholstery fabric. Surprisingly, eight were overhauled in March 1947, being outshopped in the current malachite green livery; these were 998 and 1006/19/20/22/58/68/90. By the start of 1948 trailer set operation was virtually confined to the Central section, with only scarce Eastern section workings into Holborn Viaduct and nothing at all on the Western section. The last of the trailer sets was withdrawn in the latter part of 1948 with the disbanding of nine sets, 1005/42/51/68/78 and 1106/28/75/78 in August, leaving two stragglers, 998 and 1111, which survived until the following month. Use of trailer sets was officially discontinued from 27th September. It is interesting that some of the original LSWR sets in the 1001-1024 series originally dating from 1919-22, basically unaltered save for the substitution of more modern bogies, survived almost until the end of trailer set operation.

Remaining un-augmented three-coach motor units, by this time mostly confined to services on the Hounslow loop from Waterloo (and occasionally to Windsor) and on the Charing Cross–London Bridge–Caterham/Tattenham Corner line, were withdrawn in 1948 and 1949. The first to go were remaining units from the 1631-1657 and 1702-1716 batches, all of which had ex-LBSCR 'bogie-block' bodywork, originally dating from the turn of the century, on standard SR 62ft underframes. The sixteen remaining, 1632/35/40/41/46/55-57 and 1702-05/08/10-12, were mostly withdrawn during 1948, with only a few lasting into the following January. The few augmented units with bodies of similar origin were also withdrawn at this time. Their bodywork was scrapped at Horley or Lancing and their frames reused under vehicles of new all-steel 4 SUBs numbered in the 4621-4666 series. On the Hounslow loop the last three-coach units ran in November 1948, concurrent with the belated extension of the platforms at Barnes Bridge to fit eight-coach trains composed of two 4 SUBs, while they disappeared from the Tattenham Corner/Caterham services in March 1949.

These withdrawals left only SECR-bodied units of the '1401' and '1601' types in existence. 1404 was condemned in January and 1528 in August 1949, but the remaining 27 were taken out of service more-or-less en-bloc in November 1949. These were 1401/21/25/30/32/38/40/45/48/49/58/61/63/65/79/81/82/87/92/95 and 1606/07/14/16/19/22/27. Officially, some lingered on (probably on paper only) just into 1950. These two batches were both broken up at Horley, their frames and bogies going to SUBs in the 4667-4754 series.

6: THE 4 SUB UNITS 1939-83

INTRODUCTION AND ORIGINAL PLANS

This chapter deals with two distinct groups of rolling stock. Firstly, it continues the story of the Southern Railway's fleet of three-coach suburban electric multiple units through their reformation into four-car units and eventual withdrawal. Secondly, it deals with the second-generation replacement stock completed between 1941 and 1951, which had equipment compatible with the pre-war stock and interworked indiscriminately with it while both types remained in existence. As in Chapter 5, while the information is as complete as the author is able to make it (within the bounds of reasonable space), no attempt has been made to trace the complete history of every vehicle due to the extreme complexity of the story. Both new four-coach and existing three-coach units augmented with a fourth vehicle were classified 4 SUB, and from the start no operating distinction was made between old and new stock. As the old units were withdrawn, many of their underframes and bogies were recovered for use in the new coaches. The last of the SUBs with bodywork of pre-Grouping origin was finally taken out of service in February 1960, while those units built with new steel-panelled bodies in 1925 had all gone by January 1962. Withdrawal of the second-generation 4 SUBs commenced at the start of 1972 and was completed in September 1983, although one unit (4732) was preserved and remains in existence as this is written.

The situation is further complicated because from the end of 1951 further new units were built to continue the replacement of pre-1939 suburban stock, of virtually identical construction to the post-war SUBs and also built on reclaimed underframes, but with significantly more advanced control and braking systems that made them incompatible with the older stock. These units formed the major part of the EPB fleet.

As described in Chapter 5, about four-fifths of the existing fleet of electric suburban stock on the SR in 1939 was composed of three-coach motor units. The remainder comprised a smaller number of two-coach trailer sets which worked between pairs of motor units to increase rush-hour capacity, an arrangement which dated back to the LSWR in 1919. (The two-coach WIM/SL units 1801-1812 and the London-area 2 NOLs 1863-1890 are not included in these totals.) Apart from the 55 units built new with steel-panelled bodywork in 1925 (1285-1310 and 1496-1534), all vehicles had been constructed by making use of existing wooden carriage bodies. Without exception of pre-1923 design and with many dating from before the turn of the century, it was never

intended that these mostly Victorian and Edwardian relics would have a very long life following conversion. By the end of 1938 most of the planned main line electrification programme was either completed or well in hand, and it was therefore at last possible to direct attention and finance towards the urgently-needed modernisation of the suburban fleet.

Apart from the advanced age of the bodywork of most existing suburban rolling stock, there were two further matters that required immediate attention. Firstly, traffic on the suburban lines had soared inexorably through the 1930s to levels never-before known. Inner-suburban traffic had been in decline, but the fast and frequent electric services had encouraged large numbers of people to move to the new housing being erected in the middle and outer suburbs. Considerable developments had taken place in areas such as Bexley, Sidcup, Orpington, Purley, Sutton, Epsom and Surbiton for the benefit of office workers employed in the City and West End. At the same time, the two daily peaks were being concentrated into a shorter time span, and these factors led to increasing overcrowding. Owing to the long average journey distance, SR policy had always been geared towards providing a seat for everyone, and thus suburban trains of greater capacity were required.

Secondly, it was urgently necessary to make peak-hour operation more efficient. LSWR electric operations had begun with three-coach motor units which operated singly or in pairs to make six-coach trains. With an increase in passenger numbers after 1918 however, two units provided insufficient capacity for many rush-hour duties, but there were not enough of them to make a significant number of trains up to nine coaches. Lengthening of units to four coaches was resisted at the time, as this would have resulted in unnecessary vehicle mileage at slack periods when three-coach trains were adequate, and would also have impaired performance. The eventual solution adopted by Herbert Jones, the LSWR electrical engineer, was to use unpowered two-coach trailer sets, marshalled between pairs of motor units during peak periods. Following Jones's appointment as the SR's Chief Electrical Engineer following Grouping, this three+two+three arrangement was perpetuated for nearly all the SR suburban electrifications, even though it resulted in awkward and inconvenient shunting before and after peak periods as the trailer sets had no cabs or handbrakes. With traffic steadily rising through the decade, by the late 1930s the trailer sets were proving an increasing impediment to the provision of a reliable service.

The appointment in 1937 of O.V.S. Bulleid and A. Raworth as Chief Mechanical and Electrical Engineers respectively, following the retirement of their predecessors, resulted in policy changes with regard to the future design and operation of SR suburban stock aimed at dealing with the difficulties just outlined.[14] Firstly, by the introduction of welding techniques, it proved possible to construct an all-steel coach body side of adequate stiffness without thick wooden framing. Furthermore, by curving this to give a maximum width of 9ft at the shoulder level of seated passengers, it proved possible to seat six (rather than the previous standard of five) across the width of the compartment, which went some way towards providing the increase in seating capacity required. The new design was described to shareholders at the SR Annual General Meeting in February 1939, following a visit by the Chairman to Eastleigh Works where he and five other men 'of ample proportions' sat in a mock-up compartment and apparently found it (according to his AGM report) 'very comfortable'. Secondly it was decided to revise the formation of existing suburban units by adopting the obvious solution of augmenting some of them to four coaches with the insertion of an additional centre trailer, withdrawing the trailer sets, and building or rebuilding coaches to provide replacements.

The two strands of the 4 SUB story are illustrated in this view photographed at Waterloo East, probably in the summer of 1947. On the right, LSWR 'nutcracker' unit 4145, augmented from three-coach unit 1259 with an additional vehicle from a disbanded trailer set, forms an Orpington and Sevenoaks service. On the left, new all-steel 'six-a-side' unit 4128, one of a batch of ten experimentally given saloon accommodation to gauge passenger reaction, is bound for Charing Cross. *F.G. Reynolds*

Eventually, suburban formations would be either one or two four-coach units, and trailer set shunting, with its attendant problems, would be eliminated.

A programme was prepared, for implementation over ten years from 1939, to cover the modernisation and reformation of the suburban fleet. The first stage of the intended programme comprised the construction of thirty entirely new four-coach units and withdrawal of trailer sets 1001-1024, which were life-expired. Later stages would involve the withdrawal of 125 two-coach trailer sets. These were of the types in the 989-1000, 1038-1167 and 1188-1200 series with one LSWR-bodied coach on a standard SR 62ft underframe and one coach with SECR or LBSCR bodywork and a non-standard underframe. The vehicles with standard underframes were to be rebuilt with new steel-sided bodies, and those with non-standard underframes would be scrapped. Following the completion of the thirty new four-coach units, 55 new trailer coaches were to be constructed, to enable the SR-bodied three-coach units of the '1285' and '1496' classes to be augmented to four coaches and further trailer sets to be withdrawn and scrapped.

---

14 In connection with these, it is significant that Alfred Raworth, Jones's equivalent on the SECR and subsequently Electrical Engineer for New Works on the SR, had originally specified four-coach units for the SECR suburban electrifications. However, as related in Chapter 5, his plans were overruled by Jones, ostensibly in the interests of standardisation.

It was intended to commence withdrawal of wooden-bodied motor units as soon as enough of the first thirty entirely new units had been placed into traffic. Their standard 62ft underframes would then be reconditioned and new bodies built onto them to create further new units. In each of the years 1941 to 1945, forty units would be dealt with. The re-bodied units would have been made up to four coaches either with rebuilds of vehicles with SR underframes originally taken from the trailer sets or with an entirely new trailer. These completely new vehicles would, in turn, allow the remainder of the trailer sets to be withdrawn. Only standard 62ft underframes newly built between 1925 and 1940 would be re-bodied. Those lengthened from former ac frames under the majority of vehicles in units of the 1717-1772 and 1780-1782 groups would eventually be scrapped with their bodies. It is tempting to suppose that eventual re-bodying was in mind when production of the original suburban stock was being planned, although no known evidence supports this. In view of subsequent events, it is worth pointing out that there was at this stage no intention of augmenting any existing unit (other than the 1925 contractor-built units) with a new wide-bodied trailer prior to that unit being rebuilt with new bodywork.

Instructions to build the first thirty entirely new four-coach units were issued on 28th December 1938 to HO 1060. Allocated numbers 4101-4130, they were to be constructed at Eastleigh on Lancing underframes. Although about fifteen of them would have been required to prime the rebuilding programme and they were needed to provide additional capacity when replacing old coaches on a one-to-one basis, no specific purpose was mentioned under the expenditure heading, but they were eventually referred to as 'additional rolling stock'. The order for the first 55 augmentation trailers, to HO 1094, followed on 16th May 1939; exceptionally, both bodywork and underframes were to be built at Eastleigh. It was intended that only seven of these would have new bogies, the remainder being recovered from withdrawn trailer sets 1001-1024 which had been given new replacement bogies in 1934-36, but were not on standard 62ft frames and were therefore due for complete disposal. Contracts were placed with English Electric early in 1939 for electrical equipment to equip these thirty new units and 55 trailers.

The outbreak of World War Two did not immediately halt construction of the new suburban stock, and production of underframes at both Eastleigh and Lancing was able to continue until February 1940 by which time about thirty had been built. By then about half of the equipment for the first ten units had also been manufactured, while materials to complete them were on hand at Eastleigh. By the time that non-essential work ground to a halt in May 1940 a number of motor coach underframes, for units up to 4108, had been fitted with basic bodywork but without window glass. These unfinished vehicles then had to be stored, in the open, at various locations, with only tarpaulins to protect them from the weather. Apart from the first unit, 4101, which was nearly complete by this time, electrical equipment for the remainder was probably stored in sheds around the Works yard. Although production was badly delayed, wartime service cuts allowed the withdrawal of some trailer sets, and augmentation of three-coach units to 4 SUB was commenced as part of a greatly altered programme.

The break down of intended production of further new suburban stock year-by-year in 1940-45 was as shown in the table below, taken from the Minutes of the SR Rolling Stock Committee meeting of 20th March 1945. Although this production schedule had been approved by the Committee, nothing on it had reached the HO Order stage by this date.

Order Date	*Construction Authorised*	*Total Units*
2.4.40	40 Trailers (New) 80 Motor Coaches + 40 Trailers (Existing Frames)	40x four-coach
23.1.41	40 Trailers (New) 80 Motor Coaches + 40 Trailers (Existing Frames)	40x four-coach
19.2.42	25 Trailers (New) 80 Motor Coaches + 55 Trailers (Existing Frames)	40x four-coach
25.3.43	20 Trailers (New) 80 Motor Coaches + 60 Trailers (Existing Frames)	40x four-coach
20.3.44	20 Trailers (New) 80 Motor Coaches + 60 Trailers (Existing Frames)	40x four-coach

These original 1940-44 approvals were reconsidered at the March 1945 Rolling Stock Committee meeting in the light of war-imposed difficulties, and the subsequent programme was to follow an entirely different building sequence from that originally intended, although the end-result was similar. The effects of the war, post-war shortages of staff and materials, changing traffic levels and the political situation all resulted in substantial changes to the original plans. In particular, the rebuilding part of the renewals programme eventually started only in 1949, as a surge in traffic caused by demobilised servicemen returning to civilian life meant that the old units could not be withdrawn for re-bodying as rapidly as had been hoped. However, the annual increase in traffic levels characteristic of the pre-war boom years was gone.

Although the new suburban stock was nominally the responsibility of Bulleid, the actual design work continued to be under the direction of L. Lynes, who had effectively been responsible for the mechanical parts and bodywork of all SR electric stock from the 1925 suburban units onwards. The need to interwork with, and be fully compatible with, the earlier stock gave very little scope for innovation, and it is therefore unsurprising that the new designs were relatively conventional, being a direct development of the 1939 2 HAL type. The compartment arrangement with hinged doors was preferred as a matter of SR policy, as it provided the maximum number of seats and made station stops as brief as possible.[15] Formation was two motor coaches with driving cab and brake van at the outer ends, sandwiching two trailers. The driving ends had the large self-contained Spencer-Moulton side

---

15 Station dwell times with slam-door coaches were remarkably brief, even at the height of the peaks. Stops of twenty seconds were standard except at major stations.

buffers, while the standard centre-buffer/rubbing block arrangement was used to close-couple coaches within a unit. As on the three-coach units the motor coaches had rubbing blocks but, in common with the 4 LAVs, it was necessary for one trailer to have a centre buffer at both ends and the other a buffer at one end and a rubbing block at the other. Other than the use of curved and welded body sides to give a greater internal width, construction, dimensions and equipment were standard. Thus the units were built on 62ft underframes with 8ft 9in wheelbase 'central' type motor bogies and 8ft trailer bogies. Above the floor, the coach profile consisted entirely of arcs, that of the sides from solebar to cantrail height being a continuous smooth curve of 22ft radius.

English Electric electro-pneumatic contactor control gear, identical to that on the last six pre-1939 suburban units 1579-1584 and all post-1936 semi-fast stock, was utilised, and the motors were of the EE 339 type. (As will be described later, many production SUBs were given a new lightweight motor, type EE 507C, but the control system remained identical.) The basic electrical arrangements otherwise remained fundamentally the same as on the 1914 LSWR units. Heating and lighting were series-wired and operated at line voltage, hence special 70V light bulbs had to be used which could only be replaced by depot fitters, some of whom were on hand at London termini for this purpose. Separate circuits were provided for cab heating to save electricity when working empty, but no cab lighting was provided other than for illuminating the headcode panel. The compressors, one under each motor coach, were of the Westinghouse DH25 type and provided air for the brakes, control system and whistles (or horns, later in the units' life). They were controlled by governors which detected any significant drop in main reservoir pipe air pressure below 90-105psi, and all were linked throughout the train by means of a synchronising line in the control cable so they all operated simultaneously. The air brakes were of the Westinghouse automatic type and operated with a train-pipe pressure of 70psi.

Over the period of SR suburban stock renewal four significant changes occurred which were not envisaged in the original 1938 plans. Firstly, there was a changeover to all-steel construction after the first ten new units and 45 additional trailers in order to speed production and reduce maintenance. Secondly, a centre-gangway saloon layout, rather than the previously universal closed compartments, was introduced to improve passenger circulation and comfort in overcrowded conditions. Thirdly, an entirely new design of electrical and braking equipment was introduced about halfway through the construction programme to produce the 4 EPB type. Lastly, ten-coach trains were introduced on Eastern section suburban lines from 1954, requiring the production of new two-coach motor units of class 2 EPB. Overall, construction of the second-generation SUB and EPB stock, together with a few other miscellaneous units (the two experimental 4 DDs and fifteen former 'Tyneside' 2 EPBs) resulted in a net increase in the SR suburban fleet from roundly 2,000 to nearly 2,300 vehicles by 1963.

The second-generation 4 SUB fleet was built during a period of considerable upheaval for the Southern, with World War Two and its aftermath closely followed by nationalisation. One effect of this was that the various groups of units were outshopped when new in a variety of different livery styles as policy on this matter changed frequently in the 1941-51 period. For this reason, livery details are mentioned within the descriptions of each batch rather than here.

The seat upholstery material patterns used, on the other hand, cut across the various orders, and descriptions of those in general use are therefore included at this stage to avoid repetition later. (The same patterns were also used in other electric and steam stock constructed or receiving a general overhaul while they were in use). While each of the patterns concerned was used for upholstering new stock over a relatively short period (between two and eight years – the period to which the dates below refer), all of them survived in service for at least ten years, the working life between suburban unit body overhauls. In practice, patterns could be seen around for much longer, as roll ends kept for replacing the odd vandalised cushion were often used to retrim complete coaches towards the end of the working life of the main batch of material. Small remnants were also used for motorman's and guard's seats. Descriptions of the six patterns used over the span of 4 SUB production are given first, followed by their distribution among units and (where known) augmentation trailers.

Pattern A: Moquette with a repeated dark brown flower motif (resembling an elaborate *fleur-de-lys*) on a lighter brown background. This, the Medway pattern, was the first of a new idiom replacing the jazz-age designs of the 1930s, and was initially used in 2 HALs 2601-2676. Despite a slightly threadbare look, it proved tough almost to the point of indestructibility, but appeared depressing once dirty or worn. It was in use from 1939 until 1946.

Pattern B: Moquette with a slightly larger flower motif and speckles, this time in fawn on a darker brown background. Introduced in 1946 and in use for two years, it was a slight redesign of pattern A. Again very hard-wearing, it appeared just as depressing once grubby.

Pattern C: Moquette with reddish-brown speckles and brown trailing leaf-spray outlines on a fawn background. This was the first 1946 attempt to produce a more cheerful pattern, but it did not wear well and was discontinued in 1948. However, roll-ends were used for fifteen new motor coaches (12650-64) in 1950.

Pattern D: Moquette with a fawn diamond-shaped flower-and-leaf pattern on a crimson background. This was the second, and much more successful, 1946 attempt to produce a brighter design, and was a further development of the original 1939 pattern. By a small margin the most common upholstery design in post-war SUBs (71 units), it was also extensively used in other electric and steam stock until 1954. (The last new units to have it were 4 EPBs 5053 and 5104). There were three recognisably different background shades of crimson during its long production run.

Pattern E: Moquette with fawn leaf-spray outlines on a

plain maroon base. Although not introduced until 1949, this successful design was of purely SR origin and was in widespread use in SUBs (67 units) and other stock until 1954. (The last new unit with it was 4 EPB 5046.)

Pattern F: Repp with fawn branchlets on a plain wine-red background (described by G.T. Moody as 'rust'). This odd material, completely out of character for the SR at this time, was used briefly in 1949-50, but its use other than in SUBs was rare. (Repp is a very tough, coarse variant of tapestry.)

The distribution of patterns among the second-generation 4 SUB fleet was as shown in the table below. The symbol * after the unit number series concerned indicates that only some coaches in each unit, usually the third motor brakes, had that particular pattern. Note also that when augmentation trailers were reformed from pre-war units into new steel-bodied SUBs from 4667 upwards they were not reupholstered, so references to these units refer only to the three saloon vehicles although, in practice, the pattern was the same in many cases anyway. Such units are indicated by †.

Pattern A:	Units 4101-10, augmentation trailers 10346-90
Pattern B:	Units 4115-20, 4121-23/25/26, 4285-89, 4364-65*, 4367-77, 4382, some augmentation trailers, including 10391-10400
Pattern C:	Units 4112-14, 4355-56* 4357, 4358-9*, 4360-61, 4362/66*, MThB 12650-64 (in 4590, 4601-07), some augmentation trailers
Pattern D:	Units 4124, 4127-30, 4280-84, 4290-93, 4355-56*, 4358-59/62*, 4363, 4364-66*, 4378-87, 4621-40, 4665-66, 4667†, 4671-72†, 4734-54†, some augmentation trailers
Pattern E:	Units 4294-99, 4673-4733†
Pattern F:	Units 4641-64, 4668/69†

Significant reformations during the lives of the units concerned are included in tables in the main body of the text, as are the original formations of various odd units where they help to clarify a particular point in the story.

THE PROTOTYPE 'SHEBA' UNITS 4101-4110

As a result of almost total suspension of work, the first new 4 SUB unit, numbered 4101, which should have appeared towards the end of 1939, did not actually enter service until October 1941. Work on new construction did not then recommence until about September 1944, and following this the remainder of the first ten entirely new SUBs, 4102-4110, were outshopped between December 1944 and March 1945. The motor coaches of these units had Lancing-built underframes as specified in HO 1060, but at least some of the trailers were built on frames constructed at Eastleigh in late 1944 to HO 1094 and originally intended for augmentation trailers.

Other than the curved and welded body sides to enable six passengers to sit across a compartment as already described, construction was entirely conventional. These body sides were built-up from steel sheets welded to vertical ribs (which formed the edges of the door openings) and to a bottom flange which was in turn welded to the underframe solebars. Welded construction meant that galvanised steel could no longer be used, and this necessitated alterations to the priming and painting sequence. The roof was of the usual deal planking covered in canvas and with curved rainstrips but the driving cabs, including the domed roof, were also of welded steel sheet, being virtually identical to those of the 1939 2 HAL units. The cab sides were straight and inclined slightly inwards, and the motorman's door had a wood-framed droplight. Even more than on the HALs, the cabs looked as if they had been stuck on as an afterthought. The quarterlights were curved to match the body-side contour and were rubber-mounted in separate bolt-on frames. The compartment doors had frameless self-balancing droplights without a locking device, and were surmounted by a lozenge-shaped toplight characteristic of Bulleid coaching stock from this time onwards, both electric and steam-hauled. The door droplights tended to stick at first, and there are several recorded incidents of glass shattering when attempts were made to force them, resulting in temporary plywood replacements.

All accommodation in 4101-4110 was in compartments, each being formed of two nine-compartment motor coaches (diagram 2118), one eleven-compartment trailer third (dia.2012) and one ten-compartment trailer (dia.2312) which was fitted-out as a composite only in 4101 with six wider first class compartments at the centre and two thirds at either end. The motor third brakes were numbered 10941-60, and allocated in pairs; the eleven-compartment trailers 10419-28 and the ten-compartment trailers 11471-80. These latter had the rubbing block at one end and the centre buffer at the other. Motor coaches and trailers had approximate tare weights of 43 and 29 tons respectively. Just before 4101 entered service, first class was abolished on the suburban lines 'for the duration' and the remainder of the units had the wider compartments trimmed as thirds from the start. In order to achieve this number of compartments within the standard coach length they were narrower than previously, thirds being a cramped 5ft 6in between partitions and firsts only 12in wider, while at just under 7ft 6in the motor coach brake vans were also smaller. The additional compartments gave a massive seating capacity for a four-coach unit of 468, but their narrowness caused passenger's knees to touch when full, making standing extremely uncomfortable. The compartments adjacent to the van in each motor coach were designated LADIES ONLY, a feature repeated in every other SUB with all-compartment accommodation, ancient or modern.

Internal partitions were of plywood, and panelling mainly of hardboard or plywood, finished in cream linen fabric on the ceilings and partitions above the seats, and mid-brown

Right The first new 'Sheba' 4 SUB 4101, originally completed in 1941, approaches Brentford Central with an anti-clockwise Hounslow loop line service from Waterloo on 10th September 1966. Similarity in basic design to the 1939 2 HALs is obvious. Wearing the second BR green livery with small yellow warning panels, air horns on the roof have replaced the original whistle by this time. *Brian Stephenson*

'Rexine' on the doors and lower panels. Window surrounds were covered in cream fabric in 4101, the remainder having 'Rexine'. The third class seating was similar to that in the HALs, with narrow fixed wire-framed interior-sprung bench seats and thin backs without additional padding at head-height. The tops of the seats were scalloped, each arc denoting one seat, and upholstery moquette was the depressing beige/brown Medway design (pattern A above). The first class compartments in 4101 were designed to seat ten passengers, the seats being divided two+one+two across the compartment with fixed side and two folding intermediate armrests in the manner of the non-corridor third class compartments in the 1932 4 LAV units. The backs were not scalloped at the top, each place had its own individual seat cushion, and upholstery was in jade green moquette with a fawn floral pattern as used in the HALs. All compartments had lamps on projecting bases with individual shades, the last SR suburban stock to be so fitted. Quarterlights were fitted with green roll-down sunblinds (again, the last so equipped), and to make these effective for blackout use the sides and lower edges of the windows of 4101 were painted internally to a depth of about 2½ inches. This unit had channels on the window frames to locate the blinds, but the remainder had small metal brackets. The blinds and blackout paint were removed soon after the war ended, but the brackets not until 1955-56. 4101 retained original upholstery in its former first class compartments until overhaul in July 1954, and its blackout blind channels remained as late as 1962.

4101 was outshopped in an unlined bright green livery, probably the same shade as applied to HALs 2677-2692, with black intermediate coach ends, underframes and bogies and grey roofs. Coach numbers were in small highlighted yellow figures below the cantrail at each end, and unit numbers appeared in the usual position above the headcode panels in large hand-painted figures. The word SOUTHERN appeared in shaded sans-serif 'sunshine' lettering below the quarter-lights between the fourth and fifth compartments of the motor coaches, and block letters 3 and 1 below the droplights of compartment doors as appropriate. In order to comply with wartime blackout restrictions and to provide blast protection, large areas of the cab lookouts were blanked off and gas-detector paint applied to the offside forward facing window. 4102-4110 were delivered in the definitive malachite green shade, with clear compartment windows, but without class designations on the doors as all SR suburban services were by this time third class only.

Numerical headcodes, identical in design to those on the main-line stock, were introduced on the suburban lines with the new 4 SUB stock. 4101 first entered service on the Victoria–Orpington line, which was particularly subject to over-crowding at this time. The Government Order imposing the temporary abolition of first class came into effect on 6th October 1941, so 4101 actually entered service as a 'third class only' unit and its first class compartments were never officially designated as such. 4102-4110 also went to the Eastern section when new, and were first utilised on Charing Cross–Dartford services. 4102 was actually first used in

traffic on New Year's Day 1945. Their first recorded appearance on the Central section was in December 1945 (4102) and by the following month they could also be seen working out of Waterloo. Notwithstanding being new, these units were not popular with commuters due to their cramped, narrow compartments.

In view of their unusual width and high capacity, 4101-4110 quickly became known among some railwaymen as 'Shebas' from the Bible: 'And when the Queen of Sheba heard of the fame of Solomon … she came to Jerusalem with a very great train...' (I Kings, x, 1-2). The commuters of Orpington, however, tended not to travel '...with camels that bear spices, and very much gold, and precious stones'! These units were also dubbed 'Queen Marys' in view of their straight-backed third class seats, a feature shared with the Royal lady in question. The term 'Mary' was also applied to later SUB units, but for a different reason.

THE FIRST AUGMENTED UNITS AND NEW AUGMENTATION TRAILERS

In spite of the war situation and a halt on new construction, withdrawal of the trailer sets and augmentation of existing units was pressed ahead with, as elimination of trailer set shunting would make operation more flexible and promised staff savings. This was made more urgent by the increased number of minor depot collisions resulting from shunting in blackout conditions.

As related in Chapter 5, trailer sets were withdrawn progressively from 1942 onwards, the first to be disbanded being from the 989-1000, 1038-1167 and 1188-1200 groups formed with one 62ft LSWR-bodied and one shorter LBSCR or SECR vehicle, as in the 1938 plans. The 62ft coaches were then inserted into units of the '1201' class, which became 4 SUB and were renumbered into the series 4131-4171 and 4195-4234 following augmentation. The new numbers were assigned in the sequence in which the units were augmented, grouped by subtype, but otherwise unrelated to their former numbers as three-coach units. It is presumed that they were done as they became due for revarnishing. Units 4131-4171 were augmented from units of the '1203/4' subtype with compartment trailers by adding a ten-compartment trailer, giving a seating capacity of 350. The remainder were made up from those units with ex-first class saloons using an additional eleven-compartment trailer, and seated one or three more. 4195-4215 were the former '1201' subtype (with diagram 772 trailer composite), while 4216-4234 were the '1206' subtype (with dia. 771 trailer composite). A few units had vehicles originating from more than one three-coach unit, mostly as a result of earlier wartime reformations. (Note that the quoted seating capacities for these and all other augmented pre-1939 SUB units assumes that five passengers could sit each side of the former first class compartments, which in reality was not always possible.)

Work on making the necessary alterations to the 62ft vehicles from the trailer sets was officially authorised for the first twenty augmentations by HO 2149 of 1st August 1942. In reality, work had by this date already been under way at

4 SUB 4233 was augmented from original LSWR unit 1266 with additional LSWR-bodied coach 9221 from trailer set 1133 in February 1948. It is seen here on 12th May 1949 leading the 5.31pm Victoria–Coulsdon North service departing from Clapham Junction. It is painted in the earliest interim BR livery, basically Southern malachite but with BRITISH RAILWAYS in sunshine lettering on the van sides. *J.H. Aston*

Eastleigh for some months, as the first unit to be augmented had been noted in traffic the previous April. This was 4131, augmented from three-coach unit 1204 using vehicle 10411 from set 989. Modifications to the former trailer set coaches included removal of the prominent full-width transverse 'box' carrying waist-level jumper cables and sockets from one end, their replacement by new fittings at roof-height, and substitution of the original side buffers with centre buffer or rubbing block. When formed into units, the additional trailer coaches all had a centre buffer at one end and a rubbing block at the other, as this arrangement then required no further alteration to the intermediate couplings of the unit being augmented.

Following alteration, these additional trailers were all given revised diagram numbers. These were 742 for the eleven-compartment vehicles (formerly 727), 743 for the two 61ft ten-compartment coaches 9078 and 9298 (ex 739), and 740 or 741 for the standard 62ft ten-compartment trailers (ex 732 and 731 respectively). The reason for this latter division was that, as originally formed in a trailer set, those vehicles now to diagram 740 had a centre-buffer at the inner end so

the outer end buffing-gear was replaced by a rubbing plate. On diagram 741 vehicles the opposite arrangement applied, a new centre-buffer being required at the outer end. An exception in this batch was vehicle 9169, which for some reason became diagram 738 after alteration. All of the eleven-compartment vehicles had a centre buffer added at the former 'outer' end, so only one diagram number was needed.

On augmentation the units were given a fresh coat of green paint in a new shade which was to become the definitive malachite colour used by the SR, Railway and Region, for electric stock until 1957. Lettering and numbering were in the shaded 'sunshine' style. There was no lining, but the destination board clips on the cab sides were picked-out in bright yellow – odd because the use of these boards had been abandoned 'for the duration'. In some cases the coaches were also re-upholstered, generally using the Medway pattern, opportunity being taken to retrim the downclassed first class compartments as 'proper' thirds with no armrests (although at this stage it was still intended to re-introduce first class on suburban trains when the war ended).

The first twenty augmentations were complete by about

March 1943, and a further order dated 29th April 1943 (HO 2525) authorised the conversion of forty more. When the war ended a final 59 augmentations using 62ft LSWR-bodied vehicles from trailer sets were authorised by HO 3226 of 5th May 1945. The first part of this order covered augmentation of the remaining 23 '1201' series units. As we shall see, by this time Eastleigh had been able to resume new construction work, and the rate of augmentation using existing trailers then slowed down. Thus it was not until early 1948 that all had been done, the last being 4234 (formerly 1274) in April. In a few of these post-war augmentations, including 4147/61/70, only the additional trailer was repainted in malachite, giving a piebald look as the other three coaches remained in pre-war dark green, by now weathered to an almost blue shade. Of the 82 original LSWR units rebuilt in 1934-40, only one (1283) was never augmented, as it had been disbanded following the destruction of motor coach 8125 during the 'blitz' in December 1940. Not all augmented LSWR units existed at once, however; 8124 and 9371 of 4222 (ex 1282) were destroyed in the Motspur Park collision on 6th November 1947, but its eleven-compartment trailer 9220 was later repaired and reformed into unit 1681 in September 1948, which became 4 SUB 4242 on augmentation.

The other part of HO 3226 involved the augmentation of 38 three-coach units from the 1658-1701 series. These too had LSWR bodywork, but had been converted by the SR in 1928-29. As the disbanded trailer set coaches used were of the same origin, in common with the earlier augmentations they were presumably chosen to go into these units in an attempt to produce at least some stock of uniform appearance. Following lengthening, the 23 units given an additional diagram 740/41 ten-compartment trailer were renumbered 4172-4194 and seated 350, while the remainder given a diagram 742 eleven-compartment vehicle became 4235-4249 and seated ten more. These reformations took place between January 1947 (4172, formerly 1658) and April 1949 (4249, ex 1669). Renumbering took place in order of augmentation.

Other than 4131-4249, the only four-coach SUBs to be formed at this time without using new trailers were a group of eight 'scratch' units, made up from the serviceable vehicles of three-coach units which had been bombed or involved in accidents over a period of nearly five years from August 1943 to early 1948. Numbered 4250-4257, they were formed mainly from vehicles with bodies of LBSCR origin, but scant regard was paid to placing matching vehicles in particular units in the later examples, and most had a fairly short life before further reformation or withdrawal. These units were formed as shown below, with numbers in brackets showing the origin of each vehicle. Vehicles not otherwise identified had LBSCR bodywork.

Unit	MThB	TTh	TTh	MThB	Date formed
4250	8678 (1709)	9722 (1722)	9709 (1709)	8844 (1709)	by 8.43
4251	8705 (1736)	9741 (1741)	9736 (1736)	8871 (1736)	circa 2.44
4252	8738 (1761)	9472 (1761)	9728 (1728)	8896 (1761)	circa 7.44
4253	8556 (1774)	9316* (1667)	9650 (1774)	8802* (1667)	circa 7.45
4254	8373† ‡ (1474)	9527† (1474)	9730 (1730)	8865 (1730)	circa 10.46
4255	8194* (1673)	9322* (1673)	9350 (1701)	8836 (1701)	circa 12.47
4256	8672 (1703)	9703 (1703)	9505† (1415)	8838 (1703)	circa 2.48
4257	8653 (1649)	9693 (1649)	9670 (1600)	8654 (1649)	circa 2.48

* denotes vehicle with LSWR bodywork
† denotes vehicle with SECR bodywork.
‡ 8373 replaced by 9876* in 1951. This resulted in a unit uniquely formed of vehicles with bodywork of all three constituent companies.

Returning to 1945, with the end of the war in sight it was hoped to continue with the 1938 suburban stock renewal programme, but this did not prove possible at once. Apart from shortages of labour, particularly of skilled craftsmen, there were also difficulties in obtaining supplies of steel and electrical equipment, many categories of which remained under Government control. Moreover, there were considerable arrears of maintenance and repair to be taken in hand. SR works managers and production planners therefore had a difficult task in trying to satisfy competing demands with limited and uncertain resources, and frequently had to change their plans. Nevertheless, it proved possible to continue with the construction of badly-needed new suburban coaches on a limited scale.

After completion of new unit 4110 a start was made at Eastleigh on the 55 new trailer coaches ordered in 1939, which were used to augment existing units. This had the advantage of putting many new vehicles into stock without requiring any new traction equipment. Many underframes built for the purpose at Eastleigh in 1939-40 had been used for most of the units 4101-4110, so some frames used for the 55 were fabricated at Lancing and intended for new four-coach units 4111-30, which had been deferred due to traction equipment being unavailable. Although similar to the trailer thirds in 4101-4110, notice was taken of passengers' complaints and these coaches had only ten (rather than eleven) compartments 6ft 1½in between partitions, the slightly increased legroom giving fewer seats but at least somewhere to stand. (They differed from pseudo-composites 11471-80 in 4101-4110, in that all compartments were of equal width.) With a seating capacity of 120 and weighing 28 tons, the 55 trailers 10346-10400 were given the diagram number 2013. All but the last ten had wood and canvas roofs with curved rainstrips, the last SR EMU vehicles to be so constructed (other than some express stock replacements for vehicles destroyed in the war). Internally, they featured clip-on internal panels that originally tended to rattle and become detached, but it meant that a compartment could be stripped for reconditioning in about fifteen minutes. Other internal changes included the adoption of end armrests and seat backs

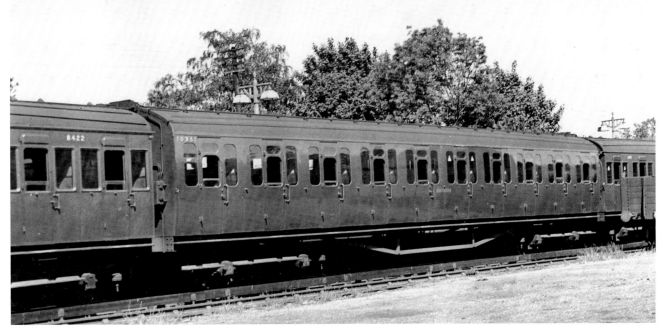

Ten-compartment 'six-a-side' augmentation trailer 10351, one of the first batch of 45 constructed in 1945-46 with wooden roofs, stands in as-built condition at Hayes in about 1948. It is formed in 1925 long-framed unit 4328, formerly 1498. *H.C. Hughes*

without scalloped tops but with additional headrest padding, and bare bulbs in shadeless sockets recessed into the ceiling.

The last ten vehicles from this batch, 10391-10400, had redesigned bodywork of all-steel construction, a momentous change which then became standard for the remainder of second-generation 4 SUB production (as well as much of the EPB fleet). The construction methods are dealt with below, but the main external change was the lack of a cantrail strip, now unnecessary as the roof was formed continuously with the sides. As a consequence, the bodyside paintwork was carried up around the roof curve to the straight rainstrip (which formed the joint between the side and roof panels), producing an appearance hitherto unfamiliar on British rolling stock, but unfortunately not matching the other vehicles of the unit into which they were formed. Rather than the lozenge-shaped toplights, the doors of 10391-400 initially had two recessed semicircular air-intake slots feeding an adjustable slotted ventilator inside.

These trailers entered service at the rate of about one per week from spring 1945 and went to the pre-war units with the newest bodywork, 1925-built 1285-1310 and 1496-1524, which were renumbered on augmentation into the series 4300-4325 and 4326-4354, in their original order. Revised seating capacities of the two types were 330 and 360 respectively. In order that the contrast between the shining new trailer and the three war-weary old coaches in each unit should not be too great, the old coaches were 'revarnished' – effectively this meant repainting them unlined malachite. Additionally, on reformation the short-framed units 4300-4325 were given the through lighting control cables along the roofs and associated jumpers under the headcode panels (the long-framed ones already had these from new).

THE FIRST ALL-STEEL UNITS 4111-4130

The redesign of the bodywork of the new suburban rolling stock to be of all-steel construction, first applied to augmentation trailers 10391-10400, was carried forward to the final twenty entirely new units completing the initial 1938 order, 4111-4130. Quite apart from the benefits of greater durability and fire-resistance, an all-steel structure enabled all bodywork to be pre-formed and assembled on jigs. The production of the post-war SUBs was the responsibility of Messrs C.A. Shepherd and G. Forder, the latter devising the welding and jigging techniques for the all-steel bodywork. Particular advantages of jig-construction were that few men trained in the old coach-building skills were required, although an increased number of welders was necessary, and that vehicles could be constructed quickly at a time when they were urgently needed. Three carriage jigs were set up at Eastleigh Works – one for a SUB motor coach, the second for a SUB trailer and the third for a Bulleid main-line corridor coach.[16] The body side panels were supplied, ready curved, by Fisher and Ludlow (a division of the Pressed Steel Co.), a company better known for its 'Prestcold' refrigerators. Coach ends other than cabs had vertical ribs pressed into them to increase their stiffness.

A consequence of motor coach construction using only one jig was that all were built facing the same way, and one of the pair of motor coaches for each unit therefore had to be turned on the triangle of lines round the back of Eastleigh Locomotive Works before the unit could be marshalled. This reversing

---

16 Bulleid main-line corridor coaches, although of similar general appearance to the electric suburban vehicles, used seam welds in the body side skinning but were otherwise of conventional wood-framed construction.

The first all-steel 4 SUB unit, 4111, poses outside Eastleigh Works for its official portrait in April 1946. Features to note include the six wider compartments in the 'pseudo-composite' (second vehicle back), the semi-circular ventilator recesses above the droplight on each passenger door and the lack of a cantrail, allowing the malachite green livery to be extended on to the roof. *SR Official*

operation was usually done after the coach was completed and numbered. If there was a rule that all odd-numbered or all even-numbered vehicles should be turned, it was certainly not followed consistently, and this resulted in some all-steel SUBs having their motor coach pairs numerically reversed in relation to their trailers compared to other units in the same batch.

All-steel construction required a redesigned driving cab. On the new version, the sides were of the same curved profile as the rest of the coach, and the inward-opening motorman's doors were not inset. The driving ends continued to be formed of a central narrow panel parallel with the buffer beam and wide side panels at a slight angle, but the traditional domed roof-end was abandoned and the front panels continued up to end square with the roof.

The first complete all-steel 4 SUB to leave the Eastleigh production line was 4111, completed in April 1946 as the first of a sub-batch of ten units numbered up to 4120. All accommodation was again in compartments, with each coach having one fewer than its equivalent in 4101-4110. The guard's vans were slightly larger than on the earlier units and were marked with an increased loading capacity of 1½ tons. Provision was made for the reinstatement of first class accommodation so one trailer had six wide compartments, no less than 7ft 2in between partitions, which could be converted to first class at a future date if required. These were flanked by two standard-width third class compartments at one end of the coach and one at the other. The total seating capacity of 4110-4120 was 420. Doors again had semi-circular air vents in place of toplights. Livery was identical to the earlier units except that the word SOUTHERN was prominently displayed across the top of the cab above the unit number, both of which were in the shaded yellow sans-serif 'sunshine' style. As on the first all-steel vehicles 10391-10400, the body side paintwork was carried up onto the roof on these and all subsequent SUB units, giving an entirely spurious streamlined, modern look. The seats were the same as those in the first augmentation trailers, with straight tops, and most interior panelling was covered in mid-brown rexine. Upholstery moquette in 4111

was of a unique pattern with a fawn and black foliage motif on a russet background, never used in any other vehicle, while the remainder of the batch had the standard patterns as indicated earlier.

The eight-compartment motor third brakes of this batch were numbered 10961-80, the ten compartment trailer thirds 10429-38 and the nine-compartment pseudo-composites 11481-90. All were formed up in exact numerical order of coach numbers with the motor third brakes allocated in numerical pairs. In these and subsequent SUBs with the same formation, as well as 4121-4130, the nine-compartment trailer had a rubbing block at one end and centre buffer at the other. As with 4102-4110, some of the trailers in these units incorporated Eastleigh-built underframes originally intended for augmentation trailers. Diagram numbers were 2119 for the motor coaches, 2014 for the ten-compartment trailers (different from the otherwise-similar augmentation trailers because they had a centre-buffer at both ends) and 2314 for the nine-compartment trailers. These diagram numbers were continued for the same vehicle types in subsequent new steel SUBs of this type (and nine-compartment trailers used as augmentation vehicles). The all-steel MThBs had a tare weight of 43 tons and trailers, of both types, 28 tons.

4111-4120 were followed directly off the Eastleigh produc-tion line between August and October 1946 by 4121-4130, the final units of the original 1938 order. Externally, they were virtually identical to the earlier batch except that 4121/23/24/27 had doors with glazed toplights rather than air vents. Inside, however, they were very different as it was decided to experiment with saloon accommodation, previ-ously a feature only of express stock (6 PUL, 4 COR etc) motor coaches. Each unit incorporated one nine-compart-ment trailer with six wider compartments (11491-11500), but the other vehicles had an arrangement which came to be known as 'semi-saloon'.

In the motor coaches (10981-11000, diagram 2120), the passenger accommodation comprised two four-bay saloons with a solid partition between them, while the ten-bay trailer (10439-48, diagram 2015) had two partitions with the accom-modation arranged three bays + four bays + three bays. At the ends of the saloons were full-width seats for six, as in compartments. Other seats were arranged two + three either side of an off-centre gangway. This arrangement combined the improved passenger flow and standing room of open saloon stock with the speedy loading and unloading of a door to every seating bay, and was made possible by the improved rigidity of the welded steel bodywork. Separate hammock-slung seat cushions were used except for the full-width seats

All-steel SUB 4369 from the 4355-4377 batch, which were the last to be built new with all-compartment accommodation before the general adoption of centre-gangway saloons, stands at London Bridge on 10th March 1948 leading a Dartford–Cannon Street working. Having been delivered just after nationalisation, BRITISH RAILWAYS is displayed and the unit number is prefixed with an S, but otherwise livery is still the final SR style. Note the grab handles and step-plates on the cab front to assist headcode changing, necessary due to the non-opening offside cab window. *J.H. Aston*

adjacent to partitions, which continued to be of the wire-framed bench type. Saloon seats had no armrests by the gangway, and the rexine-covered seat ends were lower than the cushions. Steel tube luggage racks, doubling as handholds for standing passengers, were fitted above seat backs – on 4130 these were of chromium-plated brass with steel mesh instead of the string netting normally employed. Livery was the same as the previous units, but seating capacity was reduced to 382. These internal rearrangements made no effective difference to vehicle tare weights, which (with the exception of 4130 – see below) were the same as for 4111-4120.

Of rather greater significance than its luggage racks, an important innovation in unit 4130 was its experimental equipping with the four prototype English Electric 'lightweight' traction motors, designated type EE 507A. Designed by Dennis Lightband just prior to World War Two at the SR's

instigation, the new design had a significant weight advantage over the existing 339 type, being only 1.92 tons including gears instead of 3.6 tons. The armature speed of the type 507 was increased, and it drove the wheels via 17:65 ratio gears. At an initial rating of 185hp, this gave a balancing speed of 56mph. It was designed to have the characteristics of a suburban motor (type 339) when working in parallel, and of an express motor (type 163) when working in weak-field. The type 507 motor was self-ventilated, and an air duct ran up the cab partition in the van to two large square ventilators on the roof of the motor coach.

Inevitably, the term 'tin can' quickly became used to describe the new steel-bodied SUBs by observers and staff. The soubriquet 'Queen Mary' (or simply 'Mary') was also widely used, in this case by analogy with wartime RAF fuselage road carriers known as 'Queen Marys' (after the ship) due to their length.

MORE NEW COMPARTMENT UNITS AND AUGMENTATION TRAILERS

At this stage, the production of further new all-compartment 4 SUBs and new trailers to augment existing units to four coaches became intertwined. For the sake of clarity, therefore, the new-build vehicles are dealt with here, and the augmentation, reformation and disposal of the remainder of the pre-war stock in later sections.

4130 was followed off the Eastleigh production line by a further 116 diagram 2013 augmentation trailers, numbered 10230-10345 (to HO 3351 of 2nd April 1946), delivered between October 1946 and June 1947. These were virtually identical to the ten-compartment trailers in 4111-4120 and augmentation trailers 10391-10400. One difference was that the doors were redesigned with the lozenge-shaped toplight now recessed and incorporating air vent slots at each end feeding an internal slotted ventilator above. This feature was perpetuated on all subsequent new SUB vehicles.

It is worth mentioning here that the doors of all-steel SUB (and SR EPB) vehicles were made to be fully interchangeable, which resulted in most of them being loose-fitting and hence prone to rattling noisily. Doors were frequently exchanged among coaches during overhaul, which over the years resulted in the early doors with semicircular ventilator recesses being distributed randomly among the SUB and EPB fleets. Conversely, the 'standard' door with toplight and ventilator slots appeared in time on units 4111-4130.[17]

The next batch of completely new 4 SUBs comprised 23 units numbered 4355-4377, ordered to HO 2231 on 5th May 1945 with sublime optimism a few weeks before the end of the war, but not turned out from Eastleigh until September 1947 –June 1948. It was originally intended that use would be made of the six underframes ordered as replacements for 1202/10 (subsequently cancelled) and fourteen other existing motor coach underframes from scrapped pre-war units, but in the event all the underframes used were of new construction. These units, which were budgeted for as 'additional stock', were intended to be internally identical to the 4111-4120 batch, comprising two eight-compartment motor coaches, one ten-compartment trailer and one nine-compartment trailer, the latter with six wider compartments. The compartment arrangement was perpetuated because further time was needed for the semi-saloon units (4121-4130) to be evaluated in traffic before the design was generally adopted.

The trailers intended for 4355-4377 were built in the summer of 1947, comprising ten compartment vehicles 10449-71 and nine-compartment 11448-70. However, a severe shortage of traction equipment, particularly motors, meant that construction of the motor third brakes, numbered 10895-10940, again to be formed in numerical pairs, did not start until September 1947. Even so they then had to be stored awaiting electrical equipment, and the units appeared in

reverse numerical order probably because their motor coaches were formed into them out of storage on a 'last in, first out' basis. Motor coaches awaiting traction motors and trailers awaiting formation into a four-coach unit were held, complete except for their upholstery, in the carriage sidings at Micheldever, 15 miles up the line from Eastleigh and long-used as a dumping ground for out-of-service vehicles.

A further 63 ten-compartment augmentation trailers to diagram 2013, numbered 10167-10229, were completed concurrently between January and July 1948, the first three having been ordered to HO 3386 (23rd May 1947), and the remainder to HO 3463 (24th November 1947). Because of the late completion of their motor coaches and in order to get the new vehicles into service as quickly as possible, some of the trailers intended for 4355-4377 were used to augment pre-war units, and some of the augmentation trailer batch went into the entirely new units. In the event, 4364-4376 were formed as intended, including a nine-compartment trailer, but the use of augmentation vehicles gave units 4355-4363 two ten-compartment trailers, giving a revised seating capacity of 432. (As a result, nine nine-compartment trailers ended up as augmentation trailers in otherwise pre-war units.) 4377 also had a nine-compartment trailer, but its other trailer was an experimental vehicle, 10463, described below. All were painted in the same livery as previously, but those delivered from January 1948 onwards (4369 downwards) had BRITISH RAILWAYS across the cab fronts but no evidence of ownership at all on the sides, and the unit number had a small s prefix. 4369 appeared at a livery exhibition at Kensington Addison Road in January 1948 when it was being decided in what colours publicly-owned trains should be painted. The indicated carrying capacity of the motor coach vans in these units reverted to 1 ton, although at just over 8ft in length they were identical in size to those of 4111-4130.

Externally, two minor alterations to the cab fronts were the provision of step plates above the buffers and grab-handles above and on the outer edges of the windscreens. These were to enable staff to attach and remove headcode stencils from the outside, necessary because, unlike all other SR dc units built until then, the offside cab windscreen on these units could not be opened. 4355-4366 had step plates and grab handles on both sides, while 4367-4377 had them on the offside only. The grab handles, also fitted to some later SUBs and to the post war 2 HALs (see Volume 2), were originally painted yellow and gave the units a somewhat fierce 'eyebrowed' look. Internally, an odd feature of all the vehicles built to HO 2231, whether formed in units 4355-4377 or used as augmentation trailers, was the use of a Norwegian cork flooring material embossed to resemble tiling, rather than the ubiquitous granite-coloured linoleum generally used. It proved unsuccessful as it wore quickly and was difficult to keep clean, and was replaced on first overhaul.

Four vehicles with non-standard experimental features were included in the 4355-4377 batch. Motor coaches 10939 and 10940 in 4377 had a small ventilator above the nearside windscreen, but these were removed and plated over in 1966. MThB 10896 in 4355 had a wiper on the guard's periscope

---

17 As an aside, the almost identical doors for Bulleid steam coaches were, by contrast, not interchangeable but tailor-made for their own doorway, and indeed had the carriage number stamped on the door edge.

4191, one of the LSWR-bodied units converted in SR days and augmented with a further vehicle of the same origin from a trailer set, forms the 12.32pm Charing Cross–Sevenoaks at London Bridge (Eastern) on 14th April 1949. It was originally unit 1685 and coach 10408 (the second vehicle back, with steel plated sides) came from trailer set 1051. *J.H. Aston*

and had the headcode shown by means of a pair of numerical roller blinds behind a glass panel rather than external stencils. Both features were approved for general use, although roller blinds did not become a standard fitting on new stock until 1952 after SUB production had ceased.

The final non-standard vehicle was trailer 10463, formed in 4377 in place of the ten-compartment trailer. This was a full saloon with no intermediate partitions, seating 102, and given diagram number 2016. Unlike those in 4121-4130, the inner seat ends had armrests, and ornate steel tube and wire-mesh luggage racks were fitted above the seat backs, together with additional grab rails. A peculiar feature was the inclusion of small advertisement panels between the top of each seat and luggage rack, slightly reminiscent of those in the original 1909 ac side-gangway coaches. These panels were removed in about 1979, but otherwise this unusual experimental vehicle survived, latterly running in unit 4277, until the very end of SUB operation in September 1983.

Interior of unique diagram 2016 full-saloon trailer third 10463, formed in unit 4377. Note the ornate luggage rack with additional handrails, and the advertisement panel above the seat back, both features omitted from the production diagram 2018 vehicles in new units 4277-4299 and 4378 upwards. *B.W. Rayner*

FURTHER AUGMENTATION, REFORMATIONS AND WITHDRAWALS OF PRE-WAR UNITS

To summarise those three-coach units already mentioned as being lengthened to four coaches, the first to be augmented were the ex-LSWR '1201' type, which became 4 SUBs 4131-4171 and 4195-4234 between 1942 and 1948. The 1925-built units of the '1285' and '1496' types gained new 'six-a-side' trailers to become 4300-4354 in 1945-46, while 38 further SR-built units from the 1658-1701 group with LSWR bodywork became 4172-4194 and 4235-4249 when augmented with the remainder of the 62ft vehicles from trailer sets in 1947-49. Finally, eight units numbered 4250-4257 were made up between 1943 and 1948 using spare vehicles from units rendered incomplete by enemy action or accidents.

All other pre-war units to be made up to four coaches were given one new all-steel 'six-a-side' trailer apiece. The remainder of the augmentation process was a complex and untidy affair, made more so by a dearth of new units due to materials shortage and of older coaches due to wartime damage and maintenance arrears. Originally, it was intended to select those units with bodywork in the best condition for lengthening with new trailers, and blocks of new unit numbers in the 4xxx range were allocated to the various groups of units to be made up to four coaches. Those not selected for augmentation would be withdrawn as new four-coach units came into service, once wartime and other accidental losses had been made good. However, as mentioned above, it did not prove possible in the event for systematic withdrawal of the pre-war units to commence until the start of 1949. This was partly due to the peak periods becoming more concentrated just after the war, requiring a net increase in suburban rolling stock anyway, and partly because new units were not produced as fast as had been hoped. Some of those pre-war units already augmented had to be disbanded due to the poor condition of their wooden-bodied coaches, and the new 'six-a-side' trailers released were reformed in further units not originally intended to be so treated. Most units augmented with a new all-steel trailer seated 360, but there were variations.

The 116 new trailers in the 10230-10345 series, which were ordered in April 1946, and turned out from Eastleigh between October 1946 and June 1947, were immediately formed into a variety of former three-coach units, which were then renumbered into the series 4401-4516. The new vehicles were added to the old units without regard to their numerical sequence, but the new unit numbers were assigned systematically, in distinct blocks for the various types and within these blocks in the same order as the old unit numbers. Units chosen were selected as having bodywork in the best condition, and no repainting or other refurbishment was done prior to augmentation. The new numbers and origins of the various units concerned are given in the table below:

New Numbers	From the series	Bodywork Origins
4401-4405	1773-1785	LSWR
4406-4410, 4430, 4431	1786-1796	LSWR
4411-4423	1585-1599	LSWR
4424-4429	1579-1584 (all)	LSWR
4432-4494	1401-1495	SECR
4495-4501	1525-1534	SECR
4502-4516	1601-1630	SECR

The last SECR-bodied electric vehicle remaining in passenger service was trailer third (formerly composite) 9527 formed in unit 4254, seen here parked at Orpington on Sunday 18th May 1952. Uniquely, at the time this unit had vehicles with bodywork from all three constituent companies; the ends of LBSCR-bodied TTh 9730 (left) and LSWR-bodied MThB 9876 (right) can be glimpsed. *J.H. Aston*

History repeats itself: SECR-bodied SUB 4492 (formerly 1490), reformed for its last year in service with an additional SECR trailer from a with-drawn unit in place of a steel 'six-a-side' vehicle, approaches East Croydon with a Victoria to Coulsdon North service on 30th April 1950. *Pamlin Prints*

Following completion, the new trailers were generally stored at Micheldever for a short while awaiting electrical equipment, and following the fitting of this were hauled up to Selhurst in fours or sixes ready for incorporation into an existing unit[18]. As a result they did not arrive in numerical order and this accounts for the random sequence in which they were formed into their units. For example 10230 itself, carrying a paint date of 18th October 1946, did not reach Selhurst until the following 8th January, three weeks after 10242. By early February 1947, 36 new vehicles had been delivered, of which thirty had been formed into units and placed in service.

However it soon became apparent that a small modification to the bogie springing was needed to ensure complete clearance between the wheels and the diagonal underframe members when the coach was heavily loaded, so the six unused trailers were sent back to Eastleigh for alteration, and all further deliveries were to the new standard. A careful eye was kept on the first thirty augmented units and as soon as practicable the all-steel trailers were removed and replaced by a modified example, enabling them to be returned to Eastleigh for modification and reuse. This resulted in even further mixing of the new trailers within units. For example, 10230 was originally formed in otherwise SECR-bodied unit 4488 early in January 1947, was replaced in 4488 by 10291 in July, and finally went to 4436 in the following month. Most of these trailers went into service without heaters, these being fitted later.

The final 63 trailers used for augmentation purposes also went into a variety of pre-war units during 1947 and 1948. It appears that the original intention was to place them into LBSCR-bodied units in the 1631-1657 and 1717-1771 groups, the resulting augmented units taking the numbers 4517-4579. In the event these plans were revised and very few of the former group were in fact used, probably due to poor bodywork condition. Following augmentation, the 63 4 SUBs actually formed were numbered within the range 4517-4614, but not all existed at any one time, and a few numbers (4595-4600, 4609/11/12) were never used. As described below, these numerical over-runs resulted from last-minute changes of policy, which seemed to be continuously short-term and ad-hoc during this period.

Those units given standard ten-compartment all-steel trailers were renumbered in the series 4517-4571 – of these, 4520 and 4527-4571 were augmented from units in the 1717-1771 group, which were still in reasonable condition as most had bodies converted from ac vehicles dating from 1911-23. 4522-4526 were made up from the 1631-1657 type, but 4517-19/21 were from miscellaneous LSWR-bodied units 1784, 1599, 1728 and 1679 respectively. On augmentation, these units were not all renumbered in their original order.

The nine nine-compartment steel trailers 11448-56 origi-nally intended for 4355-4363 were used in 1947 to augment LBSCR-bodied units 1600, 1707 and seven more from the 1631-1657 series to form units 4601-4607, 4613 and 4614. 4602 and 4607 were disbanded quickly, and their steel trailers then went to augmented units 4608 and 4610. All this batch had been withdrawn by September 1949, but by this stage it was apparent that pre-war vehicles were having to be kept in service for longer than had been intended because new stock was not being produced as fast as had been hoped. The steel trailers released were therefore re-used once more to create yet further augmented SUBs, mostly numbered in the range 4572 to 4594. These were formed-up on an ad-hoc basis from 1949 using various miscellaneous units. Tracing the story of individual units or vehicles is complicated, as not all units existed at once and some were withdrawn after only a few months. A number of all-steel trailers released from these and other previously augmented SUBs were reused in further units, as by this time some earlier units were being with-drawn systematically, and others in the lower-numbered series had already been condemned following mishaps.

Rostering of stock became very difficult in the transition from three to four-coach units. Inevitably, seven-coach forma-tions were common and sometimes even nine coach trains (4 SUB + trailer set + 3) could be seen in traffic with the conse-quent problem of platforms being too short. Several instances of this were recorded by G.T. Moody. For example, on 10th July 1946 three-coach 1798, trailer set 1191 and 4 SUB 4251 formed the 7.23am Horsham–London Bridge, while on 8th July 1947 the 8.23am Bickley–Holborn Viaduct was formed of 4 SUB 4413, 2 NOL 1872 (running as a trailer unit) and an unidentified three-coach unit. To illustrate the problems caused by these over-length formations, the latter train was half a coach too long for platform 5 at Holborn Viaduct, and on leaving had to cross onto the Up line then back again onto the Down. This phenomenon was apparently much rarer on the Western section than elsewhere.

The appearance of the various augmented pre-war units varied considerably. The neatest and most uniform were those formed with LSWR-bodied stock and an additional vehicle of the same external appearance from a trailer set. The 1925 units looked reasonable too, as the roof and (mostly) cantrail heights were the same in both the original and post-war vehicles. Other units with new wide-bodied steel trailers looked untidy to varying degrees, the worst match undoubt-edly being with vehicles having LBSCR-type bodywork. Not only were the new coaches wider and taller than the old, but the arc roof and sharp cantrail of the LBSCR coach profile contrasted severely with the smooth curves of the Bulleid vehicle. All this was, of course, of only academic interest to the SR maintenance and traffic staff struggling to keep enough units serviceable, and vehicles were frequently swapped between units in order to keep as many as possible in traffic.

There were a significant number of units formed up with coaches of two constituent companies as a result of reforma-tions of this type and following accident damage, and one unit (4254) uniquely ran with coaches of all three body-

---

18 The match vehicles used for these movements included a pair of 'Van C' four-wheeled parcels/guard's vans with modified couplings and buffing gear. Pairs of underframes from withdrawn trailer set vehicles were also utilised.

Clearly demonstrating the unfortunate mismatch between arc-roofed LBSCR-bodied vehicles and all-steel augmentation trailers, unit 4555 stands at London Bridge (Central) on 23rd June 1949, waiting to depart with the 1.40pm to Sutton. *J.H. Aston*

patterns from 1951 until withdrawal in 1956. Incidentally, this unit had the last electric vehicle with SECR bodywork (trailer 9527) in traffic. Undoubtedly the strangest unit running around during this period was 4590. From 1950 to 1954 this was formed of new all-steel saloon motor coach 12664 (one of a batch built in 1950, see below), all-steel nine-compartment trailer 11451, and LBSCR-bodied motor coach and trailer 9482 and 9806 originally from 1771. In 1954, steel-bodied motor coach 12664 was reformed in new 2 HAL 2700, and was replaced in 4590 by LSWR 'bullet-nosed' MThB 8023 from unit 4153; in this formation it lasted until 1956.

Other than units withdrawn or disbanded as a result of mishaps, the first four-coach SUBs to be taken out of service systematically were those lengthened from the 1631-1657, 1702-1716 and 1797/98 groups. These had LBSCR bodywork from Billinton 'bogie block' sets dating from c.1900, which was by this time in very poor condition. The 26 units concerned, 4256/57, 4522-25/57/62/63/75-78/81-84, and 4601/03-05/07/08/10/13/14, were withdrawn between January and October 1949, at the same time as their non-augmented sisters, the last survivors probably being 4256/57, 4576/78/81 and 4613. (Records are not always entirely clear regarding exact withdrawal dates.) Following scrapping of their body-

work at Horley or Lancing, underframes and bogies were recovered for use in new all-steel 4 SUBs of the 4621-4662 batches. The 24 all-steel augmentation trailers released were, for the time being, used to lengthen other pre-war units to four coaches as mentioned above, but eventually all were rewired and renumbered for use in 4 EPB units.

Following withdrawal of the final three-coach SECR-bodied units by the end of 1949, as related in Chapter 5, augmented units of the same origin in the 4432-4516 series followed in 1950-51, next in line because of bodywork age and condition. Underframes, bogies and augmentation trailers were re-used in 4 SUBs in the number range 4667-4753 as explained below (and also in the first EPBs which followed). Exceptionally, six units of this type were reformed once more in April and May 1950, their 'six-a-side' vehicles being swapped for a wooden-bodied trailer from a similar unit already condemned. This enabled their augmentation trailers to be released for forming up with new steel motor coaches (in units 4601-4606, the second SUBs with these numbers) before there were enough new units to enable them to be withdrawn. These rearrangements were only of a stop-gap nature, none of the reformed units lasting much over a year. Their formations are listed in the following table.

Unit	MThB	TTh	TTh	(ex unit)	MThB	Date Formed	All-Steel TTh to unit
4441	8372	9506	9609	(4442)	8254	April 1950	10276 to 4602
4445	8261	9552	9550	(4458)	8262	May 1950	10265 to 4604
4456	8295	9563	9495	(4462)	8296	April 1950	10297 to 4603
4463	8314	9555	9541	(4465)	8313	May 1951	10248 to 4606
4478	8361	9561	9558	(4480)	8362	April 1950	10259 to 4605
4492	8405	9521	9493	(4448)	8406	April 1950	10245 to 4601

The withdrawal of the remainder of the pre-war stock following the entry of the last all-steel 4 SUB unit, 4754, into service is covered later in the chapter.

THE PRODUCTION SECOND-GENERATION 4 SUBS

After the start of 1948, supply difficulties with electrical equipment became less acute, and it was possible to commence production of entirely new units in earnest. Following the successful operation of the 'semi-saloon' units 4121-4130 and of experimental fully-open vehicle 10463 in unit 4377, it was decided that the majority of accommodation in the production 4 SUBs would be of the open saloon type. The chosen formation was a pair of open motor coaches, each with eight bays, flanking a ten-bay open trailer and a ten-compartment trailer, giving a seating total of 386. None of the saloons were subdivided and all accommodation was third class, as by this time it had been decided that first class was definitely not to be reinstated in suburban trains.

The interior arrangements in these units were arrived at following passenger surveys, and in this respect a paper given by L. Lynes (co-written by C.A. Shepherd) to The Institution of Locomotive Engineers in January 1948 is interesting. 'It is well-known that compartment stock, with its transverse seats, favours the seated passengers during the maximum traffic periods at the expense of the comfort of the standing passengers. With expanding traffic and concentrated working hours of travellers, the need for improving this state of affairs became a matter deserving of attention, as more people were daily being called upon to stand throughout their journeys, often in discomfort, owing to overcrowded conditions of travelling.' After describing the steps leading to semi-saloons and then full length saloons he went on. 'By means of mass observation tests, a process by which persons are questioned in large numbers and their replies analysed, the passengers' opinions were obtained. The results showed a majority preference for the new style of unit.' [19]

___

19 What was not said was that another option, that of LT-style sliding-door stock, received very little enthusiasm from the travelling public. This fact has tended to be ignored when SR historians compare the relative design features of the 'old-fashioned' slam-door 4 SUB stock and roughly contemporary sliding-door EMUs built for LT, Liverpool Street–Shenfield and the Liverpool area electric lines of the LMSR.

The first ten new units with this new standard formation, numbered 4378-4387, were ordered on 23rd May 1947 and completed in two simultaneous lots (4378-4382 and 4383-4387) between September and November 1948. They were justified financially as 'replacements' for war losses. The two lots were identical apart from minor wiring layout details, and all were given EE 339 motors. Oddly, although the technical split was five and five, they had been ordered in two sub-batches of eight (4378-4385, to HO 3384) and two (4386/87, to HO 3385). The reason for this division is not known. Motor coach (MThBO) numbers were 10829-48, (in pairs) compartment trailers (TTh) 10472-81 and saloon trailers (TThO) 12351-60. The eight-bay open motor third brakes were to diagram 2126 and the ten-bay open trailers to diagram 2018. All subsequent SUB vehicles of these types were given the same diagram numbers, regardless of underframe origins, motor bogie or traction motor type. The diagram 2013 ten-compartment trailers were identical to the standard augmentation vehicles built previously, with a centre buffer at one end and rubbing block at the other.

There followed directly a further 23 units, 4277-4299, ordered on 24th November 1947 to HO 3464 as additional stock. They were identical except for the fitting of the new EE 507C traction motor, the first production version of the prototype 507A type which had been successfully tried in unit 4130. Motor coaches fitted with (or intended to have) the newer design of motor were built with two square air-intakes on the roof above the van, connected to ducting down the body sides to ventilate the motors. Coach numbers for these units were 10849-94 (MThBO), 10144-66 (TTh) and 10121-43 (TThO). Use of these lightweight motors reduced the tare weight of the motor coaches to 39 tons.

4378-4387 and 4277-4299 were all constructed on new underframes with 'central'-type motor bogies, and were turned out in malachite green with coach numbers at cantrail height and the unit number preceded by a small 's', there being otherwise no evidence of ownership. They had non-opening offside cab windows and hence were given cab-front step plates and grab rails around windscreens (those on 4378-4387 were on the offside only). All were marshalled in strict order of vehicle numbers.

The saloon vehicles in all these units had internal arrangements which perpetuated the more successful features of units 4121-4130 and of coach 10463 in 4377. The simple above-seat luggage racks fitted to the '4121' series were preferred to the over-complicated arrangement in 10463, and only the end panels of each saloon had advertisement frames. All seats, including the full-width ones at the ends of saloons and in compartments, now had separate hammock-slung cushions. Seat ends adjacent to the gangway had armrests as in 10463, and were originally covered in tan-coloured rexine, as were the panels on the lower halves of doors and around the quarterlights.

By 1949 mass withdrawals of pre-war suburban stock were at last taking place, as explained previously, and this released numbers of standard 62ft steel underframes which could be reconditioned for incorporation into the final, and largest, batch of new 4 SUBs to be built, as envisaged in the original 1938 plan. Following withdrawal and stripping of reusable equipment at Durnsford Road (Wimbledon) and Strawberry Hill depots, the old vehicles found their way to railway-owned scrap sidings at Horley or Lancing Works, where their wooden bodywork was demolished, largely by hand, and burnt. The underframes, sometimes after a period of storage at one of various locations around the system, were then sent to Lancing. Here they were dismantled and cleaned prior to being reassembled with additional strengthening pieces, and were then hauled to Eastleigh to be fitted with new all-steel bodies. A large majority of the vehicles of these later units were built on reclaimed underframes in this way. The release of nearly new all-steel augmentation trailers from withdrawn pre-war units only commenced in 1950 and these were incorporated into new 4 SUBs from June of that year, commencing with 4667.

The SECR wooden bodies of withdrawn unit 4446 in the process of being smashed from their underframes at Lancing Works on 5th September 1951. The frame of the leading vehicle 8264 was reused under all-steel 4 EPB MThB 14039 in unit 5020. *J.H. Aston*

Recently-completed 4 SUB saloon motor third brake 11333, to be formed in unit 4637, parked in Eastleigh Works yard on 17th September 1949. Painted in the plain BR malachite green adopted at this time, note that the unit number is prefixed S, the vehicle number is towards the left hand end, and there is no 'lion on wheel' badge. The underframe for this coach was recovered from LBSCR-bodied MThB 8674. *J.H. Aston*

The 134 units of this final SUB production run were numbered 4621-4754 and were turned out in four distinct lots between May 1949 and December 1951. Most had the same formation as the '4277' and '4378' batches, but six had nine-compartment 'pseudo-composite' trailers. There were also fifteen motor coaches with new underframes which originally went into SUBs of non-standard formation. The cab fronts reverted to having an opening offside windscreen for head-code changing, so the grab handles and step plates were omitted.

4621 and 4622 were outshopped in the same livery as 4277-4299 with shaded numbering at cantrail height. By this time, however, BR had finalised liveries for its electric trains and units from 4623 were outshopped in a revised scheme, although (except where noted) the shade of green remained all but identical to the Southern Railway malachite.

Numbering and lettering were now in old gold with thin black edging. Coach numbers initially appeared at waist level on the left hand ends of vehicle sides, but policy on this changed in about October 1950 and units from 4700 upwards were outshopped with them at the right hand end, which then became the standard position. (Earlier units had them re-positioned on first revarnish or before.) Coach numbers were prefixed, and from 1951 suffixed, S. An S also sometimes preceded the unit number, but was inconsistently applied. The BR 'lion on wheel' emblem was applied to the lower body panels between the third and fourth compartment doors (from the driving end) on the motor coaches from 4707 onwards, and it was quickly added to earlier units which had entered service without it. Remaining augmented pre-war SUBs passing through shops from early 1950 onwards also received the same livery.

Two all-steel 4 SUB units from the 4621-4754 production series, parked side-by-side at Selhurst on 28th February 1967 and showing a number of important detail differences quite apart from contrasting liveries. 4628 on the left has 'central' type 8ft 9in motor bogies, recognisable by straight guard irons in front of the leading wheels, and a standard stencil headcode panel. On the right, 4721 has 9ft 'eastern' motor bogies with kinked guard irons, and a roller-blind headcode panel. 4628 is in blue with full yellow ends, one of the first to be repainted in this livery, while 4721 retains the later BR green with a small yellow panel. *R.E. Ruffell*

The first sub-batch covered units 4621-4655, ordered to HO 3504, 7th September 1948, and turned out from Eastleigh between May 1949 and January 1950. They were followed by virtually identical 4656-4666 between January and March, which had been ordered on the same date to HOs 3505 (4656-4659) and 3506, and which differed from 4621-4655 only in respect of the seating in the compartment trailers, where there was a reversion to fixed benches with wire-framed cushions. For some peculiar reason these were divided 2¼+1½+2¼ rather than the more usual two+two+two, not improving the ride for those sitting over the gap. The inner seat-ends in the open saloons of all units from 4621 upwards were of polished wood rather than being 'Rexine'-covered. Motor third brakes were numbered 11301-92, the compartment trailers 8901-46 and the open trailers 12361-12406. Note that the new compartment trailers reused the coach numbers of withdrawn ex-LSWR trailer sets 1001-1024.

A total of 133 vehicles, comprising all but the last seven motor coaches and about half the trailers, were built on underframes recovered from scrapped pre-war units. These came mainly from the 1631-1657 and 1702-1716 batches which had bodywork of converted LBSCR steam-stock origin, but a few came from LSWR-bodied 1773-1796 series units and from other miscellaneous withdrawn vehicles. All the trailers of the 4656-4666 batch had new underframes. The motor coaches all had either new or reconditioned 'central'-type motor bogies modified for the mounting of new EE 507C traction motors. However, a shortage of these meant that 4621-4649 went into service with the older EE 339 type, but all had been replaced by 1960. Coaches were formed into units in numerical sequence, resulting in 4663-4666 being formed entirely of vehicles on new frames.

Fifteen extra open saloon motor coaches, numbered 12650-64, were ordered to HO 3618 of 2nd November 1949 and completed in April 1950, all having new underframes with 'central' motor bogies and EE 507C motors. Fourteen of them were paired up with existing all-steel 'six-a-side' trailers from augmented pre-war units to form 4 SUBs 4601-4607. These had the non-standard formation of saloon motor third brake + trailer compartment third + trailer compartment third + saloon motor third brake, and seated 404. As noted earlier, it was actually necessary to reform, with old trailers, six SECR-bodied augmented units due for early withdrawal in order to release sufficient all-steel coaches for these units, while 4607 initially included wooden-roofed 10373 from withdrawn 1925 unit 4350. The fifteenth vehicle, 12664, initially formed part of the unique SR/LBSCR hybrid unit 4590, but in 1954 was paired with a new all-steel driving trailer composite to form 2 HAL 2700, in which guise it collected a second periscope. This coach finally ended its days in unit 4369 as a replacement for 10923, damaged in an accident in 1968. It is convenient to mention here that the wooden-roofed trailer in 4607 was swapped for newer all-steel vehicle 10449 from 4333 in May 1960, at the time when the 1925 units were being taken out of service, and was subsequently scrapped.

Following the mass withdrawal of the remaining un-augmented SECR-bodied units of the '1401' and '1601' classes towards the end of 1949, and of their augmented versions in the 4432-4516 series shortly afterwards, their underframes and bogies reappeared under most bodies of the final production 4 SUB units, numbered 4667-4754. These 88 units were built in two distinct lots between May 1950 and December 1951. The first lot was covered by HO 3617 of 2nd November 1949 and included units up to 4709, and the remainder were to HO 3638 of 16th January 1950. (There were to be a further fifteen units to HO 3638, but in the event these were turned out as the first 4 EPBs, similar in basic design but with differing control and brake systems). Motor coach numbers of 4667-4754 were 12665-12800 and 8616-55, and those of the open trailers 8957-9034. As the planned number series for new motor coaches had become exhausted, 8616-55 (in 4735-4754) reused numbers from withdrawn MThBs in LBSCR-bodied units in the 1631-1657 series.

All SUBs in these two batches were given one existing augmentation trailer, originally built in 1946-48, recovered from a withdrawn pre-war unit. Those in 4688/96 and 4723/28/33/39 were some of the nine-compartment vehicles originally intended for units in the 4355-4363 batch, but instead used to augment existing stock; this gave these units a reduced seating capacity of 374. It was normal practice to haul the three new coaches of each unit from Eastleigh to Selhurst, where the existing trailer was marshalled in. Although these trailers were revarnished externally to match the new coaches, interiors were generally left as they were.

These units were otherwise generally identical to previous SUBs from 4378 onwards, but their underframe origins resulted in all but two of the motor coaches having 9ft wheel-base 'eastern'-type motor bogies, recognisable by their kinked guard irons in front of the leading wheels. The original DK 77 motors fitted to these bogies were scrapped at this time, the new SUBs entering service with the EE 507C type. The MThBOs of final 4 SUB 4754, 8654/55, were built on new underframes with 'central'-type motor bogies. Units were again formed with consecutively-numbered motor third brakes and saloon trailers. Those from 4739 upwards were originally outshopped in a lighter shade of green due to a specification error – this 'bog grass' hue did not wear well and the SUBs concerned were among the first to be repainted. Internally, these same units had plastic ceiling panels rather than the hardboard hitherto used, but they proved unsuccessful and were replaced on first overhaul.

Although the appearance of unit 4754 in December 1951 signalled the end of 4 SUB construction, the jigs at Eastleigh were not dismantled until nearly a decade later, latterly being used in the construction of SR-type 4 EPB and similar units which followed the last of the SUBs off the production line. As with the SUBs, these used salvaged 62ft underframes following the scrapping of the remainder of the pre-war suburban stock; indeed, the number of EPB vehicles built with Bulleid (rather than BR Standard) bodywork exactly matched the number of recoverable 62ft underframes remaining.

There were few odd vehicles in the fleet of 'standard' 4 SUB units as built. Following the success of the trial roller-blind headcode panel fitted to MThB 10896 in unit 4355, similar equipment was fitted to the motor coaches of 4694-4700, 4721 and 4736. The odd number sequence of units fitted with this equipment allegedly resulted from two of the supplied sets being mislaid in Eastleigh Works and then later rediscovered. Initially all had square-cornered glass panels flush with the cab fronts, behind which were two blinds

In final condition with 'central' motor bogies, self-contained buffers and reinstated ventilator over the headcode panel, augmented 1925 'long-frame' unit 4337 accelerates away from Wimbledon with a Waterloo–Hampton Court service in about 1959. *F.W. Ivey*

carrying large numerals of similar dimensions to the standard stencils. Each blind had numbers 0-9 in white on a black background, plus a white blank for tail-end display (not illuminated at night) and a black blank for use with single-digit codes. Several were modified in later years and further units were so equipped, as detailed below.

THE LAST YEARS OF THE PRE-WAR UNITS

Following the emergence of the last new all-steel 4 SUB 4754 in December 1951, withdrawals of the pre-war units continued, although not at a steady rate. Standard 62ft underframes and bogies released were used for the 4 EPB units, as were the all-steel augmentation trailers, which were rewired and renumbered for their new role.

A few of the 1925 units, which had been the first to be augmented with new 'six-a-side' trailers, had these swapped for others from augmented units already withdrawn. For example in December 1949, 4313 had its original wooden-roofed trailer 10376 replaced by nine-compartment all-steel vehicle 11456 which had previously been formed in 4594. Of greater significance, all-steel coach 10398 was removed from 4333 in 1951 and replaced by 10449 from 4569. 10398 was then rewired and renumbered to 15001, becoming the compartment trailer third in the prototype 4 EPB unit 5001.

Between 1951 and 1953, the motor coaches of long-framed 4326-4354 had their 9ft wheelbase 'eastern' motor bogies substituted by spare examples of the 8ft 9in 'central' type from withdrawn units originally in the 1601-1630 series. (The original DK 77 motors were scrapped and replaced by new EE 507Ds in the 9ft bogies, which then went to 4 EPBs from 5016 upwards then being constructed.) At the same time, the original buffers at the driving ends were replaced by the Spencer-Moulton self-contained type fitted to express stock and second generation SUBs. These came from a large stock of spares, some of which had originally been supplied for the 5 BEL and 6 PUL Pullman cars, and as a result a number of very lowly suburban units ran around with PULLMAN cast on their buffer housings!

The rate of withdrawal of pre-war stock slowed down significantly after 1951 as the construction of replacement units was cut down from approximately fifty per year (in 1949-51) by about two thirds. This was a result of Government controls interrupting the supply of sheet steel to railway workshops, diverting it instead to an armaments programme and to the motor industry, which was supposed to pursue an export drive. This resulted in no new units being turned out from summer 1952 until spring 1953.[20] Therefore, in 1952 particularly, few old units could be withdrawn, but individual vehicles in poor condition were condemned and others moved between units to cover the gaps, resulting in many mixed formations. From later in 1953 the rate of production of new EPB stock picked up again, enabling wholesale withdrawal of wooden-bodied SUBs to start up once more. At this time the scrapping of bodywork was transferred to sidings at Newhaven Town, and virtually all remaining pre-1939 suburban coaches, as well as sundry other withdrawn EMU vehicles, met their ends there.

Systematic withdrawal of LSWR-bodied units began in 1951, the first to go being those in the 4401-4423, 4430/31 and high 45xx groups which had been augmented from 1773-1796 and 1585-1599 with new all-steel trailers. These had all gone by the end of 1953, their augmentation vehicles going to new 4 EPBs. Seven vehicles from these units had been converted using lengthened LBSCR ac stock underframes and, probably because these were not required for further use under new coaches, only one motor coach (9816) was actually scrapped at this time. Three were reformed into other units, while the original vehicles of 4579, the erstwhile 1782, were retained following withdrawal in July 1953 for conversion into a three-coach Instruction Unit. Initially numbered S10, this survived until May 1976 and is described in detail in Volume 2.

Withdrawals of units in the 4172-4194 and 4235-4248 groups commenced in 1953; augmented from 1658-1701 with another LSWR-bodied trailer, all vehicles were condemned. From 1954, units 4131-4171 and 4195-4234, the original LSWR 1201-1284 similarly augmented, were also steadily withdrawn. It is thought that they lasted this long because, having been substantially rebuilt with new frames between 1934 and 1940, they were in better condition than others. The last of both types went in 1956, as did 4424-4429, the former 1579-1584 with 1936-type control gear, augmented with steel trailers which now went to further EPBs.

Following this, there remained few units with pre-Grouping bodywork other than those in the range 4527-4590, composed mostly of vehicles from units in the 1717-1772 series. These had bodies of LBSCR design from former ac vehicles, mounted on lengthened former ac stock underframes which were not intended for reuse under new coaches. The majority were condemned in 1956, the wooden-bodied vehicles being entirely scrapped at Newhaven and their augmentation trailers rewired for use in new 4 EPBs. However, 72 coaches were retained, including three surviving LSWR-bodied ones originally from units 1780/81, also with lengthened ex-ac frames, and these were reformed into eighteen 4 SUBs numbered 4501-4518 between June 1956 and January 1957. 4501 had an LSWR-bodied motor coach and trailer and 4511 a similar trailer, but otherwise these units presented a much neater and more uniform appearance with all coaches of the same arc-roofed profile, by now looking positively ancient! Their decrepit appearance was accentuated by undulating wooden stepboards and cantrail strips, but conversely some wooden body panels had been plated-over with steel sheet by this time, and all vehicles were given a thick coat of green paint with light silver-grey roofs on reformation. The formations of these units are shown in the table opposite.

SUB 4501 from the second 4501-18 series was unique in having a LSWR-bodied motor coach, 9815, formerly from 4573 and also on lenghened ex-LBSCR designed frames. This vehicle leads as the unit enters Clapham Junction with a Waterloo to Chessington South train in about 1958. As on most remaining pre-1939 suburban stock, the ventilator above the headcode panel has been blanked-off. *F.W. Ivey*

20 The spare capacity at Eastleigh Carriage and Wagon Works during this period was used to completely refurbish about 100 Maunsell-design Hastings line steam corridor coaches.

The second 4 SUB unit to carry this number, LBSCR-bodied unit 4503 draws to a halt at Blackfriars with an unidentified evening peak service out of Holborn Viaduct in about 1958. This was one of seventeen such SUBs, 4501-17, formed up in 1956-57 using vehicles having lengthened LBSCR ac underframes not required for new EPB stock. *F.W. Ivey*

Formations of 4 SUB Units 4501-4518 (the second units with these numbers), formed in 1956-57 (Numbers in brackets denote the previous unit in which each vehicle ran.)

Unit	MBS	TS	TS	MBS
4501	8895(4526)	9730(4254)	9656(4573)¶	9815(4573)¶
4502	8733(4553)	9720(4571)	9467(4553)	8891(4553)
4503	8718(4546)	9478(4573)	9733(4534)	8868(4534)
4504	8721(4549)	9463(4549)	9724(4527)	8859(4527)
4505	8736(4559)	9461(4547)	9470(4556)	8894(4556)
4506	8717(4545)	9719(4133)	9748(4545)	8883(4545)§
4507	8703(4535)	9728(4134)	9731(4532)	8866(4532)
4508	8707(4538)*	9472(4134)	9738(4538)	8873(4538)
4509	8712(4541)	9726(4529)	9743(4541)	8878(4541)
4510	8739(4528)	9746(4543)	9725(4551)	8860(4528)
4511	8731(4551)	9737(4537)	9657(4551)¶	8889(4551)
4512	8708(4539)*	9729(4531)	9739(4539)	8874(4539)
4513	8722(4550)	9475(4557)	9464(4550)	8888(4551)
4514	8701(4533)	9747(4544)	9732(4533)	8867(4533)
4515	8694(4555)*	9462(4548)	9473(4555)	8897(4555)
4516	8734(4554)	9734(4535)	9468(4554)	8892(4554)
4517	8742(4558)	9727(4530)	9746(4558)	8900(4558)
4518†	8705(4251)	9741(4251)	9736(4251)	8871(4251)

Notes:

¶   LSWR-bodied vehicle.

*   These three vehicles had bodywork from SL driving trailers, which had in turn been converted from Billinton 'bogie block' third brakes, dating from 1899-1901.

§   MBS 8883 in 4506 was replaced by similar 8719 (previously formed in 4339) in April 1958.

†   4518 was the former 4251, renumbered into the new series.

These units were withdrawn between October 1959 and January 1960, with 4511 officially lasting another month, and all were broken up at Newhaven. Their demise saw the end of electric stock with bodywork of pre-Grouping origin in passenger service on the SR, although a few such vehicles survived in departmental service a while longer.

Augmented 1925 'short frame' unit 4322 halts at the down Windsor line island platform at Clapham Junction in about 1959 with what is probably an ECS working from Waterloo to Wimbledon Park depot. Like its long-framed cousin 4337, it too has regained a ventilator bonnet above the headcode panel, in this case curved to match the 'bullet' cab end. *F.W. Ivey*

The last remaining pre-war suburban units in passenger traffic were augmented 1925-built units 4300-4349 and 4351-4354. (4350 had been withdrawn in 1950, although three of its four vehicles were reformed into other units.) Remarkably, they underwent a minor modification shortly before withdrawal, when in 1958-59 ventilators were reinstated over the headcode panels of the motor coaches, unit numbers then being painted on them. Although this work, carried out at operating depots, was officially sanctioned by HO 4496 of 5th June 1958, it would appear that certain '4326'-type long-framed units had been altered unofficially prior to this. In their last years three units, 4309/35/48, had their 1925-built trailer replaced with a second 'six-a-side' augmentation trailer from a unit already withdrawn. 4309 was running with 10372 (from 4310) by April 1958, 4335 incorporated 10376 (from 4313) from March 1961, and the motor coaches of 4348 ran with trailers 10352 and 10361 (from 4339 and 4351 respectively) from about the same time. Finally, it was perhaps inevitable that a 1925 unit ended up with a long-framed motor coach at one end and a short-framed 'bullet-nosed' one at the other. When unit 4339 donated LBSCR-bodied MBS 8883 to 4506 in April 1958 (see page 179), it was replaced by short-framed 8148 which had previously been formed in 4310.

Virtually all the 1925-built 43xx series units survived until withdrawals commenced in earnest in December 1959, most having gone by the end of 1961. A few of the long-framed batch lasted into January 1962, the last survivor being 4329 which was officially withdrawn on 15th January but probably ran in traffic for the last time on Friday 12th January. With the exception of 4328 and 4330, which had been painted in the later BR dark green with roundels on the motor coaches in March 1957 and December 1958 respectively, all were taken out of service still in 1950-style malachite livery with the first BR emblem. With them went the last of the letter headcodes. Twenty long-framed motor coaches were retained for conversion into ten two-coach de-icing units 92-101, replacing those ex-LBSCR vehicles converted from trailer set coaches in 1946-47. Five further vehicles of the same type were also kept, one as a replacement following fire-damage to de-icing unit 92, two to form test unit S15, and two as a shunting unit at Durnsford Road. Finally, short-framed motor coaches 8143/44 from unit 4308 were retained for official preservation by the National Railway Museum, being stored at York in 'as-withdrawn' condition until about 1977. 8143 was then restored externally to Southern Railway lined olive green livery using parts cannibalised from 8144, which was afterwards scrapped.

Following withdrawal the 1925 units, in common with most other pre-1939 suburban stock, had some electrical and brake parts removed at Durnsford Road and the rest of their electrical equipment at Strawberry Hill. They were then towed to Gatwick sidings where the augmentation trailers were taken out for onward dispatch to Micheldever, while a few days later most 1925-built coaches not otherwise retained were taken to Newhaven Town sidings for scrapping. Some of the 103xx 'six-a-side' augmentation trailers were subsequently stored on the closed Didcot, Newbury and Southampton line south of Winchester (within sight of the Bournemouth main line); then at Fullerton (near Andover); and then back at Micheldever. Short-framed motor coaches 8175/76 from unit 4325 were used as match wagons for these movements, and a few other motor coaches also found their way to Fullerton and Micheldever.

A number of the wooden-roofed 103xx trailers saw further use. For example, 10356 went into 4108 as an accident replacement in January 1961, while 10359 went into 4 LAV 2926 for the same reason a year later. Four others were formed into electrically-heated trailer set 900 (later 701). This peculiar formation was used, diesel-hauled, exclusively in peak-hour service on the Oxted line from September 1963 until September 1967. Following its disbanding, three were subsequently used with 2 HAL motor coaches to form additional 4 SUBs 4131 and 4132 in 1969, while the fourth went into 4 SUB 4364 as an accident replacement in 1970. As mentioned elsewhere, 4131 and 4132 lasted until 1971, and 4364 until 1974. With no further use in prospect, the remainder of these coaches were broken-up at Newhaven in 1963 and 1964.

The eight 10391-10400 series all-steel trailers still formed in the 1925 units on withdrawal were all retained for further service. Of these, 10392/97/99/400 were converted into four EP-braked de-icing trailers for the Kent Coast electrification in 1959-60. 10394/95 were rewired and renumbered for use in 4 EPB units, while 10393/96 went into SUBs as accident replacements.

Limitations of space preclude listing the formations of 4 SUB units numbered in the 4131-4257 and 4401-4614 series, augmented from three-coach suburban units, as originally formed in the years 1942-48. In many cases, further reformations took place following accident damage, or to enable particular vehicles in very poor condition to be withdrawn.

Although 205 4 SUB units (in the 4401-4614 series) were augmented from existing units having wooden bodywork of pre-Grouping origin with an additional new all-steel 'six-a-side' trailer, only 179 of these augmentation trailers were built, and therefore not all units existed at the same time.

There was a certain amount of swapping around of new augmentation trailers in the 10230-10345 series between units when first formed, to allow unforeseen problems with body flexing to be rectified. Some trailers which had been intended for augmentation purposes were instead formed into entirely new 4 SUB units in the 4355-4363 series, and therefore the vehicles actually built for these units were used as augmentation trailers in existing units instead.

Of the 466 three-coach 'first generation' units, more than

400 were wholly or partly involved in the augmentation programme. About 60 three-coach units were withdrawn or disbanded without being augmented, because of life expiry, unserviceability or war damage. These were:
    1202/10; 1401/04/08/21/25/27/28/30/32/38/40/45/48/49;
    1454/58/61/62/63/65/73/76/79/81/87/92/94/95;1528/30/98;
    1612/14/16/19/22/27/32/33/35/40/46; 1654/55/56/57;
    1702/05/08/10/11/12/22/45/58/60/63/70; 1800.

LIVERIES, INTERIORS AND MODIFICATIONS OF THE SECOND-GENERATION UNITS

Liveries carried by second-generation 4 SUBs followed the same pattern as earlier stock. By about 1953 all those units delivered in a non-standard scheme had been repainted into the early BR (SR) malachite green with 'lion on wheel' emblems midway along the motor coach sides and coach numbers at the right hand ends of vehicles. Inner coach ends were black with yellow lettering. From 1957 the green was replaced by a darker shade and the carriage stock roundel replaced the 'cycling lion', but it was well into the 1960s before all had been reliveried. In 1962 unit 4378 was chosen to receive an experimental yellow panel on the cab front, in the form of a narrow horizontal rectangle under the cab windows, to improve its visibility when approaching. This shape was not approved by Southern Region management and a narrower but deeper panel, almost square, was chosen instead, presumably because it was less obscured by jumper cables and the dirt which collected around them. It took more than three years for the entire SUB fleet to gain these small yellow warning panels. In 1965-66 a few Eastleigh green repaints had a semi-matt 'eggshell' finish applied with an airless spray and, on these units, the inner coach ends were also painted green.

The new 'rail blue' was applied to SUBs receiving overhaul at Eastleigh from July 1966 onwards, again initially with the semi-matt sprayed finish and now with dark brown underframes. The first few, including 4117/21/24/26/27, 4284/88/96/98 and 4358/65/67/69/72/75, had small yellow warning panels and smaller 'double arrow' symbols than later became standard. Selhurst continued repaints in green until December 1968 (except for 4379 outshopped in blue in October 1967). The sprayed-on finish was found to wear very quickly and was abandoned in 1969 in favour of a glossy one-coat thixotropic paint, applied by brush and giving the traditional varnished appearance. From the latter part of 1966 full yellow cab ends with black numbers were adopted, and during this transition period some units were outshopped following overhaul in green with yellow ends, while others had yellow ends applied over existing paintwork. (Perhaps inevitably, a reformation in March 1968 resulted in blue MBSO 10915 being formed into otherwise green 4627, and it had to be revarnished back to green at Selhurst in order to match the rest of the unit.)

By early 1969 all SUBs were being finished in the glossy blue with full yellow ends, large double arrows between the cab and van doors and white numbering using larger figures than had hitherto been used, and this livery was retained until withdrawal. Only a small number of units withdrawn in 1972 or earlier were never repainted in blue. From the early 1970s underframes and bogies reverted to black. The special livery applied to 4732 in 1982 is dealt with later. Finally, the BR standard red triangle NO SMOKING transfers, replacing the previous SR green-on-white design, were attached very firmly to appropriate quarterlights. They were superseded by various round versions from the end of the 1960s, but many of the hard-wearing originals remained.

Given the size of the second-generation 4 SUB fleet, external modifications during the life of the units were remarkably few. As built, no all-steel SUB vehicles had guttering at cantrail height, the smooth curve from the sides onto the roof being one of their distinctive features. However in 1955-56, units 4112/15/18/29 were fitted with a thin steel strip along the sides level with the tops of the door openings. On 4118 and 4129 these were formed into a continuous gutter, whereas on 4115 they were plain except directly over the doors, but in all cases they were added mainly for strengthening purposes. Further strengthening also came to be required along the bottoms of the body sides of most post-war SUB coaches, where serious corrosion began to show up after about fifteen years' service.[21] The remedy here was to weld or rivet reinforcing strips over the affected areas, a process usually carried out during overhaul. No attempt was made to add these strips uniformly along the bottom of a particular vehicle, with the result that several units looked decidedly tatty in this area by the mid-1960s, especially as in some cases more than one strip had been affixed over a particularly weak area. Plastic bodyfiller was also used from about the same time to repair corrosion damage around window openings.

It has already been mentioned that a number of SUBs were given roller-blind headcode equipment when new, and later two further units were given them. 4718 was equipped in about February 1952 following accident repairs, and 4660 followed in about July 1965. On those motor coaches which had them from new, some were altered during first or second general overhaul in the 1960s. MBS 10896 from 4355 was the first to be dealt with in this way, being modified in January 1965, followed by 4694 (March 1969) and 4695/97. Some were simply given a wider retaining flange around the glass, but others had entirely new protruding headcode boxes. Following this, it appears that there were three different types in use – for example 4721 retained the original flush type, 4694 had slightly-protruding boxes, and newly-equipped 4660 had boxes which were considerably deeper. New blinds with smaller numbers and incorporating red blanks for use in place of a tail lamp were gradually introduced from early 1960, although 4721 still retained the old style in 1967. The appropriate SUBs still had to carry a tail lamp however, as the panel could not be back-lit at night when the power was

---

21 This problem was also to affect the first generation of BR-designed steel rolling stock. It was caused by water ingress exacerbated by the acid in carriage washing chemicals.

Production all-steel 4 SUB 4277, in later BR green livery, passes St Mary Cray Junction with a mid-day Holborn Viaduct to Sevenoaks service on 16th May 1959. In the foreground, track quadrupling has just been completed in preparation for the Kent Coast (Phase I) electrification. *R. C. Riley*

4118, from the first batch of ten all-steel units, was one of very few post-war SUBs to be fitted with cantrail height guttering on first overhaul. Repainted by this time into the first BR green livery with 'cycling lion' emblem and an S prefix to its unit number, it was photographed passing Peckham Rye shed on the Tulse Hill line with a London Bridge to Epsom service on 28th February 1957. *R.C. Riley*

isolated because SUBs had no battery back-up. Following reformation in 1978, 4710 ended up with one roller-blind equipped motor coach (12767 from 4718). All second-generation 4 SUB conversions for departmental purposes were fitted with this type of headcode panel in the course of rebuilding.

4 SUBs were initially equipped with whistles mounted outboard of the motorman's lookout but, as on pre-war main line units which survived into the 1960s, from 1963 they were gradually replaced by two-tone air-horns mounted on the cab roof. It took some years to convert the entire fleet, and it was not until 1971 that all had been done. A number of later units had their cab windscreen wipers altered to swing from above (as on the EPBs) rather than bottom-right; no details of this alteration can be found in official sources

but it seems to have occurred from about 1965. To complete details of alterations in the cab area, in their later years a number of motor coaches with square roof-mounted motor ventilators had these removed and plated over.

Originally, both door and commode handles were brass castings as on all previous SR electric stock, the commode handles having a flattened section in the centre. From about 1970 there was a spate of incidents in which these fittings were stripped and stolen from units berthed overnight. As an example, the whole lot were stolen from 4663 and 4116 while parked at Hampton Court in March 1970. (It is suggested that disposal was not a problem because BIL and HAL units with similar handles were being scrapped in quantity at this time.) In 1968, 4641 had experimentally been fitted with a

Originally built with stencil panels, the motor coaches of SUB 4660 were re-equipped with roller-blind equipment in 1965. These stood proud of the cab fronts rather than being flush, an arrangement which occupied less space in the cab. In its final blue livery and displaying headcode 15 on its blinds, 4660 waits to depart from Horsham with the 07.24 to Waterloo via Dorking and Epsom on 15th June 1982. *John Scrace*

new type of commode handle bent from steel rod and painted white, and between 1972 and 1976 the remainder of the SUB fleet was fitted with this cheaper and less criminally-desirable version.

Electrical modifications too were few, the main changes concerning the traction motors fitted. As stated earlier many units intended to have the lightweight 507C type motors were initially delivered with type 339 motors due to shortages. Although these had all been replaced by 1960, it appears that some were given them again, probably in the early 1970s when there were large numbers of spares following the withdrawal of the LAV, BIL and HAL fleets as well as earlier SUBs. To confuse matters further, several motor bogie exchanges also took place in the 1950s and 1960s, the first

known example being the swapping of the 'central' bogies of 4754 with the 'eastern' bogies of 4680. By 1975, units recorded as being fitted with EE 339s included 4622/25/27/29/36/38/40 /41/43-45/47/64/77. The earlier motor was by now not standard and expensive to maintain, and to eliminate them from the fleet several of the units concerned swapped motor bogies with just-withdrawn 507C-powered units in May 1976, at the same time as compartment trailers in units to be retained were swapped for saloon trailers from the same withdrawn units. Units given 507C-equipped motor bogies at this time were 4627/29/36/38/41/43/64, the bogies coming from withdrawn 4604/07/24/65/76/90. The prototype EE 507A motors fitted to 4130 were replaced by type 339s in December 1955 and it then retained these until withdrawal. 4288/89 had wiring modifications to enable their type 507C motors to work at higher speeds on a weak-field setting during the first six months of 1950.

Experiments with beamless shoegear were undertaken on various SUBs, 4630 being the first to be equipped early in 1957, followed by 4672 in May 1959. In March 1960, the equipment on 4630 was transferred to 4663 until removal late in 1961. These tests were possibly in connection with development of the new Brighton line express stock (4 CIG etc), but their success or otherwise is not recorded. As on the pre-war express and semi-fast stock, in 1959 a small number of SUBs were equipped with lightweight sprung current collector shoes attached to a conventional shoebeam, replacing the gravity shoe-gear originally provided. This proved successful and all were eventually re-equipped, the replacement equipment also proving more efficient at brushing aside debris from the surface of the live rail.

A major programme of internal modifications covering fully-open saloon vehicles of the production 4 SUBs (and 4 EPBs 5001-5015) was commenced in March 1953 (HO 3962) with the aim of attaching the seating units more securely and rigidly into the body structure. The wooden legs which fixed the gangway ends of the seats to the floor were replaced by metal brackets, the seat frames were bolted to the body ribs and two vertical tubular extensions were attached from the inner end of the luggage rack to the ceiling. The work, involving SUB vehicles to diagrams 2018 and 2126, was carried out at Eastleigh, Lancing and maintenance depots, and had ceased by the end of 1956. The 'semi-open' 4121-4130 batch were not altered, while some others were not given the ceiling extensions.

There were a number of more minor internal alterations over the years, but most proved unsuccessful and were removed at the first opportunity, showing the soundness of the basic design. 4277 was given additional hand-rails on its full width luggage racks at saloon ends and in compartments when new, and these were not removed until December 1958. In November 1955 coach 11496 of unit 4126 was given vertical

A typical 4 SUB saloon interior in final condition following the fitting of tubular extensions from the luggage racks to the ceilings in 1953-56 and the replacement of netting by steel bars in the racks twenty years later. Upholstery in this 1977 view is the grey-based Trojan pattern in repp, ubiquitous in SUBs in their final years. *BR Southern Region*

grab-rails fixed to the inside of the door pillars of compartment D; these were not a success and were taken out in February 1958, after less than three years. Anticipating possible passenger complaints about draughts in full-length saloons, MThB 10843 of 4385 was built with glass screens fitted above the seats between the fourth and fifth bays to partially divide the saloon in half without restricting passenger movement, but again they were found to be pointless and were removed on first overhaul. 4280 had non-standard droplights manufactured by Widney-Solex fitted in its doors. Saloon trailer 12403 in 4663 was fitted with fluorescent lighting between 1956 and 1958. To enable this to work from the traction supply, dc/ac inverters were provided, carried under the seats at the ends of the coach.

There were successive alterations to interior finishes over the life of the second-generation SUB fleet. On many units, the original tan rexine on window surrounds, doors and saloon seat ends was replaced by a maroon shade on first overhaul while a few others, including 4118, were given polished wood. A more common alteration was the complete replacement of side and door internal panelling with Hardec, a plywood laminate with plastic wipe-clean surface, generally in a light beige fabric pattern. On partitions and coach ends Wareite, a similar material, replaced the original fabric covering. These latter finishes were virtually universal in SUBs remaining in traffic after about 1975. From the mid-1970s the traditional framed pictures, advertisements and mirrors were gradually removed from compartments and saloon ends, and the string netting in luggage racks replaced by wire grilles; in both cases this was a consequence of increasing vandalism by schoolchildren and others. Finally, the armrests fitted under the quarterlights were progressively removed on overhaul from 1978 onwards, leaving only a narrow ledge.

Changes to upholstery fabrics used in SUBs followed the sequence of other stock in service over the same period, the final SR designs of the 1939-51 period giving way to BR standard patterns. There were three designs in general use in the 1952-65 period covering the first post-war SUB overhaul cycle. The first of these was a shallow horizontal V pattern in shades of maroon, hunting pink, blue/green and black. This material, which appeared in about thirty SUBs, was widespread in other new and overhauled electric stock.. The other two, both much tougher, were crimson moquette with vertical light brown chains and a faint horizontal blue stripe, and a maroon repp fabric with a pattern of twigs and amoeba-like shapes (dubbed 'sprig and octopus' by upholstery spotters of the time). These styles survived into the 1970s, but from about 1965 green/black and red/black horizontal striped patterns, designed to differentiate non-smoking and smoking accommodation respectively, were introduced. They became quite common and in a number of cases survived until the end of SUB operation, although by this time smoking accommodation in SUBs had been reduced and seat colour was no longer a reliable indication. However the most widespread design in the later years of the fleet was the grey pattern with repeating red, blue, yellow and white squares

known as Trojan, thought to have been originally used in Eastern Region standard FOs circa 1954, and first used in SUBs in 1966. Initially a tapestry and later an uncut moquette, it was initially in saloon accommodation only, the matching compartment pattern being a plain mid-grey. The vast majority of SUB vehicles spent their last ten years of service upholstered in Trojan. The blue/green check introduced in 1966 was very rare in SUBs; it appeared only in 4101 on its last overhaul in 1971 and in the compartment coach of 4654 in 1974. A few vehicles were given a green tartan tapestry of rather poor quality on final overhaul.

SERVICE, DECLINE AND WITHDRAWAL OF THE SECOND-GENERATION UNITS

Following the introduction of the first units, the area of operation covered by the second-generation SUBs was initially the same as that of the pre-war units, with which they interworked entirely. To recap, this area covered the routes from the SR London termini as far out as Gillingham and Maidstone West (via Gravesend), Sevenoaks via both Swanley and Orpington, Crystal Palace (High Level), Hayes, Sanderstead (via Woodside), Caterham, Coulsdon North, Tattenham Corner, Horsham via Dorking, Guildford via Effingham Junction, Hampton Court, Weybridge via Chertsey, and Windsor.

After 1951 new 4 EPB units gradually superseded the remainder of the pre-1939 suburban stock, entering service first on the Waterloo to Guildford via Cobham service. In 1954 a scheme was developed for running ten-coach rush-hour trains on the South Eastern routes out of Charing Cross and Cannon Street utilising trains formed of four-coach and two-coach EPB units which, as mentioned previously, could not work in multiple with SUBs. With this scheme completed in 1957, 4 SUB units were almost totally banished from the former SER suburban routes, although until sufficient 2 EPB units had been delivered some ten-coach trains were formed of a combination of 4 SUB and 2 HAL units as a stop-gap measure. For a short time SUBs continued to monopolise services on the former LCDR routes out of Victoria and Holborn Viaduct/Blackfriars, including rush-hour trains onto the Dartford lines via Nunhead and Lewisham, but by 1960 most Eastern section suburban services were EPB worked.

From this time, for the next fifteen years the pattern of SUB operation remained basically constant. With the exceptions noted below, they worked about two thirds of suburban services on the Central and Western sections, but none on the Eastern. On the Central, exclusively EPB-worked lines included Charing Cross – Purley – Caterham/Tattenham Corner and Holborn Viaduct – Wimbledon – West Croydon – Victoria, the latter in order to simplify terminal working at Holborn and Blackfriars. South Western routes operated by 4 EPBs included the Guildford New line from 1952 and Waterloo–Windsor/Weybridge from 1956, following withdrawal of the NOLs. (Between October 1959 and January 1960 these services were gradually taken over by new 2 EPBs built on ex-NOL frames.) Thus from the early 1960s to the mid 1970s the Southern Electric suburban scene was largely

SUB units were widely used for seaside excursions and bank-holiday extras. In this view 'Sheba' unit 4109, in malachite green with 'lion on wheel' transfer, passes Three Bridges leading a summer Eastbourne–Victoria extra sometime in the 1950s. *F.W. Ivey*

constant, with second-generation SUBs ubiquitous on all Western and Central suburban services other than those just mentioned, but only very rarely seen on the Eastern.

As with all SR electric stock SUBs were originally without official depot allocations and, after the last three-coach units and trailer sets were withdrawn, diagrams frequently took the units from services on one section to another in the course of a days work. Units were nominally allocated to one of the three sections for planning, maintenance and accounting purposes however. As an example, for the winter of 1958-59 the allocations were: Eastern 53 units, Central 138 units, Western 74 units and maintenance cover 33 units, giving a grand total of 298. Of these only 227 were second-generation units, the remainder being pre-war units which had not yet been withdrawn, including the 54 augmented 1925-built units and mainly LBSCR-bodied 4501-4518 – as mentioned earlier these were treated as common user with the post-war units in spite of their lower seating capacity.

After the comparative standardisation of the previous decade, the 1970s saw major changes in suburban stock diagramming which resulted in 4 SUBs appearing in greater numbers on services where they had previously been unusual, at the expense of their traditional haunts. From 1973 onwards there was also a period of retrenchment, with service cutbacks and stock withdrawals for economy reasons. Being by then the oldest suburban units, the SUB fleet bore the brunt of these withdrawals, without (except in a few cases) being replaced by new stock until 1981. Consequently, an increasing proportion of trains on the Central and South Western divisions became EPB worked. Depot allocations were finally introduced in 1973 with SW SUBs being allocated to East

Wimbledon (WDON) and Central examples to Selhurst (SHST); from this time they did not generally stray from their respective divisions unless re-allocated.

Significant workings taken over by 4 SUBs from May 1973 included an early morning turn into Blackfriars and, more surprisingly, almost the entire Waterloo–Guildford New line service via Cobham, in place of 4 EPBs which had worked this route since their introduction in 1952. This lasted for only five months, as in the following October they were displaced once more, this time by new 4 VEPs. Regular weekday operation of SUBs into Blackfriars and Holborn Viaduct started once again in 1978, when Central division timetable alterations resulted in SUBs being diagrammed for the Wimbledon–Sutton 'wall of death' line. This change was not popular with train crews due to the number of stations with curved island platforms and the absence of guard's starting bells. At this time, SUBs were still working seven days a week on their traditional routes, although Sunday turns had already become limited in number. From August 1980, following the introduction of replacement class 508 stock, there were none scheduled out of Waterloo at week-ends, although a few Central division workings clung on into the following year. From May 1981, however, it was strictly Mondays to Fridays only, except at times of disruption, and yet another round of service reductions in 1982 saw further SUB withdrawals and consequently fewer trains worked by this stock. The sequence of withdrawals of the second-generation SUB fleet is detailed on pages 190-192.

Although basically suburban units, 4 SUBs were entirely compatible with the fleet of main line semi-fast units introduced between 1932 and 1954. They therefore frequently appeared on main line stopping services and even occasionally operated to the coast, often in the company of 4 LAV, 2 BIL and 2 HAL units. For example, in some years they were diagrammed for odd peak-hour Waterloo–Woking services, and occasionally one was rostered for a Waterloo–Portsmouth stopper. They were also used for parcels services on the same routes, some all year round and some only in the pre-Christmas period, when extra mail trains were run. On these, SUBs regularly reached such exotic locations as Bexhill, Chichester and even (on at least one occasion) Bournemouth. In December 1971 units 4103/04/05/09/15/18 were used on special mail trains prior to withdrawal, and in other years units so employed were usually those due for overhaul, then going into Works immediately after Christmas. Hence it was logical to use 4124 on a Woking–Bournemouth special on Christmas Eve 1972, the unit then running to Eastleigh.

Until its closure in 1964, 4 SUB units received their general overhauls at Lancing Works, running there and back under their own power. This work was then transferred to Eastleigh, but locomotive haulage was necessary until completion of the Bournemouth line electrification in July 1967. From this time SUBs worked electrically to and from overhaul once more, with the proviso that the 660V heating and lighting circuits were disconnected, due to the higher nominal voltage of 750 between Brookwood and Eastleigh. It is suggested that on one occasion a SUB reached Basingstoke in passenger service at a time of service disruption, but there is no record of any such journey beyond this point.

The number of 4 SUBs reflected the quantity of stock required to operate the weekday peak service, so there were many spare in off-peak times and at weekends, an inescapable economic consequence of commuter railway operation. However, these spare units with their high capacity could be put to good use for excursion, holiday and race traffic, all features of Southern Electric traffic through the 1950s but declined into virtually nothing thereafter. In the London area, the SR served racecourses at Epsom, Sandown Park (Esher), Kempton Park, Hurst Park (near Hampton Court and now closed) and Ascot; meetings at all these courses were served by additional trains, nearly all formed of SUB stock. Derby Day at Epsom, on the first Wednesday in June, was the last race meeting for which SUBs were regularly used on relief trains, this also being the only time when the class could be seen on the Tattenham Corner branch. In 1981 some units due for withdrawal were specially retained and used for this traffic. In 1982 a few were kept on hand but none was actually used. Another sporting venue served was Twickenham Rugby Ground, and SUBs also worked specials here.

Post-war, it again became customary on Bank Holiday Mondays to run many additional services and excursions to cater for the huge number of day-trippers from the London suburbs to the south coast. To operate these, all available spare rolling stock was trawled from around the electrified network, regardless of age, type or facilities, and inevitably on these occasions many of the services were SUB worked. Similar, but less intensive, arrangements applied in the summer months when additional seaside excursions to the coast, mainly from London Bridge and Victoria but also from suburban stations such as Streatham Hill or Tooting, were operated. Services also worked between Wimbledon and Littlehampton/Bognor Regis via Epsom and Dorking. Many of these trains were also formed of SUBs, although prior to 1962 these could be of pre-war or second generation types. Some summer Sunday Brighton services and numerous excursions were formed 12 SUB (three 4 SUB units coupled), with approximately 1200 seats, but otherwise SUBs rarely worked trains longer than eight coaches.

As with race traffic, demand for such additional services reduced dramatically into the 1960s, and this was finally recognised by the authorities in 1962, perhaps influenced by Beeching's researches. In that year the traditional intensive Bank Holiday timetable was operated on Whit Monday, but was cut drastically to a standard Sunday timetable with a few extras the following August Bank Holiday Monday, when appropriately it rained all day. No intensive Bank Holiday operation was ever mounted again, but a few extra summer-dated coastal services survived through the decade. The last additional SUB-worked seaside excursion ran on Sundays in the summer of 1970, when an 8 SUB formation was booked to work a 10.23 East Croydon–Brighton (non-stop) and 17.47 return to Victoria. The Up working called at Three Bridges and East Croydon but still did the journey in 63 minutes, only seven more than the preceding non-stop *Brighton Belle*.

A shortage of suburban rolling stock following mishaps led to the formation of two 'scratch' 4 SUB units, numbered 4131 and 4132, in May and September 1969 respectively.[22] They were made up of motor coaches from withdrawn 2 HAL units and spare suburban trailers and therefore bore a superficially similar appearance to the '4101' series, but with significantly fewer (380) seats. Both were in blue livery with full yellow ends throughout their short lives. Three of the trailers used were wooden-roofed 103xx ten-compartment vehicles previously formed in trailer set 900/701. 4131 and 4132 were the shortest-lived SUBs, being withdrawn in October 1971. Their formations are shown in the table below (The numbers in brackets are the unit in which the vehicle ran previously).

Unit	MBS	TS	TS	MBS
4131	10740(2622)	10149(4282)	10346(701)	10777(2659)
4132	10755(2637)	10349(701)	10351(701)	10806(2688)

Until 1972, the only second-generation 4 SUB units to be withdrawn were those involved in accidents and too badly damaged to be worth repairing. In that year however some of the oldest, including the prototype 4101-4110 'Sheba' units, were taken out of service. At least one of the first batch of

---

22 It appears that 4131 and 4132 were specifically replacements for 4282 and 4365, officially withdrawn in April and February 1969 respectively following shunting collisions at Wimbledon depot some time earlier. In fact, four undamaged coaches from these units were later reformed into other units (including 10149 into 4131).

The 4 SUB numbered 4131 shown in this photograph was one of a pair made-up in 1969 with motor coaches from disbanded 2 HAL motor coaches and spare suburban trailers. Shortly after its formation, 4131 snakes out of platform 17 at Clapham Junction leading a Victoria–Epsom Downs service. *Denis Battams*

all-steel units, 4115, was withdrawn still in green livery. Following withdrawal of 4106 in January, motor coach 10952 was formed in 4355 for a few months, but this unit had gone by May that year.

The first mass withdrawals followed in 1973, when many of the older all-compartment units went. These were also among those still fitted with the heavyweight EE 339 traction motors, by now non-standard and more costly to maintain than the newer 507C type used on other stock. A large number of further SUBs went for scrap in April 1976, when service cutbacks made considerable inroads into the quantity of suburban stock required for service. Withdrawn at this time

were all surviving non-standard units, including all those remaining with compartment motor coaches, and also a significant number of saloon units. As mentioned above, by carrying out a number of motor bogie exchanges at this time it also proved possible to eliminate EE 339 motors from the fleet while still retaining those units in the best mechanical condition.

Included in the April 1976 withdrawals were the remaining five units from the 4121-4130 replaced by 'semi-saloon' batch. The previous year two of these, 4126/27, had their compartment trailers replaced by 'semi-saloon' vehicles from withdrawn units, while similar reformations were carried out

All 4 SUB units remaining in service by 1982 had been (with one exception) reformed to become all saloon in an attempt to deter vandalism and other crime. Two such reformed units, led by 4666, approach West Barnes Lane level crossing (between Raynes Park and Motspur Park) with a Waterloo–Chessington South service on Friday 8th April 1983. Also prominent in this view are the white-painted steel commode handles which had replaced the original brass variety by 1976. *David Brown*

to three other SUBs. It was then decided to use available saloon trailers from units just withdrawn to carry out substitutions in order to remove compartment trailers from other SUBs remaining in traffic. This measure was intended to reduce vandalism and provide greater passenger security at a time when petty crime was on the increase, especially in the inner London suburbs. 44 units were reformed in this way to become all-saloon between April and July 1976. Together with the withdrawals mentioned above, these reformations enabled all the remaining 114xx nine-compartment 'pseudo-composite' trailers to be eliminated from the SUB fleet, although three remained in store at Micheldever for some

time. In all cases, it was necessary to modify the saloon trailers being used to replace compartment vehicles by substituting the centre buffer at one end with a rubbing block.

After withdrawal in 1976, unit 4748 was equipped with a thyristor control system, doing away with conventional resistances and contactors. Dubbed the 'Super-SUB', it ran tests from Strawberry Hill for about a year.

The next significant withdrawals came in 1981, following introduction of new class 508 stock on the South Western division. Again, compartment trailers in surviving SUBs were replaced by displaced saloon trailers, sixteen units being reformed in this way between March and July that year.

Mention should be made here of the fate of non-standard 4 SUB units 4601-4607, originally formed in 1950 from new saloon motor coaches and existing compartment augmentation trailers. In June 1972 4602 was reformed with a saloon trailer and, now having the standard '4621'-series formation, was renumbered 4620. In May 1976 it was further reformed to become all-saloon and survived until May 1983. 4607 was given a motor coach and trailer from 4661 following a depot collision in December 1973, but retained its original formation with two compartment trailers and was withdrawn in April 1976, as were unaltered 4604 and 4606. 4605 was given one saloon trailer in July 1975, while 4601 and 4603 were both reformed with pairs of 'semi-saloon' trailers from withdrawn 4126 and 4127 respectively in June 1976. 4601/03/05 were then renumbered 4617-4619, in that order, in May 1977. 4619 was withdrawn in February 1981 without having been made all-saloon, while 4617 and 4618 survived until June and October 1982 respectively.

The table below gives a summary of 4 SUBs reformed to become all-saloon in 1975/76/81, totalling just over sixty units. Note that not all units existed at the same time, and in a few cases particular saloon trailers were reformed into more than one unit.

Date	Units reformed to become all-saloon
January 1975	4126.
March 1975	4127, 4284, 4639/49.
April-July 1976	4277/79/85/91/93/94/97/98, 4601/03/20/21/26/27/33/37/51, 4654/56-59/62/66/68/70-72/78/80/82/87/96, 4710/18/21/22, 4725/26/38/39/43/49/50.
March 1981:	4287
May-July 1981:	4278, 4629-31/60/69/73/83/84, 4714/16/42/51/54.

Up to their very last weeks in traffic, 4 SUBs remained in service on both the Central and South Western divisions based at Selhurst and Wimbledon depots respectively and were not (as might have been expected) concentrated on a single depot. This appears to have been a deliberate ploy by management to avoid confrontation with motormen, who were expected to feel unfairly treated if all old stock was to be used only in a single area. 'Spreading the load' among two divisions was a means of avoiding this. By October 1982 just 33 units remained in traffic, of which only eight were based at Selhurst: these were 4726/32/38/42/43/47/51/54. The remaining 25, 4277-79/91/94/98, 4620/29/30/57/60/66/68/70/78/80/82/87/92 and 4710/14/16/19/21/22, were allocated to Wimbledon.

From April 1983 onwards the introduction of new class 455 suburban units accelerated the withdrawal remaining 4 SUBs, and the last diagrammed working on the South Western division took place on Monday 11th July, when 4277 and 4298 were used on the 08.16 Waterloo–Kingston–Richmond–Waterloo 'roundabout' service.

Remaining units continued in use on an ad hoc basis for several weeks however, working on various services including trips to Guildford via Cobham. The last recorded run on a SW timetabled service occurred on Saturday 6th August, when 4291 formed the 12.10 Windsor and Eton Riverside to Waterloo. No doubt these odd workings would have continued beyond this date, had the last two Wimbledon-based units, 4279/91, not been transferred away two days later.

On the Central division, the eight units remaining at Selhurst from October 1982 worked three Monday–Friday 8 SUB diagrams, with the other two units spare. These workings remained remarkably reliable until mid-August 1983, after which ad hoc replacement of SUBs by spare EPBs began. Consequently, the final runs on Tuesday 6th September went largely unrecorded. 4279 and 4754 came out of the carriage sidings at Dorking to run to Victoria via Sutton, and then took a stroll down to West Croydon via Crystal Palace and return, with the usual crawl behind empties at Streatham Hill. There followed a final trip down to East Croydon, returning to Victoria with the 10.21 departure, and then, as booked, an ECS run to Selhurst. However, the two SUBs did not follow their diagram and run empty to Victoria later that day to form the 15.35 to Epsom Downs, EPB stock being used instead. Hence Wednesday 7th September 1983 saw a weekday without SUBs for the first time in over forty years (strikes and Bank Holidays, etc. excepted).

Green-liveried 4732 was retained at Selhurst to work a '4 SUB Farewell' railtour on Saturday 1st October. Organised jointly by the SEG and LCGB, a wreath was carried on the leading cab end and many participants were appropriately attired as 1950's 'commuters'. Starting and ending at Waterloo, the tour visited all the SR London termini and travelled as far out as Windsor, Reading, Alton, Guildford, Slade Green and Bromley North. Following this tour 4732 was not sent for scrap, but was instead placed in storage at Brighton. Although not known at the time, it was destined to be retained by BR in operational condition for a further eleven years, and its subsequent history is dealt with at the end of this chapter.

Following withdrawal, vehicles were generally stripped of reusable parts at Selhurst depot and elsewhere. Apart from mechanical and electrical equipment such as motors and compressors, with SUBs this also included seat units, cushions and even doors, all of which could be utilised in the SR-type EPB fleet of virtually identical construction. In particular, seat units were used in 4 EPBs when their compartment coaches were opened out into saloons in the course of 'facelifting' (a refurbishment programme described on page 194 and in Volume 2). A main dumping ground for withdrawn and stripped vehicles was Micheldever, which held little else but derelict SUB coaches from the mid-1970s until about 1982, when the site was cleared. Norwood Yard and Selhurst were also main storage points, and other sites used at various times included Lancing, Crystal Palace and Feltham. The 1981 withdrawals from the South Western resulted in condemned units being stored in Wimbledon West Yard, while two years later Hither Green Up Sidings (adjacent to the closed Continental depot) and Fratton were used, the withdrawn stock working to these locations under its own power. Thus in the summer of 1983 it was possible to see 8 SUB ECS workings down the Portsmouth Direct line en route to oblivion. A few withdrawn units were used for fire brigade rescue or civil defence exercises at various locations throughout the SR before being disposed of.

Once stripped, SUB vehicles were formed up into various odd combinations for the final haul to the breakers. Scrap merchants who purchased significant numbers included Cashmores of Newport, Wards of Briton Ferry, Birds at Long Marston, Frank Berry of Leicester, Booths of Rotherham, Marple and Gillott of Attercliffe, Cooper Brothers of Brightside and Kings of Wymondham and Snailwell. A small number of vehicles were also cut up on railway premises such as Micheldever and Hoo Junction by railway staff or contractors. Most were accident victims which could not be moved long distances for scrapping. An interesting arrangement used to haul unbraked scrap SUB vehicles to Long Marston in 1981 involved marshalling four or more between fitted ferry wagons, generally two at the front and three at the rear to provide sufficient brake-power. The van brakes were connected by a temporary external brake pipe attached along the running boards on one side of the scrap SUB coaches.

A significant number of 4 SUB coaches survived beyond the September 1983 withdrawal from passenger service of the class, some as departmental conversions, some converted to work in 4 EPB units, and four as a complete preserved unit in working order. Of the departmental units made up from former post-war SUB vehicles, Stores Unit 024, converted from the motor coaches of 4378 in 1973, survived in service until the end of 1984, while Instruction Unit 055, converted from all of 4367 in 1974, was taken out of use in November 1985. Eleven new de-icing conversions, mainly to replace the

1925 units, were heavily modified from pairs of SUB motor coaches between 1977 and 1982 and numbered 003-013. All these departmental conversions are described fully in Volume 2.

84 of the 'six-a-side' steel-bodied SUB compartment thirds (seconds from 1956), mainly augmentation trailers originally marshalled in pre-war units but a few from post-war SUBs, were modified, renumbered and reformed into newly-built 4 EPB units, mostly in the 1950s, and two additional coaches were converted to replace accident victims. Four were nine-compartment vehicles, including 15084 (formerly 11485) which went to 5115 in 1969 after running as a composite in 7 TC 701. Alterations were few other than the addition of 27-wire control cables, 70V lighting circuits and EP brake valves (and cantrail guttering in some cases) and many survived in original condition until withdrawn. They were numbered 15001-84, and the two later conversions were 15228 (formerly 10394) and 15278 (formerly 12392). The origin of each individual vehicle is listed below. Although many of these vehicles were later converted into open saloons as part of the EPB facelifting programme mentioned overleaf, about thirty remained unaltered until finally withdrawn in 1990-91.[23]

A programme of 'facelifting' or light refurbishment, which went beyond the usual body overhaul routines, of much of the EPB fleet was instigated following the formation of a prototype unit, originally numbered 5263, in 1976. No. 5263 was

---

23 Following a murder in a compartment of coach 15084 in unit 5115 in March 1988, all remaining EPB compartment trailers, including the ex-SUB examples, were concentrated in pairs into 32 reformed units, numbered 5501-5532 and reclassified 4 COM (for 'compartment'). The compartment coaches were given red cantrail stripes to warn prospective passengers, and the class was used only for peak-hour services.

Awaiting final breaking-up, 4673 stands in Booth's scrapyard, Rotherham, on 15th March 1984. *Andrew French*

New No.	Old No.	New No.	Old No.	New No.	Old No.
15001*	10398	15031*	10192	15061	10226
15002*	10345	15032	10280	15062*	10178
15003*	10333	15033*	10460	15063*	10194
15004*	10203	15034	10470	15064	10469
15005¶	11454	15035	10229	15065*	10212
15006	10253	15036*	10459	15066*	10186
15007	10228	15037*	10222	15067*	10453
15008	10335	15038¶	11451	15068*	10183
15009*	10201	15039*	10246	15069*	10225
15010*	10391	15040*	10285	15070*	10180
15011*	10174	15041*	10322	15071*	10191
15012*	10169	15042*	10283	15072	10179
15013	10189	15043	10275	15073*	10185
15014	10184	15044*	10224	15074*	10168
15015	10277	15045*	10452	15075*	10187
15016	10251	15046*	10466	15076*	10227
15017	10292	15047*	10468	15077*	10204
15018	10238	15048	10299	15078*	10182
15019*	10332	15049	10176	15079	10195
15020*	10177	15050*	10260	15080¶	11456
15021	10254	15051*	10211	15081	10208
15022	10175	15052*	10223	15082	10207
15023*	10309	15053*	10471	15083	10395
15024	10266	15054*	10167	15084¶	11485
15025	10456	15055*	10451	15228§	10394
15026	10298	15056*	10190	15278§	12392
15027*	10281	15057*	10193		
15028	10272	15058*	10188		
15029*	10202	15059*	10450		
15030*	10278	15060*	10467		

Notes:-

Vehicles later facelifted (see notes in text) to become trailer open seconds are indicated *.

Nine-compartment "pseudo-composite" vehicles are indicated ¶.

Vehicles which were accident replacements and given the same number as the 'EPB' vehicle they replaced are indicated §. 15278/12392 was a TSO, not an TS.

made up of two former 2 SAP motor coaches (virtually identical to MBSOs of existing 4 EPBs, but constructed on 2 NOL underframes in 1958) and two former SUB compartment trailers 10337 and 10480, renumbered 15450/49 respectively on conversion. These two vehicles were subject to the EPB alterations mentioned above, but were also extensively modified internally at Eastleigh Works, including opening out by removal of the partitions and the fitting of fluorescent lighting and a public address system. 15449 was additionally fitted with a lowered false ceiling formed of plastic panels. Seat units recovered from withdrawn SUB saloon vehicles were used, but the seat cushions were reprofiled to resemble those in VEP stock. Other improvements included better draught proofing and new floor coverings.

Following this, it was decided to facelift a major proportion of the EPB fleet in an effort to improve the amenities of the stock slightly at a time when finances to build new trains were not available. This work, which commenced in 1980, was initially split between Eastleigh and Horwich (Bolton), but the latter was closed down at the end of 1983 after which all remaining coaches were facelifted at Eastleigh. Units in this scheme involving former 4 SUB vehicles were of two types. Some were refurbished from existing 4 EPB units already incorporating a former SUB compartment trailer. In many cases units were reformed before being sent for facelifting, the open trailer in the unit to be facelifted being swapped for the compartment trailer in the unit remaining unfacelifted. As part of the facelifting process involved 'opening-out' former compartment vehicles, both units concerned were then all-saloon, in line with the need for greater security mentioned above. 52 former SUB compartment trailers were dealt with in this way. They included 15001, one of the ten prototype all-steel coaches dating from 1946, then converted to run in the first 4 EPB 5001 and ending its days formed in facelifted unit 5446. The others were made up from ex 2 SAP motor coaches and spare SUB trailers from withdrawn units in the manner of 5263/5401. In all, 33 'new' EPB vehicles, numbered 15449-81, were converted in this way from withdrawn SUB coaches, mainly to run with ex-SAP motor coaches.

Of the 97 SR-type facelifted 4 EPBs, no less than 55 contained at least one former SUB trailer. All these vehicles survived until 1993-95 when remaining EPBs, facelifted and not, were withdrawn and scrapped, mostly by Gwent Demolition at Margam. This resulted from the introduction of new-technology class 465/466 'Networker' stock, which represented a complete break with a basic design philosophy for SR suburban stock which had survived since before World War One.

Although it had been intended that all remaining 4 SUB units would be made all-saloon by July 1981, owing to an administrative oversight compartment trailer 10239 was left in unit 4732. In 1982 this unit was chosen to be the last 4 SUB to receive a classified overhaul, and was repainted in a special livery at the same time. It was originally intended to paint it blue/grey, as on the first 'facelifted' 4 EPBs then entering traffic, but as the idea caught on with SR manage-

Showing off its approximation to the Southern Railway livery applied to the first all-steel 4 SUBs, 4732 approaches journey's end at Effingham Junction with the 10.38 service from Victoria on 29th October 1982. Unusually, it is carrying whistles (to the right of the motorman's lookout); these were normally removed other than for special trains. *David Brown*

ment this was changed firstly to BR green and then to Southern Railway malachite, the livery in which 4732 finally appeared when outshopped from Selhurst that August. Entirely spuriously, as the unit was built well into BR days, it was given a livery which resembled that of the first all-steel SUBs. The lettering was yellow shaded black in 'sunshine' style, with the coach numbers at both ends at cantrail height and the word SOUTHERN at the centre of each coach side just below the windows. Intermediate coach ends were black with yellow lettering. While the driving ends were necessarily yellow, the upper portion was green with the unit number and SOUTHERN emblazoned across it. The green paint was specially mixed by a firm in Derby, while a signwriter at Selhurst was responsible for the complex lettering. 4732 also had whistle connections reinstated, but whistles were only carried when working special trains. Internally, pictures and mirrors were refitted in compartments and saloon end walls. Following an appearance at Ashford Chart Leacon Open Day shortly after being outshopped, the unit returned to normal passenger service on Central division suburban lines, and was also used for a number of railtours.

After withdrawal of the remainder of the SUB fleet in 1983 this unit was retained in operational condition, appearing at several depot open days and being used for a number of railtours over the next eleven years. On many occasions it operated coupled to 2 BIL 2090, preserved in the National Collection, the only other extant SR electric unit

with which it could work in multiple. Indeed, one of the main reasons why 4732 was retained was to act as a 'runner' for 2090 which, having only one motor bogie, was not considered reliable enough on its own. Following new Department of Transport directives in 1991 it was no longer possible to operate the BIL and the future of the SUB was in doubt, particularly as arrangements for forthcoming railway privatisation left little room for 'unofficially preserved' rolling stock. On the weekend of 31 May – 1 June 1994 it worked a number of specials from Brighton to Hastings and return, billed as 'the last ever', following which it was offered for sale. However an agreement was reached with Waterman Railways, new operators of the former BR Special Trains Unit, and 4732 was reinstated once more to work a special shuttle between Tunbridge Wells and Hastings on 10th-11th September 1994, in connection with an open day at St Leonards Depot. The agreement with Waterman Railways was not, in the event, progressed and following a period parked in the open at Brighton, its paintwork gradually fading, the unit was moved to Long Marston for storage in 1996. 4732 was privately purchased by a preservation society in 1998 and the following year was moved by road to an open-air site in Coventry.

APPENDIX 1

SUMMARY OF CARRIAGE NUMBERS, WITH HO ORDER, DIAGRAM AND UNIT NUMBERS FOR FIRST GENERATION DC SUBURBAN STOCK.

Numbers listed are as allocated to units or sets when newly ex-works. Allocations and later re-allocations of individual coaches are not shown. 2 NOL units allocated to main line duties are included in this summary.

Carriage numbers	SR Order No./Date	SR Dia. No.	Ex-works	Unit Nos.
Motor third brakes (MThB)				
8001-8126	LSWR	660 (a)	11/14-8/17	1201-1284
8127-8178	SR Board 12/23 (Not HO)	661	-/24-7/25	1285-1310
8179-8222	HO 206 – 3/9/26	671	8179 – 9/27	1658-1701
			others – 1-4/28	
8223-8225	HO 584 – 5/6/30	671	11/30-1/31	1783-1785
8226	HO 584 – 5/6/30	682	1/31	1786
8227-8246	Pre-SR (Joint Cttee) – 11/22	662	1925	1401-1410
8247-8258	Pre-SR (Joint Cttee) – 11/22	665	1925	1411-1416
8259-8297	Pre-SR (Joint Cttee) – 11/22	666	1925	1417-1436
8298-8326	Pre-SR (Joint Cttee) – 11/22	665	1925	1437-1452
8327-8417	Pre-SR (Joint Cttee) – 11/22	662	1925-26	1453-1495
8417-8474	Pre-SR (Joint Cttee) – 11/22	670	1925-26	1496-1524
8475-8494	HO135 – 8/9/25	662	1926	1525-1534
8495-8524	HO 206 – 3/9/26	653	8-11/27	1601-1615
8525-8538	HO 206 – 3/9/26	667	11-12/27	1616-1622
8539-8548	HO 206 – 3/9/26	669	12/27-1/28	1623-1627
8549-8553	HO 206 – 3/9/26	668	1/28	1628-1630
8554	HO 206 – 3/9/26	664	1/28	1630
8555-8563	HO 553 – 1/2/30	671	6-8/30	1773-1781
8564	HO 553 – 1/2/30	671	8/30	1782
8565-8571 (odd)	HO 584 – 1/2/30	680	1/31	1786-1789
8566-8570 (even)	HO 584 – 1/2/30	682	1/31	1787-1789
8572	HO 584 – 1/2/30	683	1/31	1790
8573-8580	HO 584 – 1/2/30	683	1-2/31	1790-1794
8581	HO 584 – 1/2/30	683	2/31	1794
8582-8585	HO 584 – 1/2/30	683	c12/31	1795-1796
8586-8589	HO 584 – 1/2/30	674	c12/31-c1/32	1797-1798
8590-8595	HO 584 – 1/2/30	674	c1/32	1799-1801*
8596-8615	HO 874 – 7/6/35	686	2-3/36	1863-1882
8616	(number left vacant)			
8617-8639 (odd)	HO 206 – 3/9/26	672	1631/2: 9/27; others: 7-8/28	1631-1642
8618-8638 (even)	HO 206 – 3/9/26	673	as 8617-39	1631-1641
8640-8644	HO 206 – 3/9/26	673	8-9/28	1642-1644

8645/47/49/51	HO 206 – 3/9/26	672	9/28	1645-1648
8646/48/50	HO 206 – 3/9/26	673	9/28	1645-1647
8652-8656	HO 206 – 3/9/26	673	10/28	1648-1650
8657/59/61	HO 206 – 3/9/26	672	11/28	1651-1652
8658/60/62-70	HO 206 – 3/9/26	673	1651-55: 11-12/28; 1656: 5/28; 1657: 4/28	1651-1657
8671-8685	HO 206 – 3/9/26	672	1702-05: 10/27; others 7-12/28	1702-1716
8686-8692	HO 373 – 25/8/28	675	1-2/29	1717-1723
8693-8696	HO 373 – 25/8/28	675	5-6/29	1724-1727
8697-8705	HO 373 – 25/8/28	678	6-8/29	1728-1736
8706/07	HO 374 – 25/8/28	675	6/29	1737-1738
8708	HO 374 – 25/8/28	675	6/29	1739
8709-8722	HO 398 – 14/11/28	678	6-8/29, 1/30	1740-1753
8723-8730	HO 372 – 25/8/28	681	4/29	1901-1908*
8731-8733	HO 396 – 10/11/28	678	11-12/29	1754-1756
8734-8745	HO 480 – 28/6/29	678	1-6/30	1757-1768
8746	HO 515 – 5/9/29	678	6/30	1769
8747/48	HO 553 – 1/2/30	679	6/30	1770-1771
8749	HO 553 – 1/2/30	678	6/30	1772
8750	(number left vacant)			

Motor composite brakes (MCB)

8792-8792	LSWR	690 (b)	11/14-8/17	1203/4/7/8 etc
8793-8836	HO 206 – 3/9/26	691	8793: 9/27; others 2-4/28	1658-1701
8837-8851	HO 206 – 3/9/26	692	1702-05: 10/27; others 7-12/28	1702-1716
8852-8858	HO 373 – 25/8/28	693	1-2/29	1717-1723
8859-8862	HO 373 – 25/8/28	693	6/29	1724-1727
8863-8871	HO 373 – 25/8/28	694	6-8/29	1728-1736
8872-8874	HO 374 – 25/8/28	693	6/29	1727-1739
8875-8884	HO 374 – 25/8/28	694	6-8/29	1740-1749
8885-8888	HO 398 – 14/11/28	695	1-2/30	1750-1753
8889	HO 396 – 10/11/28	694	1/30	1754
8890-8891	HO 396 – 10/11/28	695	1/30	1755-1756
8892-8900	HO 480 – 28/6/29	695	2-3/30	1757-1765

Trailer thirds (TTh)

8901-8912	LSWR	720	*	1002/4 etc
8913-8924	LSWR	721	*	1001/3 etc
8925-8948	LSWR	722	*	1001/2 etc
	*Sets 1001-12: 2/20; 1013-1018: 12/21; 1019-1024: 12/22			
8949-8974	HO 67 – 10/24	723	4/25	1025-1037
	(dia. 735 or 736 after altered buffing gear)			

8975-8998	HO 214 – 30/9/26	725	3-4/28	1121-1144
8999, 9001/10/11/13/14/20/22/25-34, 9060-9116			5-12/25 to 9110,	1051-1109
	HO 53 – 11/7/24	723	note (k)	

(9078 lost in mishap, replaced by another, to dia. 739, 1937)

9117-20	HO 136 – 11/9/25	726	1/26: 9111-9120	
	9000/02-09/12/15-19/21/23/24, 9035-59		1051-1109	
	HO 53 – 11/7/24	724	note (k)	
9121-9132	HO 136 – 11/9/25	726	2-3/26	sets in 11xx

(dia. 733 (9123/5/6/8/30/2) or 734 (9121/2/4/7/9/31) after set reforms)

9133-9155	HO 214 – 30/9/26	725	10/28-2/29	1145-1167

(9140 replaced by another conversion, 12/37)

9156-9166 (even)	HO 585 – 5/6/30	725	2-3/31	1189-1194
9157-9167 (odd)	HO 585 – 5/6/30	727	2-3/31	1189-1194
9168-9175	HO 791 – 25/11/33	731	c8/34	note k
9176-9191	HO 844 – 12/2/35	731	c7/35	note k
9192-9199	HO 853 – 29/3/35	731	c7/35	note k
9200-9208	HO 901 – 8/1/36	731	c12/36-3/37	note k
9209-9255	HO 214 – 30/9/26	727	3/28-2/29 1121-1167	

(9240 changed to dia. 740 after altered buffing gear)

9256-9277	HO 375 – 25/8/28	728	7-9/29	1168-1178
9278-9281	HO 399 – 14/11/28	728	1/30	1179-1180
9282/88/90	HO 455 – 7/5/29	730	2/30	1181/4/5
9284/86/92	HO 455 – 7/5/29	729	2-3/30	1182/3/6
9283-9293(odd)	HO 455 – 7/5/29	728	2-3/30	1181-1186
9294/95	HO 516 – 5/9/29	728	7/30	1187
9296	HO 516 – 5/9/29	725	7/30	1188
9297	HO 516 – 5/9/29	727	7/30	1188
9298	HO 901 – 8/1/36	739	1/37	1098
9299	HO 929 – 28/5/36	732	7/37	998
9300	HO 929 – 28/5/36	739	7/37	999

Composite trailers

9301	HO 584 – 5/6/30	759	11/30	1783
9302/03	HO 584 – 5/6/30	760	11/30	1784-1785
9304-06	HO 584 – 5/6/30	765	1/31	1786-1788
9307-9343	HO 206 – 3/9/26	759	9307: 9/27	1658-1694
			others: 2-6/28	

(9316 changed to dia. 774 after altered buffing gear for augmentation)

9344	HO 206 – 3/9/26	760	6/28	1695
9345-9350	HO 206 – 3/9/26	759	3-5/28	1696-1701
9351-9371	LSWR	750 (c)	12/14-8/17	1202/06 etc
9372-9413	LSWR	751 (d)	11/14-8/17	1203/4/7/8 etc
9414-9434	LSWR	752 (e)	11/14-8/17	1201/05 etc
9435-9460	SR Board 11/23 (not HO)	753	-/24-7/25	1285-1310

9461-9464	HO 398 – 14/11/28	761	1-2/30	1750-1753
9465-9467	HO 396 – 10/11/28	761	1/30	1754-1756
9468-9479	HO 480 – 28/6/29	761	2-4/30	1757-1768
9480	HO 515 – 5/9/29	761	6/30	1769
9481-9483	HO 553 – 1/2/30	768	6/30	1770-1772
9484	HO 584 – 5/6/30	766	1/31	1789
9485-9579	Pre-SR J C 10/22, 11/22	1925-26	1401-1495(j)	
9485-9504, 9519, 9524-44, 9556, 9558-79		754		
9505-9518, 9520-23, 9545-55, 9557		755		
9580-9608	Pre-SR J C 10/22, 11/22	758	1925-26	1496-1524 (j)
9609-9618	SR Board 1926	754	?-6/26	1525-1534
9619-9624	HO 206 – 3/9/26	756	8-9/27	1601-1606
9625-9628	HO 206 – 3/9/26	757	10-11/27	1607-1610
9629-9631	HO 206 – 3/9/26	756	11/27	1611-1613
9632	HO 206 – 3/9/26	757	11/27	1614
9633-9648	HO 206 – 3/9/26	756	1/27-1/28	1615-1630
9649-9655	HO 553 – 1/2/30	760	6-8/30	1773-1779
		(SR underframes)		
9656-9658	HO 553 – 1/2/30	760	8/30	1780-1782
		(LBSCR underframes)		
9659-9661	HO 584 – 5/6/30	766	1/31	1790-1792
9662	HO 584 – 5/6/30	767	2/31	1793
9663	HO 584 – 5/6/30	767	2/31	1794
9664/65	HO 663 – 12/6/31	767	c12/31	1795-1796
9666-9670	HO 663 – 12/6/31	762	c12/31-c1/32	1797-1798
9671-9674	HO 900 – 8/1/36	770	c12/37	1579-1582
9675-9701	HO 206 – 3/9/26	762	9675: 9/27; others: 7-12/28	1631-1657
9702-9716	HO 206 – 3/9/26	763	9702-04: 10/27; others: 7-12/28	1702-1716
9702 replacement	n/a	764	1929	1702
9717-9736	HO 373 – 25/8/28	761(f)	1-8/29	1717-1736
	(9722/28/41 changed to dia. 773 after altered buffing gear for augmentation)			
9737-9749	HO 374 – 25/8/28	761	6-8/29	1737-1749
9750	number left vacant	-	-	-

Trailer thirds (TTh), motor third brakes (MThB), trailer composites (TC), motor composite brakes (MCB), driving trailer composites (DTC), driving trailer thirds (DTTh):

9751-9758 (DTC)	HO 372 – 25/8/28	793	4/29	1901-08 *
9759/60 (TC)	HO 900 – 8/1/36	770	c12/37	1583-1584
9761-9765 (TC)	HO803 – 23/3/36	770	7-8/34	1595-1599
9766-9775 (TC)	HO 842 – 13/2/35	770	c10-11/35	1585-1594
9776-9780	numbers left vacant	-	-	-
9781-9788 (MThB)	HO 899 – 8/1/36	688	c7/36	1883-1890

9789-9800 (MThB)	HO 900 – 8/1/36	689	c12/37	1579-1584
9801-9803 (MCB)	HO 480 – 28/6/29	695	3-4/30	1766-1768
9804 (MCB)	HO 515 – 5/9/29	695	6/30	1769
9805-9807 (MCB)	HO 553 – 1/2/30	695	6/30	1770-1772
9808-9814 (MCB)	HO 553 – 1/2/30	697	6-8/30	1773-1779
9815-9817 (MCB)	HO 553 – 1/2/30	697	8/30	1780-1782
9818-9821 (MCB)	HO 530 – 4/11/29	696	c6/30	1909-12*
9822-9824 (MCB)	HO 584 – 5/6/30	697	11/30-1/31	1783-1785
9825/28/29 (DTTh)	HO 933 – 18/6/36	732	7-9/37	note k
9826/27/30 (TTh)	HO 933 – 18/6/36	731	7-9/37	note k
9831-9860 (MTB)	HO 803 – 23/3/34	687	c10/35	1585-1589
9861-9871 (MTB)	HO 804 – 23/3/34	686	11-12/34	1813-1823
9872-9910 (MTB)	HO 807 – 23/3/34	686(g)	c3-5/35	1824-1862
9911	number left vacant	-	-	-
9912-9919 (DTC)	HO 899 – 8/1/36	795	c7/36	1890/89/83-88
9920-9939 (DTC)	HO 874 – 7/6/35	795	2-3/36	1863-1882
9940-9950 (DTC)	HO 804 – 23/3/34	795	11-12/34	1813-1823
9951-9954 (DTC)	HO 530 – 4/11/29	794	c6/30	1909-12 *
9955-9960	numbers left vacant	-	-	-
9961-9999 (DTC)	HO 807 – 23/3/34	795	c3-5/35	1828/27/26/24/25, 1829-1862
10401-10418 (TTh)	HO 965 – 16/4/37	731 and 732(h)	1-5/38	note k

Notes:

* Units 1801 and 1901-12 were renumbered in 1934 to 1600 and 1801-12 respectively
(a) rebuilt to dia. 676 or 685 in 1934-40
(b) rebuilt to dia. 690 in 1934-40
(c) rebuilt to dia. 771 in 1934-40
(d) rebuilt to dia. 769 in 1934-40
(e) rebuilt to dia. 772 in 1939-40
(f) on incorporation into 4 SUB units as augmenting trailer, altered to 773 (ie one buffer removed)
(g) altered to dia. 684 when coupé comp was removed (second use of dia. 684)
(h) 731 altered to 740, 732 to 741, on reform into 4 SUB units.
(j) 9485-9579 and 9580-9608 not allocated in numerical order at any time. Some were initially in temporary four-car formations in 1925, and re-allocated to three-car units.
(k) allocated in random order; many reallocations of earlier vehicles in 1934-38 trailer set reforming programme and more in 1940-45.

Note on AC electric stock in Southern Railway fleet in 1923-1929:

The Southern Railway allotted the following stock numbers and diagrams to AC electric stock. Most of the numbers were used again for DC coaches:

8567–8600	'Crystal Palace' motor third brakes: dia. 676
8601–8616	'South London' motor third brakes: dia. 677
9169–9208	'Coulsdon–Wallington' driving trailer thirds, dia. 738
9655–9674	'Coulsdon–Wallington' composites, dia. 768
9811–9824	'South London' driving trailer composites, dia. 790
9825–9892	'Crystal Palace' driving trailer composites, dia. 791
9893–9914	'Coulsdon–Wallington' driving trailer composites, dia. 792
10101–10124	'Coulsdon–Wallington' motor brake vans, dia. 830

APPENDIX 2

SUMMARY OF CARRIAGE NUMBERS WITH INITIAL ALLOCATIONS
TO FIRST GENERATION SUBURBAN STOCK

This Appendix includes all vehicles formed in three-coach motor units (listed in SR working books as '3'), to two-coach motor units (2 NOL, '2 SL', '2WIM') and to two-coach trailer sets. Subsequent changes (principally in the 4 SUB augmentation programme) could only be shown by lengthy and complex tabulation which would, unfortunately, have exceeded the practicable scale of this history.

War and accident losses are listed, with final unit numbers where relevant.

Motor third brakes:

8001-8126   **1201-1284, allocated to 1201/2/4/6 etc in pairs and 1203/4/7/8 etc as singles; most to 4 SUB units in 41xx, 42xx; most withdrawn 1953-56**

8003 of 1202 lengthened with new cab, to underframe of 8581 and renumbered 10/40

8101		war loss South Bermondsey 26/10/44
8033		original car acc loss 27/11/37, replaced by newly converted body on new frame /38
8064		acc loss 26/4/48
8124		acc loss Motspur Park 6/11/47
8125		war loss Selsdon 18/10/40

8127-8178   **1285-1310 allocated in pairs; all to 4 SUB units 4300-25; most withdrawn and cut up 1960/61 (last in traffic were 8171/2 in 2/62)**

8143 of 4308 (was 1293)		preserved NRM York
8127 of 4300 (was 1285)		acc loss Selhurst depot 4/3/58

8179-8222   **1658-1701, one to each unit; most to 4 SUB in 41xx, 42xx; last in traffic 8193 in 12/54**

8188	1667	acc loss Caterham 26/6/45
8222	1701	acc loss Swanley 7/3/47

8223-8226   **1783-1786, one each unit; withdrawn 1947-56**

8226	1786	acc loss Motspur Park 6/11/47

8227-8416   **1401-1495, allocated in pairs; many to 4 SUB in 44xx, 45xx**

8234	1404	acc loss Caterham 26/6/45
8249/50	1412	acc loss Cannon Street 2/49
8253	1414	war loss Selhurst depot 30/10/40
8255/56	4442 (was 1415)	acc loss Crayford 11/2/48
8278	1426	war loss Selhurst depot 14/10/40
8280	1427	war loss Peckham Rye depot 6/1/45
8281	1428	war loss Peckham Rye depot 6/1/45
8283	1429	acc loss Spa Road Bermondsey 21/1/47
8289	1432	war loss Charing Cross 8/10/40
8290	1432	war damage 11/40, repaired and to 1428 circa 4/41, then war loss (?Greenwich 1/7/44)
8294	1434	acc loss Woolwich Arsenal 11/11/40
8321	1448	war loss Victoria 8/9/40
8330	1452	acc loss, withdrawn 11/47; location not traced
8334	1454	war loss Peckham Rye depot 8/9/40
8336	1455	acc loss Mottingham 19/3/46
8340	1457	acc loss Dorking North 12/41
8350	1462	acc loss Dorking North 12/41

8371	1473	original body acc loss Battersea Park 2/4/37
8378	1476	war loss near Hampton Court 16/8/40
8379	1483 (was 1477)	acc loss Cannon Street 21/2/49

8417-8474 **1496-1524, allocated in pairs; all except 8466 to 4 SUB 4326-4354; most withdrawn and cut-up 1960-62 but some retained for departmental use; last in traffic were 8424/28 in 4329, probably 12/1/62**

8429	4332 (was 1502)	acc loss Woolwich Arsenal 18/11/48
8466	1520	acc loss Woolwich Arsenal 11/11/40

8475-8494 **1525-1534, allocated in pairs; withdrawn 1949-51**

8495-8554 **1601-1630, allocated in pairs; most withdrawn 1949-51, but 8553/54 in 1/55**

8517/18	1612	war loss Charing Cross 14/5/41
8523	1615	acc loss Battersea Park 2/4/37; replacement with LSW body, new underframe.
8536	1621	war loss West Croydon 23/6/44

8555-8564 **1773-1782, one for each unit; withdrawn 1951-56**

8564	4579	(was 1782) converted to Departmental DS40 in instruction train S10 in 4/56

8565-8573 **1783-1790, one for each unit; withdrawn 1951-56 except 8565**

8565	4406 (was 1786)	acc loss Motspur Park 6/11/47
8572	1790	acc loss London Bridge 19/4/34; replacement with LSW body, new underframe.

8574-8585 **1791-1796, allocated in pairs; withdrawn 1951**

8581	1794	body acc loss Horsham 9/39; replaced 1940 by rebuilt body from 8003
		(ex unit 1202) with new cab, van and adjacent compartments.

8586-8595 **1797-1800, 1801, 1801 renumbered 1600 in 4/34, allocated in pairs. Most withdrawn 1948/49**

8590	1799	war loss Elmers End 11/5/41
8594/95	4607 (was 1600)	acc loss Crayford 11/2/48

8596-8615 **1863-1882, one to each unit; withdrawn 1956-59**

8616	Number not allocated to DC stock	

8617-8670 **1631-1657, allocated in pairs; withdrawn 1948-49**

8622	1633	acc loss Waddon 4/11/42

8671-8685 **1702-1716, one to each unit; withdrawn 1948-49**

8678	4250	(was 1709) acc loss Herne Hill 6/11/47

8681-8692 **1717-1723, one to each unit; withdrawn 1951-56**

8693-8722 **1724-1753, one to each unit; most withdrawn 1956**

8711	1742	acc loss Dorking North 12/41
8714	1745	war loss Orpington 25/10/40

8723-8730 **1901-1908, renumbered 1801-1808 in 4/34, one to each unit**

		Withdrawals: 1807 in 1940, 1802 in 1951, others in 1954
8729	1807	war loss Peckham Rye depot 2/10/40 (but officially written off 3/45)

8731-8749 **1754-1772, one to each unit; most withdrawn 1956-59**

8737	1760	war loss Chelsfield 4/11/40
8740	1763	acc loss South Bermondsey 10/3/48
8744	4559 (was 1767) withdrawn 10/54, towing unit Durnsford Rd 3/55-9/55 and again in 1957; condemned 10/57	
8747	1770	acc loss South Croydon 24/10/47

Motor composite brakes

8751-8794 **1203/4/7/8 etc, one to each unit; all to 4 SUB 4131-4171 and 4246, withdrawn 1953-56**

8793-8836 **1658-1701, one to each unit; most withdrawn 1953/54**

8814	1679	war loss Norwood tunnel 9/12/41
8823	1688	acc loss Waddon 4/11/42
8827	1692	war loss Bickley 30/6/44
8832	1697	war loss Selhurst depot 14/10/40
8837-8851	**1702-1716, one to each unit; most withdrawn 1948/49**	
8844	4250	(was 1709) acc loss Herne Hill 6/11/47
8852-8857	**1717-1722; most withdrawn 1951-56**	
8857	1722	war loss Charing Cross 17/4/41
8858-8900	**1723-1765, one to each unit); most withdrawn 1955-59**	
8863	1728	war loss Walworth 28/6/44
8876	1741	acc loss Slades Green 4/2/44
8898	1763	acc loss Bermondsey 1/5/48

Trailer thirds

8901-8924	**1001-1024 series, one each, not in number order;**	
8925-8948	**1001-1024, one each, not in number order; most withdrawn 1947-48**	
8907/37	1013	acc loss Hampton Court 19/11/37
8910/45	1021	acc loss Sevenoaks Tubs Hill 6/5/43
8914/27	1003	acc loss Effingham Junc 29/6/38
8917/33	1009	war loss Selhurst depot 14/10/40
8924/47	1023	war loss South Bermondsey 26/10/44
8949-8974	**1025-1037, pairs; most withdrawn 1947/48**	

8951/2 of 1026 converted to departmental stores vans 434s, 435s, Lancing works c12/46

8975-8998	**1121-1144, one to each set; withdrawn 1942-47**	
8976	1122	acc loss Mottingham 19/3/46
8983	1129	war loss Victoria 8/9/40
8992	1138	war loss New Cross Gate 25/11/44
8999-9116	**1051-1109, never allocated in numerical order; extensive reforming circa 1934-38; withdrawn 1942-48; set number shown below is as at time of accident or war loss**	
9000	1039	war loss, 16/10/40, probably Stewarts Lane
9015, 9016	1063	war losses Charing Cross 19/9/40
9019	1120	war loss Plumstead 7/9/40
9032	1109	war loss Peckham Rye 6/1/45
9036	1048	war loss Waterloo 12/11/42
9037	1081	war loss Victoria 9/10/40
9043	1080	underframe to ex-LBSC steam ThB, SR 3851, c5/42
9053	1070	acc loss Selhurst depot 17/7/44 (cut up Lancing 12/47)
9061	1065	war loss Peckham Rye 6/1/45
9063	1061	war loss Vauxhall (Loco Junc) 24/2/44
9075	1090	acc loss Selhurst depot 7/1/48
9078	1078	original coach presumed to be acc loss, withdrawn 12/35, cut up 7/36; replaced by LSW steam body on SR 'Continental' type underframe blt 1927; withdrawn in unit 4190 in 1/56
9086	993	war loss South Bermondsey 26/10/44
9100	989	acc loss Horsham 4/9/39
9115	1055	war loss, 12/40, location not recorded
9131	1197	acc loss Shepperton 11/9/39

The following were converted to deicing trailer vans:
9003 (1060) to 356s, 11/45; 9010 (1065) to 351s, 12/45; 9013 (1053) to 353s, 11/45; 9060 (1060) to 355s, 11/45; 9069 (1053) to 354s, 11/45; 9079 (1083) to 398s, 11/46; 9089 (1083) to 399s, 11/46; 9116 (1109) to 352s, 12/45. The Southern Region replaced the 's' suffixes by DS prefixes.

The body of 9043 was cut up 9/42 and the underframe transferred to Push-Pull set brake third 3851.

9117-9132   **1110-1117, in pairs, in order; withdrawn 1942-47**

9131   1197   acc loss Shepperton 11/9/39

9133-9155   **1145-1167, one each; most withdrawn 1942-48**

9135   1147   acc loss Waddon 4/11/42

9140   1152   acc loss Epsom Downs 14/8/37, replaced by another (similar) 9140, withdrawn 8/48

9147   1159   war loss, ?Selhurst depot, cut up 20/11/40

9156-9167   **1189-1194, allocated in even-odd numbered pairs to each set**

9156   1189   acc loss Cannon Street 19/1/42

9164   1193   war loss near Brockley 1/11/44

9168-9208 (dc) 1195-1198 in pairs, then to 1038-1050, 1087, 1115-1117, 1195-1200 as singles; most withdrawn 1953-56

9198   1055   war loss 12/40; location not recorded

9200   1038   war loss 18/9/40; location not recorded

9169-9208 (ac) were CW DTC, all withdrawn for conversion to DC 1928/29

9176-9191 (dc) nominally for 1087, 1115-17, 1195-98, but possibly direct to 1043-50, 1064/70/71/92/97, 1111/12/13 (one each)

9198   1055   war loss 4/12/40 location unknown

9192-9199 nominally for four unspecified sets, but de facto to 1039-42, 1055/59/73/96 (one each)

9200-9208 (dc) nominally for 1038, 1118-20, 1199, but de facto to other sets (one each)

9198   1055   war loss, location not recorded, body cut up 4/12/40

9200   1038   war loss, location not recorded, body cut up 18/9/40

9209-9255   **1121-1167, one each. Most withdrawn 1953-56.**

9227   1139   war loss Selhurst depot 14/10/40

9256-9281   **1168-1180 pairs; sub-lots 9256-77 for 1168-78, and 9278-81 for 1179-80**

9261   1170   war loss Selhurst depot 14/10/40

9282-9292   **even, 1181-1186 (one each set)**

9289   1184   acc loss Cannon Street 19/1/42

9290   1185   acc loss Effingham Junc 9/10/40

9283-9295   **odd, 1181-1187 (one each set)**

9289   1184   withdrawn and cut up 20/11/40: presumed war loss

9290   1185   acc loss Effingham Junction 9/10/40

9294   1187

9296   1188 (withdrawn 7/47; 9297 for 1188 (withdrawn in 4211, 1954)

9298   1076 (withdrawn in 4176, 1956); 9299 for 998 (withdrawn in 4250, 1955)

9300   999 (withdrawn in 4164, 1955)

9301-9306   **1783-1786, one to each unit; most withdrawn 1951-56**

9304   1786/4406   acc loss /47

Trailer composites:

9301-9306   **1783-1788, one for each unit; most withdrawn 1951-56 except 9304, (1786/4406) acc loss /47**

9307-9350   **1658-1701; most withdrawn 1953-56**

9341   1692   war loss Bickley 6/44

9351-9371	**1202-82 series: 9351/53 (1202/06) withdrawn 12/39; rest withdrawn 1953-56**	
9371	4222	acc loss /47
9372-9413	**1203-1284 series: withdrawn 1953-56**	
9414-9434	**1201-1281 series; withdrawn 1953-56**	
9435-9460	**1285-1310; withdrawn and cut up 1958-61**	
9455	1305	war loss Lancing works 25/4/41
9461-9480	**1750-1769; most withdrawn 1956-59**	
9471	1760	war loss Chelsfield 4/11/40
9474	1763	acc loss South Bermondsey 1/5/48
9481-9483	**1770-1772; withdrawn 1954-56**	
9484	1789;	withdrawn 1954

9485-9579 for 1401-95. Not allocated in numerical order at any time; some units temporarily formed as four-car when first in traffic c1925 had two trailers of this series

9489	1427	war loss Orpington 25/10/40
9497	1454	war loss Peckham Rye depot 8/9/40
9540		war loss
9568	1476	war loss near Hampton Wick 16/8/40
9579	1462	acc loss Dorking North 12/41
9553	1428	war loss Peckham Rye depot 6/1/45

9580-9608   1496-1524. Not allocated in numerical order at any time; some units temporarily formed as four-car when first in traffic c1925 had two trailers of this series. Most withdrawn and cut up 1960-62

9609-9618	**1525-1534; not in numerical order; withdrawn 1949-51**	
9618	1530	war loss 19/10/40 near Durnsford Road.
9619-9648	**1601-1630; most withdrawn 1949-51 (9648 in 1/55)**	
9630		war loss Charing Cross 14/5/41
9649-9655	**1773-1779; withdrawn 1951-54**	
9655-9674	**numbers allocated to ac trailer composites, withdrawn 1929 and rebuilt to dc**	
9656-9658	**1780-1782; withdrawn 1959/59/54**	

9658 with both motor brakes of 1782 altered to Instruction Unit S10; 9658 became DS41.

9659-9663	**1790-1794; withdrawn 1951**	
9664-9670	**1795-1801, 1801 renumbered 1600 in 4/34; withdrawn 1946-51**	
9671-9674	**1579-1582; all withdrawn 1956**	
9675-9701	**1631-1657; withdrawn 1948-49**	
9702-9716	**1702-1716; withdrawn 1948-49; original 9702 acc loss London Bridge 9/7/28, replacement with same number assembled 12/28**	
9717-9736	**1717-1736; most withdrawn 1956-59 (9722 withdrawn 12/47)**	
9737-9749	**1737-1749; most withdrawn 1956-59**	
9728	1728	war loss Walworth 28/6/44
9741	1741	acc loss Slades Green depot 4/2/44
9742	1742	acc loss Dorking 12/41
9745	1745	war loss Orpington 25/10/40
9750	number not allocated	

Driving trailer composites

| **9751-9758** | **1801-1808, converted 4/29 as 1901-08, renumbered 4/34** | |
| 9757 | 1807 | war loss Peckham Rye 2/10/40; others withdrawn: 1802 in 1951, remainder in 1954. |

Trailer composites

9759-9760   1583-1584; withdrawn 1956

9761-9765   1595-1599; withdrawn 1950-54

9764   1598   war loss Bickley 30/6/44

9766-9775   1585-1594; most withdrawn 1951-54

9776-9780   numbers not allocated

Motor third brakes

9781-9788   1883-1890; withdrawn 1957/58

9789-9800   1579-1584, allocated in pairs; withdrawn 1956

Motor composite brakes

9801-9804   1766-1769; one each unit; withdrawn 1954-56

9805-9807   1770-1772; one each unit; 9806 withdrawn 1956; 9807 withdrawn 1955

9805   1770   acc loss South Croydon 25/10/47

9808-9814   1773-1779; one each unit; withdrawn 1951-54

9811-9914 (ac)   Numbers allocated to DTCs; 9811-9824 (SL), 9825-9894 (CP), 9895-9914 (CW); all converted to dc

Motor third brakes

9815-9817   1780-1782; one each unit; 9815 withdrawn 1959; 9816 withdrawn 1951; 9817 altered for training unit S10, as DS42

9818-9821   1809-1812, converted 6/30 as 1909-12, renumbered 4/34; withdrawn 1954

9822-9824   1783-1785; one each unit

9824   1785 war loss 11/40 (location unknown)

9825-9830 for trailer sets (various reforms);

9830   war loss 11/40

9831-9860   1585-1599, allocated in pairs; most withdrawn 1951-54

9857/58   1598   war loss Bickley 30/6/44

9861-9910   1813-1862; most withdrawn 1957-59

9863   1815   acc loss Hastings 5/57

9876   to 1799 c7/41, to 4254 in 10/46, withdrawn 3/56

9901   1853   acc loss Barnes 2/12/55

9903   to 1679 c1/42, then to 4521, withdrawn /53

9911   number not allocated to DC stock

Driving trailer composites:

9912-9919   1889/83-88/90

9920-9939   1863-1882

9940-9950   1813-1823

9946   1819   acc loss 1/51

9961   war loss Portsmouth and Southsea 4/5/41

Driving trailer thirds

9951-9954   1809-1812 (converted 6/30 as 1909-12, renumbered 4/34); withdrawn 1954

9955-9960 numbers not allocated

Driving trailer composites

9961-9999 for 1828/27/26/24/25/29-62

9990   1853   acc loss Barnes 2/2/55

9992   1855   acc loss Staines 24/11/41

Trailer Thirds:

10401-10418 for trailer sets; withdrawn 1953-55

APPENDIX 3:

ROUTE LETTER HEADCODES USED ON FIRST GENERATION SUBURBAN STOCK

A feature peculiar to the SR three-car suburban units and to the 4 SUB units augmented from them was the use of letter headcodes to indicate route and destination. With the final demise of these units at the beginning of 1962 these codes ceased to be used, and the numerical headcodes introduced on the Brighton main line in 1932 became universal on suburban, as well as main line, services. As with many other distinctive features of the Southern Electric, the letter headcodes were first introduced by the LSWR, and the principle was extended by the SR to its other suburban lines as they were electrified. By no means all the letters of the alphabet were used, but only those which easily formed a stencil and which were easily distinguishable during the hours of darkness. To indicate route variations and to give more choices, bars above the main code were provided; single dots and double dots above the main code were introduced for the 1925-26 Eastern section electrification. The construction and fixing arrangements of the headcodes are described in Chapter 5. The list of headcodes was extended and amended in detail over the years as further lines and spurs were electrified, and the letter headcode list given here is for about 1939.

The list which follows covers codes for timetabled regular passenger services. On the Western section additional variants were added for special passenger trains and some empty stock workings. Letters with two dots were generally ECS workings. J, N, U and d (inverted P) were generally race or football specials. Inverted V is shown in the list as A. Letter headcodes were allocated for use on excursion and bank holiday workings of suburban stock to the coast etc., but were in practice seldom used. Suburban stock used for Central section bank holiday services between London and the south coast was provided with sets of main line type number plates for the day.

Notes:

a) Services routed 'via Parks Bridge Junction' avoided Lewisham, running directly from St Johns to Ladywell (on the Mid-Kent line) or Hither Green (on the main line).

b) '-' between starting and destination stations implies that a headcode applies to the particular service in *both* directions.

c) 'to' between starting and destination stations implies that a headcode applies in *one direction only*.

d) Stations separated by '/' indicate starting or destination stations on the *same* route.

e) Stations separated by 'or' indicate starting or destination stations on *different* routes.

f) 'etc' means that the headcode also applies to services starting or ending their journey at other intermediate stations on the same route.

Western Section

Headcode	Route
H	Waterloo – Hampton Court Waterloo – Weybridge/Windsor (via Brentford)
H (+ bar)	Waterloo – Effingham Junction/Guildford (via Cobham) Waterloo – Weybridge/Windsor (via Richmond)
I	Waterloo – Dorking North/Holmwood/Horsham Waterloo – Woking (via Brentford and Camberley)
I (+ bar)	Waterloo – Effingham Junction/Guildford (via Epsom) Waterloo – Woking (via Richmond and Camberley)
L	Waterloo – Chessington South Waterloo – Reading or Aldershot/Farnham (via Brentford and Ascot)
L (+ bar)	Waterloo – Epsom or Leatherhead Waterloo – Reading or Aldershot/Farnham (via Richmond and Ascot)
O	Waterloo to Waterloo (via Brentford, Hounslow and Richmond)
O (+ bar)	Waterloo to Waterloo (via Richmond, Hounslow and Brentford)
N	Woking – Alton

P	Waterloo – Wimbledon (via East Putney)
P (+ bar)	Waterloo – Wimbledon Park (via East Putney)
S	Waterloo – Shepperton (via Wimbledon and Kingston)
S (+ bar)	Waterloo – Shepperton (via Richmond)
T	Waterloo – Woking/Guildford (via Weybridge) Waterloo – Windsor (via Brentford)
T (+ bar)	Waterloo – Virginia Water (via Weybridge) Waterloo – Windsor (via Richmond) Waterloo – Woking (via Weybridge)
V	Waterloo to Waterloo (via Wimbledon, Kingston and Richmond)
V (+ bar)	Waterloo to Waterloo (via Richmond, Kingston and Wimbledon)
A	Waterloo – Strawberry Hill (via Wimbledon and Kingston)
A (+ bar)	Waterloo – Strawberry Hill (via Richmond)

Eastern Section

Note that Blackfriars was named St Pauls until February 1937.

Headcode	Route
H	Victoria or Holborn Viaduct/St Pauls to Herne Hill Sevenoaks (via Swanley) or Orpington to Holborn Viaduct (via Herne Hill) Cannon Street – Hayes (via Lewisham) Charing Cross to Hayes (via Lewisham)
H (+ 1 dot)	Sevenoaks to Holborn Viaduct (via Swanley and Catford) Hayes to Cannon Street (via Parks Bridge Junction)
H (+ bar)	Sevenoaks/Orpington to Holborn Viaduct (via Catford) Cannon Street or Charing Cross to Hayes (via Parks Bridge Junction) Hayes to Charing Cross (via Lewisham)
H (+ 2 dots)	Crystal Palace High Level to Holborn Viaduct Hayes to Charing Cross (via Lewisham)
I	Cannon Street or Charing Cross to Beckenham Junction (via Lewisham) Sanderstead or Beckenham Junction to Cannon Street (via Lewisham)
I (+ 1 dot)	Cannon Street or Charing Cross to Sanderstead (via Lewisham) Sanderstead or Beckenham Junction to Cannon Street (via Parks Bridge Junction)
I (+ bar)	Cannon Street or Charing Cross to Beckenham Junction (via Parks Bridge Junction) Sanderstead or Beckenham Junction to Charing Cross (via Lewisham)
I (+ 2 dots)	Cannon Street or Charing Cross to Sanderstead (via Parks Bridge Junction) Sanderstead or Beckenham Junction to Charing Cross (via Parks Bridge Junction)
J	Holborn Viaduct/St Pauls to Slades Green or Dartford (via Nunhead and Bexleyheath) Holborn Viaduct/St Pauls to Dartford (via London Bridge and Bexleyheath) Gravesend/Dartford etc to Holborn Viaduct (via Bexleyheath and Nunhead)
J (+ 1 dot)	Holborn Viaduct to Dartford/Gravesend (via London Bridge and Bexleyheath) Gravesend/Dartford etc to St Pauls (via Bexleyheath and Nunhead) Orpington to Holborn Viaduct (via Grove Park and London Bridge)
J (+ bar)	Holborn Viaduct to Gravesend (via London Bridge and Bexleyheath)
J (+ 2 dots)	Holborn Viaduct/St Pauls to Gravesend (via Nunhead and Bexleyheath)

L	Victoria or Holborn Viaduct/St Pauls to Bickley (via Herne Hill) Sevenoaks to Holborn Viaduct (via Orpington and Herne Hill) Cannon Street or Charing Cross to Dartford (via Sidcup) Gillingham/Gravesend/Dartford etc to Cannon Street (via Sidcup)
L (+ 1 dot)	Cannon Street, Charing Cross or Holborn Viaduct to Dartford (via London Bridge, Lewisham and Sidcup) Gillingham/Gravesend/Dartford etc to Cannon Street (via Sidcup and Lewisham)
L (+ bar)	Victoria or Holborn Viaduct/St Pauls to Bickley (via Catford) Sevenoaks to St Pauls (via Orpington and Catford) Cannon Street or Charing Cross to Gravesend/Strood/Gillingham (via Sidcup) Gillingham/Gravesend/Dartford etc to Charing Cross (via Sidcup)
L (+ 2 dots)	Cannon Street, Charing Cross or Holborn Viaduct to Gravesend/Strood/Gillingham (via London Bridge, Lewisham and Sidcup) Gillingham/Gravesend/Dartford etc to Charing Cross (via Sidcup and Lewisham)
N	Holborn Viaduct to Dartford (via Nunhead, Lewisham and Woolwich) Gravesend/Dartford etc to Holborn Viaduct (via Woolwich, Lewisham and Nunhead)
N (+ 1 dot)	Holborn Viaduct to Dartford (via London Bridge, Lewisham and Woolwich)
N (+ bar)	Holborn Viaduct to Gravesend (via London Bridge, Lewisham and Woolwich) Gravesend/Dartford etc to Holborn Viaduct (via Woolwich, Lewisham and London Bridge)
N (+ 2 dots)	Holborn Viaduct to Gravesend (via Nunhead, Lewisham and Woolwich)
O	Sevenoaks to Victoria (via Swanley and Catford) Cannon Street, Charing Cross or Holborn Viaduct to Orpington (via London Bridge and Grove Park) Orpington to Cannon Street (via Grove Park)
O (+ 1 dot)	Victoria to Orpington/Sevenoaks (via Herne Hill) Orpington to Cannon Street (via Grove Park and Lewisham)
O (+ bar)	Victoria or Holborn Viaduct/St Pauls to Orpington/Sevenoaks (via Catford) Orpington to Charing Cross (via Grove Park)
O (+ 2 dots)	Holborn Viaduct/St Pauls to Orpington/Sevenoaks (via Herne Hill and Petts Wood) Cannon Street or Charing Cross to Orpington (via Lewisham and Grove Park) Orpington to Charing Cross (via Grove Park and Lewisham)
P	Victoria or Holborn Viaduct/St Pauls to Crystal Palace High Level Cannon Street or Charing Cross to Barnhurst/Dartford (via Lewisham and Woolwich) Gillingham/Gravesend/Dartford etc to Cannon Street (via Woolwich and Lewisham)
P (+ 1 dot)	Bromley North to Cannon Street
P (+ bar)	Cannon Street or Charing Cross to Gravesend/Strood/Gillingham (via Lewisham and Woolwich) Gillingham/Gravesend/Dartford etc to Charing Cross (via Woolwich and Lewisham)
P (+ 2 dots)	Charing Cross or Cannon Street to Bromley North Bromley North to Charing Cross Holborn Viaduct – Orpington (via Nunhead, Lewisham and Beckenham Junction)
S	Victoria or Holborn Viaduct/St Pauls to Sevenoaks (via Herne Hill and Swanley) Sevenoaks to St Pauls (via Swanley and Herne Hill) Orpington to St Pauls (via Herne Hill) Cannon Street or Charing Cross to Slades Green or Dartford (via Bexleyheath) Gillingham/Gravesend/Dartford etc to Cannon Street (via Bexleyheath)
S (+ 1 dot)	Sevenoaks to St Pauls (via Swanley and Catford)

S (+ bar)	Victoria or Holborn Viaduct/St Pauls to Sevenoaks (via Catford and Swanley) Sevenoaks/Orpington to St Pauls (via Catford) Cannon Street or Charing Cross to Gravesend/Strood/Gillingham (via Bexleyheath) Gillingham/Gravesend/Dartford to Charing Cross (via Bexleyheath)
S (+ 2 dots)	Crystal Palace High Level to St Pauls
T	Cannon Street or Charing Cross to Addiscombe (via Lewisham) Addiscombe to Cannon Street (via Lewisham)
T (+ 1 dot)	Addiscombe to Cannon Street (via Parks Bridge Junction)
T (+ bar)	Cannon Street or Charing Cross to Addiscombe (via Parks Bridge Junction) Addiscombe to Charing Cross (via Lewisham)
T (+ 2 dots)	Addiscombe to Charing Cross (via Parks Bridge Junction)
U	Holborn Viaduct to Dartford (via London Bridge and Sidcup) Gravesend/Dartford etc to Holborn Viaduct (via Sidcup, Lewisham and Nunhead)
U (+ 1 dot)	Holborn Viaduct/St Pauls to Dartford (via Nunhead, Lewisham and Sidcup) Gravesend or Dartford to St Pauls (via Sidcup, Lewisham and Nunhead)
U (+ bar)	Holborn Viaduct – Dartford/Gravesend (via London Bridge and Sidcup)
U (+ 2 dots)	Gravesend/Dartford etc to Holborn Viaduct (via Sidcup, Lewisham and London Bridge)
V	Sevenoaks/Orpington to Victoria (via Herne Hill) Cannon Street, Charing Cross or Holborn Viaduct to Barnhurst or Dartford (via London Bridge and Greenwich) Gillingham/Gravesend/Dartford etc to Cannon Street (via Greenwich)
V (+ 1 dot)	Sevenoaks to Victoria (via Swanley and Herne Hill)
V (+ bar)	Sevenoaks/Orpington to Victoria (via Catford) Cannon Street, Charing Cross or Holborn Viaduct to Gravesend/ Strood/Gillingham (via Greenwich) Gillingham/Gravesend/Dartford etc to Charing Cross (via Greenwich)
V (+ 2 dots)	Crystal Palace High Level to Victoria Holborn Viaduct – Bromley North (via London Bridge) Gillingham/Gravesend/Dartford to Holborn Viaduct (via Greenwich)

(Note that headcode "inverted V" is shown here as "A")

A	Cannon Street or Charing Cross to Sevenoaks (via Grove Park and Orpington) Sevenoaks to Cannon Street (via Orpington and Grove Park)
A (+ 1 dot)	Sevenoaks to Cannon Street (via Orpington, Grove Park and Lewisham)
A (+ bar)	Sevenoaks to Charing Cross (via Orpington and Grove Park)
A (+ 2 dots)	Cannon Street or Charing Cross to Sevenoaks (via Lewisham, Grove Park and Orpington) Sevenoaks to Charing Cross (via Orpington, Grove Park and Lewisham)

Central section

H	London Bridge to Victoria (via Tulse Hill and Streatham Hill)
H (+ 1 dot)	Victoria to London Bridge (via Streatham Hill and Tulse Hill)
H (+ bar)	Victoria – Crystal Palace Low Level (via Streatham Common)
H (+ 2 dots)	London Bridge – Caterham (via Forest Hill)
I	Victoria – Coulsdon North (via Streatham Common)
I (+ 1 dot)	London Bridge – Coulsdon North (via Forest Hill)
I (+ bar)	Victoria – East Croydon (via Streatham Common)

I (+ 2 dots)	London Bridge – Coulsdon North (via Tulse Hill and Crystal Palace Low Level)
L	Victoria – Coulsdon North (via Streatham Hill)
L (+ 1 dot)	London Bridge – Dorking North/Horsham (via Mitcham Junction)
L (+ bar)	Victoria – Caterham (via Streatham Common)
L (+ 2 dots)	London Bridge – Effingham Junction/Guildford (via Mitcham Junction)
O	Victoria – Epsom Downs (via Mitcham Junction)
O (+ 1 dot)	London Bridge – Epsom Downs (via Forest Hill)
O (+ 2 dots)	London Bridge – Wallington (via Forest Hill and West Croydon)
P	Victoria – Beckenham Junction (via Streatham Hill) Purley – Caterham (shuttle)
P (+ 1 dot)	London Bridge to London Bridge (via Forest Hill, Crystal Palace Low Level and Tulse Hill) Purley – Tattenham Corner (shuttle) St Helier to St Pauls (via Wimbledon and Tulse Hill)
P (+ bar)	Victoria – Holborn Viaduct (via Streatham Hill, West Croydon, Sutton, Wimbledon and Tulse Hill)
P (+ 2 dots)	London Bridge to London Bridge (via Tulse Hill, Crystal Palace Low Level and Forest Hill)
S	Victoria – Wallington/Sutton (via Streatham Common)
S (+ 1 dot)	Victoria – Epsom Downs (via Streatham Common) Cannon Street or Charing Cross to Caterham Tattenham Corner or Caterham to Cannon Street
S (+ bar)	Victoria – Selhurst (via Streatham Common)
S (+ 2 dots)	Cannon Street or Charing Cross to Tattenham Corner Tattenham Corner or Caterham to Charing Cross
T (+ 1 dot)	Victoria [Eastern] – Sutton (via Herne Hill, Tulse Hill and Wimbledon)
T (+ bar)	Victoria – Tattenham Corner (via Streatham Common) London Bridge – Holborn Viaduct (via Forest Hill, West Croydon, Sutton, Wimbledon and Tulse Hill)
T (+ 2 dots)	London Bridge – Tattenham Corner (via Forest Hill)
V	Victoria – Epsom/Guildford (via Mitcham Junction) London Bridge – Selhurst (via Forest Hill)
V (+ 1 dot)	London Bridge to London Bridge (via Forest Hill, Selhurst and Tulse Hill)
V (+ bar)	London Bridge – Selhurst (via Tulse Hill and Streatham Common)
V (+ 2 dots)	London Bridge to London Bridge (via Tulse Hill, Selhurst and Forest Hill)
A	Victoria – Horsham (via Mitcham Junction)
A (+ 1 dot)	London Bridge – Horsham (via Forest Hill and West Croydon)

APPENDIX 4:

NUMERICAL HEADCODES USED ON MAIN LINE ELECTRIC STOCK AND POST-1941 SUBURBAN STOCK

Two-digit numerical route headcodes were introduced in 1932 in connection with the London–Brighton/Worthing electrification. Numerical headcodes were certainly allocated to the Eastern section in 1939 with the Medway electrification, and may have been used a year or two earlier for the small number of peak hour 2 NOL and 2 BIL workings between London and Sevenoaks. Numerical codes were allocated for most Western section suburban routes on the introduction of 2 NOL units 1863-82 in 1936. These codes continued in use and became standard on trains operated by the new wide-bodied suburban stock introduced from 1941 on the Eastern section, and 1946 on the Central and Western sections.

Route headcodes on main-line stock built between 1932 and 1948, and on nearly all suburban stock built between 1941 and 1951, consisted of one or two black number stencils each half the width of the letter stencils carried by suburban stock. These number stencils slotted into a carrier frame which was to the same dimensions as a letter-headcode stencil and slotted into the frame of the opal-glass headcode panel. As only one of each number was carried, headcode 11 and multiples thereof could not be used. A black blank was carried for use in the frame with single-digit codes.

From the end of 1951, roller blinds were fitted to new units instead of stencil plates, but existing units continued to be operated with stencil plates, except the Portsmouth express stock, which was fitted with roller blind equipment circa 1960.

The same headcode applied to a route in both directions unless otherwise noted. Except where a separate headcode was specified, a headcode applied to trains terminating at 'stations short thereof'. Some routes from Blackfriars and Holborn Viaduct had separate headcodes for each direction, others were the same in both directions. On some routes on the Central and Western sections, separate headcodes were allocated to distinguish fast, semifast and stopping trains.

Central section headcodes for trains to/from London were generally odd numbers for London Bridge and even numbers for Victoria. Eastern section headcodes were generally odd numbers for London Bridge (terminating) and Cannon Street, and even numbers for Charing Cross. Eastern section headcodes for Holborn Viaduct/Blackfriars were generally odd numbers; those for Victoria were generally even numbers. Some Holborn Viaduct/Blackfriars codes, for the Dartford routes, were even numbers. In 1959, The 'Eastern Victoria even' rule was broken by the allocation of odd numbers to main line services via the Catford loop and even numbers via Herne Hill.

The headcodes usually applied from the date of electrification or stock introduction; in the period from 1945 to circa 1980, changes were made from time to time, either by abandonment of some codes or changes in the code allocations. New codes, including the introduction of 'doubles' such as 22, 33 and 88, were needed for the Hastings diesel-electric scheme in 1957, and some alterations to existing codes were made when the large number of additional codes were introduced for the Kent Coast electrifications in 1959, 1960 and 1961. Some Eastern section changes were made in 1965, and more in 1976. Most Eastern Section (South Eastern) headcodes have remained otherwise unchanged; some were altered in detail to suit the revised layout in the London Bridge area c.1977 or to suit revised service patterns – for example, headcode 40 originally applied to Charing Cross – Dartford or stations short thereof; but after 1976, short workings carried the headcode 46, which formerly applied to Charing Cross – Dartford – Maidstone West, a service which was discontinued in the 1970s.

Most Western section (South Western) main line codes changed piecemeal from about 1957 onwards, with the introduction of diesel electric trains, and more extensively with the electrification of the Bournemouth line in 1967.

Until 1962, there were also a few letter headcodes allocated to Western section main-line services which could be diagrammed for suburban stock. These included N (plus one dot) for Woking–Alton and T (plus two dots) for Waterloo–Woking.

From 1957 onwards, headcode numbers were required for diesel electric services, which were put into the same numerical series as electric services. Exact dates for some changes can be difficult to identify, and copies of the working timetables which showed most (but by no means all) codes are rarely available for research.

In addition to the headcodes which applied to regular services, there were other codes which applied only to special workings, including race and football specials, excursions to the coast from London suburban stations, military specials between Gillingham and Portsmouth. or when engineering work caused diversions off the booked line. Empty coaching stock trains were denoted by a bar above the number, or in some cases, such as 'all sidings or depots to Waterloo via Earlsfield', a dedicated number.

The following lists relate generally to the period from 1932 to about 1980, after which changes became more extensive than hitherto.

Central Section (later Central Division)

Headcode	Route
1	Arundel – Littlehampton
1	Bognor Regis – Barnham
1	Brighton – West Worthing (direct)
1	Eastbourne – Ore
1	Horsted Keynes – Haywards Heath
1	Lewes – Seaford
1	London Bridge – Beckenham Junction via Tulse Hill (from 6/63: replaced 3)
2	Eastbourne – Polegate
2	Horsted Keynes – Brighton
2	Redhill – Reigate
2	Three Bridges – Horsham
2	West Croydon – Wimbledon via Mitcham
2	Victoria – London Bridge via Denmark Hill
3	Arundel – Bognor Regis via Littlehampton
3	London Bridge – Brighton via Quarry line (fast)
4	Arundel – Bognor Regis (direct)
4	Victoria – Brighton via Quarry line (fast)
5	London Bridge – Brighton via Quarry line (semi-fast)
5	Three Bridges/Horsham – Littlehampton
6	Three Bridges/Horsham – Bognor Regis (direct)
6	Victoria – Brighton via Quarry line (semi-fast)
7	London Bridge – Brighton via Tulse Hill and Quarry line (stopping at suburban stations)
7	Three Bridges/Horsham – Bognor Regis via Littlehampton (code deleted 1959)
8	Victoria – Brighton via Quarry line (stopping)
9	Bognor Regis to Three Bridges via Littlehampton and Horsham (code deleted 1959)
10	Victoria – Brighton via Redhill (fast) (code deleted c1945)
12	Bognor Regis – Portsmouth Harbour
12	Victoria – Brighton via Redhill (semi-fast)
13	Littlehampton – Portsmouth and Southsea¶
13	London Bridge – Brighton via Redhill (semi-fast)
14	Victoria – Brighton via Redhill (stopping)
15	Chichester – Portsmouth & Southsea¶
15	London Bridge – Brighton via Redhill (stopping)
16	Brighton to Hastings/Ore via Eastbourne
16	Victoria – Littlehampton via Quarry line and Hove
17	Brighton – Lewes
17	London Bridge – Littlehampton via Quarry line and Hove
18	Brighton – Eastbourne
18	Victoria – Littlehampton via Redhill and Hove

19	London Bridge – Littlehampton via Redhill and Hove
20	Victoria – Portsmouth Harbour via Mitcham Junction and Horsham
21	London Bridge – Portsmouth Harbour via Mitcham Junction and Horsham
23	London Bridge – Portsmouth Harbour via Quarry line, and Horsham
24	Victoria – Brighton via Redhill (fast)
25	London Bridge – Portsmouth Harbour via Redhill and Horsham
26	Brighton – Hastings/Ore (direct)
26	Victoria – Portsmouth Harbour via Quarry line and Horsham
28	Brighton – Seaford
28	Victoria – Portsmouth Harbour via Redhill and Horsham
30	Victoria – Wallington/Sutton via Streatham Common and West Croydon
30	Brighton – Portsmouth Harbour via Littlehampton
31	Brighton – Bognor Regis via Littlehampton
32	Brighton – West Worthing via Preston Park
34	Victoria – Reigate
35	Brighton – Littlehampton
35	London Bridge – Selhurst via Tulse Hill and Streatham Common
36	Victoria – Beckenham Junction via Crystal Palace
37	London Bridge – Reigate via Forest Hill
37	Horsted Keynes/Haywards Heath – Seaford
38	Victoria – Tattenham Corner via Streatham Common
39	London Bridge – Epsom Downs via Forest Hill (from 1948)
40	Victoria – Bognor Regis via Mitcham Junction and Horsham
41	Charing Cross – Reigate via Forest Hill
41	London Bridge – Bognor Regis via Mitcham Junction and Horsham (deleted c1950)
41	London Bridge – Brighton via Crystal Palace and Quarry (deleted by 1960)
42	Bognor Regis to Victoria via Littlehampton, Horsham and Redhill (from 6/58; other direction see 98)
43	London Bridge – Bognor Regis via Quarry line and Horsham
45	London Bridge – Bognor Regis via Redhill and Horsham
46	Horsted Keynes/Haywards Heath – Lewes
46	Victoria – Bognor Regis via Quarry line and Horsham
47	Haywards Heath – Ore (direct) (deleted c1950)
47	London Bridge – Bognor Regis via West Croydon and Horsham
48	Victoria – Bognor Regis via Redhill and Horsham
49	Horsted Keynes/Haywards Heath – Eastbourne
50	Victoria – Littlehampton via Mitcham Junction and Horsham
51	London Bridge – Ore via Quarry line and Eastbourne (deleted c1950)
52	Victoria – Ore via Quarry line and Eastbourne
53	London Bridge – Littlehampton via Quarry line and Horsham (deleted c1950)
53	Special workings across section boundaries (c1946-c1960)
54	Victoria – Ore via Quarry line (direct, not via Eastbourne)

56	Victoria – Littlehampton via Quarry line and Horsham
57	London Bridge – Littlehampton via West Croydon and Horsham
58	Victoria – Littlehampton via Redhill and Horsham
59	London Bridge – Littlehampton via Redhill and Horsham
60	Brighton – Portsmouth Harbour (semi-fast)
60	Victoria – Ore via Redhill (direct)
61	London Bridge – Ore via Redhill and Eastbourne
62	Brighton – Portsmouth Harbour (stopping)
62	Victoria – Eastbourne via Quarry line
63	London Bridge – Eastbourne/Ore via Redhill
64	Brighton – Bognor Regis (direct)
64	Victoria – Eastbourne via Redhill
65	London Bridge – Eastbourne via Quarry line
67	London Bridge – Eastbourne via Redhill
68	Victoria – Seaford via Quarry line
69	London Bridge – Seaford via Quarry line
70	Victoria – Portsmouth Harbour via Mitcham Junction, Horsham and Littlehampton (deleted c1950)
71	London Bridge – Portsmouth Harbour via Mitcham Junction, Horsham and Littlehampton (deleted c1950)
72	Victoria – Eastbourne/Ore via Redhill
73	London Bridge and Portsmouth Harbour by Quarry line, Horsham and Littlehampton
74	Victoria – Seaford via Redhill (deleted c1950)
75	London Bridge – Portsmouth Harbour via Redhill, Horsham and Littlehampton
76	Victoria – Portsmouth Harbour via Quarry line, Horsham and Littlehampton
78	Victoria – Newhaven Harbour via Redhill
79	London Bridge – Crystal Palace via Forest Hill
81	London Bridge – Caterham via Forest Hill
82	Victoria – Crystal Palace via Selhurst
83	London Bridge – Selhurst via Forest Hill
84	Victoria – Epsom Downs via Selhurst
85	London Bridge – Tattenham Corner via Forest Hill
86	Victoria – Horsham via Mitcham Junction
89	London Bridge – Horsham via Mitcham Junction (deleted c1962)
90	London Bridge – London Bridge via Selhurst and Norwood Junction
90	Victoria – Bognor Regis via Mitcham Junction, Horsham and Littlehampton
91	London Bridge – Bognor Regis via Mitcham Junction, Horsham and Littlehampton
93	London Bridge – Bognor Regis via Quarry line, Horsham and Littlehampton (deleted c1946)
93	Cannon Street or Charing Cross to Tattenham Corner via Forest Hill
94	Victoria – Coulsdon North via Selhurst (service ceased 9/83)
95	London Bridge – Bognor Regis via Redhill, Horsham and Littlehampton
96	Victoria – Bognor Regis via Quarry line, Horsham and Littlehampton
98	Victoria – Bognor Regis via Redhill, Horsham and Littlehampton (down only from 6/58; see 42)

01   London Bridge – Victoria via Tulse Hill and Streatham Hill

01   Tattenham Corner or Caterham to Charing Cross via Forest Hill

02   Victoria – Guildford via Mitcham Junction

03   London Bridge – Guildford via Mitcham Junction

03   Crystal Palace and Beckenham Junction (1941-46)

05   London Bridge and Coulsdon North via Forest Hill

06   Victoria – Blackfriars/Holborn Viaduct via Crystal Palace, West Croydon, Sutton, Wimbledon and Herne Hill.

07   London Bridge – Littlehampton via Quarry and Horsham

08   Victoria – East Croydon via Selhurst

09   London Bridge to London Bridge via Norwood Junction and Selhurst

Note: Direct trains between Lewes and Hastings/Ore avoiding Eastbourne ran via the Polegate – Stone Cross spur.

Trains terminating at or starting from Portsmouth and Southsea used the low-level platforms.

Trains between Norwood Junction and Selhurst (station) ran via a loop closed in the 1980s.

Western Section (later South Western Division)

Headcode   Route

2   Waterloo – Portsmouth Harbour via Richmond and Chertsey

3   Waterloo – Portsmouth and Southsea via Bookham

4   Waterloo – Portsmouth Harbour via Bookham

5   Waterloo – Portsmouth and Southsea via Cobham

6   Waterloo – Portsmouth Harbour via Cobham

7   Waterloo to Portsmouth and Southsea via Worplesdon (stopping) with rear coaches for Alton detached at Woking.

7   Portsmouth and Southsea to Waterloo via Worplesdon (stopping), attaching coaches from Alton at Woking; combined train to carry 7 to Waterloo.

8   Waterloo – Portsmouth Harbour via Worplesdon (semi-fast, not calling at Havant)

9   Waterloo – Portsmouth and Southsea via Richmond and Chertsey

10   Waterloo – Woking via Surbiton

12   Waterloo to Alton via Surbiton (stopping) with rear coaches detached at Woking for Portsmouth and Southsea via Worplesdon. To carry 7 from Woking to Portsmouth.

13   Waterloo – Woking via Richmond and Chertsey

14   Waterloo – Virginia Water via Weybridge

15   Waterloo – Alton via Richmond and Chertsey

15   Waterloo –Effingham Junction via Epsom (code replaced by 16 from 6/54)

16   Waterloo – Guildford via Epsom

17   Waterloo – Horsham via Epsom

17   Waterloo – Weybridge via Hounslow (with or without portion for Windsor detached/attached at Staines)

18   Waterloo – Weybridge via Richmond (with or without portion for Windsor detached/attached at Staines).

18   Waterloo – Chessington South

19   Waterloo – Worcester Park/Epsom/Leatherhead

20   Waterloo – Ascot via Earlsfield, Woking and Frimley

20   Guildford – Farnham/Alton

21   Waterloo – Guildford via Richmond and Ascot (or portion of Waterloo – Reading train detached/attached at Ascot) (not after 1965)

21	Guildford – Aldershot
21	Waterloo to Waterloo via Kingston and Richmond (from c1965)
22	Empty trains Waterloo to Farnham depot via Richmond (c1954-65)
23	Empty trains Waterloo to Farnham depot via Brentford (c1954-65)
24	Waterloo – Shepperton via Earlsfield
25	Waterloo – Woking via Brentford and Ascot
26	Waterloo – Woking via Richmond and Ascot
27	Waterloo – Reading via Brentford (with portion for Aldershot line detached/attached Ascot)
28	Waterloo – Reading via Richmond (with portion for Aldershot line detached/attached Ascot)
29	Empty trains on transfer between between Western and Central sections
30	Waterloo – Hampton Court via Earlsfield
32	Waterloo – Alton (stopping) via Earlsfield and Woking (no portion for Portsmouth line) (not after c1965)
32	Waterloo – Waterloo via Richmond and Kingston (from c1965)
34	Empty trains from any station (except Waterloo) to Durnsford Road depot
35	Portsmouth – Gillingham (Kent): special trains by any available route via London
37	Waterloo – Alton via Brentford
38	Waterloo – Alton via Richmond
42	Waterloo – Guildford via Cobham
43	Waterloo – Effingham Junction via Earlsfield and Cobham (deleted 6/54)
43	Waterloo – Guildford via East Putney and Cobham (from 6/56)
47	Waterloo – Shepperton via Richmond
52	Waterloo and Farnham via Earlsfield (semi-fast)
53	Waterloo – Aldershot/Farnham via East Putney
57	Waterloo – Portsmouth and Southsea via Earslfield (stopping); no portion for Alton line.
57	Waterloo – Staines/Windsor via Brentford (no portion for Chertsey line)
58	Waterloo – Staines/Windsor via Richmond (no portion for Chertsey line)
61	Waterloo – Waterloo via Earlsfield and Richmond (not short workings)
62	Waterloo – Waterloo via Richmond and Earlsfield (not short workings)
63	Waterloo to Strawberry Hill via Earlsfield
64	Waterloo to Strawberry Hill via Richmond
68	Waterloo – Kingston via Richmond (from 9/58)
70	Waterloo – Portsmouth and Southsea via Worplesdon (semi-fast, calling at Havant)
71	Waterloo – Haslemere (fast between Waterloo and Woking)
72	Waterloo – Farnham (not calling at Surbiton) (from 2/59)
80	Waterloo – Portsmouth Harbour via Worplesdon (semi-fast, calling at Havant)
81	Waterloo to Portsmouth Harbour via Worplesdon (stopping) with Alton portion in rear detached at Woking; Portsmouth Harbour to Waterloo, Alton portion attached at Woking; ran as 7 from Woking to Waterloo c1954, thereafter as 81 throughout.
85	Waterloo – Wimbledon Park via East Putney
86	Waterloo – Wimbledon via East Putney
87	Waterloo to Waterloo via Richmond and Hounslow
89	Waterloo to Waterloo via Hounslow and Richmond

91	Waterloo to Bournemouth (fast)
92	Waterloo to Bournemouth (semi-fast)
93	Waterloo to Bournemouth (slow)
97	Brockenhurst to Lymington (from 1967, code later discontinued)

94/95/96/97/98 Special workings (Race meetings, football, etc)

04	Windsor – Portsmouth Harbour via Chertsey (usually Royal journeys)
05	Waterloo – Portsmouth and Southsea via East Putney and Worplesdon
06	Waterloo – Portsmouth Harbour via East Putney and Worplesdon
07	Waterloo and Portsmouth and Southsea via Earlsfield (non-stop)
08	Waterloo and Portsmouth Harbour via Earslfield (non-stop)
09	Waterloo – Ascot/Reading via Earlsfield and Chertsey

Note: Trains terminating at or starting from Portsmouth and Southsea used the low-level platforms

Two-digit numerical headcodes were allocated for most Western section suburban routes, on the introduction of 2NOL units 1863-82 in 1936. These codes continued in use and became standard on trains operated by the new wide-bodied suburban stock introduced from 1946.

Until 1962, there were also a few letter headcodes allocated to Western section main-line services which could be diagrammed for suburban stock. These included N (plus one dot) for Woking – Alton and T (plus two dots) for Waterloo – Woking.

Eastern Section (later South eastern Division) including Kent Coast headcodes introduced in 1959 and subsequently

Headcode	Route
0	Elmers End – Hayes (replaced by 04 in 6/65)
0	Maidstone East – Ashford (from 6/61)
0	Strood – Gillingham
1	Ashford – Margate via Canterbury West
1	Grove Park – Bromley North (replaced by 01 in 6/65)
1	Sittingbourne – Sheerness (replaced by 01 in 6/65)
1	Strood – Maidstone West (replaced by 01 in 6/65)
2	Charing Cross – Cannon Street (empty stock) (from 6/59)
2	Elmers End – Addiscombe (replaced by 06 in 6/65)
2	Nunhead – Crystal Palace High Level (line closed 9/54)
3	Holborn Viaduct – Ramsgate via London Bridge and Greenwich (from 6/59, prob to 6/65)
3	Holborn Viaduct – Kent House or Beckenham Junction (prob from 6/65)
3	Elmers End – Sanderstead (replaced by 08 in 6/65)
3	Slade Green – Gillingham (empty stock) c1958/59, then replaced by 61, 63 or 65
4	Charing Cross – Orpington – Dover – Margate
4	Victoria – Kent House or Beckenham Junction
5	Blackfriars – Kent House or Beckenham Junction
5	Cannon Street – Orpington – Dover – Margate
5	Ramsgate – Dover Marine (empty stock) c1962-65
6	Ashford – Folkestone (dot from rear of Charing Cross via Swanley/Maidstone train) (c1962-65)
6	Charing Cross – Ramsgate – Margate via Maidstone East and Folkestone (6/61-6/65)
6	Gillingham – Victoria via Swanley (CEP stock trials, 5/56)

6	Victoria – Bellingham
7	Cannon Street – Ramsgate via Maidstone East and Folkestone
7	Victoria – Herne Hill – Orpington – Dover – Margate (from 6/65)
8	Charing Cross – Ashford via Orpington (from 1961)
8	Orpington to Slade Green via London Bridge (empty stock) (until 1961)
9	Cannon Street – Bromley North via Parks Bridge
9	Cannon Street – Grove Park sidings (passenger between Cannon St and Hither Green)
9	Cannon Street – London Bridge (shuttle service)
9	Holborn Viaduct – Bellingham
10	Charing Cross – Bromley North via Parks Bridge
10	Charing Cross – London Bridge (shuttle service)
10	Grove Park sidings – Charing Cross (passenger from Hither Green)
10	London Bridge – Charing Cross
10	Stewarts Lane – Dover Marine or Folkestone Harbour via Herne Hill and Orpington (empty stock) (1962/63)
11	Cannon Street and Charing Cross (empty trains) from 1957
11	Cannon Street – Blackfriars/Holborn Viaduct via Metropolitan Junction (from 6/65 vice 76)
11	Charing Cross and Coulsdon North (engineering works diversion of Tattenham Cnr service 1962)
12	Charing Cross – Orpington via Parks Bridge and Chislehurst
12	Charing Cross and Grove Park sidings (passenger between Charing X and Hither Green)
12	Victoria – Dover Marine via Herne Hill and Maidstone East (from 6/60)
13	Cannon Street – Orpington via Parks Bridge and Chislehurst
13	Victoria and Dover Marine via Catford loop and Maidstone East (from 6/60)
14	Charing Cross – Orpington via Lewisham and Chislehurst (code extended to Sevenoaks, 1959-61)
14	Victoria – Folkestone Harbour/Dover Marine via Herne Hill, Swanley and Sevenoaks (from 6/60)
15	Cannon Street – Orpington via Lewisham and Chislehurst (code extended to Sevenoaks 1959-61)
15	Victoria – Folkestone Harbour/Dover Marine via Catford, Swanley and Sevenoaks (from 6/60)
16	Charing Cross – Sevenoaks via Parks Bridge and Orpington
16	Stewarts Lane – Ramsgate or Dover Marine via Herne Hill and Chatham (empty stock)
17	Cannon Street – Parks Bridge – Orpington – Sevenoaks
17	Holborn Viaduct to Sevenoaks via London Bridge, Parks Bridge and Orpington (from 6/59)
17	Sevenoaks – Maidstone West (1961/62; replaced by 59)
18	Charing Cross – Sevenoaks via Lewisham and Orpington (until 6/59)
18	Charing Cross – Margate via Orpington and Minster (not via Lewisham)
19	Cannon Street – Sevenoaks via Lewisham and Orpington (until 6/59)
19	Cannon Street – Margate via Orpington and Minster (not via Lewisham)
20	Charing Cross – Beckenham Junction via Lewisham
21	Cannon Street – Beckenham Junction via Lewisham
21	Holborn Viaduct/Blackfriars – via Herne Hill, Tulse Hill, Wimbledon, Sutton, West Croydon, Forest Hill.
22	Holborn Viaduct/Blackfriars – Hayes via Nunhead and Lewisham (not before 1960)
23	Cannon Street – Dover Priory via Greenwich and Chatham (1957-59 only: no Charing Cross equivalent)
23	Holborn Viaduct – Bickley via Herne Hill

23	Tonbridge – Hastings, DEMU from 1957
24	Charing Cross – Hayes via Lewisham
24	Victoria – Bickley via Herne Hill
25	Blackfriars – Bickley via Herne Hill
25	Cannon Street – Hayes via Lewisham
26	Charing Cross – Addiscombe via Lewisham
26	Victoria – Bickley via Catford loop
27	Holborn Viaduct – Bickley via Catford loop
28	Charing Cross – Selsdon/Sanderstead via Lewisham (until closure of Woodside – Sanderstead)
28	Charing Cross or Holborn Viaduct – Lewisham – Beckenham Junction – Orpington/Sevenoaks (after closure of Woodside – Sanderstead)
29	Cannon Street – Selsdon/Sanderstead via Lewisham (until closure of Woodside – Sanderstead)
29	Cannon Street – Lewisham – Beckenham Junction – Orpington/Sevenoaks (after closure of Woodside – Sanderstead)
29	Blackfriars – Bickley via Catford loop
30	Charing Cross – Beckenham Junction via Parks Bridge (until 6/59)
30	Victoria – Faversham, Canterbury E or Dover Priory via Herne Hill and Chatham (from 6/59)
31	Cannon Street – Beckenham Junction via Parks Bridge (until 6/59)
31	Orpington or Grove Park – Barnehurst/Slade Green via Lee spur (empty stock) (after 1962)
31	Victoria – Canterbury East or Dover Priory via Catford loop and Chatham
32	Charing Cross– Dover Priory – via Chislehurst and Chatham
34	Charing Cross – Hayes via Parks Bridge
34	Holborn Viaduct/Blackfriars Dover Western Docks via Herne Hill and Chatham
35	Cannon Street – Hayes via Parks Bridge
35	Holborn Viaduct – Ramsgate via Catford loop and Chatham
36	Charing Cross – Addiscombe via Parks Bridge
36	Holborn Viaduct – Sheerness via Herne Hill and Sittingbourne (1959-65)
37	Cannon Street – Addiscombe via Parks Bridge
37	Holborn Viaduct – Sheerness via Catford loop and Sittingbourne (1959-65)
37	Holborn Viaduct/Blackfriars – Sutton or West Croydon via Tooting and St Helier
38	Holborn Viaduct/Blackfriars – Grove Park or Bromley North via Nunhead and Lewisham (after 1976)
38	Charing Cross – Selsdon/Sanderstead via Parks Bridge (until closure of Woodside – Sanderstead)
38	Charing Cross or Holborn Viaduct – Parks Bridge – Beckenham Junction – Orpington/Sevenoaks (after closure of Woodside – Sanderstead)
38	Victoria – Canterbury West or Margate via Herne Hill, Orpington and Tonbridge (empty stock) (1962-65)
39	Gillingham or Fawkham to Blackfriars via Catford loop (until 6/59)
39	Cannon Street – Selsdon/Sanderstead via Parks Bridge (until closure of Woodside – Sanderstead)
39	Cannon Street – Parks Bridge – Beckenham Junction – Orpington/Sevenoaks (after closure of Woodside – Sanderstead
39	Holborn Viaduct/Blackfriars – West Croydon via Selhurst (prob from 1960)

40 – 89 Most of these codes originally applied to services between London, Dartford, Gravesend and Gillingham or intermediately. Some have been altered; from 1959 use of some of the numbers was duplicated for routes (mostly on the 'Chatham' lines) not overlapping or conflicting with the previous uses.

In the following summaries, even numbers are to/from Charing Cross unless noted as Victoria or Blackfriars/Holborn Viaduct; odd numbers to/from Cannon Street or London Bridge unless noted as Blackfriars/Holborn Viaduct:

40 – 49 via Sidcup, avoiding Lewisham (Loop Line)

50 – 59 via Lewisham and Dartford loop (Sidcup line)

60 – 69 via Lewisham and Woolwich (North Kent line)

70 – 79 via Lewisham and Bexleyheath line

80 – 89 via Greenwich and Woolwich

40, 41, 50, 51, 60, 61, 70, 71, 80, 81: London and Dartford

42, 43, 52, 53, 62, 63, 72, 73, 82, 83: London and Gillingham (until 1965); London and stations to Ramsgate (from 1959)

46, 47, 56, 57, 64, 65, 74, 75, 84, 85: London and Gravesend or Maidstone West (until 1965);

also 68, 69 Blackfriars or Holborn Viaduct: 68 via Nunhead, 69 via London Bridge.

44, 45, 54, 55, 64, 65, 74, 75, 84, 85 London and Gravesend or Maidstone West (from 1965)

46   Charing Cross – Sidcup or Slade Green avoiding Lewisham (from 1965)

47   Cannon Street – Sidcup or Slade Green (avoiding Lewisham) (from 1965)

49   Holborn Viaduct or Blackfriars – Dartford or Gravesend via London Bridge and Sidcup (not via Lewisham) (until 6/65); HV/B – Sidcup, Slade Green or Dartford (from 6/65); code deleted c1976.

57   Cannon Street – Sidcup or Slade Green via Lewisham (from 1965)

58   Holborn Viaduct or Blackfriars to Gravesend Central until 6/59;to Gillingham and Ramsgate via Nunhead, Lewisham and Sidcup, 6/59-6/65; HV/B – Sidcup, Slade Green or Dartford (from 1965).

58   Victoria – Dover Priory via Catford loop and Chatham (from 6/65)

59   Gillingham to Holborn Viaduct or Blackfriars via London Bridge, Lewisham and Sidcup (until 1976); HV/B – Sidcup, Slade Green or Dartford (from 6/65).

66   Charing Cross – Plumstead or Slade Green via Lewisham and Woolwich (from 1965)

67   Cannon Street – Plumstead or Slade Green via Lewisham and Woolwich (from 1965)

68   Holborn Viaduct or Blackfriars – Dartford or Gravesend via Nunhead; HV/B – Dartford via Nunhead (from 6/65)

69   Holborn Viaduct or Blackfriars – Dartford or Gravesend via London Bridge (until 6/65); HV/B – Dartford via London Bridge (from 6/65)

78   Victoria – Dartford via Nunhead and Bexleyheath (from 6/65)

79   Holborn Viaduct or Blackfriars – Dartford via Nunhead and Bexleyheath

86   Charing Cross – Plumstead or Slade Green via Greenwich

87   Cannon Street – Plumstead or Slade Green via Greenwich

89   Holborn Viaduct or Blackfriars – Dartford via London Bridge and Greenwich (until 1959, then stations to Ramsgate)

Headcodes 40 – 89 for Services between London and destinations other than Dartford, Gravesend, Maidstone West, or stations to Gillingham or Ramsgate via Chatham; and local services outside the London area. Some codes were allocated in 1960/61 to be carried by diesel locos if required.

40   Victoria – Margate via Herne Hill and Chatham (from 6/59)

41   Victoria – Margate via Catford loop and Chatham (from 6/59)

42   Victoria – Folkestone Harbour via Herne Hill and Maidstone East (from 6/60)

43   Victoria – Folkestone Harbour via Catford loop and Maidstone East (from 6/60)

44   Charing Cross –New Romney via Orpington and Ashford (1957 until closure of NR branch)

45   Orpington or Bromley North to Holborn Viaduct via London Bridge (not via Lewisham) (until 6/61)

45   Chart Leacon or Slade Green depots – Wimbledon Park sidings (from 6/61)

46   Victoria – Dover Marine (later Western Docks) via Herne Hill and Orpington (from 6/60)

47   Victoria – Dover Marine (later Western Docks) via Catford loop and Orpington (from 6/60)

48	Holborn Viaduct or Blackfriars – Bromley North via London Bridge (not via Lewisham)
50	Victoria – Ramsgate via Herne Hill and Chatham (from 6/59)
51	Victoria – Ramsgate via Catford loop and Chatham (from 6/59)
54	Eastern Section special workings, 1939-62
54	Charing Cross – Maidstone West via Orpington (6/62-6/65)
54	Victoria – Ramsgate via Herne Hill and Chatham (from 6/65)
56	Victoria – Folkestone Harbour via Herne Hill and Orpington (from 6/60)
59	Sevenoaks – Maidstone West (from 6/62)
60	Victoria – Sheerness via Herne Hill and Sittingbourne (from 6/59)
61	Blackfriars – Orpington or Sevenoaks via Herne Hill and Petts Wood
61	Strood – Paddock Wood
61	Tonbridge – Margate via Ashford and Dover Priory, not via Minster.
62	Victoria – St Mary Cray or Swanley via Catford loop (from 1965; previously 82)
63	Blackfriars – Orpington or Sevenoaks via Catford loop and Orpington
64	Victoria – Sheerness via Catford loop and Sittingbourne (from 6/59; finish date unknown)
64	Victoria – Chislehurst – Swanley – Sevenoaks – Dover – Margate (start date unknown)
65	Blackfriars – Swanley or Sevenoaks via Herne Hill (until 1965; then Blackfriars – Swanley)
66	Victoria – Sheerness via Herne Hill and Sittingbourne (from 1959)
67	Cannon Street – Plumstead or Slade Green via Lewisham and Woolwich
68	Charing Cross – Chislehurst – Swanley – Sevenoaks – Dover – Margate (no Cannon Street equiv)
69	Victoria – Sheerness via Catford loop and Sittingbourne (from 1965)
70	Victoria – Orpington or Sevenoaks via Herne Hill and Petts Wood (until 1965; then Victoria – Orpington)
71	Holborn Viaduct – Orpington or Sevenoaks via Herne Hill and Petts Wood (until 1965; then HV/B – Orpington)
72	Victoria – Orpington/Sevenoaks via Catford and Petts Wood (until 1965; then Victoria – Orpington; then deleted)
72	Stewarts Lane – Folkestone Harbour or Dover Western Docks via Nunhead and Orpington (empty stock)
73	Holborn Viaduct – Orpington/Sevnks via Catford and Petts Wood (until 1965; then HV/B – Orpington; then deleted)
73	Blackfriars carriage sidings – Folkestone Harbour or Dover Western Docks via Nunhead and Orpington (empty stock)
74	Victoria – Herne Hill (until 6/59; replaced by code 76)
74	Victoria – Dover Marine (later, Western Docks) via Herne Hill and Chatham (from 6/59)
75	Victoria – Dover Marine (later Western Docks) via Catford loop and Chatham
75	Holborn Viaduct or Blackfriars – Herne Hill
76	Charing Cross – Hastings via Orpington and Ashford (DEMU, 1957 to 1965)
76	Victoria – Herne Hill (from 6/59)
77	Stewarts Lane – Herne Hill – Streatham Hill (empty stock)
78	Charing Cross – Margate via Chislehurst, Swanley, Sevenoaks and Canterbury West (until 1965)
80	Strood or Faversham – Dover Priory via Margate or Canterbury East
80	Victoria – Sevenoaks via Herne Hill and Swanley
81	Holborn Viaduct and Sevenoaks via Herne Hill and Swanley
81	Strood – Ramsgate via Margate or Canterbury East
82	Victoria – Sevenoaks via Catford loop and Swanley
83	Holborn Viaduct or Blackfriars – Sevenoaks via Catford loop and Swanley
84	Sheerness – Dover Priory (from 1959)

85	Holborn Viaduct or Blackfriars – Orpington via Nunhead, Lewisham and Beckenham Junction
85	Sheerness – Ramsgate
86	Victoria – Crystal Palace High Level (until 9/54 closure of the branch)
87	Holborn Viaduct – Crystal Palace High Level (until 1954)
90	Victoria – Gillingham via Herne Hill until 6/59; from 6/59, to Sheerness direct, not via Sittingbourne
90	Charing Cross – Margate via Orpington and Canterbury West
91	Cannon Street – Margate via Orpington and Canterbury West
91	Holborn Viaduct – Gillingham via Herne Hill until 6/59; from 6/59, to Sheerness direct, not via Sittingbourne
92	Victoria – Gillingham via Catford loop until 6/59; from 6/59, to Sheerness direct, not via Sittingbourne
93	Holborn Viaduct – Gillingham via Catford loop until 6/59; from 6/59, to Sheerness direct, not via Sittingbourne
93	Charing Cross or Cannon Street or London Bridge (Brighton side) to Caterham via Forest Hill
93	Caterham or Tattenham Corner to Cannon Street via Forest Hill (see 01)
94	Charing Cross – Sheerness via Greenwich (from 6/59) (direct, not via Sittingbourne)
94	Victoria – Maidstone East via Herne Hill until 1961; from 1961, to Margate via Canterbury West
95	Cannon Street – Sheerness via Greenwich (from 6/59) (direct, not via Sittingbourne)
95	Holborn Viaduct – Maidstone East via Herne Hill until 6/61; from 6/61, to Margate via Canterbury West
96	Charing Cross – Sheerness via Greenwich and Sittingbourne (from 6/59)
96	Victoria – Maidstone East via Catford loop until 6/61; from 6/61, to Margate via Canterbury West
97	Cannon Street – Sheerness via Greenwich and Sittingbourne
97	Holborn Viaduct – Maidstone East via Catford loop until 6/61; from 6/61, to Margate via Canterbury West
97	Charing Cross – Reigate (until 1965)
98	Victoria – Folkestone Central via or Margate via Herne Hill and Maidstone East (from 6/61)
99	Holborn Viaduct/Blackfriars – Nunhead – Ladywell – Beckenham Junction or Swanley
01	Charing Cross or Cannon Street or London Bridge (Brighton side) to Tattenham Corner via Forest Hill (see 93)
01	Bromley North – Grove Park (replaced 1)
01	Maidstone West – Strood
02	Charing Cross – Orpington – Tonbridge – Maidstone West (6/61-6/62) (replaced by 54; 02 reinstated 6/65)
02	Charing Cross or Cannon Street to New Cross Gate or Selhurst (empty coaching stock) (not after 1962
02	Victoria – Ramsgate via Lewisham, Woolwich and Chatham
03	Cannon Street – Dover Priory via Chislehurst and Chatham
03	New Cross Gate to Charing Cross (empty coaching stock) (not after 1962)
03	Holborn Viaduct – Streatham Hill via Herne Hill (empty coaching stock)
03	Nunhead – Crystal Palace High Level (1945/46)
03	Victoria – Stewarts Lane (empty coaching stock)
04	Hayes – Elmers End (replaced 0 in 6/65)
04	New Cross Gate to Cannon Street (not after 1962)
05	Cannon Street – Sevenoaks via Chislehurst and Swanley
05	Holborn Viaduct – Sutton via Herne Hill, Tulse Hill and West Croydon (deleted unrecorded date before 1959)
06	Addiscombe – Elmers End (replaced 6 in 6/65)
06	Charing Cross – Sevenoaks via Chislehurst and Swanley
06	Holborn Viaduct – Sutton via Herne Hill and Wimbledon
07	Cannon Street – Ramsgate via Swanley and Chatham

07	Victoria – Blackfriars or Holborn Viaduct (empty coaching stock)
08	Charing Cross – Ramsgate via Swanley and Chatham
08	Victoria (Eastern) – Sutton via Herne Hill, Wimbledon and St Helier
09	Cannon Street – Maidstone East via Chislehurst and Swanley
09	Stewarts Lane – Slade Green via Nunhead and Woolwich (empty coaching stock)

Notes:

All empty stock trains to display bar above code number.

Suburban services avoiding Lewisham are shown in Southern working books as running via Parks Bridge junction and loop, on the main line between St Johns and Hither Green.

Dover Marine: later operating instructions describe this as Dover Western Docks.

APPENDIX 5:

SIDE DESTINATION AND ROUTE BOARDS

Initially, no indication as to the route or destination of a service was carried on suburban trains other than the headcode. From 1928 side destination boards began to be introduced, initially on the Tattenham Corner branch, and their use soon spread to virtually all suburban services worked by electric stock. They were carried on the upper sides of the guard's vans on the three-coach suburban units (and also on main-line electric stock of the 4 LAV and 2 NOL types) and they slotted into four brackets arranged in a rectangle. The boards themselves comprised cream lettering on a green background and were of two types. When not in use they were stored in racks at principal stations.

a) The more common type were large rectangular boards which utilised all four brackets. They showed the main calling points and destination and were painted on both sides, so they merely had to be reversed at termini. For example, on the Victoria – Coulsdon North service the two sides of the destination board read:

CLAPHAM JUNC	and	PURLEY
EAST CROYDON		EAST CROYDON
PURLEY		CLAPHAM JUNC
COULSDON NORTH		VICTORIA

b) Some services carried small horizontal boards attached to the upper pair of brackets only, just below cantrail height. They generally gave the destination only or destination and brief route details.

The use of destination boards continued until the end of 1939, when wartime conditions and shortage of staff caused their disappearance. The larger type made a brief reappearance on some Central section suburban services in about 1946. (Some, possibly most, were sent to Lancing in the late 1940s where they were used for carriage internal repairs, good-quality timber being in short supply at the time.) The smaller type were also briefly reintroduced after the war on certain routes. They lasted longest on main line stopping services, finally disappearing in the mid-1960s.